Back to Front

A True Story of Growth and Redemption

AN INTIMATE MEMOIR
❖ THE SKANEATELES KIDS ❖
CROSS COUNTRY—NEW YORK STYLE
THE 2006 CAMPAIGN

Jack Reed

authorHOUSE®

AuthorHouse™
1663 Liberty Drive, Suite 200
Bloomington, IN 47403
www.authorhouse.com
Phone: 1-800-839-8640

Cover Art: Brian Kinney, Toxic Snoman Industries
Editing: Dave Sipley

First published by AuthorHouse   3/31/2009

ISBN: 978-1-4389-5557-5 (sc)

Printed in the United States of America
Bloomington, Indiana

This book is printed on acid-free paper.

Contents

Back to the Front

This story is raw. It's real and unfiltered as it chronicles the lives of a teenage cross country team with something to prove. It's a rollercoaster of deep emotions replete with tunnels of darkness and successful strides taken in the blinding sun. An insider's story like this has never been told in such a personal way. There's the somber letter from state prison, the e-mails from an Olympian with one arriving on his high school coach's computer just a few hours before the 5000-meter prelims in Athens, Greece. There are heart-wrenching e-mails that drip with grief and bravado. This is New York State Cross Country—the best in the United States—and it's the storied history of the girls and boys from Skaneateles Lake. Passages are stolen from the private conversations of good high school kids courageously searching for truth, for salvation and a light in the vast emptiness of too many dimensionless and lonely nights when dreams seem to fade-away and die. Nothing has been left out. One went to the state penitentiary for killing a childhood friend. Two others faced arrest in an incident involving alcohol the weekend before the mid-week race to keep the girls 14-year unbeaten streak alive. One poetic soul was senselessly eliminated from the human gene pool. One was a wiry-haired and ever-smiling Athens Olympian and high school superstar intent on breaking the 4-minute mile. His story is told here for the first time. What happened during the 2006 Skaneateles Cross Country season is revealed intimately and starkly in jaw-dropping detail. Excited to have their story told, the high school kids were all anxious about being caught naked in such a personal and public way. In every instance and in every way, the student-athletes in this book

1

achieved ultimate victory as each courageous Harrier never stopped fighting to conquer their most stubborn and ominous demons. And that's the goal of every coach and every teacher who seeks to make a difference. The legends who paved the way had won 10 New York State cross country and 4 x 800 championships and the 2006 team had vowed to write their own special chapter. This is their topsy-turvy story. Don't be too judgmental. With luck, this could be you.

Warm-up

Perfect harmony exists. UCLA's Bill Walton found it on the hardwood during the NCAA championship game in 1973. Michael Johnson achieved it on the track in 1996 and Jesus found it on the cross 2000 years ago.

The runner most often finds perfect harmony when he's alone in solitary pursuit of the ultimate run. Expecting to exert the requisite amount of grunt work while fulfilling the daily dose of Spartan living, he's inexplicably rewarded with a heavenly-sent euphoria. Entering the zone, the blessings of life lie exposed in all their glory. It's the dew rising from the morning grass, the orange light glowing from just beyond the eastern horizon as the sun shines its approval. It's the smell of a baby lathered in powder and the wagging tail of a puppy excitedly discovering her new home. When the swirling vortex of spirit, body and universe whirl in a flawless, give and take symbiosis, the runner intuitively understands that he's just completed the unblemished run and is in perfect harmony with the universe—if only for those few precious moments. The delicate balance of the perfect run emerges only when the punishing pace, pain, the body's demand for oxygen, miles of training and his robust desire has jelled wondrously like never before. Everything flows effortlessly as if called by Mother Nature herself, the feet verily floating across the terrain, the breathing deep and silent, the air ruffled only by a chain of exhales.

This state of heavenly harmony is a bit like good needing evil before it can truly be appreciated, synthesized and understood. The good run—the perfect run—can only be fully internalized and appreciatively recognized for what it is when it leaps free of the long shadow cast by too many runs that went wrong as they veered from the plan and fell apart as legs grew weary or the lungs shriveled in the face of the body's respiratory demands. Change any one thing leading up to the perfect run and the balance is replaced by a sudden tumble into destruction. Think about Hasbro's tower-building game, Jenga: the tower is in perfect harmony with the gravitational forces of Earth until you extract one block too many—or the right stick, but in the wrong sequence--tipping the tower and sending it tumbling into a jumbled pile of meaningless, formless sticks, one indistinguishable from the others.

Perfect harmony, elusive and tantalizing, does exist. Though it's not a pain-free state, it's ravenously sought by people of every nationality and shape who dare to dream and to chase their vision of perfection. The vision of perfect harmony, once given life, mutates insidiously within your bones, your soul. Festering as days become weeks and months become years, it gains control of your every conscious thought while utterly dominating your life. Beauty passes by you unseen. Spicy Cajun dishes go unappreciated as the culinary arts are replaced by the urgent and simple need to refuel the running machine. At this point, the goal of achieving the perfect run has taken hold of all your senses, your conscious state-of-being and even your subconscious thinking processes as it haunts your dreams. Reaching critical mass, you've become the dream's vehicle and it drives you into a maniacal mindset where madness and the unrelenting pursuit-of-perfection chase away your few remaining friends who don't understand your pursuit. Your abiding belief in the mission is the force that makes the heart beat reliably and pulls you from your bed at the crack of dawn for yet another solitary run.

Belief, the lifeblood of every runner's viable dream, moves from the heart into the deep and mysterious crevices of the mind and flows throughout a beastly evolutionary brew, a frothy mix of spirituality and fleshy sinew. Entangled in twisting, fibrous strands like the infrastructure of a mighty city, belief enters a world consisting of blood and its transporting web of vessels and arteries that weave throughout the body seeking the remotest of cellular outposts like the Mars rovers, Spirit and Opportunity, searching the rugged terrain of the Red Planet for water, life and 'neighbors.'

Pulsating muscles, directed in their movement by microscopic cells, move to the heart's rhythmic beat as rapacious, hungry lungs covet oxygen—the substance of life—like whales opening their cavernous mouths to devour plankton, herring and other small coastal fish of a slower sort. Runners are a lot like the old Pac-Man video game as they gain strength while devouring the slow, the weak and those spiritually empty vessels wearing heavily marketed shoes and hoping for the best.

If some are to be believed, ghosts and spirits inhabit old architectural structures as unfinished and tragically-ended lives dance darkly in the cold shadows of a world they can no longer inhabit. Lurking deep within Homo-sapiens is a shared, kindred spirit, a dancing and bubbling cousin from the spirit world, that's as exciting and awe-inspiring as the Aurora Borealis flashing brilliantly in the northern skies as supercharged ions traveling at warp speeds from the sun ignite the earth's magnetic field. The onset of a runner's spiritual awakening is an explosion of will, desire and devotion and a divine bliss much like the northern lights pulsating across the skies in a sudden and dazzling display of power, beauty and harmonic motion. The rising clouds of amorphous, mysterious and misunderstood human spirits that wash over the daring and chosen few who have experienced the perfect run is a heavenly reward for those who not only believed and dreamed, but prepared.

Swirling and pulsating in a galactic dance of life and death, the human spirit exists in all its manifestations and incantations. It maneuvers the human body's chemistry and enjoins the genetically encoded strands of our DNA as it translates wordless desires into human actions as the messages hidden along the twisted double helix are called to duty and into productive activity. This collision of physical preparation and an uproarious self-belief yields a hauntingly beautiful spectacle of sweat and bodily poetry-in-motion with flying heels and piston-pounding arms ridden hard by an edict-giving ten pound head that is at once grimacing toothily and howling in euphoric happiness at the successful harnessing of life's forces.

Running with purpose is unguided, dangerous and uncharted, more Lewis and Clark than the Travel Channel's confident and experienced hosts who take their viewers on trips through Europe. Competitive hoofing is nowhere near as assuring and directive as a road map compiled by Rand McNally, but it leads us nonetheless on a road trip into self-understanding like no other by answering questions that we haven't yet asked.

Waiting for practice to begin in a cold and sterile Skaneateles main entryway as our high school vacation coincides with a college semester break, I'm surrounded by high school athletes of various talents; some are more akin to stick-figure-artists from the Middle Ages where emotionless and motionless drawings greet the art devotee while others are developing into full-fledged realists who understand the secrets of Renaissance art that lays darks against light colors while appreciating and glorifying the human body in all its magnificent dimensions and understanding its potential. While standing among this group of teens in the midst of being transformed from kids to young adults, I'm greeted by the sight of girls who have formed an outer ring encircling the current team. They're All-State titans Jessica O'Neill, Zandra Walton, Erika Geihe, Lia Cross, Vanessa Everding and Katie Figura. Toned, buff, roiling with confidence and possessing new knowledge garnered from a collegiate life that's wholly lived outside the small, intimate and limited Skaneateles Circle-of-Knowing, they are ebullient and seeing life from a more distant and telling perspective. They look upon the current team with a concern as they shake their heads. "This isn't the mystery of life we're dealing with here. The game of running isn't that hard to unravel," they think. "Surely they can connect the dots," they tell each other. "Blinders. Why aren't these girls removing 'em and roaring down the freeway that Coach has built for them? The path's so wide open and clear. It should be as simple as a baseball player on a hitting streak swinging at beach ball-sized projectiles?"

The human species is bright, engaging, social and curious, and it sends its newborn into the world bereft of inherited knowledge and without any sense of institutional history. Everything must be learned from scratch in a hurried rush to catch up and match the older generation's accomplishments while preparing to surge past them into the unknown completely trained and hell-bent on creating a better existence-on-earth for everyone.

From the first day standing tall in the tightly laced running shoes with enormous trepidation pulsating through their body, it's a game of catch-up, a constant learning experience, a race against time and opponents from other continents. It's a tense chess match of mind versus doubt, body against fatigue, us against them. "Look ahead," they're each told. "Learn from the past. Don't look behind you. Do better. Follow the deepest ruts. Control yourself. Be patient. Respect the process. Be aggressive and stay relaxed. That's how you defeat your opponents." Yes, it's a jumbled pile of puzzle pieces, but the pieces are bigger and fit together more easily than kids think.

Finishing a run in mid-December long after the cross country season has been put to rest, I run past the school's southern brick facade. In the windows I see the bright red petals and green leaves of healthy geraniums, pot after pot displayed in windows blackened by weekend inactivity. The scene juxtaposes day and darkness, hope and despair as a rare and bright sun soothingly shines down upon me as if some benevolent divinity is thinking kindly of me on this Christmas Eve.

I casually ask myself if there's an omnipotent God, some all-knowing intelligence that we look to for guidance and salvation as we traverse the hills and valleys on our way through this complex maze called life. Or is there some other creator—another definer of life—some other force that we've yet to discover and worship?

All I know is that we each share a special spirit—the human spirit— and we each contain in our soul a portion of the magical whole. When we join forces in shared purpose, impossible is no longer an obstacle as the USA hockey team discovered in the Lake Placid Winter Olympics in 1980. The mystical spirit that we each possess has many names, but no true identity, as the search continues.

Life can be tedious, a head-shaker, a dizzying mystery waiting to be unraveled. We tread down many roads only to find out that the faster looking by-pass led to nothing more meaningful. We discover that merely dressing seductively for the dance doesn't count. Looking regal in a team uniform doesn't send runners dashing across home plate with the winning run. Making shots in basketball warm-ups fails to inch you closer to notching another victory. In running, feeling ready, having a bouncy stride, possessing ultimate confidence on the eve of battle, counts for naught. It's more than mechanics and more than preparation. Success takes more than team dinners, drinking, and sleeping in a proper fashion. Those things, though necessary, often pull the unwary teen into a disillusioning snare like quicksand engulfing unwary wanderers. These trappings to a runner are like a lure is to a fish as too many runners climb the seductive steps toward a race but forget about the destination and the real reason for the long, steady climb.

Becoming a winner takes spirit, a dreamy whimsy, sometimes a concocted aura of invincibility that can literally scare opponents shitless before the race has begun. Succeeding requires a certain bearing, a physical hands-on-hips swagger, a kick-ass facial expression, lips snarling and curled at one corner that begins to convince the body that it can actually do the deed. Everybody is watching. Everyone is looking and wondering as they anticipate something eventful to mark this day in history.

Give 'em a show. The time to race is here, the race being a cerebral and physical series of private and deeply personal tests played out in public, sometimes painfully. One test asks us to red-line the third 400 of the mile as we strip the varnish from the wood to expose its grainy essence, the bent of our timber. Another exam directs us to accelerate past the crest of a gut-wrenching hill as we sandblast the brick facade to expose original color—and all the cracks and flaws that need our attention. Seeking its truest essence, its core, we're forced to stare down the homestretch as we shuck the husks from the corn to get to the golden and life-giving juicy kernels. That's our reward if we do it right. We get to suck the juice from life when we successfully enter the chute in harmony with the forces of life.

When the starter raises his blackened steel .32 caliber pistol, the purity of the sport takes center stage and it stands tall and majestic. It isn't the shoes, the visualization, the pep rallies, the uniform or the sweat suits that foretell the future or the truth about each of us. It isn't personal bluster, the press clippings or the genre of pre-race music played from techno-charged iPods that separates inveterate posers from intrepid runners who have learned to conquer the ageless enemy, thy self. Perfect harmony comes from doing a thing well.

To be a good racer, sacrifice is the first step taken, to be followed by persistence and steadfastness, then prudence, then gall and bellowing bravado. Finally, there's the step called reflection. For the distance runner, becoming comfortable as both predator and prey is the holy creed.

Becoming one-with-the-race is the goal. You must become the race, sensing it, feeling its ebb and flow, smelling those who are rapidly becoming victims and picking up the scent-of-the-trail left by the true leaders who have learned their lessons well.

Despite everything that the pop-culture magazines, sociologists and psychologists propose about effort, camaraderie, learning and healthy living, it's the race, stupid. All that truly counts is the race. So, ask yourself just one question: Did ya pass the last test?

Tranquility Base

We're a lightning rod. We draw fans. We draw raves. We capture peoples' attention. We're fast. At times we've swept through a race course, through an entire season, like the Mongols swept unfettered out of Asia. We've gone from being the prey to being the respected and pitiless hunter.

For the better part of two decades, an invisible force-shield has protected us from every threat and attack. No foe has beaten the girls of Skaneateles in our last 79 league dual cross country meets. The bull's eye draws attention to us, puts us on notice, perks our interest and fills a vacuous life—compliments of modern contrivances that ease all of life's struggles. The struggle of athletic competition lays bare our basest instincts while reconnecting us with our evolutionary past where only the fittest survived.

To our continual amazement—maybe chagrin—we tend to bring out the best in our opponents, and I guess that's a form of flattery, a positive sign, a show of respect towards us and what we've become: a juggernaut. Every race is someone's chance to knock us off and sometimes the opportunity to race against us is the pinnacle of their season, the single event that will define forevermore their efforts, their season, their summer of preparation, their dreams and hopes to attain greatness. Teams get more cranked-up for us than their other competition. In a smaller world, a most personal and intimate world, where the battle against opponents is over-shadowed only by the greater battle of one's body against one's soul, these match-ups can be bigger than Michigan vs. Ohio State or more life defining than USC vs. Notre Dame in South

Bend with Touchdown Jesus gazing down upon 60,000 fans, as we've become the measuring rod of success. As sportsmen we value beating opponents on their best day as it's the true measure of worth and merit. We know, regardless of winning or losing, whether we pass the internal test of success, whether we pass muster, knowing intimately how much fuel we expended, how much our soul withered, how well we battled the demon, that angry devil called Fear.

We always have to be on our game, focusing incessantly on the little details, for each one of us is only a bad meal or one-cup-of-water-too-few from meltdown. Living precariously, filling and draining our reserves, we gallop over hills and burn glucose in our mitochondria at a ravenous rate. Running through muggy wooded trails drains water from the cooling system faster than planned and no matter how powerful the internal will-of-life, when drained of nutrients and other life sustaining elements, we die.

We draw praise. We're feted in small, intimate ways. Names of our runners go up on our "Blue Ribbon School" sign in front of our campus, and our walk grows springy and taller, not because of the recognition, but because of the pride, because of the work, because of the choice to suffer, and because of the social, physical and personal sacrifices each accepted in order to have a shot at ultimate success.

We draw condemnation. We're referred to as a cult, for anyone who runs must have experienced a mind-altering sort of brainwashing. Accomplishments have been pooh-poohed as everyone knows that only non-athletes end up running. Grudgingly, year by year, a token few begin to understand our sport, and word spreads that we're okay.

And within our own school, we draw more than our fair share of jealousy. Yup, we're a lightning rod. And it's a point of pride.

We've gotten the job done year after year with different coaches, different kids, challenging schedules, and like most athletic programs, not as much assistance as we'd like.

But things have changed, and at times I wonder how we've gotten here because for so long we did it right, got the right response from the kids, from their parents, and, at the end of the day, we reaped, from meets, what we sowed in practice: Victory. We're still in the hunt and there's still a thrill derived from training and preparing for competition, but the effort has become more of a struggle lately, like that of a runner worn down from the effort with hollow, sunken eyes, feet blistered, bloodied and virtually useless, with legs that wobble like a table with broken legs, the sinew of life awash on some forlorn starting line in the distant past. It's been coming for a while as my pleas for help have been scoffed at. "You'll find a way to win," the administration said. And we did, but the success was increasingly harder to come by, and now we've reached the day of reckoning. We either get help from staff who need to send us some bodies, coaches who need to cut some kids from other teams, or we'll die and the program will be eliminated. It's no idle reality that I speak of. At the first hint of problems with the indoor program in the early 1990s, it was eliminated from the budget. We're running out of kids, the raw material of our existence.

Launching

As I write this, there are just 360 school days between retirement and me. With the transformation from a day riddled with too little time to plan, even less time to execute, and almost no time to sleep save the five hours I squeeze in at night, I'll have unbounded time to, well, to do what? I don't know right now. My kids are grown, so life is teaching and coaching. I'm growing weary of both, though when I'm "on" and in the zone, I'm still good.

In teaching terms, 360 days can seem like an eternity. In coaching terms, 360 days means one cross country season—just one more summer of enjoyable, unpaid volunteer work with the teams—until I plan to take my final walk off the muddy, sometimes scenic and raucous 3.1-mile race course and board the yellow school bus with our driver Gary Martin, for the final time. We're going out together. He's retired from everything except helping me take care of our runners—our kids. He's the best.

Gary is a stalwart of our program, as valuable as any coach could be and absolutely trusted by the kids and their parents. I don't even fear falling asleep with Gary at the helm on those race days when the elements make you feel as if you'd just finished 10 rounds with Joe Frazier or Ali; the pummeling bloating the face, puffing the eyes, fattening the lips while leaving you feeling like a street sign that stood in the face of Hurricane Katrina: all twisted, bent and unsightly. Gary studies the sport, understands how our kids operate, and keeps things nice and low-keyed in order to reduce unnecessary stresses that are very likely to erupt on a bus ride when a driver isn't a good fit. Gary doesn't have to stop the bus on trips to get anyone's attention. He doesn't yell. He gets results because he's earned respect, he's understood to be on the side of the kids, he's patient, accommodating and complimentary. He's a normal guy, a man's man.

Getting places with Gary is a snap. He studies routes, asks about shortcuts that actually work, picks great places for us to camp, and oftentimes gets the bus into places that other drivers could only dream of. He's a rock of stability and he not only recognizes kids from other teams, he understands how they compete. He's our volunteer assistant coach who truly helps us in the meets. His post-race analysis is right on the mark. Plus, he's a Yankee fan, which makes it hard to figure out how we got lost twice on one important trip through New York City to Long Island for a state championship.

We were making good time on our longest, most important trip of the season while the kids sang, ate, slept, held a daytime slumber party in the bus aisle, and did homework, but there was a time-warp problem as the hours spent on the little yellow bus kept piling up and the distance remaining wasn't lessening. Around midnight, we approached the GWB—the George Washington Bridge—and I was cursing at all the people who thought it important to be out clogging the highway at such an hour on a weeknight. "What the shit gives?" I asked, speaking in a hushed tone to Gary and Rob Tuttle, my young, aspiring and astute co-coach. In due course we escaped that madhouse but then we entered the Twilight Zone. There was a massive bridge construction project right where we needed to make some critical moves, and on a bus on the highway in New York, you don't get second chances.

Moving slower than the speed limit, we three literate adults somehow managed to miss an exit sign that would get us onto Long Island. We ended up on some God-forsaken marshy lowland where the Mafia dumped bodies. I'm sure of that. It looked like a crime scene from the television drama "CSI". Decrepit warehouses dotted the marsh, swaying reeds designated no-man's land, rusted barrels popped up everywhere and must have contained body parts, and ditches meandered while stuff oozed, glistening black and syrupy along the bottom. Maneuvering precariously on rutted dirt paths that passed as roads around the swamp, we headed toward the city lights as we slowly high-tailed it out of there by taking some turns that seemed, at the time, to make sense.

We ended up going round and round on something called the Hugh J. Grant Circle. Coach Tuttle and I kept our eyes open to help Gary get the school bus through a portion of the Bronx that probably had never seen a school bus on its medieval roads; narrow, winding corridors with no beginning or end.

Suddenly Rob shouted out, "Gary, the pole!" We were underneath the railroad track—maybe it was an elevated portion of the subway— and Gary slammed the brakes hard and avoided more travel delay. There were black iron support poles all over the place, some right in the middle of the road. We were stuck in a Bronx maze and we couldn't get off the circle for nearly 15 minutes. Traffic! Damn traffic! There were kids all around on bikes, walking, just hanging out on street corners. And it was a school night. It's true: New York City never sleeps.

"Good God, what can go wrong next," I said as I exhaled fully, my diaphragm rising toward my lungs to squeeze every bit of air from my body into the city atmosphere that was at once a mix of vehicle emissions, the aromas of exotic foods, and a general staleness found only in crowded places where piles of garbage waited to be collected.

Well, Gary got us back on the highway in the midst of the disaster known as the bridge construction, and we excitedly sighted the exit sign for Long Island—just a wee bit too late. We ended up back in the mafia burial ground and once again did laps around the Hugh J. Grant circle somewhere in the Bronx, a place we couldn't ever find again if we tried. The exit sign was a small 2 x 2 foot sign—and I'm being generous—about 20-feet up on a pole, an Al Oerter gold medal Olympic discus throw away from where we were driving.

We were scheduled to stay at Hofstra University and were following the next batch of directions perfectly. And then the directions failed us. We stopped at an all night gas station on a street that featured crotch rocket motorcycles whizzing up and down the boulevard, and we asked quite simply, "Are we anywhere near Hofstra?" The guys shook their heads and spoke something in a language we didn't understand. So we drove on. We stopped at the Post Office, a branch of the U.S. Postal Service—our postal service—that was midnight-busy and once again asked some workers, "Is Hofstra anywhere near here?" "Uh, I don't know anything about Hofstra," one said, shaking his head and shrugging his shoulders dismissively. Back on the bus I mumbled something about wondering how any piece of mail ever got to its intended destination with those guys in charge. In school we call it being geographically challenged—and stupid.

So we drove another mile and there was Hofstra University; a mile away and the U.S. Postal service had never heard of it. With a sigh of relief we found our dorm and settled in for the night. It wasn't Gary's fault. We were traveling through the universe on our way to Long Island, and we'd gotten sucked into a wormhole to nowhere. I felt like Billy Pilgrim in Kurt Vonnegut's "Slaughterhouse-Five".

Together, Gary and I have seen assistant coaches come and go for a wide variety of reasons. And they're all legitimate. Some had terrible times with a parent or two—something that's becoming more and more common in the coaching ranks regardless of sport—and just decided to move on with their lives. While most parents are very supportive and will do absolutely anything to help coaches and teams raise money for uniforms, sweats and trips, some just can't separate their ego from the life and activities of their children. In this politically correct environment, schools, when confronted by one of these belligerent and demanding parents with tunnel vision, often take the course of least resistance and acquiesce, thereby empowering the off-site parents—who lack insight into practices and team camaraderie—and disemboweling their coaches and teachers. Assistant coaches who are verbally assaulted and undermined and who aren't making a dime for all of their time, really have no reason to continue in the coaching ranks. And it's getting difficult to find adults who are willing to enter our profession. Some of our assistants simply grew tired of dealing with the kids. It isn't just coaching anymore, it's a multi-faceted job that on some days becomes a real grind as the day never seems to end, and the endless drama can quickly drain all of your energy while leaving you feeling ratty, sluggish and defeated for your teaching job the next day. To do the job right, to be true to the basic precepts of the profession, and to be a positive factor in the kids' lives, you have to be an effective psychologist, a social worker, a college recruiter, a cheerleader. You have to provide a shoulder to cry on while being a confidant, a morale booster, a doctor, a physical therapist, a chiropractor, an English teacher, a dean-of-discipline, a tutor and an entire tapestry of other roles in order to keep some kids afloat.

Some of our coaches finally had kids of their own, and family must come first as those precious, incredibly fleeting childhood moments fade into mere memory far, far too fast. And soon you might find yourself alone in your car sobbing uncontrollably—empty crates in the trunk—on the way home after dropping your son or daughter off at college, after realizing that your family, the sinew and core of your Earthly existence, is forever changed. No matter what you do, you can't ever put it back together again. You soon find yourself driving alone on country roads as dusk falls on the landscape; driving, searching, looking for peace from the emptiness that envelops you. Months go by and the heart still hurts; the pangs of despair unrelenting. Poring over photo albums, as the lonely nights without your child pile up, leads you to the awful realization that arms can't hug memories, and putting your lips on a picture isn't the same as softly kissing your kid's cheek as you put them safely to sleep.

Losing good coaches isn't quite the same as being cut-off from daily interactions with your son or daughter, but good coaches are rare, and having a good coach who is also a trusted colleague and friend is even rarer. So, when they go, it hurts, but we understand.

Some of our former coaches have needed more money than high school coaching affords as the meetings, conferences, courses, health re-certifications and state license requirements grow too intrusive as they overtake your evenings and rob you of too much of your private life. At times you wonder if you're even allowed a private life as insulting e-mails, haranguing phone calls, snail-mail letters from crackpots, and letters to the editor leave you nowhere to hide. It's amazing how smart some people can be who sit in the stands and never attend a practice.

Some of our coaches just got hired away, which we look upon as a supreme compliment. Some coaches finally left, thank God. Two punished the little 7th and 8th graders for actually behaving like little 7th and 8th graders, and made them run. That's right: they used our sport as an instrument of punishment.

Gary and I have seen this program rise and rise from nothing. And just when we thought we were at our peak, we'd get it to rise even more. The biggest victories earned us both a nice cold brew at Morris' Grill at the corner table near the bar and the pool table after we'd put the big yellow school bus back into its corral. Our table, rickety and slicked smooth with a dozen or so coats of polyurethane, was close to the urinals, so on a bad night we could smell old piss.

But the celebrations are growing rarer. That was yesterday, and yesterday's gone. As Bob Dylan and Joni Mitchell said in their battling versions of Big Yellow Taxi,

> *Don't it always go to show,*
> *You'll never know what you got till it's gone?*
> *They paved paradise and put up a parking lot.*

With a slew of great kids, a supportive, organized and aggressive booster club, and a high turnout for the team, we had our version of paradise. And we want it back. We're trying to pull back from the abyss. Haltingly, we appear to be making some progress at the upper levels.

When our fabulously talented girl's lacrosse team won its first of two consecutive New York State titles here at Skaneateles High, I told the coach and the crowd at the senior athletic awards banquet that what they accomplished won't truly sink in with full understanding until she knows, in her heart, that she can't win it again, no matter what she and the girls do. You don't know what you've got till it's gone—and your gut of guts tells you that there ain't nothing you can do to get it back again. When you hear athletes or coaches say a championship hasn't sunk in yet, it's true. When the realization hits that the run to the top can't be achieved again, true understanding and appreciation finally settles into the soul like when you realize that a former hot love is forever gone and isn't coming back into your life no matter how often you cry or pace around the house, alone and forlorn. When that epiphany strikes, the heart grows heavy with the bite-of-sorrow turning your inners a face-wrenching sour, and you finally understand that new goals must, of necessity, be born because life is going on with or without you.

We were good here in Skaneateles. We wear blue and gold, sometimes yellow, and in a mere 13-year span, our Laker boys won a state title behind the efforts of Olympian Jonathon Riley while the girls were crowned four times, with three coming as the "Three-Headed Monster" led the way. Rival coach Rob Schemerhorn from Jordan-Elbridge gave the girls that moniker in abject frustration and sincere admiration. Taylor Strodel, Taylor Lind, and Liz Bevier were tough to break. Whenever you saw one, you were sure to see three, oftentimes stride for stride, looking like a team of synchronized swimmers.

I started out coaching at Marcellus, just east over the hills from here. I was driving east on business on the Thruway one day back in the summer of 1986 and I realized that over a dozen years of purposeless life was enough. I got home from Albany and applied for a coaching opening at Marcellus. My heart said I needed a change. Mert Raner, a former football player at Syracuse and a Marcellus athletic legend, hired me on a hunch over a more qualified applicant from Syracuse University. I was 36 years old with no experience, no resume, and no real college running to speak of.

I had been at Ithaca College during the end of the debacle of Vietnam and our coach was a drill sergeant who was big into small heads of hair. We didn't get along. I was more concerned with people like my neighbors who were dying unnecessarily for reasons of political insanity. Secretary of Defense Robert S. McNamara finally set the record straight decades later, 58,000 deaths too late. Some of those same people are at it again in Iraq and repeating McNamara's mistakes. Some people will do anything in order to advance a personal agenda and secure their hold on power so long as it's other people who are being sacrificed on the altar of twisted politics. It's fast becoming the American-way, and I call the people traitors, enemies of the people as they desecrate the Bill of Rights and fail to truly protect us while, in reality, sacrificing us to a private and very strange God.

So, there I was, without portfolio as they say, but there was a noticeable burning passion to get started. I needed to coach, but little did I know how much. In quick succession I quit my job, enrolled in grad school, signed up to be a substitute teacher and began coaching. At one time I was coaching kids from Marcellus, Jordan-Elbridge and Skaneateles together during an indoor season. When I saw one out in public, I'd find myself in a quandary as I tried to tie the face to the right school and the right name. Talk about wracking your brain.

Mert was the salt-of-the-earth, a pipe smoking gentleman who had the kid's true interests in mind. Under his athletic department leadership there were no favorite teams; girls' sports were honored as much as the boys and I think that was the beginning of his downfall. There were a number of disgruntled football parents who were convinced that their diminutive Marcellus kids weren't getting D-1 scholarships because of Mert. D-1 is social status for parents. People say that Mert played football with Jim Brown. If anyone understood what a D-1 football or basketball player looked like, it was him. He bled green and red, the colors of his hometown Mustangs, but it wasn't enough. They ran him out on a rail.

Mert was cutting edge. In 1990 we hosted the double dual cross country meet that would determine the Central Division championship. Each of the boys and girls teams was undefeated, Jordan-Elbridge, Skaneateles and Marcellus. Mert developed a program to score the meet on his computer. It was 1990! It was quick. It was portable. And it worked. No one did that back then.

Eric Roschick from Skaneateles, who I would coach a year later, won the race in 15:50 for the 3-mile mountain climb at Marcellus. It was a course record. My Marcellus Mustang David McShane was next in 15:52. Both boys would make it to the state championship. JE beat my Marcellus squad 27-30 while my Marcellus boys beat my future Skaneateles team 21-34. On the girls' side we saw a course record by Skaneateles legend Christina Rolleri as she won in 17:57, with my Tonya Fuller in second at 18:44. Tonya, an artist from a dysfunctional family, liked to shave her head. She was cool. Skaneateles beat my Marcellus team 26-29 while JE beat my Marcellus girls 22-33.

I learned a lot at Marcellus. It was my proving ground. We came in second a lot, most often to Corcoran from the City of Syracuse school system. I was force-fed humility. I learned to trust myself, to ask questions and to seek answers from other high school coaches, college coaches and Olympic team coaches. Olympic coach Brooks Johnson, then of Stanford, was instrumental in helping me to form my philosophy on speed training. Ask and most will respond. I also realized that I would win some day. Year after year I got practice with learning how to lose and how to come in second in championship races. I think I lost graciously, but I didn't like it and Mert heard about it. My Skaneateles girls have been in that runner-up spot at the XC sectional championships the past two years after ten years of being crowned champ. We want to get back to the top.

I also learned I should treat my runners better, be more understanding, less judgmental and more patient while helping them to develop a mindset that desired a higher personal standard of success. I want them to develop their own goals. A year after that battle of three undefeated teams, I was coaching at Skaneateles with Sheila Card, and the boys, who my Marcellus team had just beaten in the dual meet, would now be mine: Roschick, Jeff Lego, Ted Hahn, Dan Miles, Brett Bradley and Dan Naas. With the addition of John Kelly and Jeff Welch, we took a big step forward and began our ascent.

The nice thing about the runners from the three neighboring schools was that they became friends. We had a big summer running club and for $25 they had the opportunity to run during their summer evenings. We'd often end up in the lake on Lakeview Circle's beach rights. It was private, but no one seemed to mind. Runners from all three schools joined, plus some from league rival Westhill. Some kids even started dating and a few of the relationships have lasted into adulthood. We worked hard to break down the ridiculous walls that had formed over the better part of a half-century between these schools because of the contact sports and a bevy of adults who continue to instill in their kids a sense of hatred toward people who live on the other side of an arbitrary border. We broke bread together, had pizza dinners with each other, and partied at my place along the lake after hot evenings on the road.

Yet, like with all serious athletes, the in-season competition was fierce. Some of the most intense competition came after the invitationals on Saturdays as the boys from Marcellus and Jordan-Elbridge would stake out a claim on a field and play 'touch' football. We filmed these games and the coaching staffs kept hoping that no one would get injured. Today we play hacky-sack with enough gumption that it serves as a sort of ballistic warm-up. Times have changed.

On September 21st, 1993 my Skaneateles boys received their first No. 1 state ranking in New York. Jonathon Riley, Adam Cross, Jamie Riley, Jeff Welch, Dave Crowther, Brett Bradley and Todd Jackson read in the morning newspaper that they were ranked atop the state by the New York State Sportswriters Association. The number-one ranking had taken two seasons of work, sacrifice, and dreams to eliminate the stigma of being the worst team in Section III, which cuts a huge swath through the central region of New York. At times I felt like Peter-the-Great dragging everyone kicking and screaming into the new era. Gone were the days of incomplete teams. Gone were the days of being the doormat for any school with five guys who could waddle to the starting line and somehow finish.

At the Newark Invitational east of Rochester, the site of the state championship later in 1993, we defeated the 2nd, 3rd and 4th ranked teams in New York at the pre-state meet where we all got our first look at Stuart Park, the state meet race course. Skaneateles tallied 99 points with the mighty orange and green-clad Beaver River squad right behind with 109. East Rochester scored 111 and Lafayette finished with 114. Needless to say, we all knew the state championship was wide open. Within a few years, East Rochester would be coached by Skaneateles alum Jim Bathgate and they'd go on to great success.

At the Sectional meet at Green Lakes State Park, Beaver River beat us 74 to 87 as experience won the day. At the state meet a week later, back at Stuart Park, they pulled farther ahead and won 75 to 121 as the spectators were held at bay behind an endless array of ropes that kept everyone from watching the race. My brother Hugh nearly got into a fight with an official. Despite placing second, we'd arrived. And we knew it.

A year later in 1994, Beaver River, our nemesis-from-the-north, beat us at the Sectional meet 43-63, and a week later we were the ones to close the gap as we ran an inspired race before losing the state meet 62-65 at Albany State. But the next week at the Federation Championships that invited the top teams for a one race showdown, we placed an astounding 5th overall while beating Beaver River 243 to 301. The sportswriters designated us co-state champs. We were on the map. We were somebody. People began to know the Skaneateles name.

Getting to coach full-time at Skaneateles took some time. My oldest son Kirk was entering 7th grade and there really wasn't a modified program, and the varsity boy's program was close to being cut from the budget. It was important to me to coach in my adult hometown. There's a heavy dose of pride that I think I've inherited from my grandmother, the late Ina Miller Kirkendall, and it drives me to succeed. I guess I also fear failure the way some of my runners fear success. After a hallway walk with Superintendent Dr. Walter Sullivan, who promised me that the 6-lane cinder and grass track would be replaced by a real all-weather one, we agreed to terms and I began working with my hometown kids. I scouted elementary school basketball games. I haunted the little league fields. I approached kids who were out playing. No one escaped me. And I got the best athletes in the school district. I wanted to put the Skaneateles name on the map. I wanted people to look into the sea of yellow school busses on race day and pay attention when they saw the one with Skaneateles emblazoned on the side. I wanted them to look at us with nothing but respect, maybe even awe. It was that hellfire burning desire that pushed me day and night to be the best.

The drive to the top of the state included battles with Mother Nature, too. Assistant coach John Covell, an aggressive emergency room doctor, who took over cases like Patton took over battlefields, was a 'take-no-prisoner' sort of guy. Big, thick bodied, deep voiced and a former champion hurdler, he was used to giving orders and getting things done, "STAT". One day we were scheduled for a home track meet and he wasn't satisfied with the slow progress of the grounds crew after a few days of spring rain. John came up with shovels, pumps and piping and began to drain off the cinder and grass track. He ended up face-to-face, nose-to-nose with the head grounds-man who was upset about someone encroaching on his professional turf, and Doc said, "What's the matter with you? I'm doing your God-damn job." Smack, Doc was called into the principal's office like a slime-ball kid who told a teacher to 'f-off', and he was reprimanded. With a shrug, he said he had to go out and apologize. Being the good man he is, Doc's apology was sincere and I believe the two men smoothed out some ruffled feathers. The new track brought an end to such confrontations.

The boys and girls both toiled through the flooded course at St. Lawrence University in Canton, NY, compliments of an angry Grass River that rose over ten feet the night before the state championship. You want mud? You want a show of character? Everyone in that race showed America's true colors that day, but none more than Jen Nyzio (Assumption College). Running far out of position after the first of three boring laps on the weather-altered race course, I gave her 'the look' that told her I wasn't a happy man and I yelled a few words that I hoped would rally her spirit, words that I wouldn't necessarily feel comfortable saying in church. It wasn't until after the race that I found out she took a header in the frigid, muddy, thigh deep 200-meter long 'stream' that the runners had to ford three times in the race—while snow fell from an ugly sky. It was freakin' miserable. I was very slow to emerge from the building that housed the indoor track and the ever-popular showers where the comforting steam floated into the track area where the huddled masses stood together. It was dark, clammy, but warm. So we claimed it as our home.

We lined up at Lake Placid in just our skimpy uniforms, with the great mountains that surrounded the Olympic biathlon course around Mirror Lake shrouded in a nasty snowstorm. The temperature on the starting line was 25 degrees. The temperature at the higher elevations must have been real bad as the storms would blot out the magnificent mountains from time to time. The ground was crunchy with a thin layer of frozen snow. Yeah. Frozen. It had fallen hard two nights before the race, melted a bit and re-frozen into a crust. Nasty stuff. We placed a credible fifth after having the race in the bag at the two-mile mark. A senior, lovely as you could want, melted down on that cold day on the Lake Placid tundra.

Local rival Jordan-Elbridge, coached by Roger Roman, won the boys "B" race that day. Jeremy Cornue, who led the nation in the 3k steeplechase the following spring, and Zach Bennett led the Eagles. I tried this summer to hire both of them to take over our modified program, but their careers got in the way. I also tried to get Kevin Collins, who I saw working at Dick's in the athletic shoe department. Once one of the best marathoners in America who represented the nation at the Worlds in Paris, he was interested, but I think he wanted to give competitive running one more shot once his injuries healed. The man had given up his life from college graduation until he was in his mid-30s in pursuit of running and representing his country. He was working at Dick's in order to one day qualify for health benefits so that he could have surgery to fix an injury he'd incurred by training over 100-miles a week. And he ends up selling running shoes at Dick's Sporting Goods. Kevin was the runner-up at our National Championship in 2003 in 2 hours, 15 minutes. I wish we could have struck an agreement so that a new path in his life could have been started right here in Skaneateles. The kids would have loved him.

Year after year we were buffeted by the weather. We battled gale force winds at New York Tech on Long Island. The team and I broke into class buildings to try to stay warm and dry because there was no shelter. We had to escape the bus because parents had migrated to it and were countering my messages with theirs. I'm not sure how much angst we caused the custodians, but they seemed unfazed by our presence. We shared one building with the kids and coaches from Queensbury and it's always fun to casually observe another great team as they reach the final stages of race-day preparation. There's never a bad time to learn. Outside, the dirt turned to mud, and the sand turned into a quagmire that sent runner after runner to their hips at every right angle turn, and those deadly turns were everywhere. What a lousy course. What lousy hosting. There was absolutely no official shelter, no scoring. Why those people were allowed to host a championship is far beyond my understanding. Callous, disorganized, angry, they just messed-up everything. The course was as fan-unfriendly as you could get. And they charged for parking, five bucks, during what would be called a nor'easter during the winter. They should have paid the few spectators who showed up. Using the Beaufort gale force numbering system, the winds were an 8 on a 16-point scale. A full-fledged hurricane is declared when the number rises to 12.

We've done it all and kept winning, kept being in the hunt for titles, and that's my definition of good. Counting the track team's 4x800 relays, the school has won ten state titles in that baker's dozen time-span. But things have changed as titles that we once naturally assumed we could capture are now off of our radar.

Included in the glorious span was "The Streak" when the girl's teams won 10 straight sectional crowns in cross country, and the wins weren't even close. With an ever-changing line-up that just naturally occurred with graduation, the margins of victory hit triple figures against runners-up Cato-Meridian and Sauquoit Valley. Poor South Jefferson from the western fringes of the Tug Hill Plateau was the runner-up three times during the streak, and they had a helluva team that could have won state titles of their own.

Unfortunately, the 'wise' men and women who run the state athletic association haven't figured out how to get the top teams into the state meet. You could be the 2nd ranked team in the state behind a team from your own section, and you don't get to go to 'states if they beat you in your section's qualifying meet. By God, in 1989 Cicero-North Syracuse and Baldwinsville were one-two in their division of our league. They finished in the same order at the Onondaga High School League

(OHSL) Championship. C-NS won the sectional title with Baldwinsville second. CN-S won the state title and Baldwinsville couldn't go. At the Federation Championship, that included the top public high school teams plus champions from New York City, the private conferences and the Catholic Conferences, C-NS was first with 104 points and Baldwinsville was second with 107 points. Amazing! Yet we couldn't figure out a way to get them both into the public state championship race, and we still don't have a high school state championship with the top public schools teams, despite having this problem for decades. Inertia. Damn inertia. We're like a Confucian society that does things today exactly like we did it yesterday. Progress is just not in the cards as the status quo reigns supreme.

There's just an endless array of cases like that. We don't wear school uniforms at the state championship either. Several times, when I argued for the wearing of team jerseys, section and state coordinators actually told me that it's too difficult for officials to call out shirt colors when the kids enter the chute en masse. In the old days before our foolproof automated timing systems, maybe they had a point. But today? It's just Stone Age thinking and it ruins the state championship, which has very small races because of the new, watered-down multi-class format. Interestingly enough, the following week's Federation Championship allows everyone in the nearly 300-runner field to wear their team uniform. Can you imagine any team championship where coaches and spectators can't identify the teams?

It's no wonder New York State is so far in debt. No wonder we're the number one-ranked state in taxation and assessments. We have a bunch of dunderheads in charge. The state track meet format is no better as its structure continually changes from year to year. You never know what's going on or who you're competing against. There is no race schedule formatted to specific times of the day. We should be able to figure out our problems, develop a championship format that is fan-friendly, and one that's predictable and makes sense for the athletes. It's just one mess after another. When you go to a basketball game you understand that the baskets will always be 10 feet off the ground and that the foul line is 15 feet from the rim. Go to a baseball game and the pitcher's rubber is 60 feet, six inches from the plate, the bases are 90 feet apart, and each side plays 9 guys. Go to a track meet and you don't know the most basic thing: the order of events. We just make things up as we go. If you want to catch a particular event or individual, you just might have to camp out for a ten hour day. And can you imagine a state track championship with no announcer, no clock? That's New York State all too often.

Our trip to the top has entailed running against the big guns. The big schools from the capital region around Albany control the state year after year in cross country. Each year they're among the best in the nation. And it's not just Saratoga that can thunder around the course disarming every challenge. Many top colleges from D-I to D-III couldn't handle those class "A" teams from Greater Albany. But the little-school division that includes Skaneateles with high school populations of less than 450 students is ruled by the schools from the Greater Syracuse geographic area. It's just what we do here. If you make it out of Section III, you'll be in contention for the state title. But getting out of here alive is tough.

Our Skaneateles running community began to expect victory and advancement to the state meet once our system caught on, and it caught on quickly. To many people, titles became an entitlement. The school population really pooh-poohed us. We win. We win every year. So what? When the streak and success began, the parents would hold festive parties to celebrate the victories. They'd host tailgate parties at invitationals and the school administration would look to spread the school name by sending us around the state for overnight trips. The girls took offense when the local masses seemed less-than-impressed by winning every year. The general retort was, "Don't they know that we work for these titles? Everyone thinks it's easy."

Everyone got used to us winning. It all became rather blasé. Winning routinely is gone now, and at times, our fight has vanished, but it's coming back as we mature and re-learn some fundamental truths about our sport and ourselves.

We have to fight for everything in Skaneateles as lacrosse—the sport that too few know about across the nation—the marquee sport of football, the community's favorite sport of hockey, and parents' devotion to youth soccer generates the majority of raves, the endless drum-roll of publicity, big chunks of budgeted money, private booster club donations that once led to oak lockers for the hockey team, chartered busses for away games, and the majority of student body attention. Lately, if a large group of 7th and 8th grade soccer or baseball players show up on day-one of their season, parents demand and get the formation of another team, replete with coaches, uniforms, money for officials, busses, and equipment. This year the school is permitting a 55-man modified football team, and in soccer, a blue and a gold team for both boys and girls. The school district, at the behest of parents who refuse to let their kids experience failure, strives mightily to cut no one, and we're left with a one man modified boys cross country team as an unintended consequence. Because we don't compete with hockey or football, I've heard that we'll have 15-20 modified girls this fall, and that should provide enough sustenance to nourish our girl's team for a few more years.

Liz Bevier was a tremendously talented athlete who was somehow stuck in goal and usually on the bench for her junior varsity soccer team. We were fortunate to get her. Experiencing failure on her soccer team, she came to us as a sophomore and finished as the number 6-ranked 3000-meter runner in the United States in her senior year while almost breaking the 10-minute barrier on less than 28-miles a week. She dared to be different, a rare quality in this follow-your-friends social world we inhabit. If she'd been cut earlier, after an honest appraisal of her talent instead of an attempt to stuff the shelves in the soccer warehouse, who knows how far she'd have gotten.

I don't understand the no-cut policy. I do understand that parents just don't want their kids to be disappointed, but it creates a predictable pattern. If the kids are cut in 7th grade, they're presented with a real-life choice: work hard and try out again the following year or try another sport. By the time the kids have spent a year or two on the bench at the middle school level, they know that their playing days are numbered. Rather than admit public defeat and risk some degree of teasing or bullying from the 'real' athletes, as freshmen, they don't try-out for their JV team. They just drop out and fade away, forever removed from our potential pool of players, cut-off from being happy and maybe successful in another sport.

The last time I really remember a deserving kid getting cut was when my son, Kirk, was cut from JV basketball as a frosh. He was devastated. But he worked hard at his game, worked hard on his academics, and ended up starting varsity games his senior year while raising his grades to a nice, acceptable level for his parents. In a JV game, he went wild, scoring 33 points with nothing but 3-pointers from out in the stratosphere. Getting cut didn't kill him. He learned, developed character, resolve, learned to work and try, try, try again. He still plays and wows those who he plays against these days. He's earned the nickname "Shooter".

Keeping the kids when they should be cut is having the exact opposite effect on the kids and our teams, and the kids who are no longer on teams are the ones getting into trouble drinking, trying drugs and expressing criminal behavior. It could all be avoided if we'd just allow some Realty 101 into their lives.

In spite all of this, we've kept winning. On a night in December 2005, the team and parents decided to present me with a plaque that recognized our girls' win streak, which currently stands at 79 and started with Coach Card at the helm. Liz Bevier's testimonial expressed the following:

> *Well, the summer before 10th grade, I remember you calling my house, and a few of my friends who ran XC kept calling me, and finally that did it. I was on the team and sure enough, as you promised, that year we brought home the state title. Well, I quit basketball after that and became a full-fledged runner.*

I can't convince kids to run any more like I could with kids like Liz, but I'm fortunate to have the good kids that I now work with. They're a rare and dying breed. They're making real progress and I like what I'm seeing from them. But our ranks are thin. We need more bodies.

I was told around 1994 that I was no longer allowed to recruit. I used to publish a paper detailing our race results and hang copies on the walls in the school. The team loved them. Someone on the coaching staff lodged a complaint and that's all it took to end my publishing career. I was told in a hush-hush closed door meeting that I was achieving an unfair advantage. I was also told I shouldn't be using the 11x17 paper for copies of my newspaper. When told that the paper was from my own stock and I copied it elsewhere, they simply said, "Still, we're telling you not to do it anymore." The problem was that I was getting a good majority of the school's better athletes and that went against custom, raising the hackles of some other coaches. Today I train whoever is brave enough to join, and fewer and fewer show up on opening day.

We're a great little community with 164 properties assessed at over a million dollars. Only about 7000 people can call this pristine place home. We're charitable in a very quiet way so that people aren't embarrassed. We have a billionaire living two miles from my house. We're professional, well-dressed, and hold many advanced degrees. We're entrepreneurs, we volunteer for everything. We're hustlers, creators, inventors, and drive little else but SUVs. (My Toyota Echo is one of the few subcompact exceptions.) But like the rest of America, we have a character flaw, as too many adults get their social self-esteem through their kids' participation in sports, and that has contributed to the no-cut policy. If a disgruntled mother calls and complains about her child getting cut, it means that kids who show up and have a pulse—but no desire or hustle—make the team, and that leads to mass lethargy as competition for spots on the team is virtually non-existent.

We have some new blood in our coaching ranks and I think that stale atmosphere is slowly beginning to change, and as it does, my runners don't look so geeky training all year long. Work ethic is once again showing the top of its head around Skaneateles as the pressure to win grows. But we've got a long ways to go.

Hearts are in the right place in our community but we have a lot of work remaining. We're making progress but not enough parents are thinking clearly. It's a competitive world and we aren't fully preparing our kids for it. Cuts enacted in a humanistic manner can help these good kids understand more about themselves and teach them that they can bounce back from disappointment. Parents from well-to-do and powerful families who undermine a coach's authority are teaching their kids about manipulation and little else. The kids know they should be cut. Teaching kids that good people move past disappointment is a better message, a better lesson to help them understand.

Pushing people around and using power in a selfish pursuit of self-aggrandizing ego gratification is the antithesis of the goal of the long distance runner. The distance runner travels the lonely trail seeking harmony between the environment and his own life-supporting systems. The runner tries to fit in like the pre-colonial era Native Americans gliding through the forest unseen and unheard. The runner measures growth step- by-step, one blister at a time, while understanding that the real fight is personal. It's gaining control over himself, not other people. The distance runner, looking aloof and self-absorbed as he runs along the shoulders of neighborhood roads—chest rising expansively with the inhalation of life-giving oxygen—applauds those who pick themselves up after being knocked down rather than finding joy in knocking them down. He encourages the valiant efforts of those who struggle instead of creating a confrontation. He lends a cheer and stands with those who are friend or competitive foe instead of jeering those who are contributing to life's enhancement. At times the obnoxious or interfering parent is just like a scab that itches, irritates and just begs to be ripped into.

Houston, We Have A Problem

2005 was a frustrating season as we felt the brunt of the community's and school's philosophies, actions, and inactions. The cross country boys were young—and awful. A tragic car accident took our top runner off the team in 2004 and into the state prison system in 2005. His 1:54.16 for the 800 was sorely missed. His leadership was missed. His guts, fortitude, drive and willingness to get under the skin of his teammates was missed. He could prod like a red hot poker. He was the knout and fire torture that Czar Peter the Great of Russia used to painfully extract the information he needed from prisoners, which on one occasion included his own son, who died while being tortured.

Steve Corsello was one of the most well-read kids I know. The articulate, tie-wearing kid was the straw that would stir the team. Kids would fear him. He'd knock out a kid for picking on a defenseless under-classman in school. He'd defend his friends. He'd protect the weak. He'd fight for anything that was of value, anything that was right. He was Superman without the cloak.

And then he made a mistake. He went drinking and driving. Steve just couldn't say "no" to his friends. And it got him into hot water. Starting in the 8th grade, as we found out in the court deposition, he succumbed to the Skaneateles pop culture and entered the drinking social scene, where too many parents seem to condone and even encourage the consumption of alcohol. Steve's house was dry as a bone and Steve's dad felt deeply deceived after the accident when he discovered, too late, the irrefutable truth about his only son becoming a binge drinker. According to community talk, newspaper columns, studies and law enforcement comments, our community continues to remain aloof to the drinking problem.

We also have too many parents who push their kids unnecessarily into work before they celebrate their 14th or 15th birthday. With work comes the desire to have adult privileges. It's just the way it goes in this country. We like to raise social drinkers. We, the community that raises children together, gave Steve the okay to party. He hid it well. I was left out in the dark when usually I hear just enough to figure out what's going on behind the scenes.

His junior track season was done and he had a little time to blow-off some pent-up steam until his academic finals hit. I got a call in the middle of the night after the deadly accident just across from Skan-Ellus, our local ice cream and burger parlor on Route 20 east of the village. I thought I was dreaming. What I heard was Steve's dad crying his eyes out on my answering machine. "Steve killed someone. He's done. This has ruined everything." I know he didn't mean it. He was just totally devastated and I knew immediately that a part of him had died. You could hear it in his voice, the voice of a dad who loved his kid. I awoke and didn't think twice about it. It was just one of those dreams, I thought, where you break out in a cold sweat, wake up frightened, and realize it's just a dream. "Thank God it wasn't real," I softly said under my breath as I rolled over and went back to sleep.

Then Julian called again the next morning. My wife brought the phone to me in bed. Steve killed one of his best friends. He was locked away. It wasn't a dream. It wouldn't go away—ever. Nothing would be normal again. The nightmare would exist for all time.

One year down, one to go. That's where Steve is today. But, there's a third year waiting for him at the state's Mt. McGregor Correctional Facility north of Saratoga. I'll never think of Saratoga the same again. Steve wasn't alone in killing friends that year. A girl from Cicero-North Syracuse did the same thing as Steve and stayed in a local jail for less than 4 months despite not obeying the terms of her probation. She and her parents didn't have the remorse or common sense to attend mandatory alcohol counseling as they awaited the sentencing. A Lafayette boy killed three girls with his car, claimed he was remorseful, had the shakes, and was out in less than 4 months. A Phoenix boy killed his best friend the same way as Steve, driving drunk during the school day. He got a slap on the wrist when he appeared before the judge with '06 carved into the back of his head. He got probation and no jail time. For some reason, Steve is paying the bill for everyone around here. But there's no excusing Steve's total lapse of judgment. Months later the Phoenix boy was back in court, having gone after a girl with intent to harm her. He was told to stay away from her as the judicial system continued to miss the mark.

A few years earlier, it was Tom Poppe who took a chunk out of my soul. He'd just waltzed to a breathtakingly easy win in the state qualifier mile with a time in the low 4:20s. 'Pop' was long and lanky, with energy systems that made running easy. He delivered more oxygen to the muscles more efficiently than most athletes. Later in the Qualifier, he just bided his time in anchoring the 4x800 to victory with my freshman son, KC, in the line-up. Within two hours, Pop, an engaging, funny, spontaneous kid who was more Stan Laurel than anything else, was at his senior ball at the Skaneateles Country Club. According to reports, he was trying to get soap from a light switch. Adults had been giving him mixed messages for several years. On one Spring Break, just months before this incident, he watched as a school board member allowed his daughter to drink at a southern coastal hotel, to the point where she had to be taken to the hospital to have her stomach pumped. Yet, adults expect kids to successfully work their way through this thicket of confusing information. In Pop's case, as in most, it just didn't work as planned.

The morning after the Senior Ball, Pop strode down the uneven steps to my log home, legs shuffling and stumbling like usual as his arms swung wildly, his head hanging sheepishly, and I could tell something was seriously amiss. With his head still downcast and shoulders slumped like an old man, he swayed back and forth on his feet and fessed up, took the blame and expressed sorrow for his actions. Despite the blunder, he was acting like a man. Pop's still a great guy and one of my all-time favorites. He nurtured and encouraged my son when he came up to the varsity in the 8th grade. He coached our modified team one year. But he just screwed up badly at exactly the wrong time. At that point I had a decision to make: insert the alternate for the 4x800 or scratch from the state championship. I scratched, believing that our job as coaches is to act in the best interests of our section and advance the best athletes and relays to the state meet the following weekend. I called Tom Wells, our coordinator from New Hartford and pulled us out. I took some heated phone calls from parents for a few days, nasty calls, because to them it was important for their kids to get into the state meet. Whether the angst was derived from wanting the just rewards for their kids or that their social prestige could be in peril, I just don't know. I did understand their disappointment, though, and I knew it was genuine. But I still felt assaulted. And I had pulled my own son from the same state meet!

In the parents' minds, their son had earned the trip to the state meet, but without Pop, we were no longer the fastest team from our section. Hopefully the greater lesson led to a higher awareness and a more solid philosophy for life, I said to myself over and over. Runner-up Chittenango got the nod and my friend, Harold Muller who coached the Bears, realized that the door-of-opportunity had opened. He didn't have to think twice about accepting the offer.

My son, KC, a strapping kid who weighed over 200 pounds in college—too much for a middle distance runner—took the news without any real show of emotion. He was young enough to be in 8th grade and I was happy that he seemed to stay on such an even keel like his older brother. It was three years later when I read his college essay and the nirvana I inhabited was shunted aside much like Peter Pan's playful Never-Never Land being overtaken by the evil Captain Hook. He'd been crushed by the withdrawal and the disappointment had etched a deep scar on his psyche. I never knew. I'll forever be shaking my head. How could I have missed that?

Fortunately, he and his teammates Erik Eibert, Adam Evans and Steve Corsello made it to the state 4x800 finals two years after the Poppe incident. They medaled. KC had persevered and climbed the podium—a hay wagon—in spite of Pop's single mistake and my ensuing decision. Pop started out at the University of South Carolina but despite all of his native brilliance, he bailed out of an unhappy situation and became a chef in Syracuse. Fortunately, he seems perfectly happy when he stops in to see me at practice. He could have been an incredible star.

Anyway, the boys stank in 2005. We had our words, I tried to be patient, I taught, they tried to learn, and we got nowhere for the first time in my career. It was a slow learning curve and it frustrated me to no end. They were just too young and physically immature, bright as the dickens, but had no upperclassmen leaders to plow the way for them. I felt awful for putting them into varsity races. They never should have had to deal with that level of competition. Years before, when I had a stable of over a dozen sub 5-minute milers, they'd have been left on the modified team, learning to race, building strength, racing a mere 1.5 miles where they could gain experience, learn to fend off challenges, and feel successful. But rules are rules and sometimes the rules only hurt the ones that need to be protected. They were my top seven, so rather than being on the modified team where they'd have a chance to grow, they were my varsity team where they got squashed.

But that's about to change. I feel it deeply. We just need to get everyone out on opening day, keep them healthy, and continue to build a sense of belief in themselves. I hope I'm not disappointed when the season begins on August 21st.

Misfiring

The Skaneateles chain of success has been broken, a chain with links between generations of athletes, the older mentoring the younger. We are now trying to find our way back. The boys have grown; they can handle a 5-miler at a nice 6:30 pace, compliments of Pete Davis, who became a strong marathoner in his 40s. He also broke the 5-minute barrier while well into his 40s. He's a stud who goes out on runs around the lake. Thirty-five or more miles later, he's done for the day.

Pete has chosen to take off Mondays during the summer instead of taking a real vacation, in order to work on his biggest weakness, track speed, while he helps push and pull our boys. He can no longer hang with the senior boys but he won't back down and our team respects that. Pete replaced Rob Shostack who, as my assistant for many years, taught the boys a lot about toughness and pace as he went stride for stride with them.

Rob started working with me back in the early 1990s when we began our assent. When I first interviewed Rob, I was less than impressed. He seemed cocky, smug, aloof, and put-off by the process of having to interview for the job—after all, he was a 4:04 miler. But we hired him anyway. And I'm glad we did because I completely missed the boat. What a sense of humor. What knowledge. And what a gift he has to convey in words, nuances, facial expressions, what kids need to understand about training and racing. He's a treasure and uses self-deprecating humor to the kids' advantage. He makes them actually feel what we all try to make them understand. I've never seen anyone do it like Rob. He could break down a course and devise a race strategy better than anyone. And his strategies worked—if you really believed in yourself and our training. He'd inspire so much confidence that he was a big reason for our success. And he could run with the boys like no one. He must have had an inborn clock, because if I asked for a 62-second 400, we'd get it. If I wanted to do a lactic acid training session that covered 195-meters in 30 seconds, he'd do it to the meter.

Rob left us to take the coaching job at Syracuse Christian Brothers Academy where he led Jason Meany to some titles and national recognition at the indoor nationals. Jason ended up being an All-American at Clemson and was just hired to teach science at his alma mater. I tried to hire him for our modified job too.

Rob left CBA for Westfield State in Massachusetts and implemented some of our tactics, most notably our LAT workout. We initially started them with a 75-second rest between reps. It was a somewhat unguided workout that relied on feel and pace perception. Run hard for 30-seconds and get the 75-second rest. Two sets of 8. Our sets gradually worked up to 12, 14 and then 16, and our rest went slowly down to 25 seconds. Rob's college kids struggled for months but got the hang of it. Within the first year Rob was producing national champions in Division III. I'd always wondered how our training would affect older runners.

Early on, beginning at Marcellus, I had a general idea about training but something was missing. And I knew it. I knew that my high school training back in the 60's was deficient, though well-intentioned. My mind kept repeating, "Paces, paces, it's the paces, stupid." But, what speed should the paces be for the different workouts? I read everything, but nothing passed the common sense test.

Then I found an article written by Jack Daniels and the skies opened for me. I was right. Training paces are the key to improvement in race performances. Training at different paces and covering an array of distances, depending on the coach's objectives, and applying different stresses by using different rest intervals produces faster races. Depending on the stress being applied, the body's engine might use oxygen, fat, glycogen, or a mixture exactly like a hybrid car, to move. The body's motor reacts much like a car as quick accelerations and fast driving speeds use more gas less efficiently than setting the cruise control on the interstate for a long trip.

Each energy system is separate and distinct and each one must draw sustenance from either oxygen or fat for the slowest paces used for long runs, or carbohydrates for the quicker paces used in the middle distance repeats ranging from 400 meters to 1200 meters. Each system has to be addressed by running specific paces with specific rest intervals in order to help the runners recover and improve. And Daniels had the answers, as he used the latest race to determine fitness and in establishing the corresponding training paces for the coming training period. Train the kids at the level they're at, not the level you want them to be. Get them fit at their current level and they'll race faster. Then train them faster. Daniels believes that less is best and that philosophy has served me well over my career. When you think you should do more, back off, take a breath, and end the workout. They're kids. With further research I learned that energy systems don't differentiate until some undetermined age in the teens, and that day is different for every kid. Until the energy systems are fully developed, it seems to me that a basic conditioning program replete with moderate distance runs ranging, depending on age and ability, from 4 to 8 miles and speed training is the way to train most teens.

Daniels spoke at a few of our cross country banquets and he attended a few of our modified meets in the early '90s. His wife said he usually booked speaking engagements many, many months in advance, sometimes a year in advance, but when I called, he accepted on the spot. And what a wonderful message he gave the kids: Train, train, train. Be prepared. If and when the door of opportunity opens, be ready. Leave nothing to chance. No wonder the guy was called the best coach in North America by Runner's World while some refer to him as the world's best distance coach.

After a cut in the budget at Westfield State, Shostack returned to us and once again helped train the teams, this time as a volunteer. He had principles, and when the Athletic Director cut the budget at Westfield, Shostack felt it sent the wrong message. So he left. Not many men would do that today. He enrolled in the Syracuse University IT graduate program and is a top dog at world famous Stickley Furniture in Manlius, the place where people like Barbara Streisand gets her furniture. I don't shop there. I'm just a teacher who coaches, getting cast-off furniture from my parents or sister-in-law.

With the loss of running stature because of the budget cut at Westfield and the new demands caused by the birth of his firstborn son, the Z-Man, Shostack helped West Genesee with their distance runners near his home. West Genny is the lacrosse giant of America and is coached by Hall-of-Famer Mike Messere. Messere gets the cream of the crop as many decades ago the community bought his strict training and Code of Behavior regimen lock, stock and barrel. Cross Country and track coach Jim Vermeulen has had to scratch out a living by poking under stairwells, behind the bus garage, and into the hallways to slowly build his program. (I'm envious of Mike, but have a lot more in common with Jim.) Mike is retired but still coaching, while I'm sure when I retire from teaching, I'll leave Skaneateles coaching, too. Our worlds are different.

Rob now has rheumatoid arthritis yet he runs and competes at a relatively high level when the drugs permit. But usually he travels to meets with his little son Zach and the two of them support his wife, Pauline, as she handles the family 5k chores. Rob also coaches the Syracuse Fleetfeet team of road racers and marathoners, and they do extremely well.

Rob will be working with my old co-coach, Lou Delsole, he with the gruff exterior and the 'don't mess with me look' who was fired from Skaneateles for defending his girls from a teacher who misrepresented an incident in the hallway during the final rep of the final indoor track practice of the season. I was there. I know exactly what happened.

Lou also called the Steve Corsello fiasco, within the school, what it really was. The official school rule, after Steve was charged with vehicular homicide, was that a kid could be kicked out of sports IF the media got involved and it became a big story. Otherwise, he could play. Lou called it what the lawyers in Syracuse called it, "The Steve Corsello Clause." If your transgression results in you becoming a hot topic, the school invokes the rule.

Someone in the office overheard Lou and ratted him out to the school officials and Lou was gone. Free speech? Private conversations? Losing Lou hurt and it was a loss for the program, the kids, the school and the community. But that's high school sports. Coaches aren't exactly the lowly 'vermin' in India called Untouchables, but they're a close cousin: here today, gone tomorrow without cause in too many instances as personalities, parent phone calls and petty parochial politics determine a coach's fate more than how well they work with kids.

I remember one time when I finally got so sick of poor indoor training facilities in Skaneateles—where the winter lasts over six months—that I proposed an indoor, multi-use facility that would enhance the well-being of nearly everyone in town. I drew up a plan, plotted an amateur architectural drawing, scouted around other facilities and met with the editor of the local paper. We went Page-One. There was a picture and a headline that said, "Coach Proposes Multi-Purpose Rec Center." The next day I was sitting with the school superintendent in a little cloak storeroom. The word "Coach' upset him. We'd always gotten along and he's always supported me. But he was bent out of shape for this one. Apparently he had a top-secret plan for a fancy school renovation and he didn't want publicity or taxpayer support to be split into two factions. Bottom line? I told him my proposal had nothing to do with the school and he needed to back off. What I did was as a private citizen and I couldn't control how the local press developed their headlines. We remain friends. But speaking your mind can result in a doomsday scenario as far as careers go in Skaneateles.

While the boys struggled in 2005, the girls were on a mission after failing to keep the 10-year sectional streak alive in 2004. Attendance at voluntary summer sessions was superb. We'd see 15 to 21 girls a day. They wanted to train together at 8 AM in the summer three days a week. Can you imagine that? This year, well, times have changed. I see four to five girls a morning. I've yet to see some members of the team this summer, while I haven't heard from others at all. I email, I stroke them, try to be personal, talk about things other than running, but still get no response. It seems disrespectful to me. I guess I have thin skin.

I heard from Jennifer Finnegan Patruno, a Wake Forest All-American who turned our modified girls into an unbreakable rubber band last fall. She told me that one of her soon-to-be frosh, who has actually been showing for summer practice, has quit so she could pursue her interest in dance this fall. Based on what I've seen this summer, it's her mom's decision. I never saw anything except the desire to improve as a runner from the girl. She'd hurt her hip and I'd have to almost physically pull her out of a practice. I haven't heard a word about quitting from either she or her mom. Basic courtesy has vanished as the nation grows coarser.

Jennifer and her husband David run the Aim High Running Camp every summer at Camp Aldersgate in the Adirondacks. They're great people who will follow the XC, indoor, and outdoor circuit every year to cheer on 'their kids'. Last summer one of their week-long guest speakers was Jonathon Riley. After camp broke they brought Jonathon, his wife, and son back to Skaneateles. We notified as many Skaneateles kids as quickly as possible about the impromptu celebrity visit. Over the years, I'd told the kids endless stories of Jonathon's exploits. Some were desperate to meet him and this was their one chance. Zandra Walton would get absolutely giddy talking about meeting Riley. And that night, her wish came true. We spent hours at Doug's Fish Fry where Jon and his wife dropped the names of Olympians like I'd drop the name of the guy who makes my pizza at Valentine's. The Olympic names that they dropped were more often than not their babysitters. We walked out on the pier into the serene and clean Skaneateles Lake as sailboats glided past, the sun reflected off the stained windows of a church, people in canoes paddled past and young fishermen dunked worms into the still water. I think people who we brushed past while walking south on the pier knew something was up, but they weren't sure who in our group was the celebrity. I do know that patrons of Doug's Fish Fry were craning their necks to hear what was being so casually discussed in the outdoor dining area about the Athens Olympics.

The Patrunos didn't have to be so charitable after a tiring week with well over 100 kids, but I'm grateful. Riley lived in Palo Alto, California and trained with the Nike Farm Team. I hadn't seen him since his senior year of high school so the brief reunion was special. Jonathan emailed me right before he left from the Olympic Village to go to the track for his 5000-meter prelims in Athens. He was a bit worried. He'd gained some weight. "The restaurants in the 'village are open 24 hours a day," he wrote.

The summer before the 2005 season, my girls were focused. We ran, we trained, we talked—man, we talked. We exchanged long, thought-provoking e-mails and we cheered each other on. I cajoled, I pushed, and by listening long and hard I soon learned that the group could not handle expectations or pep talks like previous teams. So, assistant coach Rob Tuttle and I purposely understated everything, tried to have more fun, and waited for the sectional championship. Tuttle was a Sauquoit Valley graduate, the team we'd need to beat to move on to states. Imagine that. Our former rival still has scars from a loss to us at the Sandy Creek Falling Leaves Classic in the mid 90s. We love beating Sauquoit Valley. Well-coached and always at the top of their game, a victory over them means something. With a member of the 'enemy camp' in our midst, we thought we would get a leg up on the competition, better understand their thinking, get some tips from Rob's dad who still lives in Sauquoit and keeps his eyes on them for us. Well, we got rolled by Sauquoit and it wasn't even close.

Frosh Rachel Hosie took off and led the race for a while. After her first race of the season when she did the same thing, I suggested that she hold back early in the race. Man, what a boneheaded mistake. I over-coached her. I took the natural rhythms right out of her and it took me two months to get it back. She held on well against the Sauquoit girls but had trouble repeatedly climbing up the west side of the Tug Hill Plateau in South Jefferson's mud pit. We almost moved the race to another locale early that week because of the mess Mother Nature left, but after on-site inspections and some course adjustments, we held to the original plan.

Other than Hosie, we got mugged. Looking back, Sauquoit Valley had a career day with everyone hitting their peak at the right time—in unison. We didn't stand a chance. But we were second. After ten straight first place finishes, we now had two straight second place finishes. We were crushed, disappointed, numbed that day by the 'debacle', and many of the girls cried. We'll work on that.

After 10 straight years of dominance, after earning so much respect statewide, getting regionally ranked by Marc Bloom in the XC bible, The Harrier (8th in 2000 and 9th in 2001), after having opposing kids mumble under their breaths when we arrived via the great yellow bus with Gary Martin at the helm, "Damn! Skaneateles is here," we had quickly squandered our aura of invincibility. We'd pissed away nearly everything we worked so hard to get. It wasn't a lack of talent that doomed us. It was mental, and it drove me nuts. Suddenly we were like every other team with hopes, and, in our case, a proud but faded legacy.

We had a swagger and a will to win that was hard to deny for well over a decade. Alum Cadie Cargile (Bucknell '06) wrote to the girls last year to help rally some gumption for the sectional challenge. Cadie was on her way to a stellar career when compartment syndrome felled her. Dr. Wayne Eckhardt, who along with partner Irv Raphael takes care of the Syracuse University athletes, operated on Cadie. On occasion, he dropped by the school to check on her progress. But after two years, Cadie was still not free of the drop leg syndrome. Unfortunately, she was in the 10% statistical anomaly that didn't achieve immediate rectification of the problem. Some body weight ultimately packed its way onto her small frame which finished her running career—or so we thought. This past spring, Cadie completed her first marathon with a Bucknell Bison teammate who also had left the college team. After Cadie's frosh year, she told me that there were nearly three dozen cases of stress fractures on the team and that the health department launched an investigation. Fact or fiction, I don't know. But I do know that too many college coaches ignore the mileage totals that their recruits hit in high school and quickly crank up the mileage to ungodly totals. A gradually escalating increase in mileage, drawn up in a four-year plan, would be constructive and much healthier.

Cadie put her heart into the letter to the girls, and she tried valiantly to convey some of the fighting spirit that permeated our former teams.

> *I was pushed down and fell into the mud but I got up because my coach mentioned it in the final pre-race talk. Soon, panic struck; I would be the determining factor. We would win or lose based on my race. Contradictory words of pain and team crossed my mind in incomplete sentences. The pain grew intense with every step. But it was the thought of the team that gave me strength. Crossing the line, I stumbled and cried. We won, barely. We won the state title. Six points, that's the margin. I was proud of my team, knowing that any one of the girls would have gotten up out of the mud. As we 7 stood on the victory stand, I grasped the meaning of 'team' and 'depth'. I was a senior. It finally clicked. With the clapping and camera flashes, we stood not as 7 individuals who were champions, but*

as ONE state championship team. If any link is broken, the team is lost. Hold strong, each and every one of you.

It didn't work. Sauquoit looked more like our teams than we did.

The state meet victory in 2000 that Cadie salvaged for us was to be followed by two more. The spirit we felt from our local running community was quiet, subdued, but very heartfelt. English teacher Gail Sullivan, whose daughter, Meg, raced for us years before, gave me a note to read to the girls on the bus as we headed to States.

Dear Championship Cross Country Team—

So many students who ran this year, and every adult I know who runs, would love to be in the seat you now have. Congratulations on your talent and your training. Some of you are on this bus because you are gifted by the running gods, but most of you worked and suffered and paid a high price to ride the bus to States. You know which category you inhabit. I'll be praying to those same gods of running for you, your coach, and your success on Saturday. Best of all, may good luck be with you. I envy and admire every one of you and wish I were riding there with you. Women, your custom-designed shirts were a credit to your creativity and your team spirit. You get firsties on the Twizzlers. May the winds be at your back. Mrs. Sullivan

Before the secret school renovation became reality, we had the girls stage their travel luggage in the main high school lobby on the East Elizabeth Street side of the school that featured a tile replica of our town, lake and village on the lobby floor. Except for one year when the school superintendent was in the area, the kids have felt slighted and hurt because they never saw a high school representative in the lobby to send the girls off to 'states with a wish of luck or good fortune. We're not all that important, the girls would think. And then I'd have to spend time on the bus getting them back up. You'd think that there'd be some link between the people who run the school and the highest achieving athletes who just happen to end up in the top-10 of the class rankings every year. Even though we don't do this for the accolades, it's nice to be recognized. But the girls always felt the persistent snubs, whether intentional or accidental.

With photographers snapping pictures of a thoroughly exhausted Cadie in 2000 as concerned and appreciative teammates surrounded her, she struggled to get composed in the finish chute 3.1 muddy miles from the starting line after her stellar state meet run. Her blue and yellow hair tie was still intact, but the mud had done a job on her blonde hair. We didn't leave the crowded area outside the finish chute very quickly as we surrounded Cadie in a tight and loving circle. There was something special going on amidst the hundreds of admirers and followers of our team. It was exciting and it helped refill drained batteries that had carried these girls so valiantly to the title.

Dan Doherty, famed coach of the Pearl River Pirates, knew a torch had been passed. Dan, who helps run this massive state's running championships while doing the team rankings, sent me an e-mail the following night.

> *Jack,*
>
> *It is never easy to accept defeat, and we sure as heck were disappointed by it yesterday. But when it happens to a team with girls and a coach that all show the class and dignity of true champions, it makes it a little easier to accept. Congrats to a great team, both on and off the course.*
>
> *Dan Doherty*

We'd had a rivalry for a while before the 2000 race finished, and it excited the girls. It helped make them better athletes and gave them a focus that pulled them through the doldrums of mid-season when dual meets just raised the level of boredom. Dan took it to us in 1999 at the state meet, which was held at Westchester Community College. My lakeside neighbor Lia Cross placed 4th in the team scoring. Vanessa Everding took 6th, with Cadie Cargile 8th and Simone Bras 10th. I never thought we'd lose that one. My belief is that if you get three in the top 10, you wear the crown. But not against Pearl River, who had their act together that bright sunny day. Courtney O'Keefe and Vanessa McKay went 1-2 and that was that.

The Skaneateles boys took a surprising and well-earned 3rd that same day behind Weston Cross in 9th, Tom Poppe in 11th, Andy Porter in 26th, Steve Alexander in 27th and Roger Lind in 33rd. Closing it out for us was Tom Smolenski in 41st who went on to do the animation for the Conan O'Brien Show, and Brett Searing in 57th. The boys were the unsung heroes that year as the girls simply overshadowed them. All in all, it was a pretty good showing for Skaneateles that bright day downstate. The boys wore all yellow for that one. The boys are wearing all yellow again this year. It's time to get back in the hunt.

We all got a series of unwanted medical lessons in 2000 as we looked at our 'End-Times', our athletic Armageddon, week after week. Hypoglycemia, hyperglycemia, neurally mediated hypotension, heart monitors, sports anemia, self-hypnosis and sports induced asthma entered our collective vocabulary, but we persevered.

My girls have always been creative and fuzzy warm with each other. They create buddy bags replete with healthy snacks and inspirational quotes that they exchange on the bus according to a blind name-draw a few days prior to the big meet. The bags got so creative and expensive that we had to put a temporary stop to them and get back to the original intent as Type "A" girls who are achievement-oriented took the tradition to an unhealthy and pricy level. The bags had become bigger than the meet. Sheila Card, the innovative creator of the treasured tradition, was great at reaching the girls from the emotional perspective. She was on the cutting edge with her visualization practices in the late 80s and early 90s. Emotions, that's my weakness. I'm more training oriented. But fuzzy or not, the girls would hit hard and their creativity hit a lofty peak with the Pearl River rivalry.

They took a song by the Dixie Chicks called *"Earl Must Die"* and changed some lyrics so that "Pearl" must die. That tape would be pulled out on the bus to 'states every year and once we were out of town heading to somewhere, those girls would begin to sing and sing and sing. I couldn't ever get tired of it, though. Even in December, long after the XC season had been wrapped-up, Pearl River was on our minds. Merritt Haswell, who ran through a series of very strange running injuries and illnesses at Connecticut College before graduating in 2006, emailed one night in 1999 after the loss to Pearl River at 'states. Merritt placed 42nd in the team scoring.

Next year we'll win and get Pearl River, because a lake's better than a river. Congratulations on a great season and a great job.

Love,

Merritt Haswell

And then the tradition slowly died. Rome wasn't built overnight, but neither did the Empire fall meekly into the abyss of history in a fortnight. It struggled, fought, and ultimately lost. Skaneateles sent me a lot of kids with heart, with courage, with an unusual sense of responsibility and determination. We rose. We soared, and flew across this great state with dignity, grace and a thirst for competition. The descent hasn't been swift like the depth plunge of an endangered submarine as an enemy ship with deathly depth charges and sensitive 'ears' approaches across the blank gray slate called an ocean, but the decent we're experiencing is palpable and evident to anyone with a sense of history. I have to make it stop. We need to surface, to bob back to the top.

We're all disappointed that things have changed, that fate grew fickle, that the earth's energy shifted like the magnetic-north pole. Things change and it's impossible to face the onslaught of a tsunami as a lone by-stander on a deserted tropical beach. We're a team, and we need to fight this together.

"Go with it," says the swami. "Don't desire," says the Buddhist monk. "Chill," says the beach-combing hippie. But I'm from a different world, one that says, "Produce." I recognize that life is a one-time thing, it's precious, and the battles that we deem significant are not going to be on our minds as we are sprawled across our death bed. I understand that life is good until the instant it isn't and that I should simply enjoy this precious gift.

I don't lust. I don't thirst. I don't covet. I just want to win with the kids who dare to stare at themselves in the mirror and challenge their inner being to be better, to be the best, to soar above mediocrity while vowing to never settle for average. I want to be with winners, those with the willpower to seek healthy challenges, to give up a little of the teen pop culture for greater rewards, to hold their Gang's urges at bay so that something tangible can be carried away from here in their hearts, in their minds, and deep inside where self-worth resides quietly as it brightly colors everything they will encounter for the rest of their lives.

Everything my Laker girls did with Pearl River was done in good fun and in good taste; they were great girls working hard to convince themselves that the impossible was indeed possible. Lia graduated from Colgate, Vanessa from Yale, Cadie is a Bucknell Bison for life, and Simone left Williams with a degree and a husband. America will be proud of them. They weren't average. They were different, rare like an expensive gem mined from a field of Finger Lakes shale.

Throttle Up

How dominating were the girls? The boys? Us? Our program?

Around here, we believe that our league, the Onondaga High School League (OHSL), is the largest in the nation. With more than 45 schools lining up in a one-race championship format, it's bedlam, crowded, hectic, and at times dangerous. Once at LeMoyne College, the belly of the snake hit a significant dip in the course, just 100-meters into the race. And down they went; the multitudes piling atop one another in a tangled heap. After a strong start, my Marcellus team ended up at the back of the pack, felled and trampled.

This league of ours, rough and large as it is, can proudly boast of member school Fayetteville-Manlius, a national power coached by their guru, Bill Aris, a tall, balding, brilliant and intense motivator. He's fit and possessed and has rigid features that bring to mind an eccentric Ichabod Crane, lean and lanky, skin and bone, with distinctive facial features. He's the personification of Maslow's self-actualized man and he's probably done more for our sport locally than anyone else. Rising to the top of the nation in the Nike polls had a positive effect that can't be ignored, and their 'Stotan' slogan that emphasizes a personal philosophy of toughness, dedication and togetherness has changed the face of running around here. The rest of us will either improve our game or we'll be embarrassed.

In 2000, my little group of girls took the OHSL title with a record low score of 40 points, a remarkable total considering the laws of probability. The record still stands. Fayetteville-Manlius, led by Laurel Burdick (Boston College; an FM modified coach now) in first and

Brittany Crawford (Davidson) in 9th was back in second with 102 points. Our 'Fab-5' as Neil Kerr of the Post-Standard dubbed them, included Vanessa Everding who placed 2nd and Lia Cross who took 3rd as Julie Lynch grabbed 7th with Simone Bras in 8th. Cadie Cargile took 20th while Emily Everding (Syracuse) came in 26th. Erika Geihe (Harvard) was 31st in a field of nearly 300. It was one of the most gratifying and scintillating performances of my career. We had tamed the mighty OHSL, little Skaneateles. The name on the bus was getting recognized in a vast steel forest of yellow.

Lynch went on to compete for American University and was coached by Matt Centrowitz. They fought fiercely, incessantly. A graduate of the University of Oregon Ducks, Centrowitz has coached three Olympians: David Strang, John Trautman, and Jen Rhines. Centrowitz has had great success in just seven years at American, and he's a current member of the Olympic Development Committee, but he met his match in Lynch. Eventually, after many late night phone calls from Washington D.C. and many attempts by me to get Julie to give her new coach a chance, she'd had enough and transferred, never to compete again. It was simply a match made in hell. She was getting injured, frustrated and distrustful in spite of laying down some incredible times after long spells of non-running rehab periods. The relationship just flat broke apart. They were two strong-minded individuals with willpower that, prior to their teaming up, had never really been challenged. It was such a shame, such a loss for the sport. Julie doesn't run anymore and this summer she's in Croatia on a humanitarian and religious mission.

But it wasn't just the Skaneateles girls at the OHSL championship back in 2000 that stood proudly at the meet's conclusion. The boys, who'd not done much that year, grabbed a close third in a performance that ranks as one of our special crowning achievements, even more than some state titles. They just got the job done, overachieved, believed, rallied each other and followed a collective, vibrant, human spirit. Runners do that. Together, these friends defied the odds, didn't listen to the running gods and determined their own destiny by sticking together like glue through the winding trails and up "The Wall," a steep hill that is nearly impossible to climb on a muddy day. The fans who surround "The Wall" are the cousins to those who hang around the Steeplechase water pit: sadistic and looking for trouble. They're my kind of people.

The giant from Liverpool, one of the largest schools in New York State, won that day with 114 points. Fayetteville-Manlius tallied 120 and little Skaneateles scored a nice 156 behind Weston Cross in 10th (University of Buffalo), Andy Porter in 26th (College of Environmental Science and Forestry—Syracuse), Jason Evans in 37th (Captain, Bentley College '04), Tom Smolenski 41st (Rochester Institute of Technology), Matt Zubrowski 42nd (State University of New York at New Paltz), 8th grader Steve Corsello 46th (State Prison/Amherst '11), and Adam Evans 73rd (Captain, Bentley College '06).

We weren't always good. When I was hired away from Marcellus to coach the boys, Skaneateles was, almost without argument, the worst club in the Empire State. I had a year to get it back up and running. And we did it. The girls seemed to have an unending flow of talent from the middle school team. It was different for the boys.

The old guard that I inherited was melded with some guys who I recruited hard over the summer, kids I saw hanging around the playgrounds and the school campus. There was no junior high feeder system. That would come later. I had to hit the recruiting trail.

Baseball player Jeff Welch came to us after I saw him on the school's front lawn tossing fly balls to himself. Old-timer John Kelly re-joined the team after putting on mega-pounds from weight lifting and looking more like Arnold Schwarzenegger than distance phenom Gerry Lindgren. With the added weight, he was still good. Today, he's a police officer in Richmond, Virginia. Restaurant owner Jeff Lego returned with more dedication, though one Saturday morning I could tell he'd had more than a beer the night before so I ran him until he puked. And then, over that following spring, the Riley family moved into the district, Jonathon and his brother Jamie. We began cooking right away. With the varsity holding their own until the sectional race when two of my top guys didn't make the bus, we built a modified team that was unbeatable in the early 90s. We were the New York Yankees back when they carefully groomed their minor league prospects. Long-time McQuaid Jesuit coach Bob Bradley saw what was coming during the Auburn Invitational hosted by Al Wilson. We had a group that was talented, willing to work, and willing to take my goal as their dream. Adam Cross (Cortland State), Dave Crowther (Grove City College), Scott Clearwater (Calvin College), Todd Jackson (UCONN),

Jeff Boden (Holy Cross), Kirk Reed (Ithaca) and Pete Hawley (actor, musician) put Skaneateles on the map when they teamed with James Goss (Lynchburg) and Jon (Stanford) and Jamie Riley. They were a rag-tag group that wasn't too concerned with girls, snappy dress or being on time for practice. But the boys persevered and were willing to stink up a t-shirt. Like the girls, they moved on to the big stage as they entered the state championship sweepstakes.

Chills, Choking and Growth

There are times when I get chills looking back at all the flowers that have bloomed, all the Horatio Alger stories that were written from scratch, all the memories that are reawakened when I look at yellowed, musty smelling newspaper clippings and pictures piled high in so many shoe boxes. There are times when I'll try to talk to my understanding and patient wife, Patty, about some team issue, and I get choked up. It comes out of nowhere. It happens without warning. I don't know if she's caught on yet, but I have to take a break, catch my breath, regain my composure and try to nonchalantly tell her my little story of self-importance while my voice rises and cracks. If I didn't fight it, I'd be bawling. John Madden and Andre Agassi have nothing over me.

I'm getting more and more emotional and sloppy now. There's more distance behind my run through life than before me; my quick pace slowing noticeably. I'm 54, graying, thin—I like to refer to myself as thin strips of sinewy steel—and I can still wind it up on a run if I'm slightly stuffed up and on the wonder drug known as Prednisone. Physically softening and emotionally more mellow, it's gotten to the point where I can't even speak the name of some of these kids at a team banquet.

After the 2006 track season, I was awarding Josey Witter the Track MVP at the Springside Inn on the northwestern shore of Owasco Lake, the inn owned by one of my former co-coaches, Tracy Fanning and her husband. Josey is an Eagle Scout and a growing talent in the jumps, so I tried to mention, in a matter-of-fact manner, alumni sprinter and jumper James Goss during the presentation.

James became the new head coach at Lynchburg College in Virginia after a three year stint coaching sprinters and jumpers at Emory University in Atlanta. James was one of mine. At one time he was the only local kid who could run competitively with our Olympian, Jonathon Riley, with the exception of a kid named Colt from Rome who I heard ended up in prison. James struggled when his father died after a rough divorce. His mother married Burt Lipe, owner of the World Famous Morris' Bar and Grill. Burt, ever the promoter, once sponsored a local race called the Short Fat-man Race where walking replaced running, beer filled the water jugs, and tobacco smoke swelled the participant's lungs. John Madden, who undoubtedly met the qualification criteria of having a bigger waist than inseam measurement, spent some time talking about the race during one of his NFL games back in the day. Burt's a businessman. "If the door's closed, you can't put money in the register," he'd often say. On my way to school at 7:15 on many mornings, I see Burt in Morris's serving his patrons. Burt took good care of James and James' mother, MJ, and James became a star athlete.

There was one shot in basketball that ranks as number-1 in the annals of b-ball, and I've been watching since before Elvin Hayes and his hook shot beat UCLA in the Astrodome. It was a fast break and James was flying down the left sideline of the court right in front of me. James was a sprinter, a good one, with a 100 personal best of 10.79 and a 21.57 for the 200. A ¾ court pass, thrown high and hard, led James from center court deep into the corner. With one super-coordinated jump that was part high and part long, James rose and rose—his head nearly even with the rim—grabbed the ball, turned to the right in mid-air and launched a perfect shot. He landed in the doorway of the gym and catapulted across the hallway. Three points for the Lakers.

My oldest son, Kirk, who is now the Assistant Commissioner of the NCAA Division II Central Atlantic Collegiate Conference (CACC) while pulling part-time duty at ESPN in Bristol, took James under his tutelage when they were in junior high and playing together on school teams. As a good friend should, Kirk helped trim James' highs and lows. Kirk has patience. He's moderate. But once that uniform went on, Kirk was an athlete possessed with more pride than nearly anyone I know. He's also the most loyal guy on the planet until crossed. Once scorned or burned, and the person is on 'the list', friends no more. Today, at the age of 29, Kirk and James are having babies at the same time; Kirk a boy (Jackson) and James a girl (Brenna).

James became so placid and even-tempered that his girlfriend Kenzie once thought he was too calm, too sedate, not exciting enough to ever consider marrying. He's a great man and will generate real competitiveness at Lynchburg. While I was visiting Kirk at his new home in Waterbury, Connecticut, James called and announced he was marrying my niece. Kenzie had changed her mind and realized that she'd been wrong in assessing James. He's quietly fierce with a willingness to cut you down in competition without blinking a steely eye.

Well, my voice buckled real badly when I tried to talk about James and his NCAA indoor collegiate long jump championship during the Josey Witter MVP presentation. I had to stop talking. I looked down at my speech neatly typed and spread across the podium while damning myself for folding under pressure once again. I clearly remember thinking that no one in the big audience had any clue what was getting to me. I'm not sure myself, and I can't seem to suppress these deep feelings that rise inconveniently during team banquets. Even sappy movies make my eyes well-up when I'm alone in my favorite TV chair late at night. *Peter Pan* with Robin Williams? Nothing but tears. *Dead Poets Society*? I shake with emotion, the throat actually hurting from spasms and convulsions.

Am I getting so old that my loss of poise is just the tip of the iceberg? Am I just beginning to understand the importance of these kids in my life, the role we played in each other's life? Sometimes, no matter how hard I try to pull back from this deep running hole I've dug for myself, I realize I can't escape. I'm a runner. I'm a coach. I help kids. I like kids. And I can't turn my back once we engage. I wonder what'll happen to me and my relationship with my wife when, in two years, I retire from teaching and either cut back or quit high school coaching? It could be a colossal failure. Do I really want to collect and hand in the kids' finish cards for the final time? Do I want a life without having to soothe bruised egos, temper super-euphoria, painstakingly evaluate the team's condition and develop meticulous training programs while always trying to keep kids coming to practice because they actually like being on the team?

What's become of me? I'm a coach. Kids matter. And I care. It's what I've always done. Now what?

Eric Roschick—Shooting Star

The best from my early days at Skaneateles was the late-Eric Roschick, a stalwart and vanguard of everything good that was to come. Eric stood tall and stayed true to himself. And though he was expressive, sentimental and enormously bright and civil, his competitive nature was in plain sight for everyone to see and it exploded as easily as a child twisting off the cap of a shaken can of soda. He would compete with obvious emotion and raw physical power with anyone over anything. He was a different sort of guy.

Strong, talented and possessing deep feelings that people weren't exposed to in the school system, I benched him for the Auburn Invitational during his senior year. Our schools border each other. Auburn's a member of the large school division of the OHSL and most of Eric's family resided in Auburn. It should have been the biggest moment of his life, even more so than winning at McQuaid along with teammate Christina Rolleri (Indiana/University of Delaware). But he was academically bored. On this occasion he tossed some rocks through the windows of a barn while out on his run. Benched. It hurt me to do it. Many years later, I would wonder if I'd done the right thing. He really got into running while in college. He somehow talked his way into a running scholarship in Louisiana. In August! The boy could close a deal when he wanted to. Academically bored and tired of the heat that rose hard from the bayous early in the Louisiana mornings, he transferred to the University of South Carolina. After one season the men's program was cut. I guess the administration felt the football team needed more coddling. The Gamecocks saved the football team by trimming the cheapest sport on campus. At the athletic awards banquet with other teams, Eric got on stage, turned his back on the audience and dropped his pants, mooning the administrators. That was Eric Roschick, the summer runner who would run to the golf course to do maintenance at 5 AM, and then take an even longer run back home after the workday ended. And, he always wore something black and skin tight in the summer, looking like the great Peter Snell of New Zealand.

Eric dared to be different. Here's his college essay.

> *I have chosen to tell you a little about myself through poetry. I feel the use of rhyme and scheme can in itself construct a likeness of myself unable to be obtained through just words, a certain ambiance.*

I feel it's best to tell through rhyme
The life that I've lived one day at a time:
Things that I've held most close to my heart
And days that I've sung like the notes of Mozart.
One of the things that I do so endear
Is my gift of speed to run like the deer.
Another of God's gifts bequeathed to me
Is the beauty of Dali's creativity.
Thank the Lord almighty for another
And that's the gift of strength from my grandmother.
But the gift that's held most dear to me
Is the inner persistence to be all I can be,
To be Jessie Owens and fulfill the dream
To run in the ranks of the Olympic team.
But there is a hunger that I wish to unbind
And that is the hunger of my mind:
To see by the light brought through learning
And acquire the wisdom my spirit is yearning.
Now on to those who have inspired my goals
I owe much to these beautiful souls:
Martin Luther King for peace against afflictions,
Malcolm X for the courage of his convictions,
Thomas Jefferson and his dream of democracy,

J. D. Salinger for writing against social hypocrisy.
These people have taught me to live inspiration
And to inspire the thought of this beautiful nation,
But one thing I've learned is that knowledge is power
And allows the mind to turn from bud to flower.

Eric died on February 28th, 2001, in Pomona, California where he was killed in a car accident. Eric, was killed while on his way to take the California Law Boards. He was sideswiped and eliminated from the gene pool forever. Bored to death and not exactly compliant at Skaneateles High, the news of Eric's death hardly met with a shrug, as if the school were saying, "Just another troubled kid who's no longer here." I was pissed. What no one knew is that Eric was a straight 4.0 GPA student all the way through college, all the way through Cornell Law. He'd already passed the New York Law Boards and was working for a NYC law firm and trying life in California with his fiancée when he was killed. "Just another troubled kid…" Bullshit. Do some of those teachers even care about the kids?

Jim, his dad, still likes to watch two of Eric's favorite movies, "Titanic" and "Chariots of Fire." He still, at times, thinks that Eric is away at school and will pop in any moment. Eric had a tattoo of Mercury on his shoulder and then got one of an angel on his left arm that he designed. Two months later Eric was dead. On Father's Day morning after Eric was killed, Jim remarked to his wife that he believed that Eric would still give him a Father's day present. Later that afternoon as Jim sorted through some of Eric's track clothes, he found a $50 bill in one of the pockets. "One dollar or five dollars, maybe, but $50 among his college gear is remarkable." He also found a Father's Day card, signed by Eric, among the boxes of papers.

We named one of our annual awards The Eric Roschick Harrier Award in his honor in 2001. Jim came to the banquet and presented the award for the first time to Adam Evans who was named captain of his Bentley College team in his senior year.

At the banquet, I tried to get the kids to understand that life is fleeting, that tomorrow is never guaranteed, that they can't sell their soul because they think next season will definitely arrive on schedule. At the banquet, only my youngest son, KC, had ever heard of Eric.

Growing up with a coach made it impossible for KC to ignore what was going on with my teams. I told the kids to seize their days; that their talents were precious, their time short; the trip through life brief. I begged them to live full and passionate lives and to assume nothing while leaving nothing to chance.

Of course all talk such as this is useless for kids who feel immortal. But I tried and I continue to try on Eric's behalf because I know that the song will not go on forever; that the piano will grow silent, that the concert hall doors will soon be permanently closed. I told the kids how Eric had climbed the mountain, conquered his demons and proved all his naysayers wrong. Eric had more to do, a fiancée to marry, offspring to procreate and little league games to attend. He had elementary graduation to digitally record. He had pictures to take, ideas to put down on paper, trips to navigate, friends to hug, food to cook, life to live. Life! He had so much left to experience.

I asked the kids to trust us, their coaches, their teachers, we parents; everyone who had been traveling life's bumpy roads. "We are here to help you grow, not just to race," I said. "We see things that you can't see. We know things you'll someday know. Where we see fulfillment you see nothing right now. Some of you have fought us so hard that you've let go of the hands that are guiding you."

I know I didn't make a difference. But I'll never stop trying. The sight of Eric in his coffin on a lightless and snowy night haunts me still.

Moon Unit Zappa

Runners are a different lot from the rest of society. It's like comparing Frank Zappa to Barry Manilow. They're just a bit odd, but in a good way, like a Picasso, or vegetarian pizza or squid. If they were in an orchestra, they'd be the one playing the squeezebox. You get the idea. They're the sharp key on the piano or the happy owner of a snot-snorting shih-tzu dog.

My experience tells me that runners are unusually bright and inquisitive, delving deeper into their studies than the average member of the student body, and it's that same brainpower that can destroy them in competitive running. They simply over-think everything and end up suffering paralysis-by-analysis. They uncover too many variables that they can't control—weather, footing, topography, opponents, expectations—and see too many worthy opponents while formulating two negative thoughts for every positive one.

Runners are zany, uncharacteristically witty, deadpan funny and dour as pre-race worrying has them asking convincingly, "Why am I doing this?"

At once self-reliant and dependent on their coach for support, they occupy opposite sides of the social, behavioral coin, being conservative in everything pertaining to running, but more liberal than most in the views they hold on social issues.

Runners are comfortable with their bodies, the guys feeling free to bare their upper torso regardless of being mostly skin and bones, while the girls are quick to toss away their shirt, going forth in only their jog bra, which bothers many a faculty member, especially during indoor track practice. Some see the bras as low-life decadent and unbecoming a lady. Runners see the bras as affirmation of their athletic selves as they become more than a body, more than an object or sexual being. The overweight female staff members who tend to complain will always beg to differ, and I think it's more jealously than anything else. I also see the bras as a safety issue as hot days require more diligence being paid to overheating, heat stroke, and heat exhaustion.

I remember the first day our girls went off campus with their jog bras. The administrators' telephones didn't stop ringing. Some schools, nearby Tully comes to mind, have strict rules prohibiting the wearing of jog bras on campus. So the girls, female-led by Michelle Franklin-Rauber—a Jack Daniels protégé and a multiple All-Amercian—has the girls walk to the edge of campus, toss off their shirts and hit the roads with jog bras separating skin from air.

Runners can be more off the wall than mainstream America. How else can so many people run mile after mile, day after day, year after year? Somehow, with mind games, they make running fun in the rain, sleet, snow or sub-tropical heat.

I can't say that runners live to the beat of a different drummer. Hell, most runners don't have a drummer at all, and some are missing the sticks. But, my kids are full of energy and willing to step up in class at invitationals to take on the bigger schools. We haven't been shy about accepting healthy challenges. Runners are like that. Challenge is good. The unknown is there to be explored and conquered—the mind willing.

The Skaneateles girls have seemingly always been good. They also can be eccentric, zealous about winning, fanatical about their grades, desperate to develop a complete transcript that would qualify them for a Nobel Prize of some sort, and they often combine the diametrically opposed characteristics of a cutthroat executioner and a gentle, sweet, nurturing, thoughtful and empathetic miniature Mother Theresa.

Coached by Gus Roberts and Sheila Card over the years before my arrival, they've been winning since the eighties. Unfortunately, the very institutions that teach history don't keep very good records of their own institutions as dust, decaying boxes holding mangled trophies and a 'who-cares' attitude seems to prevail.

Since the next–to-last year of the Reagan administration, my hometown Laker girls have never finished lower than second in the league while winning 15 titles, the last 13 in a row without a loss. The current league winning streak stands at 79 and very few have been a contest. Presidents Bush-the-Elder, Clinton and Bush-the-Invader of Iraq have occupied the White House since the success began. That could all change this year with a revved-up Jordan-Elbridge Eagles squad on our schedule once again. During the track season last spring, they took us to town in our traditional power events, the 400, 800 and 1500-meter distances. They even beat our girls in our annual track meet as several of our key girls had to be benched for missing far too much time before, during and after spring recess. We still owned them at the 3000 and could still handle them well in the 4x400 and 4x800. But they now have that look in their eyes, the look that says "We can run with you." We'll have to try to rise to the occasion like we did in the old days. After our dual this September, we'll know who invested more in the summer. I think we're a bit ahead on that count. Now, if we can just get around expectations. For some reason these girls falter as soon as expectations are expressed in any manner. With nothing to lose, they rise to the occasion and perform at a level that any coach would be proud of.

During our recorded history here at Skaneateles, the girls have won 39 invitationals while placing 2nd 18 times. All of these wins occurred since 1991. The boys, who somehow won the Phoenix Firebird Invitational during that horrible and largely forgettable 2005 season— they were justifiably proud that day—have won 27 invitational titles while finishing as the runner-up 15 times.

Heads turned when we first began our assault across Central New York. And then we took on the remainder of the state. Who the hell is Skaneateles? And how the hell do you say it? It's Skan-e-atlas, which means long lake according to our local Native-Americans.

I've tried to use invitationals to test our mettle. We've moved up from the small school division to take on state powers like Saratoga in the large school races. Yeah, they whooped us. Art Kranick can coach. We've picked meets that I was sure we'd win as we tried to get the kids used to running up front with confidence. We traveled so that we'd see new faces, new courses and have no preconceived pecking order to restrain our racing.

This year we're back to traveling to sights unseen. The more information these bright kids possess, the worse they seem to perform. So, we're keeping them in the dark, no maps prior to arriving at the course, no analysis of the teams or the individual opponents, no race strategy, no expectations; just run. We need to do what we've evolved to do best, and that's run. A Harvard study indicated that the whole human race should be thankful for our ancestors who could run long distances. It wasn't the sprinter from among our earliest ancestors who could run down prey for dinner. It wasn't the sprinter who kept us alive. That honorable position is the esteemed province of the distance runner who outlasted the animals.

Running blind is my goal this year. Just run. Just race. Just run our race. We need to forget about other runners. We need to stop keying off other runners who we know. I'd like to think that our kids would feel confident to race with those who they ran with at Aim High Running Camp, but I know better. This community, as great and successful as it is on so many counts, is somehow raising a lot of children who possess nothing but doubts about their abilities. They live with fear. Their confidence is shaken to the core. They believe in disbelief instead of believing in belief. Many shy from real challenges and are either choosing the smaller mountain to climb or are being steered to pursuits that are well off the main, well-worn path of American society, thus avoiding real comparisons to other kids from mainstream, Main Street America. And yet, many have been given virtually everything, without exception and without earning it. They lack for nothing, except belief in themselves.

I sometimes wonder what is going on in the homes in my hometown at night when the true family dynamic expresses itself. There's nothing normal about what the coaches are dealing with more and more frequently as the years pass. If anyone in our society should possess the balls to try things, to believe they can conquer anything, to believe they can accomplish anything, it's our Cocoon-kids who've been shielded from reality and haven't yet been scarred by defeat or a jarring reality check. But in Skaneateles, something is scaring our kids, dampening their spirit and thrusting doubt into a soul that should be alive with confidence.

We need to forget about the course we're racing on. We need to explore, to get out of our comfort zone, to hurt, take a risk and to do what others are telling us is too painful, too risky. We need to forget about the opponents and just run. We have enough talent, but our talent likes to think too much. I hope that by the end of the season we can show up for the big meets and just run the table clean.

Bronxville and Greenwich are the prohibitive favorites for the state title in Class "C", and they're already being hyped for a slot in the Nike Team Championships. They're well coached, well trained and full of tradition and dazzling power. Greenwich has, I think, only one locally-born scorer on their roster, with the others having transferred from Argyle High where they achieved legendary status with the help of Jack Daniels. With the school seemingly troubled that the team was grabbing so much of the national spotlight, the coach, along with his daughters and others, 'moved' out of the district with some joining the Saratoga team during the winter break while others were added to the roster of the Greenwich team. Yeah, Saratoga needed more national caliber runners. Last season (2005) they added the state champion from Kentucky, too.

At Saratoga something happened. Senior phenom Nicole Blood left—no senior leaves during the final weeks of their high school career—and the Argyle girls who switched to the vaunted Saratoga Blue Streaks are now back at Greenwich. They're unbeatable, unless Bronxville can add to their incredible array of talent.

We're shooting for a league title, our 11th sectional title in 13 years, and third place in the state meet. That, by my definition, is success. I'll let the girls continue to shoot for the moon. There's no need to zap that as a goal before we don our spikes for the first meet. Who knows? They just might surprise me. But reality is reality. The top two spots in New York are probably locked up.

Over the past decades, I've always seemed to have a **track** team that posed during the fall as a distance team. No more. In 1996 our boy's team was little more than a group of pure sprinters and mid-distance runners. Somehow we managed to out-leg Cortland, a **city** for Godsakes, in Auburn for the Sectional title and the right to run in the flood at St. Lawrence University where we came in dead last. I was proud of the boys that day, Pete Hawley, Jeff Boden, James Goss, Tom Poppe, Rob Janeczko (The Citadel), Chris Davis who moved mid-season the following fall to the southwest—a divorce--and my oldest son, Kirk.

This year is different. After suffering with what I thought was sub-par performances all last year, I realized that most of these girls and boys are true distance runners. I was shocked that I'd missed it. As frosh, most had turned in what would be considered strong 400s and 800s which I value as the true test of runners. The 400 reveals guts, speed and inherited talent while the 800 reveals stamina, speed endurance and a willingness to grind hard against a cactus with your bare ass. As sophomores, the girls didn't improve much at all—if at all. Some, as juniors, were on the same middle distance plateau as when they were unknowledgeable, undertrained frosh. But their 1500s and 3000s were better, in some cases competitive on the regional and state level. What I was seeing in their 400s and 800s as frosh was their max speed. That was it. There would be no more. Jack Daniels once told me that there are many elite runners who have trouble breaking 60 seconds in the 400 and yet are national caliber athletes. Those are my kids today.

There's more than one way to achieve success. In the past, we reached our goal from the speed perspective. Today, this coming year, we'll do it from the distance, threshold, lactate perspective with 100s and 200s run nearly every day after long runs to keep the neurological system popping efficiently. We'll go with longer runs, longer reps, more repeats, and then we'll begin cutting the period of rest.

So, here's the coaching conundrum. How much do I try to squeeze out of these good kids while they're in high school? I know that Saratoga and Fayetteville-Manlius not only have good coaching and talented kids, but are running far more miles than the 25-28 we run during the season. When the girls got back from Aim High after doing about 45 miles, they were dead on their feet for 4 days. Was it the running that deadened them or was it more of a teen-thing, staying up well past their usual bedtime telling ghost stories or sneaking boys into the girl's cabin? Some of the boys came back stronger. I didn't expect such a quick transformation from them.

We'll peak this summer at about 37-40 miles, but with the Skaneateles community instilling some severe college-choice paranoia in these kids, I can't send them home too tired, and definitely not exhausted.

If the Riley boys, who didn't spend much time studying, were overwhelmed by school and workouts to the point where they went home exhausted, what can I expect from these kids, some of whom will stay up until 1 AM doing homework while battling a full load of Advanced Placement courses? Erika Geihe, now at Harvard, wasn't feeling normal if she didn't have to get up for a pre-dawn ice skating workout, take all AP courses at Skaneateles, do some work with elementary kids-in-need after school, attend practice and just sizzle, go home, clean the house and do homework until 1 or 2 AM. She's still doing all this at Harvard while doing research, competing on the university record-setting 4x800 team, doing work in a political club (she's not a Republican), tutoring and carrying a full course-load in Chemistry. That's the girls of Skaneateles. The boys never seem to carry a single book home with them from school. I can relate to that. The difference in stress and academic rigor is striking, but the boys do well in school regardless. Though they're tantalizingly close, they aren't the very brightest stars in the sky. And, they aren't anywhere near burnt out either.

With the girls on such a razor thin edge, can I crank up the mileage or will it crush their immune system? Historically I've gotten unusually good summers from a majority of our boys and girls. They'd do real well in the early meets, and then some of them would crash. It's got to be the school academics, the workload, the sleep deprivation and the family drive to produce, to beat your friends regardless of the personal cost. I fully understand the benefits of mileage, long slow distance, repeat miles, but will I send the team into overload if I push that regimen?

And is there really anything philosophically wrong with squeezing all the juice out of the orange before the kids get to college? There are plenty of coaches who unabashedly admit that the goal is to get every ounce out of their girls while they are young and racing with a small chassis and big engine. Some expect to see a girl peak during the frosh or sophomore year, and if they can hang around on the team until they graduate, more power to them. College running? Forget about it. I have moral concerns about that. If the girls aren't getting faster every year, I figure I'm not doing my job. Too many high school coaches don't care about life-long running, about long term health and preparing the kid for the long haul. And who knows. Maybe they shouldn't worry about collegiate competition. "I have them now. I'm not concerned with something that they might or might not do in college," many coaches say. And maybe they're right. And some coaches don't seem to care for the present. It's just another paycheck.

When I look back, I have a good number of boys and girls who competed in college, but often they weren't the ones who were dominant in high school. They were the middle of the pack runners who ran throughout high school because they loved what it did for them. The spotlight didn't matter. And they still run, with some now getting into marathons. The most talented ones on my team had fun running, sacrificing and competing, but there would be no college athletics for many of them. And there wouldn't be any discussion about it.

My boys were few and far between when it came to joining a college team. I'm not sure many of those who did compete in college actually improved. In fact, I know most didn't with the rarest of exceptions. Some of the best coaching, some of the most intense running, some of the most exciting racing, is done at the high school level. High school running has meat on the bones while college running is mostly just bones; it's the band without the baton, the song without the chorus and refrains.

My philosophy has slowly been changing and I'm surprised to find myself in this position. Any sport in college is a job, no matter what level you're 'employed' in. My son's wife, Melissa Zurita, of Chilean descent and a fellow Ithaca College grad in Physical Therapy, played lacrosse and field hockey. There were occasions when she'd have a midnight practice in lacrosse and a field hockey practice at 6 AM. Is that crazy or am I seeing lasting peace for the Middle East? What so often happens is this: You get a Division III college coach who is using the kids to climb from their perceived lowly coaching existence to a more prestigious Division I coaching gig. D-II is 'below their station.' They're using the kids for their own professional growth, no matter what happens to the kids' love of the game, their grades, or their ability to fully experience all the advantages of college life. The professors don't do it and neither should the coaches. It's not right. College needs more balance. Even the D-1 kids could use a little more.

Parents need to begin seeing college athletics for the reality they are today, and I'm now shying away from having kids compete at the college level. It's year 'round with the coaches leading nearly every activity, every training session, every weight lifting session. And it's too much. It's depriving kids of the full college experience. A balanced experience is rare.

My son Kirk rowed during his freshman year at Ithaca. The coach was a nice guy, but expecting an 18-year old college frosh to get out of bed at 4:45 AM to run down to Cayuga Lake to row or compete on the damn erg machines and then somehow get back to campus so that they could fall asleep in their 10:00 class is pure lunacy. Kirk loved crew but folded his tent after one year. And I was happy.

Mission's A Go

There's just so much more to deal with these days that I find myself asking, "Why do I coach?" Why does anyone coach? Yes, some do it for the money, but it shows in their team's performances. Two years to go. When, and if I have the guts to leave, I'll miss getting letters like this.

Friday, June 17, 2005 8:32PM

Hey coach. I woke up this morning to my phone ringing. It was Rachel Vaivoda and she wanted to know if I wanted to go for a run. I most certainly did not want to run after staying out with friends and staying up late cleaning my room. I told her no and she said, "oh, it's okay…don't worry about it, mar." I hung up, then I sat in my bed and couldn't fall back asleep. It was 9:30 already. I kept thinking about how I should be going for a run with Rachel, and even if I wasn't' "supposed' to go on a fifty minute run for my college crew practice today, it would always be beneficial and there was absolutely no reason as to why I shouldn't get my lazy butt out of bed and run. I knew that if I didn't run it would be hanging over my head all day. So I called her back and said, "Ok, Rach. I changed my mind." She sounded so happy, and graciously said, "Thanks sooo much mar!!!" I drank some water, ate some banana, laced up my shoes, still wet from the run the day before, and headed out the door. I met her half way and we continued our 50 minute run to the left side of county line, a run that I had never taken before. As we were running, I began to really wake up, and realize what the hell I was actually doing. I was running at a moderately quick pace, and I was planning to run for just under an hour. Never in my life have I ever been able to run like this.

If you asked me in the beginning of the year if I would ever join track or xc, I would quickly respond with a "hell no". I thought that all runners were psychopaths. Sure, I wanted a bright green and yellow shirt that stood out in a crowd of 50, but I would never imagine running as a sport. The website, tullyrunners. com meant nothing to me. I had no idea running was 'real'. I love the people, the friendships, the coaches, everything about it. I joined indoor track this year to prepare for college crew at Fairfield, and basically get me off my butt during the winter. I never thought I'd become addicted.

After the lacrosse girls accomplished their state title, they had a police car escort them into town. As they drove past my house, I heard a surge of girls' voices as they all shouted my name, waved and screamed. I was outside, so I waved back and smiled and gave them all a thumbs up sign. After that, I went upstairs and cried. I cried because I was jealous of them. I cried because I was happy for them. I cried because I wished that I had played lacrosse. But then, I stopped. What made me stop crying was running. I thought about my new best friends, and about what I had been through in the past 7 or so months. I stopped because I knew that if I had played lacrosse, I wouldn't be as happy as I am now. If I had played lacrosse, I would have sat on the bench and been completely miserable. I wouldn't be in the shape that I am now. I wouldn't have this almost (kinda) six-pack(ish) stomach. And I wouldn't have had the amazing coaching that I had.

Thank you for believing in me, Coach Reed. I never thought that I was good, and you always pushed me to be better than I thought I was. I never thought that I would be participating in the track sectionals. I never thought I would understand the meaning of "1000s at thresh pace," or striders at 1500 pace. I never thought I would beat myself up over not getting sixth place in sectionals as well. And I never thought I would be friends with people like Rachel, or Kelsey, or Kaela or even Zandra. I love these girls, and I love running. On the last day of track, I cried all day as well. I have improved so much. That's what I love about track over any other sport. In lacrosse, you might be getting better, but you always have to rely on someone else's opinion. With running, you have the numbers, and the cold, hard evidence that you are improving. My only regret is starting so late. I wish that I could have found running earlier in my high school career; however, perhaps if I did, I wouldn't have loved it as much as I have.

When I started this email, I didn't know what to say, and I didn't exactly know what the point of it was, and I guess I still don't really have a point. I just needed to talk to you again, because I didn't feel as if I had closure after the season ended. I started track to get ready for crew. However, I don't consider myself leaving track. I'm still coming with Kaela, Zandra and Jess to the cross country sectionals (even though I'm not a REAL xc girl), and other pompous events to cheer on my girls. I just can't believe I'm actually leaving high school forever. But all good things must come to an end, I suppose. Otherwise, they wouldn't be so good the next time around. Thank you so much for everything, Coach Reed. I don't think this experience would have been nearly as good without your coaching. I'm most certainly coming back next year to see everyone, and perhaps I will even run during a practice, (crew training). I'm so glad that I joined the running cult, and I'm so happy that it's a new part of my life. Thank you so much.

Yours truly,

Mary Crowley.

Mary pushed herself and pushed everyone on the team. When she walked onto the Fairfield campus in August of 2005, she was the best conditioned athlete in the crew program. All she had to do was learn to row without catching a crab. I'm training her again over the summer of 2006. She just finished an 800 threshold workout and has cut her rest from two minutes to a minute, and she'll be down to thirty seconds by the time she arrives on campus this September.

Her new best friends that she gained from running were Zandra Walton (Amherst, who ran a 2:14 and change 800 at the State Meet), Rachel Vaivoda who is a senior this year and an integral member of the team), Kaela Turose (University of Rochester—she still stays up all night), and Jessica O'Neill (University of Buffalo), who ran a 4:44.81 for her final high school 1500.

These kids make coaching fun. I get a buzz from winning, from watching a pack-attack that's streaking through the field after having tempered the early pace. I love watching our uniform leading the way as the runners burst from the wooded trails with the boy's hair straight up in the wind and the girls' ponytails bobbing. I love watching a speed workout on the track with the runners doing things that absolutely no one else in the school can duplicate as they stretch toward their limits. But I like what running, my coaching, can do for kids as it gives them an arsenal of weapons that they can use to enhance virtually anything they try to do in life. It gives them purpose in the aimless years of older adolescence as they fend off the ugly, debilitating aspects of the pop-culture.

What worries me is that the pipeline is empty. And it's important to me that the program remains strong for Rob Tuttle and anyone else who takes over when I'm done and gone. The modified boy's team could boast of only two boys in each of the previous two seasons. The girls were a marvelous juggernaut but they've all moved on except one, and so far Carly Brown, who has talent, has been less than attentive to summer training. The older girls are insuring that she joins the team. She can be a strong runner.

We're not much different from any other cross country program. Most of the kids who run are those who haven't been shamed out of it by parents, classmates, youth coaches or school personnel. "Why do you run?" asks the gym teacher who also keeps pestering the best athletes to join softball, lacrosse or soccer. There's a degree of warehousing that takes place in high school sports. Cuts are discouraged by society these days, and kids who have no business being on some teams are put on a shelf in the event that they one day grow and get strong, gain skills, get fast or are just plain needed because of injuries or teen burnout.

There also just isn't much interest in supporting a sport that isn't in the newspapers much, is never on the television, and exists only in the obscure cult of internet web sites. To keep us in the local news I've written over 800 articles and had action pictures published on the front pages of the Skaneateles Press by sports editor Phil Blackwell and newspaper editor Ellen Leahy. At our annual banquets I reward as many kids as possible by giving out all the trophies we've won over the season. Fabulous trophies and plaques leave the banquet in the arms of wide-eyed and appreciative teenagers who worked hard to earn their prize. If I didn't give them out they'd end up in the trophy grave yard in the cellar of the school until some enterprising employee decided he needed the space for something more important like an empty box. Then the trophies, banged up and long-forgotten, would go to the town landfill for final disposal. .

New York State presents beautiful plaques for winning a state championship. The runner-up gets nothing, no award, no recognition, zip, the great American society at its best. Many of my state champion girls are now mothers many times over. There's still no green road sign boasting of our Skaneateles championships as you enter the village. The Olympics of the Mind championship sign is there. The hockey sign is there. But not one of our ten championships is acknowledged. And, until early in the summer of 2006, all of those state championship plaques were in a cardboard box in Rob Tuttle's storeroom outside his technology lab. We've had four athletic directors since our first championship, and it wasn't until the arrival of an outsider from the Rochester area that the plaques were properly secured to the masonry wall in the lobby outside of the new gym.

Inertia has taken hold in upstate New York. I believe it has something to do with the weather. We suffer from brain-freeze. We have learned to be submissive, to acquiesce, to give up and discount what we have. We look back to better days while many other progressive parts of the nation look forward eagerly and walk with a nice little bounce in their stride. We shuffle when we walk, an effect of trying not to fall while moving around on snowy or icy sidewalks. We just don't ever seem to get anywhere. It has nothing to do with politics. It's just a mind-set that's formed and I'm blaming the climate. You don't know what you've got till it's gone. Spending the winter in Florida will be an eye-opening experience for me in retirement as the sun replaces months of endless gray skies in a town where headlights shine at high noon on too many November days. I have to admit, the weather has worn me down and I'm tapping out of its cruel hold.

It isn't just the gloomy weather that gets us down around here. Going unrecognized for so long has had a profound effect on the kids. All the time, effort and devotion to proudly representing our school and community, and all the wins, significant and mundane, have hardly created a ripple of interest. Everything was always done in a polite manner but it was as if no one recognized the significance of championships earned in anonymity via nothing less than year 'round hard work, sacrifice and good old sweat. We run in the halls all winter, run in the halls for the first four to six weeks of outdoor track and bravely confront horrendous arctic winds that buffet our track the entire season. We start cross country in the summer with temperatures in the 90s and dew points in the tropical 70 degree range. We transition to the beauty of a short fall and the remnants of one hurricane after another that somehow wiggle their way into central New York on race day Saturdays, and finally we finish the season in the mud, bitter cold and snow in November. It does make New Yorkers tough, especially at the NIKE Nationals.

At the state championship just south of Rochester in 2003, the air temperature was 14 degrees. On that championship day, Superintendent Walter Sullivan made the drive west and stood outside the entire meet. I have to give the guy credit. I think Walter was truly on our side but some administrators didn't seem to give a damn and it hurt the kids. Walter used to get things arranged with my employer at Jordan-Elbridge High School—where I taught--so that I could travel on a school day Friday to the State Championship with the team. Money was exchanged, a sub was hired, and everyone was happy. But the first year that Walter didn't help to personally set it up, I ended up in a furious argument in the school lobby with an AD who seemed to care less about my predicament. I was told that if I wanted to go to the state meet, it was going to happen with no pay from J-E and nothing from Skaneateles. If I didn't agree, the team would go without me.

So, why do I do this? Why coach? I keep telling the kids that it's truly us against everyone else. We do it for us. Not for the village, not for the town, not for the school. We're the ones who do the work, we're the ones who feel the jubilation and angst, we're the ones who understand what we're trying to accomplish. And I let them know that there have been far too many jealous people over the years who have waited for us to fail. Our athletic department has been Balkanized with everyone digging their own trench and preparing to defend their territory against everyone else. Hopefully the new guy, Rick Pound from Honeoye Falls-Lima, can get things turned around before I leave with a bitter taste in my mouth.

We aren't where we want to be right now, though the seeds have begun to sprout. We aren't where we used to be, though the image isn't as faint, hazy and out of focus as it was a year ago. And we'll do everything we can to get back what we've lost. I'm a coach. I expect to win. It's the pressure I put on myself. It's what I do. And the goal of getting back to the front is pushing me hard this summer. I take a few steps, or read a little from the newspaper, or engage in conversation and before I know it, I'm right back to thinking, talking or writing about the team. I do feel somewhat possessed right now. But I feel alive. And I'm loving it.

Impressions and a Racing Fix

Coaching cross country is a stint in life that starts over and over and has no end, much like an MC Escher graphic design that optically has no beginning and no end, no high point and no low point; only a here and now that seemingly changes the longer you look at it. I've learned that the team and the season will never play out as I thought. My summer expectations have never survived into the deepest days of fall. Surprise is the word of the day and every day the surprise changes. Something, and sometimes everything, changes with either explosive suddenness or slowly and subtly like old age creeping up and catching you unsuspecting.

The biggest uncertainty in the summer of 2006 is how this particular season that starts on August 21st will end on November 3rd at Long Branch Park on the beautiful shores of the nation's most polluted lake, Onondaga Lake. Sectionals; it's our goal every year, really, the only goal. Not many teams can begin summer training in late June while entering Boot Camp in late August with the concrete and realistic notion of a championship on the top of their to-do list. The rest can dream, but it's an illusion that grows fainter and fainter as the miles pile up and the shoes wear out. We've been fortunate to always be in the hunt. To get the chance to hold the victor's cup, teams need to go through us. On the girl's side no one has gotten through until recently. But they did have to go through us.

Sectionals. Onondaga Lake. Ugh. Make no mistake about it, the county is spending hundreds of millions of dollars to fix what Allied Chemical and many others did to the once pristine lake that played host in the early 1900s to amusement parks, roller coasters, restaurants and some of the best white fish fishing in the world. Now the lake is a repository for mercury and raw sewage that still gets plopped into the lake when a heavy rain stresses the holding bins at the southeast end of the lake. We're working on that and we're actually making progress that surpasses the scientific predictions.

By mid-summer I'm curious. I need information. I need a racing fix. My last track meet was nearly two months ago. Coaches aren't much different from junkies. We need racing fixes more often than we like to admit, even though we all know that too much racing leads to an early end to the season as we run the stuffing and life out of some good and trusting kids. I'm hooked on races, on competition and I got a nice dose of competition at Long Branch Park tonight where the Nike sponsored Midsummer Night's Dream series of races was being hosted by Westhill High School's Dan Reid, my nemesis and friend. It wasn't but two track seasons ago that his girls edged ours by ½ point for the sectional track title. They did it again this past spring. We had nearly two dozen girls score, far more than Westhill, but they had a few studs who kept ringing up the big points while getting enough fill points from others to edge us. Damn field events.

It was fun to get together with the other coaches at Long Branch. None of them ever tell the truth because, in effect, every coach is a poker player at heart and hiding his cards for all he's worth. We all know that going into a conversation and it's part of the charm of our friendships. We all have the same desire to forge titanium-like bonds with kids, with athletes. You can see a solid relationship between F-M's Bill Aris and his top returning runner for 2006, Tommy Gruenewald (8:59.32 for 3200, 4:12 for 1600, 1:56 for the 800). Aris and Gruenewald click. It might not be that way for Tommy ever again. There's a 2-way street named 'Trust" between coach and athlete. The trick is to find the right avenue for reaching every kid. Some years you think everything is going along just right when you suddenly find yourself in the passing lane and your kids are on the arterial going in the opposite direction.

Some coaches just don't get it. These aren't football players we're dealing with. Raw emotion will not elevate your game. Running is controlled aggression. It's tempered spirit, patience. It's a waiting game, a feeling out game, a take-it-to-the-edge game for the best. And the genders are different. I just received an email from sophomore Lexie Mazzeo.

> *hi coach...I just wanted to let you know that I got shoes yesterday...they aren't the same exact model as my old ones (discontinued) but they are Saucony...we did some research before, though, and this shoe popped up as one that would fit my personal characteristics...it has high stability and I think it's made for an over-pronator...so I hope it will help my foot...and by far the most important thing about my shoes: they're pretty! today I spent a half hour just looking at them...too bad cross-country is such a muddy ordeal...anyway, my foot is feeling better lately, ever since I stopped running in those new Brooks and switched back to my old shoes...now that says something... goodbye Brooks...and Bea told me that Brooks gave her and Kelsey ankle troubles...so at least now I know.*
>
> *Lexie*

I'll never get a note like that from one of the boys. Boys and girls are not remotely alike. Girls like reassurance and compliments, but they also like to know what they need to do to get better. They don't seem to mind hearing about fixable deficiencies. You just have to blend the positive with the negative. Boys? Well, you can roughhouse with them more than the girls, but after a bad race you'd better watch your tongue and toss out compliments and warm-fuzzies. Guys race from a more primal part of their being than most girls. Reality 101 can wait until a day or two down the road when the testosterone levels and raw emotions have returned to stasis.

Coaches honestly enjoy the camaraderie that comes from within the intimate setting of cross country. There isn't any other sport that's like distance running. In wrestling you're too physically intertwined to form relationships. In swimming you've got your face in the water for 6000 to 10,000 meters a session. In football you're encouraging the boys to 'kill'. In crew you've got to have comparable talent and you're always looking at someone's back while gasping for air. In baseball you're out standing in a field alone waiting for something to happen. In cross country it's one for all and all for one, the slowest one heralded by the same applause as the first. The least is no less worthy than the leader, for they all toil to their own limits and to a state of exhaustion. The exhausted feeling is the same for the 16-minute 5000-meter runner and the 24-minute runner. Exhaustion, elation, a sense of defeating the devil all await the runner who is true to himself and his sport. Like an arch bearing a heavy load, each finisher carries the weighty responsibility of being counted in the final tabulation.

Coaches also like the power that too often is replaced by a sense of powerlessness when a kid is really messing up and you realize, at season's end, that a top-5 girl started taking birth control pills and she's gained 22 pounds in the midst of all the training. No wonder she was no longer able to be counted on. No wonder she stopped running at the two-mile mark at the state championship in Lake Placid for a brief rest. Or you find out about a nasty, contested divorce, a sexual molestation by a stepfather, or any number of ugly situations that no kid should have to live with. But the power, when things go right, is an intoxicant.

When you have kids who aren't afraid of pain, who show up every day with a positive approach to grueling training, you have to make sure that every step you ask them to take has a reason behind it. I take training very seriously. There's more to life than getting the runner to the promised-land. We also want them to have balance. We want them to have fun. And, we want them to approach the starting line with nothing but can-do and confidence in their hearts. "Run the first half with your brain, the second half with your heart."

Cross country, if taught well, is a mix of the physical—the portion that everyone sees laid bare on race day, and it's also one part spiritual or religious. Julie Lynch, perhaps the most talented natural runner we've ever had, used her deep religious convictions to give her strength and purpose in the race. It allowed her to race ruthlessly without making it personal. Erika Geihe, who was just the opposite, was cold and calculating about races, and ruthless in her own right. Julie studied the humanities. Erika is a scientist.

We all have kids who never get any respect or emotional fulfillment at home, nothing from snotty, bullying or uncaring classmates, nothing from their employers who too often use them. But here, with us, they get respect. They gain self-respect by earning it. There's no phony 'good jobs' being thrown around. We do too much of that in little league when we give every kid a trophy regardless of achievement or improvement. When good has been done, or when the effort has been extraordinary, the "good job" and a hug or hand shake are readily offered with all due sincerity.

And we talk a lot. I'm beginning to realize that what I say to the kids sometimes has real meaning. I've got to be more careful about what I say. One girl quoted me three times in her valedictory speech from the lakeside gazebo just across from Valentine's Pizza at the north end of Skaneateles Lake. I didn't attend for the first time in many, many years. Perhaps it's better that way.

Alyssa Turose opened her speech by saying,

> *As I was sitting before my blank computer screen, attempting to think of a way to start this speech, I suddenly recalled a cross country practice from the first week of last fall's season, the training period referred to as boot-camp. We had just finished two grueling back-to-back workouts, and we were gathered around coach to find out what type of a run he had in store for us the following day. Gazing off into the distance, a sage look affixed to his face, he slowly raised one hand and pointed, in a way that would have made Babe Ruth proud, and proclaimed "Tomorrow we go long. "This gesture obviously was a bit over the top, but what more could be expected from Coach Reed as well as in a graduation day speech? For we, as a class, have come a long way."*

And the speech went on discussing the many accomplishments, beginnings, transitions and endings that her class had completed. Midway through her speech, she came back to me.

> *However, community service is not the only accomplishment for which we deserve recognition. To again quote the infinitely wise Jack Reed, to be successful, one must "formulate a goal and stick it deep inside and let it burn, let it drive you, let it motivate you…let it be a constant reminder that your life has a clear and present purpose." Our class has seen a lot of goal-setting.…*

From here, Alyssa went on to highlight the big wins that her classmates achieved. But there I was again, quoted in her closing. Man, you never know what registers with the kids. I get so used to feeling like I was being ignored in class that I've got to constantly remind myself that there are indeed students and athletes who are listening and trying to find their way through life, partly with the support and guidance of my emails or conversations.

> *We've read Great Expectations in installments and practiced hand rules in physics. And now, all of the hard work and good times have culminated in this one day, an ending, a beginning, and yet, in many ways, not a new place for us at all. Coach Reed (yes, I will quote him one final time) emailed to us, the night before the first race of the season, "This is your first opportunity, after a ton of hard work, to practice what you've learned. Practice it for real." And so, I say to you, go long. Practice it for real.*

To say that I was humbled when I read Alyssa's speech in the local Skaneateles Press is an understatement of the first order. Humbled and gratified, a choking and painful knot grew in my throat. I was exhilarated and yet, fearful. What have I been saying to these wonderfully dedicated kids all these years? Who have I messed up? When didn't I zip my lips shut when I spoke in frustration after a meet? Good God, what may I have done?

Sometimes when we speak we hit the nail on the head. I think we like to soft-peddle more than we should when we deal with the kids. Tempered truth is good for them in these wishy-washy times. But truth-telling is harder than it used to be. What teacher hasn't called home with bad news and gotten royally reamed out by an ungrateful, unappreciative mom or dad?

Jessica O'Neill, who transferred to Skaneateles from rival Marcellus in what turned out to be a messy legal affair, wrote to me on Friday, June 10th, after our track banquet. The time? 1:09 AM. I tell ya, these kids don't sleep!

> *...I've had some wonderful memories these past two years, but especially this past season or two. You know what I'll never*

forget, that conversation on the indoor track bus home from Manley Field House (Syracuse University) when I was upset about the mono. I asked you, "Without running, who the hell am I?" And you told me I'd have to figure that out on my own. Thank you. That was the best thing you could have said. You helped me rediscover who I really am. I will never forget that. Thanks for always listening. Good night. By the way, everything was organized beautifully this evening. Your efforts are obvious. See ya around. Signing off. Jess

Listen to these kids long and hard, and you begin to wonder who is teaching whom. To understand Jess you had to realize that she was hooked on running. She was always a natural talent but as she got older she began to use her deep inquisitiveness to help understand what running—training—was doing to her physiologically. She was a challenge, a good challenge, every day. I loaned her several of my underlined physiology books and she actually read them and would approach me at night or at practice with thoughtful questions. She also had suggestions for her training based on what she was learning. Jessica was internalizing the information and attempting to use it to her advantage in the real world of running. I was making a difference. That's what winning means in education. She had developed the desire to learn.

Eric Roschick, as mentioned earlier, was so thoroughly bored with high school and all the silly rules that he couldn't restrain himself and he got himself into trouble. Jess was just the opposite. Boys will rebel, girls will finesse their way around the hurdle. Even though something might have bored her, Jess turned it into a challenge to leap to the next level. Why don't we listen to them more often? The discussions we have before, during and after our practices are filled with mischief, mayhem, jokes of the most-corny kind, and some very telling personal thoughts. Kids. They say the strangest things and approach running from many perspectives.

Well, my racing fix was interesting. It appeared everyone was sandbagging or they were just running poorly at the moment. Westhill's girls, who should challenge us along with the Jordan-Elbridge girls, just looked plumb tuckered out. The CBA girls, ably coached by Theresa

Trudell, one of Daniels' several protégés in the area, could take the whole thing this fall—league and sectional titles. They sometimes play games and use a race for a workout at a slower pace or they just blow it off. You never know with Theresa, who loves her beer when she's out with the coaches for a slight libation after a league meeting. She probably knows her stuff better than almost anyone in coaching. She's a true disciple of Jack Daniels who coached her to All-American status in 1997. She's brash, doesn't care what people think, and always does what's best for her kids, even though some parents often question her. But when the CBA girls approached the finish line at the Midsummer Night's Dream race, they looked exhausted and I was surprised. I think this bodes well for us. Even if we aren't the most talented team, we'll be in championship shape and raring to go. Of that, I'm certain.

On the boys side, my top guy Sam—he with the cousins in Pennsylvania who were running studs—looked good, placing 7th. When I saw Sam with his mother just moments before the gun was heard along the shores of Onondaga Lake, I started to give him some racing instructions. Catching myself, I said, "Enjoy yourself, Sam. Have fun out there." This was a night for Sam to just be a runner, not a runner who is competing for a team, a coach, a school. There was no need to interject anything about strategy, match-ups or personal expectations. Sam had fun and ran well. He looked comfortable. He's our leader this year. He's a junior. He's fast, quick, and apparently has bitten the running bullet. He never misses practice, never boasts, never causes trouble, never skips out on anything and always asks if there's anything else he should do. If we can control his propensity to shoot his wad at the start, he'll have much better results. So far, we haven't been able to do that.

Hannah, the girls' leader, is the opposite. She lags far behind until she gets her feet under her and her confidence begins to rise, and then she stages a long rally. But too many times when she held back, the race had left her and there was no way to get where she should have been. Her summer runs have been good. On a day when she was scheduled to run eight miles, she ran to the track near Lake George for her warm-up and then logged her 8 miles on the rubber oval. Her splits were 7:06, 6:56, 7:07, 7:23, 7:29, 7:44, 8:00, 7:42. Why the track instead of the wide open roads around Lake George? "I thought it might be fun." That's Hannah, a frosh sensation, a sophomore disappointment, and a junior who clicked mid-way through her outdoor track season. Providence is now after her. Hannah's mile repeat pace, based on her 10:44 3000-meter time in April, should have been around 7:50, so I think we're heading in the right direction physically and mentally. More aggression and confidence will help.

Her mother, a wise woman, said that the motto in Hannah's elementary school was, "If you had fun, you won." In the midst of Hannah's sophomore and early junior slump, mom said, "Perhaps we stressed that motto too much. Life isn't like that." The good news is that Hannah took the 8-mile run out fast. I hope Hannah's fading after mile 5 isn't her way of telling me that her summer running is fatally flawed. We're hoping that she will realize that she should be traveling with the front pack, or, in a really loaded field, at the back of the front pack. It's time to step up and play the role of talented leader. In order to keep her mind fresh and focused, I'm going to have to train her alone a lot more than anyone I've ever coached. Her strength comes from listening to her own internal rhythms which she sometimes chooses to tune-out.

A few weeks later, Hannah engaged herself in an 800-meter workout. This summer we're only doing one quality day per week and many times I'll give the team a menu of different methods that can be used to attain the same goal, letting them judge for themselves what they need to do in order to improve and gain more conditioning. Sometimes, if we're doing 400 repeats, I'll have them try to go as long as they can with a 400 jog recovery. Or they can choose to alternate an active 400 jog rest with a stationary full rest. Or they can do the first half with the jog rest and the second half with the stationary rest. The goal is to liberate them, make them self-sufficient within a system that's been proven to work for several decades now. They seem to like it as long as I can guarantee them that their personal choice won't backfire.

Hannah, in an earlier 600 workout, had done her reps at a pace that converted, when extrapolated, to a 3:09 for the 800. Her splits for the 800 repeats just seven days later were 3:07, 3:04, 3:01, 3:03, 3:05, 3:04, 3:06, 3:03. "I think I ran pretty successfully," she emailed. Hannah will be our leader and a contender for the sectional title if she keeps her head on straight. That's my job this fall. It isn't the training that will propel her to an individual title or a finish in the top five. It's my ability to keep her relaxed, calm, confident, happy and disassociated from expectations and reality.

Hannah's a piece of work. Her mind and emotions control everything for her athletically. This past spring she started eating popcorn before races. It was her intent to diminish the importance of her moment on the track. Easing her mind, the popcorn also relieved stress as she unconsciously told herself, "This is just track. It's so unimportant that I'm breaking the rules that everyone else is following." And then she went out and set another personal record. Ron Cox, my best runner at Marcellus in the late 80s, was known to down a hot dog about 10 minutes before a race. It worked for him so I didn't step in and try to be a myth-buster.

Hannah's classmate, Sofie, is all of 5' 2" and has been holding steady at an 8 minute per mile pace for her distance runs. I think that's going to be her max until she gets comfortable enough to take a risk. Sofie is young for her age. Didn't Yogi Berra say something like that? She'll be a 17-year old when she takes mid-terms in college her freshman year.

Sofie, along with Hannah and Rachel Vaivoda, were called the Brat Pack when they were up-and-coming frosh. Without them we couldn't have won the state title in 2003 at Marcus Whitman High near Canandaigua. O'Neill led us with a 3rd place finish. Lynch was 4th and Geihe was 11th. Hannah took 17th in a superb race. Sofie took 18th in her best effort and Rachel placed 19th. That's a pack by any definition. Unrefined, knowing next to nothing, worrying about nothing and being treated like little sisters fit their persona. Each of them is, in fact, a little sister, the youngest in the family. Early on they truly needed to be cared for like a little sister. I think they still need to be treated in that manner. But now they're seniors who are expected to be leaders. We'll sink or swim based on their ability to shed the little sister mindset.

Taking 20th at Marcus Whitman was Zandra Walton, whose little sister, Beatrice, is running in Ireland the whole month of July. Bea just nailed a long seven-mile run on the Irish back roads where people look at you as if something must be wrong. Bea's mile splits, using her GPS watch, were between 7:14 and 7:40 while her threshold runs have been done at a 6:50 mile pace. She's been injured so many times—broken bones in her hip and foot—that she's actually done little running since being brought up to varsity in the 8ᵗʰ grade. Morton's Neuroma? Who'd have thought that injury would incapacitate a healthy 14 year old?

Bea is experiencing the hottest summer in recorded Irish history. The temps, in the 80s, are a far cry from when her sister Zandra took the same trip, gratis and lovingly offered by her grandfather so that they could witness their heritage firsthand.

When Zandra made her trip to Ireland, she realized what home in the United States meant to her.

Hey Coach Reed,

I hope your summer is going well. I am now staying at the farm in Sligo County, but I am e-mailing you from an internet cafe in Sligo City where we are spending the day. This morning I went running. The 30 minutes and the 4x150's, the mile, and the second set of 150s went well. The quiet country roads are nice to run on. It was raining this morning but it wasn't bad. So far I have been running on schedule and I've been having no problems. I do crunches and push-ups practically every day. I am having fun, but I am looking forward to Cross-County......I will be ready.

There are lots of people here and things that I really like, but there are also people and things that they do that I don't like. But, this combination is a learning experience. Not only am I learning about Ireland and its peoples' culture, but I gained a lot of respect for the way of life I have always lived. I am proud to be an American, I appreciate my family and the way and where I was raised, and I am glad and proud that I am a runner. Running seems odd to most of the people here...they don't really understand it. But I am proud to be a runner because it's who I am and it gives my life a bigger purpose with goals always on the horizon that I work hard to achieve every day. Irish people don't really understand this....but it's who I am and I am happy that it is who I am.

I am rambling....but I don't care. I am having fun. See you soon.

—-Zandra

If that doesn't bring up the hair on the back of your neck a bit, if that doesn't toss a patriotic flutter into your heart and a little congestion in your upper chest, you're not human, certainly not an American. There wasn't an ounce of twisted or partisan politics in Zandra's message about her homeland. No unsavory tone as she spoke with the same voice that our founders used so genuinely so many years ago. From the mouth of a kid who was born in Canastota and raised on the shores of Skaneateles Lake, she speaks of freedom, of being respectful of others, and a deep appreciation for her mother country and her way of life.

Zandra was wired tight. If I said to run for 31:43 she'd run until her watch showed 31:43. If you told her to do 15 toe-lift-hip flexes, she'd do exactly that many. It took this talented girl a while to gain control over her emotions and to learn how to eat properly. She was always on a razor thin edge when it came time to 'calorie-up'. One race, at Baldwinsville, she was out in front with less than 1200-meters to go and when she came out of the woods she was far, far out of it. Her gas tank had just emptied out. Nothing left. And willpower wouldn't move her skeletal frame. She did gain mastery over the calories and is running well at Amherst College.

Bea's classmate, Kelsey, was also brought up in 8th grade but the expectations took a toll and she's trying out for soccer this fall. If she gets cut and asks to return to the team, what will I do? Kelsey has hips that seem to touch her arm pits. Her stride and turnover rate is sweet as honey. But her mind panics. Her emotions are wrapped in an egg shell-thin membrane. When she totally loses control she'll stare out at the race course from the starting line and appear to be in a drunken stupor. I can talk to her but she just looks right through me with a blank look on her ashen face. With some strong shaking of her shoulders she can respond meekly. Maybe time away from running, time to mature a bit more, will free her to run and compete again. I think there's something physical going on but I can't pin it down. Someday we'll get a diagnosis and she'll emerge whole.

Cross Country runners; they're the best. They're the truest of people. They're the meat of our nation. If I were a human resources manager in a company I'd be looking for these runners. They know how to pace themselves, they understand paying now for rewards later. Runners understand sacrifice, hard work, patience, teamwork, getting along, setting long term plans. They're winners. And they can grind out results.

Round and round we go as the revolving door brings us new athletes while spinning others off toward new pursuits. With each addition and each deletion, strategic plans are modified. But, like the bull that keeps charging toward the red cape with repeated determination, the team modifies dreams with some realized and others dashed. With more and more regularity assistant coaches join the program only to stay but a short time.

On slow hot nights during the summer when the sweat just drips off me and I'm tightly tethered to a little black Vornado fan and an extension cord, I go upstairs to the back of my deep and cluttered closet and dig out the blue folder that holds all the letters I've received from the kids over the decades. Sitting on the floor re-reading long gone thoughts penned by good kids who have graduated from the Skaneateles Sweat Factory, I continue to learn more about them with the benefit of hindsight and a reflective capacity that's sharper and more incisive thanks to a growing maturity. When the kids return from college to watch former teammates compete in track I somehow make a little time for them, but it's different as our time together has passed. My energy and time must now be given to the kids who comprise my current team. The grads understand that. We hug, I ask about their GPA, summer plans, changes in majors, significant relationships, but the reunion is too quick as I'm called back into action and rush to the starting line for the next track event or elsewhere to put out a fire. They know what we once had was special and rare as together we chased down the dreams that too many others let die from neglect. We grew stronger and wiser together while learning perspective, patience and persistence. We drove each other to be better and they understand that the new kids are now under my tutelage. They're my primary responsibility. But in my heart their spot is secure and I'll always follow them as they move through life. They're the bright lights that illuminate my existence, that prove that I once walked this earth. When I close an email, I always say 'Love ya, Coach'. And I damn well mean it.

Mission Impossible

"Julie's down," screamed a race official who was working the finish chute at Baldwinsville for our annual slug-fest in the Onondaga High School League Championship. Counting the OHSL meet, Julie Lynch had led the team in all but one meet. She was on fire, having worked hard to rediscover her competitive appetite. In terms of sticking with a few of the most elite local runners, Julz had slipped a bit. There was nothing wrong with her abilities or training. It was mental. I think Julie was having a vicious internal fight between two separate worlds, her strong religious convictions that drove best friend Erika Geihe nuts, and her secular world. I think that same battle helped drive her from a very secular American University to theologically-oriented Wheaton College in Illinois. This summer she's in Croatia trying to improve people's lives and is soon heading to Syracuse University. But for the OHSL meet, she was focused. Not every athlete can flip the switch, but Julz had the ability. When she couldn't flip it she'd been messing around with her time at home after practice, getting to her homework slowly, talking to a myriad of friends, delaying a project until the night before the due date, typical kid stuff that kept her up way past her bedtime. But running is a sport that demands time management. Sleep, dear, dear sleep, is the best friend of a high school runner, but it's hardly a reliable companion.

The Syracuse Post-Standard's Neil Kerr, who colleagues call the 'Hatman', wrote,

> *Moments after crossing the finish line at the Onondaga League*
> *cross country meet Saturday, Skaneateles junior Julie Lynch fell*
> *to the ground, writhing in pain. Lynch, who had experienced*

twinges of pain as the race wore on, had suffered a fracture of the growth plate above her pelvis.

The injury has ended the season for the 17-year old Lynch, who has been the No. 1 runner all season on Coach Jack Reed's two-time defending state Class C champion Skaneateles team. Facing four to six weeks of rehabilitation, Lynch won't be able to run competitively again until the spring track season.

She placed 10th with a commendable 20:09 on a rolling 5k layout. Her final step from that race is frozen in time by a photo that shows her taking a funny and awkward long stride into the chute in an effort to pass one more girl. That's the way it was with Julz, get one more. With the pain reaching deep into her bones, her competitive instincts and her desire to help the team still ruled the day. But, the split second she landed was the moment of the fracture. Boy, could she lay it out, even when already seriously hurt. If we'd had any hint of trouble, she'd have been by my side watching the race.

In 2002 we were bidding for our 9th consecutive sectional championship which would be held a week hence at the low lying mud-pit called East Syracuse-Minoa Schools. "I thought we were on course to win Sectionals again and maybe defend our state championship," I told Neil Kerr of the Post, "but now it'll be different. Now, Canastota will be a battle. We're still strong, but it won't be easy." In my gut, I thought we were dead. That off-the-record sentiment slowly changed and never saw the light of day as the week progressed.

Left to do the work was Zandra Walton who was shaky, still unreliable, but capable. Erika Geihe, called "Money" by former coach Lou Delsole, would be at her best. Senior Emily Everding, unheralded and in sister Vanessa's massive shadow her whole career—and hurt for most of the season—would be available after suffering a stress fracture the first week of the season. But what could she possibly do for us? Sarah Searing, Kathleen Nyzio, Kaela Turose and Lindsay Stanley would also have to be on their best game or we'd go home and 'Stota, coached by the great Andy Pino, would head to 'states at Long Island's Sunken Meadows.

Bill Meylan, who runs the fabulous web site, www.tullyrunners. com wrote this about the meet:

I spent more time analyzing this race than any other (boys or girls) ... Everything (and I mean everything) indicates that Skaneateles and Canastota are even-up ... "current form" simulations and "predictive" simulations call this a statistical tie ... amazingly, a 100,000 race simulation had Skaneateles winning exactly 50,000 races and Canastota winning exactly 50,000 races (I have never seen that before) ... clearly, an outstanding performance by any individual runner can make the difference between winning and losing.

With Julz in the line-up Bill had the meet scored 48-48. I saw Bill last night at the Midsummer's Night Dream race at Long Branch Park, and he told me that he just turned down a contract with Nike to rank the teams nationwide for the 2006 Nike Team Nationals and to serve on the selection committee for the event. Bill knows his stuff. His predictions, all scientifically calibrated by the research scientist that he is, are simply dead-on. I've heard that his web site is the most 'hit' site that deals with American high school sports. He won't take a bit of advertising and has been consistent in keeping this project of his a work of love. He won't sell out.

After learning of Julie's season-ending injury, Bill predicted a score of Canastota 44 and Skaneateles 69. It was bad news. We were in big trouble.

That week was anything but normal as we prepped for the "Big One". That title was ours. It felt like an entitlement. There was no talk from anyone all week about losing. We expected to win. "It's just what we do"—and planned to do once again. That phrase became our t-shirt motto. There was pressure on every one of the girls. They understood what this was about, the history and the special chapter they could add to the legacy. We ignored everything physical all week. We talked. We joked. We planned the trip to 'states on Long Island. We bolstered each other. We never let go of the dream. And we planned "Operation Separation." We really hadn't seen Canastota all season. We knew they were young, and we knew they were laying down fast times. Bill Meylan was not encouraged on our behalf, and he expressed that sentiment on his web site.

Regardless of the outcome, I believe that "Operation Separation" and my efforts on behalf of the kids that championship week was my best work before or since. I felt like we'd made a difference for the kids and I hoped it would show on race day.

It snowed, snowed hard. The ground was a perfect mess for the race. The temperature was 32 degrees but the air was eerily still; the crunch from shoes striking the ground was audible, crisp and perfectly clear like a spoon tapping a crystal goblet. We warmed-up in unison, minute by minute in a choreographed script that I'd developed for just this meet.

Earlier, while some of us mingled in the gym, several of my Lakers went to the bathroom and saw the Canastota girls in the hall. Rushing back to me, Erika Geihe said, "Coach, we'll never lose to them," as Julie Lynch stood nearby on crutches. I gave Erika and Sarah Searing a look that said, "What?" and they explained that the 'Stota girls were nothing more than little kids, tiny. "We're way stronger in this mud, Coach. We're taking the title."

Well, the girls did everything they could to execute "Operation Separation" as we'd planned. There was no drama, no suspense, no existential riddle waiting to be solved. The gun went off and the fun began. We took a commanding lead and ran with pure confidence as we floated effortlessly through the mud. Every cell in our bodies was at peak efficiency. We separated from everyone. It was a gamble. Could we hold tough long enough and could we maintain the lead? Would our early lead discourage the little ones from Canastota?

Mid-race Harold Muller from Chittenango yelled that we were holding. Later in the race I heard that we had it. Bill Meylan said to Harold-of-Chittenango, "I couldn't account for the mud. Skaneateles is too strong for Canastota." Cold and analytic, that's Bill. As the girls approached a beaten-up hedge row leading into the finish, I yelled for each one of them with all I had, promising that if they held on for 200-meters more, their dream would live.

When Kaela Turose, our final runner in 38th, passed me, I ran toward the finish area and forgot all about professional composure. I was running and high-stepping my way through the muck like an angry ostrich in the sand as the terrain tossed me to and fro, but I maintained enough equilibrium to stay on my feet. I picked up the girls one by one, laid a bear hug on them and gave them a peck on the cheek. We had a wild group celebration that came from a closeted corner of our emotional-being that most people never get to enter at any time in their lives. We wildly cheered our accomplishment and a few began yelping. In short order the scores came in, Skaneateles 47, Canastota 61. In the team scoring, we'd placed 2-4-5-16-20 while heavily favored 'Stota was 6-9-13-15-18. We'd done it. We'd beaten 'Stota, we'd beaten the weather, we'd beaten the computer—without Julie Lynch who stood with us all the way.

"I don't know if I've ever been as proud of one of my teams as I am today," I told the Post-Standard. "The whole team rallied together to win this race for Julie. She was watching on crutches. Sarah Searing ran the best race of her career. Emily Everding missed the whole season with a stress fracture but she came back to place sixth today."

Inconsistent Zandra took a stunning 2nd place in 19:38. Remarkable Emily in 6th forged a stunning 19:54, partly based on cross training, but mostly because she believed she could do it. Erika, the sprinter, was 7th and on-the-money in 20:11. Sarah Searing was 18th in 20:48. Kathleen Nyzio crossed in 22nd in 21:03. Lindsay Stanley was 37th in 21:48 and Kaela Turose was 38th in 21:50. Our pack time 1-5 was a solid 1:24 and we averaged 20:19 in the ankle deep mud. We had retained our headlock on Section III.

Andy Pino was a bit shocked but a gentleman in defeat as he told the newspaper reporters,

He had three, four kids who ran the race of their life. You've got to give Jack and his kids credit.

My kids. I like the sound of that. More days than not, I love 'em.

We didn't defend our state title. From 32 degrees we ended up racing in the upper 60s at 'states at Sunken Meadow on the north shore of Long Island. We got lost on the way down and didn't get into our hotel until 1 AM Friday morning. We were absolutely ready on Friday afternoon at our course preview jog, but by Saturday we had nothing left emotionally or physically. Our sleep cycle had been changed. We were spent. Yet, we took fourth behind Bayport Blue-Point (60), Rhinebeck (62) and our old nemesis Pearl River (94). We tallied 105 with Zandra placing 5th and Erika taking 8th.

Crashing Back To Earth

As I drove home from our 8 AM mid-summer practice today, my words, spoken to no one since I was alone, were, "Man, we're in trouble." I'm rumbling south on state route 41A with Zeppelin blaring from my CD player in an attempt to change my mood and put a positive spin on the day. I'm a doom and gloom coach when I'm with Rob or any one of our former coaches. I think I'm Mr. Positive with the kids and I always try to find a reason to slap 'em on the back, or give them the elbows. In our attempt to avoid passing the plaque around the team, we don't share water bottles. We don't high-five. Germs. It's a clean school but it produces more sick kids than any building I've worked in.

I do seem to dwell on the negative that I see in practice and races. I expect good things. I work hard to figure out ways to achieve excellence. I work on the mind, the body, the attention to off-site lifestyle details. I sweat the small stuff. When something goes awry, I worry, and I worry aloud. These poor co-coaches around me must hate it. But no one has said anything yet.

It was our first day for dedicated speed work, 8-10 x 400 at our 1500 paces, nothing crazy and lots of shaded rest. Rachel Vaivoda, part of the frosh Brat Pack three falls ago, went out in 81, came back in 84 and exploded to 87 and virtually collapsed on the red rubber track, exhausted; final-exam-week exhausted. It was a terrible sight. I ended her practice. If she were a horse, we'd have shot her. Sure, it was hot with 98% humidity as soph-to-be Lexie told me, but the breeze was nice, and speed with a ton of rest is the least taxing thing we do in the summer.

With the meltdown, Rachel and I had our first senior talk about being ready, not graduating with a bunch of "what ifs" being included in her memories for the rest of her life. We talked about sleep since she's a notorious criminal in that department, but she hit the sack at 11 last night. I suggested more water, picking up some ferrous sulfate and a multiple vitamin. "I don't want to look back and think I was a one year freshman wonder," said Rach. "I don't want that. I want to do this right." And, that means getting more calories into her body, probably iron, too. She took a big step in the right direction by cutting her full-time summer job in half, something she hasn't done in the previous two summers. And she's done with college visits after visiting her last two, Bowdoin and Bates in Maine. She's trying, that I know. But she should be fresh right now, and all the mileage should allow her to simply power through these little speed workouts.

Rachel's tall, dark-haired and model-perfect with a brain that really clicks. Her past two sectional runs weren't very good though. We need to break that cycle and time is running out. With 300-meters to go in her sophomore race, she dropped out. She was crazed and virtually paralyzed from the waist down. We were in the victor's circle at that point, ready to celebrate another notch in our sectional belt. Our race plan had backfired on that day when Canastota grabbed our title and broke our string of titles at 10. We had a plan to attack and run in a pack but the reverse occurred. In 2004, Canastota rallied and had career days from nearly everyone on the team while we, Skaneateles, broke. Amanda, our nut-tough frosh who stood only 4' 11" if she stretched tall, was having trouble with her blood glucose levels as her diabetes stuck its head once again into her life at an untimely moment. Zandra, a senior, fell apart mid-race and that left Rachel all alone with Canastota's pack. Hannah was a non-entity that season. Rachel was left on a string to spin and twist until she was dropped for dead.

Conflicted by emotion and beginning to doubt herself while in 4th place—even though as a frosh she had faced and conquered the same situation at the OHSL meet—Rachel broke. For nearly 30-minutes after the race she couldn't move her legs while medics worked on her. I had it figured out immediately. "Just give her a little time and some sugar water and she'll be fine," I implored. And she was. A psychological meltdown, stress induced. A simple but debilitating panic attack. The title meant the most to her and the pressure got to her. That happens in life. We all have a breaking point. I named her captain for her junior year, hoping it would show my continuing confidence in her. I figured it would come as a complete surprise and bolster her ego and self-esteem.

But that year she again ran poorly on a muddy, hilly course at South Jefferson and placed 19th on a career day for the winners from Sauquoit Valley, the alma mater of assistant coach Rob Tuttle.

My job with Rachel looks to be much the same as my job with Hannah, but for different reasons. Hannah needs a cheerleader who keeps her relaxed while downplaying the significance of the race. Rachel, too, needs a cheerleader but she needs one to help her overcome these meltdowns, to help her believe, to get her to trust her training and realize that she belongs. Rachel needs to recognize that she has all the tools to get the job done and she needs to mellow-out and accept that she doesn't have to win to perform well and help the team effort.

I have a different job with sophomore Rachel Hosie, who led the sectional race last year for a while. She ran a little last summer, but not enough, which is a common frosh mistake. Stud high school runners often make the same mistake as they cross the great divide and head to their freshman college season. After making good progress last fall, Hosie told me that her parents wouldn't let her do indoor track and her conditioning vanished even though she tried to run with Lexie, who also didn't run indoors. Hosie missed many weeks of spring track practice for a trip to visit her brother, who was nearing the end of his year overseas as a foreign exchange student in Spain. By the end of track, she still couldn't break 12 minutes in the 3k. I think she's been doing pretty well this summer in terms of attendance but quality days have been a real disappointment and an eye-opener for me.

Today we discovered that her demise in the track workouts is caused by having 2% milk with her cereal. Going to skim should settle down her stomach. I'll also have to take some other unconventional measures, soon, if she doesn't begin to come around. A few weeks ago Hosie's sub-par training was due to a thick post-nasal drip so I gave her a list of things to talk to mom about so that we'd get rid of the problem. Missing all of her stamina—her primary weapon—I think we're in big trouble. But it's important to help these kids succeed and believe in their ability. With a goal pace of 84 she was unable to close in anything under 1:40.

I couldn't believe what I was seeing from such a talented and naturally gifted athlete. It looked like we were in a ten-car pile-up.

Rays of Hope on the Horizon

Our 2006 summer attendance remains miserable; five girls today along with six boys, which is nearly everyone on the boy's team. And it isn't really improving as the summer progresses. Sam and Calvin have sizzled. I worry about Calvin, who will be a frosh this fall. His dad has different ideas about training and the duo go out on 12-mile runs every Saturday. And there is no day off, though Calvin skips Wednesday morning sessions to play golf. He reliably runs later in the day. When I look at Calvin and try to analyze his body language and the way he answers my leading questions, I don't see someone who feels as if he's being dragged to do something unwanted. Maybe the young guy will hold up. He's trustworthy, no doubt.

Calvin is strong as an ox, but he's looking gaunt already and I worry about his nutritional intake. You have to be extra careful of the young runners with strong intentions. If he doesn't break, he'll be a star. When we've been at the Paul Short Invitational at Lehigh University, the bodies of the top guy's from the college teams look like Calvin's.

Dustin, Jeff and Dan work hard but seem to have jobs and a lot of other draining things to do over the summer. They aren't able to make every practice but they're good kids who are doing positive things from what I know, and they're trying. Dustin, upon coming back from Aim High, is on a high. He finds that he's running fast and just decides to carry it forward. Getting the memory foam mattress-top for his bed is helping to relax his tight back muscles. Dan was working two jobs and will now focus on his bakery job where his mom is putting together a culinary line-up that's simply tasty. As a plus, Dan has grown taller and lost weight. His legs remain stocky, sturdy, and that can work to his advantage if we get the right stride going. Dustin landscapes and Jeff hauls hay bales around his family horse farm. His dad is a big polo player and the polo grounds are his personal domain so there's always a lot of work waiting at home We hope to host our home dual meet with Marcellus and Westhill on the finely manicured grounds of the Polo Fields this fall. The turf is so good you could almost putt on it. Doctor Michael Parker and State Trooper Dick Sterling, both accomplished Ironmen, have volunteered to develop a cloverleaf layout for us. Bottom line: None of the boys are taking it easy when they aren't with me for the morning runs, and that's a rarity in our town as privilege hasn't spoiled these fine young men.

There are some bright spots as I sit amidst my self-imposed gloomy mood. Karen, now a junior, has been stellar, a complete surprise. For the past three years she wasn't even on my radar. She hasn't been able to hit all the sessions, but she's done well in both long and short runs. And she's doing it with a big grin on her face. Since the 7th grade, she's been battling a growth plate disease in her hip with a name ending in 'itis'. Now, suddenly it's gone and she's kicking some team butt with a smile gracing her face. She's running tall and with loads of confidence. Karen's dad is totally supportive, but in a hovering way, and there's a line he's going to have to watch carefully. Back in 7th and 8th grade, you could see that there was a lot of stress developing between the two on race day. I'm guessing that they've figured out how to make their relationship work because everything about Karen this summer is manifestly different. She's relaxed, at ease with herself and having fun with her running.

Year after year I meet parents of former athletes and former JE students and they all, almost without exception, wish they could take a mulligan and rear their kids through school athletics again. They all admit that they missed the point. They drove their kids in academics and athletics to the point where there was too much stress. The kids and parents had too many inflated dreams that superseded the kid's abilities and too often they were too demanding as too many days with unreal expectations changed their precious relationship.

As soccer devotee, North Hawthorne, said to me on a typical gorgeous day in July while we were both on the track, "It's just high school sports. I wish I'd kept it in perspective." North's daughter seems very interested in Steve Corsello. She just returned from a year in Ecuador and after traveling to visit him in jail for two years, we'll see if she and Steve end up together.

When I was a frosh at Ithaca College, my neighbor in the room next to me at Langdon Hall was a citizen of Ecuador. Henry Horvath liked to start fires and I'm sure that's not endemic to Ecuadorians in general. During our frosh year his native country had a bit of a revolution. Unable to reach his family, we drove to my house in Binghamton, NY and my dad, Bill, used his contacts, found a HAM radio operator on Hospital Hill who connected us to someone in Virginia who contacted someone in Miami who got in touch with someone in Ecuador's capitol city of Quito who was able to contract Henry's father. Henry was a hell of a soccer player, but he was a better pyromaniac.

Lexie is running well and I think her upside is bright. She's inherited the gait of her dad, Rick, but she's also inherited a drive and a willpower that allows her to focus on a goal for days-on-end without it eating her apart. She has poise. I've seen her sort before, and she seems like my Fab-5 in demeanor, control and desire to win.

Kristin, a 5:17 last spring in the 1500, has begun to train better. Noted for what looks like slacking off in practice, she's always had a lion-heart and a willingness to cut down anyone in her path during a race. With improved mechanics and a few years to grow into her tall body, this might be the year the junior breaks through. In the past, she's used teammates and then kicked past them down the stretch. She's like a fly on shit. She's all over the one she's dogging in the final moments of a race. With the end of the race in sight, she gets those long lanky legs going and unleashes an internal drive that is seen only in the end moments of big races. This year Kristin just might abuse the other runners in the race instead of her teammates.

But I think we're in for some trouble. When the rocks of the line-up are showing the ability to breakdown repeatedly during the restful time of the year, it doesn't bode well for us and our shot at redemption. Gloom and doom. From Happy Jack at birth to this, and it's only July 27th.

The forecast is not very forgiving for the next seven days. Training is going to be tough and I fear that the heat will be a ready excuse for too many of the kids I'm not seeing at the relatively cool hour of 8 AM.

Dave Eichorn of WSYR-TV, the flagship station in central New York, predicts humid highs of 85, 90, 87, 91, 91, 90 and 86 with dew points nearing 70. I'm not sure we're tough enough to deal with that—yet.

We've always shied from directly confronting the many weather extremes that are normal in central New York. Few really want anything to do with the 150 to 180 inches of snow we get here annually. Jessica O'Neill and Zandra Walton were always willing to do virtually anything to stay out of the school's 800-meter hallway; 200-meters of it are a nice straight-a-way. Recently Zandra's sister Beatrice has taken to going outside, not because she likes the snow, ice and cold, but because she fears yet another broken bone from running in the halls. Those three girls wear all the right clothes, put on the right face for the challenge, and have little chains that they slip over their running shoes. And, like most of my girls over the years, they know how to entertain themselves and each other. The boys would always scowl and frown at the crazy songs the girls have slowly developed generation after generation, but it's become a part of our tradition. And yes, that part of the tradition has also slipped away.

What remains is the chant the girls sing and shout as they finish their final stride away from the starting line. They stop, circle up and spell Skaneateles while tossing their hands into the center of the circle like a wheel's spokes and rhythmically raise and lower them like fans at a football game doing the 'wave'. It's a rocking song that I still can't recite. Male genes? Music lyrics learning disability? On the jog return to the line they chant—the brave seven in unison—"We feel good. OH. OH we feel so good. OH. OH we feel so, OH we feel so, OH we feel so good. OH, OH, OH." It's the final step in their race preparation, a formal process that, if done right, takes days to complete. Step by step, meal by meal, uniforms are laid out and shoes and spikes are matched to the weather forecast. Medicines, money, course maps, key opponents' information are studied. Up until now, the girls have done a great job with this important preparation. We'll see how this team stacks up. The boys? They show up. It's what guys do. The girls will even physically rip into a bagel like instructed when they get into their kitchen on race morning. Attitude is what we preach. Swagger is what we once had naturally. We're working to get it back.

Skaneateles is an enormously wealthy community. We seem to have 30-minutes of fireworks at least once a week as someone along the lake shore celebrates something special. My little log cabin was just reassessed from $188,000 to $487,000. We worked it back down to the high 300s. President Clinton and Hillary vacation here. Actors seem to hide here without getting hounded by anyone. America's Most Wanted host John Walsh hangs out here a lot. And they all enjoy dinner at Phil Romano's Rosalie's Cucina. If you have to ask the price of anything, you aren't ready to dine there. The downside of the wealth is that all the fears and wants of so many kids are taken care of by mom and dad or grandpa. They want for nothing. The student parking lots at school are filled with everything from Italy and Germany. The teacher lot is what you'd expect. Salaries are average at Skaneateles. One superintendent actually said that teaching is a secondary job for wives, so the salaries shouldn't be any higher than they are.

With a lake that's nearly 14 miles long and a mile wide, and an indoor exercise center that can boast of ice and warm pool water all year long, there's always something for the kids to do except find time to train. The football team has been 0-for the past two seasons at a minimum. Coach Ring is working his butt off this summer to try to get the kids in the weight room—and appears to be making inroads—but you can't coach toughness. As he said, "Jack, as soon as we try toughness, the phone calls from parents begin coming in."

We've always taken a minimalist approach to training; trying to get the most benefit from taking the fewest steps. But with this team, and the rise in competition across the state, we need more mileage so that we can absorb more hard training. We need a bigger sponge to sop up more work. We just finished a two week period that looked like this:

July 16 we go 4 miles and zip through 8 x 100.

July 17 is a long day for us and we cover 8 miles.

July 18 we recover with a comfortable 4 miles and 8 x 100.

July 19 we again march through 8 miles.

On Thursday July 20th we warmed up 2 miles and did 5-7 x 800 at 5k pace with a 2:00 recovery per rep.

July 21 we go back to running 8 miles and soon we hope to see some results. For the first time we used a new web site tool to help us plan our running routes. It's called www.Favoriterun.com and it uses maps combined with satellite pictures to lay out the roads in our community. Super stuff. And no driving involved.

July 22 we take off.

July 23 we trudge through another 8 mile slug-fest.

July 24 we lengthen our short day and go 5 miles and do 8 x 100.

July 25 we pick it up and do 5 miles with 14:00 of up-tempo pace during the run. We've been gradually working our way up to doing over 20 minutes of the up-tempo running.

July 26 we're back to doing 8 miles.

July 27 we warm-up 2 miles and go through 8-10 x 400 at 1500 pace.

July 28 we return to a 5 miler with another 14-minute up-tempo run.

The younger or older rookies complete fewer reps and often simply substitute the traditional Jack Daniels workout of 3-4 sets of 200, 200, 400 with about 2:30 rest per 200 and a 5 minute break after the 400. This coming week we'll go 5 miles with 4x200 and 2 x 100; 5 miles with 10 x 100; 5 miles with 1x400, 2 x 200 and 2x 100; then a 10-miler followed by various versions of 5 miles each of the next two days. After that, it's just two weeks until I see the kids for the first official practice. In between will be a nice week at the Aim High camp that's run by Dave and Jen Patruno.

On Thursday, July 13th, we did 8-10 x 600 at 10k pace with a 400 jog recovery. The initial summer track session was July 6th and it was a shock to their system as we did 8-12 x 400 at 3k pace, something we rarely do. The rest per rep was 75% of the running time for covering the 400-meters. I'm determined this season to gradually increase the stress so that their bodies will adapt and gain whatever it is that we've been missing. The problem is that all these fancy scientific studies don't apply very well to kids. So the high school coach has to apply some art to his coaching and tinker with the study's findings.

I always worry about the kids I'm not seeing. Training high school aged kids is not an exact science, but when they never show up for summer running and, for some reason, never communicate with me and never sign up for a summer road race, it's hard to know if I'm hurting or helping them during Boot Camp. But that's the nature of the beast in the early years of the 21st Century. Yup, I'm worried already.

Strike One?

We might be developing trouble, and I think the athletic director will be involved. Hell, we aren't halfway through the summer.

Karen, tall and with short blonde hair and a Barbi doll smile, has made a strong case for 'come-back-kid-of- the-year" because of her powerful and energized summer running. He mom called and said that Karen would not be here for two of the final three weeks of voluntary summer practice, which is no problem. It's summer. Families do things. I'm easy.

But what came next troubled me: Karen, a junior to be, would also miss the first two weeks of the season, and they are mandatory practice sessions. We take it a little laid back over the summer, but once the season begins, we're a team and we're on a mission TOGETHER. No matter how fast or slow you are, we all get put through the same meat-grinder and form bonds and a unique team dynamic. Based on the Karen I've seen this summer, she's a varsity caliber runner. Mom knew that her daughter had gotten back into the game of running and was enjoying it. And she knew that taking two weeks away from practice wasn't going to be greeted with a smile from me. I gave mom the first answer that came to my mind. I told her that Karen would have to miss the entire season. She didn't drop the phone but I could hear her heart flutter.

Those first two weeks are the forge that creates a team as the individuals work to develop their own unique chemistry. Seniors have departed, kids have grown up, some have put running a bit higher on their list of priorities. This is when leaders emerge and training groups form. This is when we have to make sure that cliques don't subvert our collective goals. This is when we work hard to ensure that everyone knows that the team is the thing, not any one individual. Throughout our history here, the team has always been greater than the sum of its parts. I've preached this year after year, season after season. You want a little coverage from the paper? You want recruitment letters from colleges? Work to make the team good. A successful program gets noticed, and when it gets noticed the individuals come under further inspection by the press and the colleges. It's hard to find a diamond in the rough, but it's easy to get entranced by a program that pumps out strong teams year after year.

If the team is going to perform at a championship level, it has to develop trust among the members. Our kids always seem to get along, but they aren't necessarily all friends. And they're competitive. Winning, being the best, is the community mantra. Some years we'll find runners on our team who have a specific goal to beat a team member, and some receive gifts from their parents when they defeat their designated team-target. I keep reminding everyone that the goal is to work with teammates so that we can beat the kids in different colored uniforms.

There are an awful lot of hours spent with each other on the bus, under the pine tree canopy where we stretch, on the back roads around town and on the track where rest breaks can seem interminably long on speed day. And some of those hours can be either boring or a pressure cooker. Kids need to know about each other's hot buttons, their insecurities and the little behavioral nuances that send subtle messages out to the team. A misplaced step or poorly chosen word can trigger a team meltdown, a cat-fight. Understanding each other, knowing each other well, even though lifelong friendships aren't necessarily being formed, is what makes a team stable. We have to get along. A stable team is one that can get on with its work without distractions, public pity parties or open feuds. I've spent many a night on the phone listening to girls cry their eyes out about personal problems on the team. No one will perform well under those circumstances. And I make it a policy not to intervene. It's important for these kids to learn to settle their own problems peacefully.

It's critically important for a runner to be able to know that if they lay it all out in competition, their teammates are willing to do the same thing. They gain steely confidence in practice when people hang tough as the paces on the long run take off and they end up grinding and holding together mile after mile as everyone experiences a critical time where fatigue tries to counter-attack your every move and the breathing becomes labored and the lips reach out for air and the arms rise quickly in a clenching motion upon the chest. With every step, the pack takes on a life of its own and at times the group watches as a valued teammate tries desperately not to get dropped by the pace. Sticking with it and avoiding getting dropped, like a sack of wire-wrapped newspapers on the side of the road during the dark hours of morning, elevates people's trust in each other and gives teammates additional confidence that can be withdrawn from their psychic reserves in a race. It's on those runs where teammates take the full measure of each other. Personal mettle is being tested, forged into steel and readied for competition. They gain that confidence on the track as the reps pile up and each learns to share the workload.

It's one for all and all for one. Miss those first two weeks, and probably the first few meets, and there really isn't any reason to be a member of the team. The season has left without you and you're left on the ground looking up at a horde of spiked shoes that are making their mark at your expense.

Karen should make the varsity line-up. She's come a remarkable distance since her hip growth-plates grew inflamed almost three years ago. It just wouldn't be fair for the team to work, coalesce and ultimately have seven girls be declared a member of the varsity line-up and then to have her return from vacation and, because she's talented, bump a varsity runner from the starting line-up.

Running is different from other sports. There's no substitution. And that makes it hard to discipline a runner. In other sports you can take a starting position away from an athlete and they can still play a vital role in the game as a substitute who assumes a lesser but still important role. Perhaps that punishment brings a bit of harm to the team, but it isn't a death sentence. In cross country if you don't start a runner, they sit out the entire competition. They lose rhythm. The team suffers. It's the team that pays the heavy penalty by having to go it alone, and they've done nothing wrong.

And one thing I've discovered about most high school runners is this: rhythm is enormously important, perhaps more important than anything else we do. Break the rhythm, break the runner. Everything in science leads us to know that resting prior to a big meet—peaking— leads to certain adaptations which help the runner perform at a higher level. If I give the kids a day off prior to an invitational, their rhythm is broken and they just flop in the race. Rhythm. Keep the pattern going.

So, what do I do about Karen? I think if she stays healthy, the team will be more successful with her in the line-up, at least based on what I'm seeing this summer. She's a bonus girl who we weren't counting on at all. She gives us more options so that I can give a girl a 'blow' from a dual meet mid-week and let them crank out some much needed mileage. Racing twice a week for a month is a killer. It's child abuse. But no one who runs our sport gives a damn. I feel for the kids. But, who will feel the pinch and be pushed back to JV if I allow Karen to return on Labor Day?

Wind, Rain and Heat

Labor Day will be our day of infamy. Will we have an explosion or will all of this transpire smoothly. Labor Day has a history here in Skaneateles. We celebrate the final departure of all the vacationers with a rocking and rolling weekend of music, amusement park rides, beer, a smokin' fireworks display in Austin Park in the heart of the village, and now a mini-triathlon, a mile swim from The Judge—a tourist boat--to the shore, and a 5-mile road race.

Back in 1998 there were explosions of another sort. My garage is constructed from thick slabs of Red Pine that was left behind as Mother Nature laid a big thumping on Central New York and tore it apart tree by tree.

The big Labor Day Storm hit us with a sudden ferocity in the middle of the night. Just say the words, "Labor Day Storm," and people around here begin telling their stories unprompted. It was about 1:15 AM when it hit. I've never seen anything like it.

Taylor Strodel was a freshman at Syracuse University and living in one of the upper floors in a tower dormitory. She and her roommates could see the storm coming in from the west. When a tree flew past their window, they knew this wasn't Kansas anymore. Diaries are filled with personal accounts, some horrifying as terror struck in the middle of the night. Passing through the New York State Fair grounds, it left death behind as the unsuspecting were exposed to nature's evil side.

The village was a mess. Roads were completely impassable. The local farmers, village and town workers and general citizenry got right into disaster-mode. Many of us were without power for nearly a week.

With the CEO of Niagara Mohawk—our electric company—living just down the street from us, we were sure we'd be one of the first areas back on line. It wasn't to be. My wife, my son KC, and I watched Mark McGuire break Roger Marris' single season homerun record on a battery-powered, 4-inch-screen television in a dark kitchen. Most of the time, for over a week, we just cleaned up from the storm that turned the sky green at times as transformers blew up, compliments of a lightning storm unlike anything I've ever seen. The winds hit 110 MPH and it forever changed the landscape of Skaneateles. There was no huge Labor Day Celebration that year. We'd seen enough fireworks.

The team has always been dedicated. The community is driven to succeed. Though the teachers in town may complain overzealously at times about their students, the kids they teach are the cream of the crop who have highly educated, high profile parents who are into being successful and looking successful.

Winners don't let anything get in the way. The morning after the storm destruction we were at practice. Nearly everyone attended. It was optional, of course. The thinking was this: if you can get to the rubber track safely, you'll be safe. It was out in the open. No wires, no fallen trees. No debris. Unfortunately, the athletic director noticed us and politely, using some good humor, got his message across. I guess we weren't supposed to be there. But, my mind kept saying, "We're a conditioning sport, unlike the other sports that stress short bursts of energy and specific skills. If we stay away for a week, we're dead meat. We've trained all summer. We can't let this steal our thunder!" It didn't take more than a few days to get going again. The school year had to begin and we toed the line without losing too much steam.

We always seem to get around these little unwritten rules. During the winter snow storms that close school, the kids know that we meet for practice at the Recreation Center at 10:00 if they can get there. All things being somewhat normal, everyone is shoveled out by 10. When kids come back from college and they want to train or see us, they know where we are and what we're doing.

I don't think this 2006 team is going to cause too much trouble for me in general. They seem willing to work hard and to sacrifice. They seem to share the work ethic of that 1998 team that defied the Labor Day storm. But I worry about the pimples, our little potential problems that could turn into gangrene. So far, I think I like what I'm seeing. There's just enough mid-summer enthusiasm to give me hope.

"A big 10 miler on Wednesday... I don't think I've ever done more than 9! This is exciting... Do we even know a 10-mile loop? Haha. I'll have to get out that GPS watch."

Here we are in the depth of the dog days of summer, and Sofie is pumped and ready to run. The forecast changed a bit and the air could now heat up to 100 degrees. With that knowledge in mind, the girls decided to meet at 7 AM Wednesday to avoid the environmental blast furnace. I plotted a course that measured 9.5 miles and ended right at our neighborhood beach on Winding Way. The team had incentive for this run. There's a goal. Hit the BEACH!

At 7 AM they began to show up. Ambling out of cars with their cheeks still puffy and a bit of 'sleep' stuck in the corner of their eyes, they looked like Spartans, ready to take on the assignment, the challenge. None of them had ever run as far as we were scheduled to run. A minimalist program such as ours usually hits a maximum distance of seven or eight miles and that's it. But our challenge this year is big and our goals are bigger. The number of runners showing up was larger than any day yet this summer, the humidity was up around 60% and the dew point was higher than I've ever seen it, hitting 75. The running route was as shady as we could make it. We would be heading south for 75% of the run and there was a nice steady south wind. Coach Tuttle and I drove around to cart water, ice and a variety of sports drinks as we monitored the kids and collected sweat-soaked shirts. We saw swamp-butts early in the run as the heat enveloped them and sent salty sweat cascading down their bodies.

As the kids arrived at the beach after toiling for nearly 10 miles—sometimes in bunches, sometime alone—they swam out to the raft. Sprawling across it, young, buff and full of hope, I saw my runners shed their athlete's personas. And suddenly, there in front of me was a bunch of great teenagers acting like typical teens in the middle of a carefree summer vacation. Their bodies are chiseled, I noticed; not an ounce of fat on them. They're toned, tanned and fit, and with no apparent effort, they got organized and began doing, on their own, a core workout as the raft bobbed, dipped and rose to meet the sunny sky as spitting waves made the raft decking slick.

On the hottest day of the year, they arose at 6 AM to run. That isn't the choice of most kids today. It's on days like this that the kids and their behavior serve to remind me of their overall wholesomeness, goodness and character. They're a trusting bunch. They're great kids, just beginning to drive—which scares me to death—and I'm fortunate to have the opportunity to work with them, to know them, to have them as a part of my life. They're a big reason that my life has purpose and consequence. I really don't have a damn clue what I'd do without them. Coaching is my life but I don't understand how spouses put up with a coaching partner. It's just an insane existence that strains and tests the strongest bonds.

It's important to have fun after an arduous 10-miler. It's good for the kids to get some spark going, some sizzle and razzle-dazzle after the run. Popsicles seem to be the popular post-run snack this summer.

Even though we aren't having the sort of summer turnout I'd like, I can't complain about this group of kids—or the adult support we're getting. I used to be able to hammer the long 6-8 mile runs with them, but the hip flexors, as well as the rest of me, keep me riding along in my car. Besides Pete Davis, who ran a 34 minute 10k in his mid-40s, the kids got to run with Dr. Tony DiRubbo who gave up his general practice to take care of his own kids, to run, and to teach medical students at Upstate Medical Center in Syracuse. He's a much happier man. Tony ran for Cornell and became good friends with a member of the women's team, Debbie Coccia, who I coached at Marcellus. The older I get, the smaller the world seems.

At the state qualifier meet during Debbie's junior year, she had to run a 15.9 in the 100-meter hurdles and place in the top three to earn a coveted spot in the State Meet. She finished 3rd with a time of 15.9 and didn't move on to States. Mad Dog, who ran for the famous Jerry Riordan at Syracuse CBA, was the adult-paid official timer for third place and he recorded the 15.9. But, the second timer, provided by some school that deemed timing to be a less-than-important responsibility, was a kid who had 15.9 and change. With the round-up rule, the time was changed to 16.0 and Debbie stayed home.

The rules state that the slowest watch is the official time. If you've ever coached and had a problem where simple logic should rule, you understand that you're doomed. USA Track and Field is a mess. The sport in the United States is a mess. And I'm not even speaking about the drugs. I look at lacrosse as it tries to grow its sport and it seems to do everything right. Track? It's one disorganized blunder after another. The response from our section's coordinator was, "Coccia's a junior; she'll make it next year." Well, Debbie didn't. She lettered at Cornell and at last word had taken a leading role in raising money for the Big Red Track program. Why can't we get people to do that for a public school?

Mad Dog? The official? How did a great guy like Rick Lavin get tagged with that nick-name? There's a story behind it. There always is, right? He was out on a long run one day with his CBA teammates and a dog bit him. Jerry Riordan taught his boys to be tough. When we saw them get off the bus at our Chenango Valley Invitational just north of Binghamton back when I was a teenager, we were bummed out. "Syracuse CBA? Man, they're animals," we'd all mutter to ourselves. Mad Dog and his teammates went back after practice and the dog was dead on the side of the road. Mad Dog's name became immortal.

The kids did well today. With three straight and relatively short five- mile days leading into the 10 miler, they decided to push the pace a bit this morning. It was an open blue sky which clouded over as soon as we finished our 10x100s. The air was already thick and sticky and you could see it.

I like what I'm seeing from Sam. He's continuing to push pace. Calvin seems unafraid to push with him, looks light on his feet and has quick, short arm levers. Dr. DiRubbo and I talked about Calvin's ability to hold up throughout the season with his non-stop running. Coach Tuttle doesn't think Calvin will make it to the first meet. We all agreed that he probably needed more calories and asked him to check his multiple vitamins to ensure that he's getting 1200mg of calcium. He's taking a pounding and we need to make sure his bones will hold up.

Dustin's biceps aren't the only thing looking good this summer. He's leaving other boys behind and just running his pace.

The girls, as a group, are sticking together a bit less, which is good, but I've noticed that the pace can get sluggish quickly. That'll change once official practice commences. We've always had a problem with the girls not wanting to hurt each other's feelings so we'd end up with pace-pushers being reined in by the teammates who didn't want to work that particular day. Sofie said today that they all started together and then they just went their own paces. If we can foster a sense of independence within a team framework where you look out for your team, promote your team and have each other's backs, we'll be on our way.

Steve Corsello Strikes Out

Nobody had Steve Corsello's back that fateful night of June 14th, 2004. I'd been warning Steve to be careful. "Don't take any chances. People are looking to catch you and knock you off your pedestal. People are watching you. Don't give them any excuse to take you down. Steve, I mean it. This is important. People are out to get you." I thought we'd made progress. Steve's friends drank, and drank heavily, beginning in at least 8th grade according to court documents. Steve drank, too. Even after all this, I'm still convinced that Steve had barely touched the stuff during the school year of 2003-2004, his junior year.

On the night of June 14th, 17-year old Matthew M. Angelillo would age no more. Steve took out his dad's car without having a night driving license. Pretty much no one in Skaneateles waits until they have a night license to drive after sunset. The kids know where the cops are and they come back into the village surreptitiously and therefore away from the inquisitive eyes of the police and their radar gun. Parents don't seem to really care about it either. I don't get it.

Steve usually drove a big heavy old Mercedes but on that fateful night, the kid who was close to breaking the New York State 8th grade record in the mile was given, by his dad, the keys to the leased Ferrari. It was bright red and that more than caught the attention of the press. The fatal crash was the cause celeb. It divided the community. Too many people felt that the District Attorney and Sheriff's Department shouldn't have been questioning the locals trying to gather facts about the high speed death. People just wouldn't talk.

I talked. Too many people are afraid to lay it on the line. We have a drinking problem in this town and too much of it is parentally condoned and in too many cases encouraged. My oldest son went to a party where a father met him at the door. In order to get in the kids had to have a bottle of booze or they were barred from the party. I'm sure keys were collected. But what kind of bullshit action is that for a parent to participate in? Our job is to make illegal things a bit difficult for the kids to get into. So I talked to the press. Although I was reprimanded, I didn't lose my job. I think I was retained because of Dick Case of the Post-Standard. The renowned columnist called me a hero. I wasn't, but he said it nonetheless. Case wrote,

> *We're in the market for heroes. I noticed four this week. Jack Reed's a hero. Jack has coached track at Skaneateles High School since 1991. He coached Steven Corsello, the student charged in last weekend's car crash that took the life of Matthew Angelillo. Right now, the coach seems to stand tall among his neighbors. He's the only Skaneateles citizen we've interviewed who's been willing to say some young people in the community have a problem with alcohol; that some adults condone it. Jack shared that opinion with our reporter Monday. As the week wound on, we began to see how right he is: Law enforcers say a wall of silence fell around Skaneateles as far as cooperating in the investigation is concerned. What's the big deal, neighbors are asking the Onondaga County sheriff's and district attorney's investigators, according to DA Bill Fitzpatrick.*

> *"This is as tight-lipped as any investigation I've seen," Thomas Tubbert, chief of the sheriff's police division, said.*

> *Dozens of interviews with parents and young people provided no information to two questions: Where were the teens partying before the accident and who helped them get drunk?*

> *Our chief prosecutor's mad. He promised to throw the book at the partiers and their helpers when he tracks them down. Don't doubt he will.*

'Fitzy' singled out Jack Reed as the only citizen in Skaneateles so far who's willing to admit we've got a problem. He said he's waiting to see if the coach becomes a hero, or is ostracized in the community for his comments.

I talked to Jack on Thursday. Although school is closed, he continues to work with some of his athletes. Coaching at Skaneateles is a side job; he teaches global studies in the Jordan-Elbridge district.

No, Jack says, his opinions haven't caused him grief yet. He says he understands his neighbors' shyness, although that's not his style. "People value their privacy around here. I respect that."

Still, he's uncomfortable that adults don't' take their role in the family, and the community, seriously enough to realize that 'we're here to set an example for kids, to make them better than we are."

Also, "We can't be afraid of the truth."

Truth is, beyond the hearing of the district attorney and the cops, Skaneateles roils with gossip about the tragedy and its aftermath. It's not leaving town any time soon.

I tested my guess with a few phone calls, asking people I know what's being said behind Bill Fitzpatrick's back about the party. Randomly, coincidentally, each one had heard the same location mentioned.

The specific source of the refreshments eludes investigators so far. "If you have 100 or 200 kids at a party, you know they had to get the kegs somewhere," one neighbor said.

Who's next to join Jack Reed, Pat Waelder, Cynthia Kirby and Tommy Seals on the platform?"

I was dead set against Steve going to prison. I asked, "Why prison?" in an editorial in the Post-Standard. Steve had behaved with the utmost propriety for the year between the accident and his sentencing, which took place the day after he graduated from high school. He'd done everything the legal establishment asked of him. I didn't think there was anything constructive to gain from spending one to three years in state prison. He isn't incorrigible. He was 17 when he made a stupid mistake, the most costly mistake a human can make. But it was a mistake. It was not intentional. Steve is a bright boy. He doesn't need to be hit over the head repeatedly before something registers. The two boys who tragically ended up in the Ferrari with Steve behind the wheel had to fend off other boys who wanted the fast ride home. Matt is reputed to have said, "If I die, this is the way to go." You know that a lot of us have said the same thing at exactly the wrong time in our lives. Everyone had been drinking and they all made a stupid decision. Field parties tend to turn brain matter into mush. Steve just happened to be the one driving. He got nailed.

Many people wanted Steve to be punished just to get a pound of the kid's flesh. He'd become the poster-boy for every fear and hatred adults had toward teenagers. I don't get that. He's in the slammer north of Albany, NY. He doesn't have access to a computer. He virtually had to beg to be allowed to take correspondence courses from an Ohio college. So far he's completed three courses and gotten an 'A' in each. And he's written extensively to his professors with deep questions. He's also read everything that Dickens and Hemmingway wrote. He says Hemmingway is overrated.

I know, I know, Matt is dead. No one wanted that and no one can change that awful fact. Feeling hollow, that God-awful gutted feeling that leaves us all wanting relief, never leaves the survivors of catastrophe. But Steve is coming out. Even the draconian parole board can't keep him in prison forever. Do we want him broken or prepared to try to put the pieces of his life back together? After all, how many people come out of prison a better person? It's a macabre world. Hell, lifers in the state prison system have access to computers. Many get graduate degrees. And here we have a kid who is coming out and we don't seem to understand that a whole-Steve could still be a benefit to society. We, who know him well, fear that he'll come out a broken man who will under-perform his whole life. You wonder how anyone goes through life when the nightmare they live every day is their reality until the day they die. Steve is one tough, self-disciplined cookie. Maybe he'll make it. Maybe prison will relieve him of a small modicum of his guilt.

Steve got nailed. One to three years in the state prison system where cutthroats become 'friends' and the meaning of life can evaporate without a fight. His friends have done yeoman work making the 4-5 hour drive to see him on weekends. His friends, who were also Matt's friends, have stuck with him through the whole affair. His parents continue to make the long drive every Sunday. Yes, I know that Matt's parents can't ever see him. It's awful. But the reality is that Steve lives. He's going to be walking among us soon. What sort of Steve do we want released from prison and walking around in our community?

Steve was an average boy who reflected the society that helped to create him. We made him. The advertisers influenced him. The local community guided him to this point. We're a convoluted, split society with schizophrenic tendencies as many of our neighborly brethren are liberal boozing partiers with puritanical tendencies that constantly drive us to church where we ask for forgiveness on a weekly basis. We, the supposedly responsible adults, get kids to drink. We get them to love and crave speed. We get them to live in the moment. We gain their confidence and we alter the normal workings of their brain. Risk is the hallmark of every American. Taking chances is what we're all about. Living on the edge is normal.

The advertising money spent in this country is spent for a reason. It works. We're all nothing but guinea pigs. We know it but we don't revolt. Mass advertising worked perfectly on Steve. Combined with the community mores, advertising transformed him into the prototypical American boy, brusque, brash, brave and full of daring-do. But when the advertisers' work achieves perfection, we all step back as every one of us disowns the culprit, point fingers and abandon the malefactor to take the blame himself. He's on his own and some of us say, 'How could he be so criminally and socially messed up?"

Steve's repentant. He comes from an alcohol-free family. Both parents work with their hands: his gentle mom teachers the soft touch of the piano, and dad, a highly intelligent and educated man who suffers fools poorly, mows the lawns of the rich and famous for a dollar a minute in his retirement. Steve's a good kid and if this can happen to him, it can happen to anyone's kid. That should scare the shit out of every parent, but, too many still don't get it. We live in la-la land here in God's country. It takes a village to raise a child, and that community should hold itself responsible when it succeeds in its mission.

Steve wrote me from prison on January 15th, 2006.

Dear Coach,

I'm sorry it's taken me so long to reply. Time has a way of wandering off. I think that's probably the hardest thing about prison, the way the time goes. In many ways, time is the enemy, it is what keeps us incarcerated; a length of time we count down, measuring the days between us and our freedom. And yet the prisoner is the most incapable—though the most probable—user of time. An abundance of time is not a good thing because it creates idleness, restlessness, and lethargy; things only an active man can fight. For all my prudence and desire to maximize every second at my disposal, I sometimes slip into a mindless, unproductive state of wholly meaningless conduct. This does not arise from solitude, but instead from the company of some of the most worthless souls the world has ever seen and yet has seen them in great abundance. Left to my own devices and a quietness encouraging focus or contemplation, I fight a winning battle against the onslaught of a less than mediocre existence.

On the reflection of my high school career, both academic and athletic, the things that most stand out are the principles and lessons of my training, the metaphorical significance of repetition and sustained perseverance that running demands. The steadfast desire, composure, and endurance that running taught me has permeated my life. Those are not for the track, but for the street; for the days when we can't race, when we can't train. Throughout this mess the virtues of the runner have never been so clear to me and are part of the reason why running is the most worthy sport ever to grace this world. For all of my shortcomings and near misses my running career amounted to, that I am now fully conscious of, I would do it all again knowing the outcome.

Here and now I have taken up the sword again, pounding the pavement for a half-hour or so a day. The cold hurts and is familiar and it is only then that I find my center. I did the same during the summer immediately succeeding the accident in the midst of a looming prison sentence, baneful publicity, and extreme self-consciousness. I owe my sanity, sense of purpose and fortitude to running. Do you remember what you said to me just before I was called to the bench at my arraignment in town court? You said this is what we train for, this is what preparedness and racing is all about. I will never forget those words and have approached everything that is difficult and painful and deplorable with that in mind. The day of sentencing, just like a race, I was nervous, my heart was pounding, and my being undoubtedly shaken. And like every race that I have ever run, I did not crumble, though it wasn't about winning or losing this time, only finishing.

Steve

Nothing significant has changed since Steve went to prison. His friends went to college, some to overseas destinations for a year, the track team moved on, and drunk driving and the associated deaths continue in Central New York unabated.

Steve wanted desperately to win the state title in the 800-meter finals in June of 2005, just weeks before his sentencing. He went out and promptly got cut off. My last instructions to him were, "Get out fast and stay clean." He made a big move down the backstretch to make up a deficit and improve his position. On the homestretch of lap-one he took command. It was going to be his race to win or lose. He burned a lot of energy making up for being cut off and I was worried. I'm always worried.

I've seen the fastest 4x100 team drop the baton while in the lead. It was my team. Tommy Theobald, 6'6" and an athletic stud ran the second leg down the back stretch. He handed off to my son, Kirk, who was not the fastest on the team by far, but he could run a turn like no one. And his handoffs were automatic and flawless. Both felt that their hamstrings were a bit tight before the race so they lubed up, and with the temperatures in the 90s on the track, the sweat combined with the lube and out popped the baton with both of them having their hands around it. It just squirted out like a bar of soap. I had it on film and all that shows up on tape is them dropping the baton and my last words, "Oh Shit," uttered into a camcorder on its way to the cement stadium floor. I sent the camcorder crashing to an untimely death at the top of the stands at Rome High School. That's why I like coaching distance runners. It's more forgiving.

Steve was holding his own. He came through the 400 in 56.5 seconds; faster than he'd ever split a 400. His personal best for the 400 was 50.25 so I thought he might be able to hold up if he hadn't emptied the gas tank making up ground.

With 40 meters remaining he had a three meter lead on everyone except Fredonia's Geoff Lesch-Wragge. He was strong with thundering thighs and then nothing but a skinny leg until his calf muscles rose like the back of a Humpback whale surfacing. His biceps and shoulders made you think of a linebacker. Steve was hard but thinner. And he was saddled with a heavy burden that no one could comprehend. He wanted that victory as much for me as himself; probably more if I were to tell the truth.

Wragge's mouth was wide open in a virtual smile because he knew he had more gas in the tank than Steve, whose mouth was in a grimace as his arms came up to meet a heaving chest. It was close, 1:53.75 for the winner from Fredonia and 1:54.16 for Skaneateles Laker and state runner-up, Steve Corsello.

The defeat, yes, that's how Steve referred to it, the failure, yes, that's how Steve thought of it, was devastating. It was a school record and moved him into the Federation final the following day. But he was done. He had his crosshairs on a goal. And in his eyes, he had lost the war. I knew right then and there--watching Steve on the Award's Podium--that this setback was being taken harder than the prison sentence he was facing. He had no control over what Judge Aloi would do. But he was certain he had control over how that state 800-meter final would come out. What Steve didn't understand was the fact that Wragee had a say in the outcome, too. He'd worked hard and had his own dream and perhaps his goal meant he only had to prove himself to himself. Steve was finding out, in a harsh, public way, that he couldn't control his own destiny all the time, something his father had given only a glancing blow while teaching about being a winner. Like father, like son. Sometimes even the best can't win the race.

Steve was raised to be strong, self-reliant, tough, demanding, unforgiving, resilient and powerful. Fighting, he was told, can be a good thing. He learned to box in the city. He played basketball against the playground kids when his father dropped this suburbanite kid into the inner city so he could toughen up. Steve didn't understand quitters. And he didn't accept losing. Self-controlled to a fault, Steve broke from his training regimen in the interim between the end of track and the beginning of the state academic finals and, unrestrained, his untamed self took over and he drank, drove, and killed. Matt Angelillo is dead. And Steve Corsello is rotting in prison.

Chaos Theory

Unplanned things happen in life, and no matter how organized we get, shit happens. We can spend inordinate hours hunched in front of a computer reviewing stats, planning macro and micro training sessions, devouring the incredible scouting information that's on web sites, and shit still happens.

My interpretation of Chaos Theory is this: Nothing is predictable except the unpredictable. The unexpected is going to happen. We can count on it. So, chaos really isn't an abrupt, unexpected occurrence. It's part and parcel of the daily routine. Chaos, represented by the unexpected, always happens. Therefore chaos is normal.

No matter what we predict for our teams, the reality will be different. I never get what I expect because shit keeps happening.

I tell my teams before many meets to expect the unexpected. If something happens, they're ready for it and it's much less of a big deal. There are many occasions when I should remind myself of that truism.

Just when you think karma is on your side, a crow dumps on your newly pressed sport coat. It could be a senior who has been away over Columbus Day weekend for a college visit. Upon their return, they're sick as a dog and you're looking at two weeks of ups and downs as you try to train them while they recover. I suspect our kids are pretty good at dealing with our local viruses, bacteria and allergens, but once they cross the Hudson to the east or the Susquehanna to the south, they're sitting ducks for an immune system shocker.

Karma. I miss it. Once a year we have this confrontation: Big meet versus whale watch. It's true. Moby beats us every time as the local school kids bolt for the ocean, six hours toward the sunrise as they leave us fighting for our track meet life.

We fall to horse shows and Irish Step Dancing. We fall down stairs, fall on the ice, run into guardrails, water hydrants and parking meters and end up with swollen knees, bruised thigh muscles and black eyes. I've lost sectional titles because of pulled groins, compliments of a school dance where the kids gyrated in all directions after months or years of training to move fast forward in a nice straight line.

And then there's the young boy who fell down on the track in mid-September during a very slow warm-up jog. He broke both main bones in both arms and was in casts for months. My question and concern was primal and it hit below the belt. Did the poor kid have to call for mom or the school nurse after going number two? There was no way the kid could clean himself. I hate to admit it but it still makes me laugh. He had the most brittle bones I'd ever seen. "Mom! I need you again."

Chaos. It can be a killer. But Chaos and the unexpected can be good, too.

Simone Bras, a lover of the Latin culture and a hell of a runner, showed up in the fall of her freshman year. Pennsylvania's loss was our gain as she helped us win a few state titles. She was a classic Type 'A' personality. Everything had to be right. Control was important to Simone. One day she started having trouble breathing toward the end of races. With the pattern becoming permanent, mom found a sports psychologist who taught Simone to hypnotize herself. It worked and she returned to form.

When Simone was hypnotized by the doctor, she went to a nice, private, quiet place where she was comfortable. But then something happened. She got edgy and screamed. It began to shower paper, textbooks and notebooks. She was drowning in her school work and the pressure to excel. After one sectional race it took us nearly an hour to get her breathing under control. Despite the incredible pressure she put on herself, I'm certain that if she'd been more consistent and not skipped summers and every indoor season, we'd probably be reading her name in the sports section today.

We also accepted imports: the Riley brothers from Virginia and Jessica O'Neill from nearby Marcellus, surprises each and every one, though people didn't believe that Jessica's transfer had nothing to do with me. Team dynamics changed, new friendships developed mile after mile, and the team was richer. We've had our share of exchange students and I think we've gotten more out of them culturally than athletically. As is often said, the nations of the world send us their best.

The biggest surprise in terms of the team and championship running occurred in 2003, the year Jess O'Neill joined our team. Jess had a lot of trouble getting cleared to transfer. Things had happened over at Marcellus, including her female coach dating her father who was divorced from mom. It was just real unsettling for Jess as a frosh and sophomore. Silly things were said about me recruiting her, but I'd actually never spoken to Jess or her parents prior to her moving over here with her mom. If truth be told, Jess was the enemy and she was damn good. My job was to beat her, which we were able to do on occasion. As a sophomore, she was the state cross country runner-up—without benefit of any warm-up at all. It amazed me. Jess set PRs with us in every track distance and her cross country times on several courses were personal records, too. But the fight was getting harder for her. She started to develop hips and became a woman.

With Jess on our team we had four All-State girls leading the way. Julie Lynch led us with Jess, Zandra Walton, and Erika Geihe also returning with the All-State designation. And we had the brat-pack coming up. We were loaded. My concern was Zandra, a class valedictorian like Geihe the year before her. Zandra once said, in a very personally insightful dissection, "I like track so much better. In cross country there are just too many variables that I can't control."

For a while we weren't sure if Jess would be allowed to join us. The battle got nasty and hearings were conducted to determine the truth. In the end, after missing some meets, Jess was cleared to join her new teammates.

The Post-Standard wrote

Lady Lakers Add Ace

Defending Section 3 Class C girls cross country champion Jessica O'Neill is in the process of transferring from Marcellus to nearby Skaneateles. O'Neill last fall won the sectional Class C title and was also state runner-up in that class while running for Marcellus. Today, O'Neill ranks among the top three individual girls runners in Section 3. If O'Neill gets clearance to run for the Lakers this fall, look for Skaneateles to repeat as Section 3 champion and also improve upon its fourth-place finish at last fall's state meet.

It wasn't until September 25th that the news hit the public about Jess being cleared to race. She'd missed a month. In that time, news from our east revealed that a powerhouse Canastota team had reconstituted and was ready to take us down. Neil Kerr, the dean of high school sports coverage in New York State, wrote the following release.

High Speed Chase

Canastota cross country looks to dethrone Skaneateles

Though they remain in the lengthy shadow cast by defending Section 3 Class C champion Skaneateles, Coach Andy Pino's youthful Canastota girls cross country team is determined to chase the Lakers until they finally overtake them.

In the first set of state Class C rankings, Skaneateles is No. 2 and Canastota is No. 4.

"We've probably got the youngest girls cross country team in Section 3," admitted Pino, whose past girls teams won state titles three times (1986, 1996, 1997). "We have an outside chance of catching Skaneateles this fall but, if not, we'll certainly have a good shot at beating them next year. We don't have one senior on our team."

Andy's a good coach and I learned one important lesson from him. When scouting an opponent, he said, "Don't waste my time telling me about the kids. Tell me about the coach and I'll figure out a way to beat them." Wise indeed. But, Andy rarely had effective seniors on his team. His basic belief is that the girls peak early, so he runs them hard in 7th, 8th, 9th and 10th grades. Not too many are still real competitive after that, with notable exceptions, of course. And I can't ever remember Canastota having a junior high team. It seems that every kid who runs is enough of an athlete to pass the NYS Selective Classification physical exam. I rarely have anyone I'd like to bring up. It's an even rarer day when we see a 7th or 8th grader at Skaneateles who could even hope to pass that exam.

All season long we'd both successfully dodged each other but the time to race was getting closer and closer by the moment. Perry L. Novak, writing for the Oneida Daily Dispatch near Canastota wrote,

> *Even the most unfeeling opponent might shed a tear for Andy Pino this year. Pino has won a lot of meets with the boys, and even more with the girls. Three state titles attest to his teams' prowess, and 2003 could have been a good bet for number four except for Skaneateles. The Raiders compiled a 19-0 mark during the year and have been ranked as high as No. 2. Currently No. 3 in the girls' C poll, Canastota has the unlikely challenge of beating the state's No. 1 team, Skaneateles.*
>
> *Coach Jack Reed's Lakers were already picked to repeat as section and state champs when former Marcellus great Jessica O'Neill was allowed to join the team after transferring at the beginning of the school year. O'Neill, rated seventh in the section, headlines one of the best teams in Section III history along with Julie Lynch, Zandra Walton and Erika Geihe.*
>
> *Three of the Lakers' top runners are seniors so Pino's mighty mites have speed and experience to overcome in their 1:30 PM race. Leah McDowell, an eighth grader, leads the way with Rosemary Foran, Gina Micaroni, Kayla Curtis and Sara Foran. None of Canastota's top runners are seniors. That makes for a dynasty in the future.*
>
> *It just doesn't make for great odds in the present against a Skaneateles dynamo.*

I usually keep my thoughts close to the vest when the press calls and asks about my team. But when the Auburn Citizen called just days before the Championship, I told them,

> *"I know what we've got lined up," said Skaneateles coach Jack Reed. "This group's real good. All things being equal, I think we've got the winning team this weekend."*

As the teams lined up at Cato-Meridian, a hilly, muddy, twisting and turning course with narrow trails, I went to see Andy and wish him good luck and chaos broke out. I should have expected it. We'd always been friends and seemed to respect each other. Andy went off on me in front of his kids and other teams that were anxiously making final preparations. "I don't respect you. You have no dignity. You cheated. You went and recruited her. I know. I have sources," said Andy as his face shook and grew redder by the word. I stayed pretty calm, again wished him and his girl's good luck and said that I was sure we would get past this, and, in time, we have.

Andy had every right to be ticked off. Skaneateles having Jess on the team radically changed the equation and there was no way for Andy's Canastota team to make a counter move and draw even.

In the spring of 2003 I was on the receiving end, as two great runners from Sudan, who fortunately were able to leave the savagery of the civil war behind, relocated to nearby Tully, coached by my friend Jim Paccia. Jim and I, along with other coaches in our division, had spent one night at his place watching a collection of video tape in an effort to sort out our Sectional championship race. We had a multi-chute finish and the officials let the kids out in the wrong order to receive their finish cards. I know my boys went into that chute the winner but we had slipped from first when the final tally was announced. We drank and drank and drank until 3 AM and couldn't quite put the meet back into its proper order. It happened the next year, too. I didn't win that one either.

In the spring of 2003 my Skaneateles boy's 4x800 relay was in the hunt to advance to the state meet. The race was a yo-yo. Tully exploded from the start behind Sudan's Lopez Lemong who split a 1:55.7 while Erik Eibert from my team split a 2:02.65. Tully came back with a 2:08 leg and my son, KC, split a 2:03.15 to put us back into the game. Tully then sent out a 2:12.6 and Steve Corsello, a sophomore at the time, ran a 1:59.21. Junior Patrick Lewis closed for me in 2:03.85 and had a huge lead when he entered the final lap, insurmountable we thought. Tully closed with Sudan's tall Dominc Luka and all he did was nail a 1:52 to edge us by 0.02 seconds, 8:09.14 to 8:09.16. Poor Lewis never saw Luka coming. The crowd was going so incredibly crazy that he couldn't hear our screams of warning.

I'd lobbied for two years and took an unpopular position. Catholic Charities seemed to like giving these poor Sudanese boys a birth date of January 1st, and they always seemed to be 14 years old when they arrived in the United States so they could receive a full American education. Despite my disbelief and the furrowed brows of pediatricians who saw the boys and pegged them to be much older with one doctor saying, "Over 20," my argument revolved around proof of birth. If our taxpaying families have to prove the age of their kids in order to meet the state's age requirements, everyone should. I believed that the idea of sport is a level playing field where fairness is assured so that the best prevail. If immigrants, refugees, exchange students or anyone else can't prove their age, they should be steered to an array of local track and running clubs where they could train, learn and race to their heart's content. No one wants to punish these kids, but fair is fair. It made me sound like a schmuck.

Jonathon Riley, as a frosh, lost out on a trip to the state mile finals because Watertown had a phenom from Sweden. I made the same argument back then in the mid 1990s and no one listened. The New York State Championship is our championship. I would never dream of entering the City of London's track championship. Why? I'm not from London, no matter how long I'd been there as an exchange student or foreign resident. It's not my championship and I wouldn't belong. We deprived Riley of a valuable learning experience. As it turned out, the Olympian didn't suffer, but why make the development of our own kids so difficult? The college programs aren't helping much either, with some teams seemingly relying totally on foreign runners while our kids languish in the netherland of top coaching neglect. The influx of foreign runners grows worse year by year according the actual NCAA counts.

After my confrontation with Andy, I went to my girls and got them as fired up as any team I've ever coached. What a slaughter the race became. We placed all seven girls ahead of Canastota's 2nd finisher, Gina Micaroni, an 8th grader. Leading 'Stota was Leah McDowell. Ahead of her from my team was Julie Lynch in 2nd, Jess O'Neill in 3rd and Zandra Walton in 7th. Right behind McDowell was Erika Geihe in 9th. The Brat-Pack of Hannah, Sofie and Rachel took 13th, 14th and 15th. The shock of our relentless attack really got to the young 'Stota girls who, though ranked No. 2 in the state heading into the meet, took third with 97 points. Poor South Jefferson, with Nicole Lister (Boston College and our honoree at the track banquet as our most respected opponent) leading the way, was once again the first runner-up with 71 points. Muddied but unfazed, the Lakers were first with 34 points and every girl closed with a stirring and determined rally.

Once again, chaos can be good as often as bad.

We went on to win the state title the following weekend, beating Saranac Lake and Bayport-Bluepoint easily. But this Sectional crown—and beating back the Canastota threat—was the one we truly wanted. It marked the end of our Decade of Excellence. We haven't been to the state meet as a team since. We want to get back into the game, and we'll very likely have a tough fight with 'Stota once again this year for the right to advance to the state championship.

Advancement to Warwick, the site of the big race on November 11th, that's the purpose of meeting tomorrow at 7AM for a 10-mile run. Right now the temperature is nearing 100 degrees.

Strike 2?

Hey Coach,

I am very sorry but I will not be able to make the run tomorrow because I have something else I have to go to. I'm also writing to tell you in advance that I will be missing a meet this year because of a horse show. I have a major barrel race on September 23rd and this is when everything counts. Also my state fair show is on the 3rd and 4th of Sept. so I will be missing 1 day of practice which is Labor Day. After these 2 things all of my horse shows will be over for the year. I apologize again.

Rachel

Rachel Hosie is enormously talented, and she has a lot of interests outside of running. She has long limbs, small hips, and just loves to move fast. But since leading last fall's sectional race for an eye-opening amount of time, she's made choices that have left both of us a bit frustrated. I believe the family decided that doing three sports a school year wasn't a good idea, so Rachel passed on indoor track and didn't run from November until mid-March. When she showed up for outdoor track she was just in awful shape. She knew it and the frustration caused by horrible track times and looking at the butt-end of teammates, who couldn't ever dream of running with her back in cross country, really shown on her face and affected her demeanor.

As the summer started, she wrote and asked if she could have a summer job. She's just entering her sophomore year but I would never step in the way of anyone who has constructive plans for summer, but I made her 'sign a contract' that stated the work would not interfere with her summer conditioning. When I reflect on who has been showing up this summer, Rachel's name is not on the top of the list where it needs to be, and now this. I'm disappointed because I've spent a lot of time trying to lure her into our running web. She could be so good. We could be in trouble. I hope my mid-summer pessimism is unwarranted. We'll know soon enough.

My guess is that the team would be healthier—not better—without Rachel and Karen, who will be missing most of the first two weeks of practice, but I'm not sure how the rest of the girls would feel without them on the team. Our goal is to coalesce into a dynamic unit, unfrayed by individual agendas and unencumbered by doubt. I know both girls are fully investing mentally in our chase to the top, but there's a part of me that says team togetherness and success begins day one with all showing up.

I decided that I needed to start a fire under Rachel. It might backfire but sometimes the risk is worth it. Rachel could be a phenom. Her dad feels the same way and he told me it bothers him to see her lying on the couch when her teammates are at school preparing for the season in the coolness of the morning. But the dream has to be her own, not her dad's or mine.

I wrote back to the spunky Rach, who has a deadpan sense of humor, and I took a stern tone that was something she's never heard from me. I suspected it would shake her up. I always try to be at my corny best with her because I love the girl and we're fortunate that she wants to run with us. Hopefully my new tone didn't shatter our relationship. I've always been concerned with what the kids think of me. Many coaches could give a damn. They just do what they feel is right. I wish I could be like that but it's not in my nature. I like to be liked. It's my curse.

I really don't know how to respond to you....you're not the first to tell me that you'll be missing meets....I don't know how to coach kids who don't come to practice or meets....anything I do like any other coach in other sports, in terms like benching will hurt the kids who are sweating off their butts this summer to get back on the winning path...they want to protect the dual meet winning streak and they want to win sectionals again.... but I can't expect them to wonder who will be on the team from week to week....missing meets is totally unacceptable except for something like a death in the family....any other reason is a choice, and those choices just have consequences....I can live with Labor Day.....but the meet?...varsity athletics are not like modified where we just dip our feet into the stream...I know you realize that the F-M team would never miss a meet.... and they're not alone....we used to beat   F-M...We had our problems but never when it came to attending practice and races.....but the gradual change in the community's character has sent our success quotient plummeting....goals are reached by making sacrifices and doing everything in your power to excel....you missed a lot of time in the spring and it haunted you all season....you have talent but it's not the talent that's natural...it's the sort of talent that has to be worked....rhythm is essential and I think your lack of rhythm this summer is causing you difficulty in getting into shape....after leading sectionals last fall, I think you've been making decisions that have done nothing but trip you.... we all need to juggle schedules to make this crazy life of ours work for us and not against us....we're doing everything we can to accommodate the individuals on the team but we're losing ground....I may have to take the stern approach.... my philosophy is simple...when you join something, you show up...I know this is a bit harsh but we're only 3 weeks from mandatory practice....and we have a meet on Sept. 2 before school opens...if the team is to succeed, everyone on the team needs to be able to count on each other and to trust each other....we aren't anywhere near that this summer, and with people missing meets, it just brings everyone down to a less accomplished level....so, if the 23rd is not a race day, you may be able to join the team...if it is a race day, I'm probably going to wish you good luck with your other interests..... sorry about this Rachel....I thought after last fall that you'd be the team leader this year, and to get a note like this is very sad for me..... you're a great kid and the team likes having you around....

> *hopefully this will all work out...maybe a cooler day will alter
> my thinking....coach*

Is the note going to shake her up or cut her completely loose? Oh boy. This isn't going to go over well, but long-term it might do what we need. I have to get her on the same page as the other girls.

Having to worry about attendance is something that absolutely never happened until the past few years. The list of reasons for missing practices or meets or weeks of time in one shot has reached critical mass, and it's hurting our ability to produce while putting the kids at greater risk of injury.

I remember in high school at Chenango Valley, north of Binghamton, NY, when Chris Roser, my teammate, missed a meet to attend his sister's wedding. Coach Bob McDaniel kicked him off the team. He was let back on the squad a week later. Chris, last I knew, was principal of Hornell High School and he loyally followed his star track athlete around the state as he charged toward a state title. Bob McDaniel came from a different era. That was then. If that same decision were made now, we'd end up on the front pages of newspapers across the country—and in court. But the point remains, when we sign up for something, we're telling the organizers and everyone else that we'll show up and be responsible in our role. It's really pretty simple. I don't know what truly happens to kid's character development when families across the country let commitments fall to the wayside as soon as it becomes the least bit inconvenient.

We need Rachel Hosie. We need Karen. They're great kids, humble, eager, funny and super teammates. With Karen, the battle lines are drawn between going to Europe or staying home and getting up early six days a week to sweat and experience some real physical pain. I can't begin to win that battle. I hear that a lot of these trips that are taking students and athletes out for portions of the season across America are "Once-in-a-lifetime events". I don't buy that. They're choices. And except with the most extraordinary kids, the point of these exotic trips is being wasted. I haven't yet heard back from a kid who had much good to say about the trip. To most teens, the Louvre is boring and Chuck E. Cheese is a gas. I think the experience and time away from the team will completely change Karen's season after a summer where she'd cast off so many chains that she is now free to become a real runner of merit—if she is just given a chance.

Let me prove my point further. Hannah is one humorous and bright girl, and she can sing. She's had a charmed life. She and her guitar playing partner, my shot putter Linus Walton, continue to write their own music and entertain appreciative crowds in town. When we were traveling south from central New York to Lehigh University in Pennsylvania, we stopped at a bathroom/tourist station in Pennsylvania. Hannah, to our continuing amusement, said, "This is the same rest stop we come to when we go to our camp up north on Lake George." Hannah's camp is up near the Vermont border. So, I truly wonder what most teens are getting from these once-in-a-lifetime trips. I can assure everyone that I'd have gotten nothing from it until I was well into my 30s. Maybe it's just me. Maybe I expect too much out of people. My mother accused me of that one year. Maybe I'm too one-dimensional. But why is my generation rushing to make sure that our kids have experienced absolutely everything by the time they graduate from high school? I don't get it.

Once, when my oldest son, Kirk, was selected to compete on the local Little League All-Star team, we cut short our vacation at the ocean to get him back for a stinking practice. You'll never see Kirk cut out of a responsibility the rest of his life. He learned what it means to commit, to sign up, to join a movement where everyone depends on each other. As this high school generation begins to come of age, I can only hope for the best and shake my head. Every teacher has seen the same thing. The list of concerns is long and growing worse. We all want these kids to succeed in life.

Mert Raner, the Athletic Director of Marcellus, reassured me once by saying, "Jack, 95% of these kids are going to be fine no matter what the fuck we do." I hope his salty words are still holding water. I want life to be easy for these kids when they become adults. And I wonder what lessons they'll choose to pass on to their children, coming from an age when the signals from Hollywood, MTV, their church, school, and the pop culture are so diametrically opposed. When you're brought up with mixed messages that, on the one hand, tell you to excel, but on the other hand, tell you to give just a half-ass effort while being self-indulgent, what sort of adult do you get? I don't have the answer but the nation's sociologists will have a field day with this one. And it'll be a while before the social scientists can offer clarity. Perhaps these wonderful girls, in their hearts, know what is right. But I worry, and I wonder what course this country will be taking down the road as this generation takes over. Socrates had the same concern, but the world today seems to be unraveling in every sector at an alarming rate.

Canastota is much more focused than we are right now. Sauquoit Valley is much more talented but less driven over the summer and we're hearing rumors of discontent, rumors that claim defending sectional champ, Samantha Stedman, along with Kristina Holland (who hates cross country enough to switch to tennis in her senior season) are calling it quits. They're already losing two from last year's team to graduation from their scoring five. If true, everything changes. Jordan-Elbridge is more talented based on their track performances but they also lack depth and haven't been hitting the roads this summer like they should, based on what I saw at the NIKE Midsummer Night's Dream race. This game is ours—if we want it. I think we do, in fact, want it, but we seem to be missing something. I don't see a team and I hope it doesn't come back to haunt us. We have bricks but too little mortar right now. No, we do have mortar. I believe it. I worry too much. But my job is to worry, to produce winners on and off the field. And I don't think I'm getting through on all accounts to all of the kids. The new Athletic Director wants winners. He doesn't accept excuses. He rejects failure. He wants success. My job is pretty clear. What I've done in the past doesn't count this year. I need to produce. This is yet another audition for my 10th athletic director. Another thing is also clear. Without Karen and Rachel in the line-up, I can't produce and drive this team to the pinnacle. It isn't ability that keeps us from crossing into the promised-land, it's our approach. It's as simple as connecting the dots.

Foul Tip

Today I saw the spirit I know is necessary to produce improvement on the race courses. Running is personal. As Lexie Mazzeo's dad Rick says, "You need to learn to run alone. Running isn't boring. If you can't stand yourself for a few miles, you have more problems than any shrink can undo." The 10-miler was our longest run of the summer and we clipped along at a great pace, ending in the lake and eating bagels, cereal, yogurt and drinking OJ, compliments of Della, Lexie's mom, who works for the school at Waterman Elementary.

The girls and I finally had a chance to talk about Rachel Hosie and Karen and the dilemma that confronts us. I explained the situation to the girls and Sofie succinctly said, "We understand where you're coming from as a coach, but we need them. Not everyone on this team is totally team-oriented like some of us, but we can live with that. We need every one of them if we're going to be good."

Since I coach a team, and not individuals, I chose to respect the wishes of the team and let the matter come to a rest.

Rachel was ticked off about the tone of my email, and she had a right to be. And that's what I was looking for—some fight. If it helps to kick-start her season and propels her into wanting to prove something to me, then this little struggle will have been worth it. She's a kid who is stuck between two passions, horses and running. I wrote her with the good news.

> *I figured you'd be upset but I talked to the girls and there's good news...we talked about your situation and Karen's and they decided without a moment's hesitation that they desperately*

want you two on the team...so that's the decision...I have no problem with their decision...ultimately it's their team (yours too) and that's my focus as I mentioned in the email to you.... so, relax, good luck with the horse championship and we'll just keep plugging through the season together....we'll get over this Rachel....it's a bump in the road....I of course do realize that you have a life and lots of other interests....what I want for you is for you to be the best you can be....I'm pretty sure that's your goal, too....your eyes tell an interesting story...I grew up in a team environment and there was only one way to play....you could never miss anything or you'd be replaced....XC can be different but here's the thing....we never know if we'll be strong enough, as a team statewide, to make it to feds after the state meet....the only way to get there is to take the team into other sections and beat everyone...that was my purpose for wanting to go to these other meets instead of the regular ones around here...when good runners are missing meets, it pretty much assures us that we won't be able to beat those other teams...the result is that we can't take the team into those venues because if they beat us, it makes a case for THEM to get to feds and undermines our case....again, even the schedule is designed for the team....that's just some background behind my thinking and the reason for this little exchange we're involved in...so, keep up the running and get out there as often as you can....the girls know that they need you in order for us to have a chance to meet our team goals...hopefully there's no hard feelings.... if you're really upset, that's OK...I can understand that and respect it...if you're not feisty defending yourself, you wouldn't be the Rachel that I like...stay cool today...the weather should break tonight....the girls did a good job this morning....it was already 82 when we met at 7:00....but they did well....I think they'll be napping a little this afternoon...see ya, coach

The pre-season in the NBA is a farce. It's pretty much the same for the NFL. But in cross country, the pre-season is everything. If you want to understand anything about the championship teams that are crowned in November, study what they did back in June and July. The summer makes or breaks us. If kids don't come into camp in great condition, we can't train them without risking their health. And without the summer mileage, they'll wear down and break by the end of the season. We really have no option but to train them hard beginning the first day of mandatory practice. They either hold up or they break. There just isn't time to condition and train them during a two month season.

Dustin ran superbly today. His foot went numb once again but he seems to be working through it better. I don't think the problem is compartment syndrome but we'll have to keep an eye on it. And I can't detect that his shoe laces are causing the numbness. He was recently diagnosed with an uneven growth in his body and I suspect it's the tendons that are growing more slowly than the rest of him and at times it manifests itself in his lower extremities. As a result, his back is drum-tight and we all hope the new foam-top mattress will help. Last week he excelled over the last five of ten 400-meter runs. Today he just let loose over the final 3-4 miles of the 10-mile run. "I just felt good, coach." What was surprising was to see him run down Sam who has been untouched all summer by any teammate. Dustin even had Sam 'crying' for a slower pace as they raced down Hencoop to West Lake Road. Sam may have been a bit under-hydrated and I heard his sleep last night wasn't the best. He also had to hit the woods for a brief pit stop that allowed Dustin to close the gap. But Dustin came on today. Jeff ran much better than he did the last two long runs. Dan's good running lasted much longer into the run than usual, and he's shed his baby fat over the summer. He's quickly developing a washboard stomach.

Days like this raise my hope for the season. The boys need redemption from last year's debacle—none of which was their fault. No longer boys, they're young men and looking ready to take on the league.

Sofie was right. She usually is. She said this was an important day for the team. She always uses that term, TEAM. Becoming more of a leader every day, she's a trusted sounding board for me and has always organized the t-shirt production line and the ordering of personalized sweats. Lexie has noticed Sofie this summer and offered these thoughts.

> *I think the team did really well today...I'm especially proud*
> *of Bea...she really stayed with Rach and Sofie even after being*
> *in Ireland a month...and I'm really excited for Sofie. I've*

been sensing a lot of motivation in her right now and I think it will stay with her...I hope it does because she deserves a good senior year...she never complains and always just runs without doubt or self pity if you know what I mean...that's what I've been noticing. Sofie was the first girl and then Bea and then Rachel (Vaivoda)...I hope Rach has a blossoming season...don't you think she could potentially have one? as for me, I'm feeling a little disappointed that I fell back from the top group...do you think I could've stayed with them all the way and I shouldn't have been back where I was? I suppose if I start believing that myself I will be able to keep up...aside from that I did like the run...maybe a little too much sun and a few too many hills, but it was really scenic and the time kind of went fast... Carly and Tay? hmm...I don't know...maybe they were a little intimidated by the fact that they were going to run 10 whole miles haha...I'm really glad they're on the team though...I love Taylor...she makes me laugh.

Understanding the true pulse of a high school team is no easy task. The individual and interpersonal complexities are many and varied. If you're not willing to tap into their minds, feelings and observations, to banter with them, to listen to what they have to say, nothing good will develop. Yes, Sofie, this was an important day, and it wasn't just the running.

A week later, Rachel Hosie informed me that she won't be attending the first practice of the season. I was stunned. Her family is heading to New York City. Rachel seems genuinely concerned about what is happening. So, I'm not going to keep pushing an immovable object. She's in a family bind, so we agreed to begin anew on Tuesday, August 22nd. We'll get her into the first meet and begin the process of letting her race into shape. And from this point forward, I hope that we get all the kids to practice without a lot of fuss and fighting.

Christmas Morning in August

It isn't a depression-era 'Christmas' as the 2006 season readies to dawn in the third week of August. With excitement building to a crescendo, I can't wait to unwrap my latest team. This year it's more like a recession-era "Christmas" because I'm not certain that I see frontrunners under my tree. We're ready for action and prepared to greet the changing of the season like tourists prepped and eager to watch the changing of the guard at Buckingham Palace. We can barely wait to get going. When USA Today begins writing about the college football season as August ebbs and flows toward September's crispness, my juices begin to flow. The heat has broken after a destructive thunderstorm so walking from the local P&C grocery store to the parking lot no longer makes me melt as I leave the air conditioned store and go straight into what was earlier the black tar sauna. Towels dry on their bathroom rack now instead of staying smelly and damp; that moldering smell filling your nostrils like so much rotting vegetation in the jungle or along roadsides where carrion rot and get eaten by the insect world.

The approach of fall is a time of uplifting and joyous hope. Everyone has a dream. Everyone has a chance. Just reading about the college football top-10, the teams' turmoil, the anxieties, the hopes, the individual bios, it makes the butterflies flutter a little harder in my stomach and I begin to look ahead with anticipation instead of looking back at past results. The gears are shifting. Tomorrow is coming. And tomorrow means the season of cross.

Scouting reports get published by Bill Meylan and his one-of-a-kind, scientifically-calibrated web site www.tullyrunners.com and by www.

armorytrack.com run by the New York City-based Armory Track and Field Foundation. Teams get hyped. Individuals who decided to work hard over the summer have now risen above the crowd and climbed up the cross country ranking ladder.

Just thinking about getting the team together excites me. Will leaders show up this year? Will kids, who have been showing the sort of leadership qualities that allow Generals to command legions, take the next step and gather their 'Let's go!' voice? Will expectations be fulfilled? Will the crushing weight of skewed academic expectations take their toll and destroy what we're trying to do here as we seek a healthy balance between brains and brawn? Will we have a pack, and if we do, will it be willing to rumble up front or will it willingly die in the belly of the snake? Will we grow tough and develop intestinal fortitude when we're confronted with a challenge or will we melt like an ice cream cone on 130 degree pavement?

Demeanor, what will be the team's demeanor? Who will we be? Will we move to the raucous sound of rock and roll or will we wilt to the tunes of elevator music? Will we have a straw that can stir the drink or will we be without any carbonation, fizz, or bubble? Will we earn the respect of other runners, other coaches? Will coaches stand around during races, rub their chins and ask me, "Where did you get those guys?" Will the kids be selfless or will they shrink back into feeling great about themselves as long as they are in their 'proper' position on the team as they emerge from the chute?

As theologian Michael Novak wrote, "Most of what Americans know about the humanistic traditions—about excellence in act, about discipline, about community, about unity of body and will and spirit— they learn firsthand from their experiences in sport." Running can make you feel right about yourself and your life. I want that for these kids.

Cross Country tests the soul of each runner. It eventually rewards those who dare. It demands that you connect to nature, to your evolutionary self. It forces you to fight while being a civil person. Cross country is the fulfillment of humanity. It's being out on the course, alone in the locker room, running silently along paths, roads, splashing or tip-toeing across creeks, where you begin to understand the rhythms that control life—your life and being. You can't be a part of life if you're cloistered. You can't appreciate colors and shading until you begin to paint. I want to scream to the kids, "Wake up!" Life is just waiting to explode as the gifts of life that lay all around them are slowly recognized and opened.

I want runners who can run just a bit faster than the wind, just a bit longer than the mind is willing, just a step past the nearest opponent, and a bit farther than the crest of the next hill. I want them to see the chute and get excited to blast into it.

What a time of year it is as runners who have prepared all summer begin to take their final preparatory steps toward the formal part of the season. Some, the blessed, the most willing of the group, can hear the call in their head. It rumbles slowly, building cadence and momentum, shaking the kidneys so that their body is showered with adrenalin—the rush that enlivens their athletic life. In the deepest recesses of their being, of their soul, they feel the freedom that is promised by cross country.

They spring alert, rise to the balls of their feet and answer nature's earliest call to "Run, just run, it's so damn simple."

Dance to the music of life, stop thinking, tap your feet to the robustness of your soul, be raw, be savage, pulse with confidence and roar as you run down your prey. Leave the remains of the vanquished to the Vultures that are flying high overhead or sitting on fence posts in the cornfield eager to begin their carnage. Run, fly on with the serenade of the wind blowing through your hair and into your ears as your nostrils flare and the brittle leaves send forth their crisp chorus that amplifies your quick, steady steps across the earthen paths.

Slack-jawed and squinty eyed, the arm levers drive in short but rapid thrusts as the hands relax and the breathing provides accompaniment as you, the wolf, advance from tree to post into the open field toward the crowd, the cheers, the words of the announcer, the chute, and soon, very soon, rest and relief—the job having been done to perfection, not for you, but for the team. Run until the beast in you has been tamed. Run until you're once again ordinary and able to co-exist with those humans from a lesser God.

I worry that my numbers for Christmas 2006 are very low. Missing will be all the beautiful stocking stuffers, those hordes of kids who show up every day willing to do anything to remain on the team. They were blessed with a work ethic second to none, but possess little natural talent and worse structural mechanics. They will never be any good from a competitive perspective, but I wouldn't trade them for anyone else.

Missing this year will be the depth that gives a coach the opportunity to use one group of kids in mid-week duals and another in Saturday invitationals so that each group can experience being on the firing line and share in the responsibility and titles. Gone are the tiny packages of flowers that fill the ranks of the modified (junior high) team and grow into varsity athletes with the proper nurturing.

I think I might have two senior wildflower-surprises as we like to call them. There are two daring senior boys who are willing to stake a claim to this sport before they enter college, track high jumper and triple jumper Josey Witter, and wrestler Stephen King. Both have the bodies and both have that special ingredient of champion athletes, the will to persevere, no matter how much it hurts. They may get us over the hump just like some daring and brave kids did for us back in the early 1990s. Or they may find the hurdles a bit too high.

But it's the lack of overall numbers that has me truly concerned. Life offers so many distractions, so many pig-headed things for the kids to do that, when it's all added up, it adds up to nothing.

And then there's the most sinister thing of all, the crazed desire by some parents and communities to produce single sport stars. What we have is a generation at risk as the three-sport athlete goes the way of the dinosaur. One sport sub-wonders are being produced as they pass up a healthy variety of once-in-a-lifetime high school athletic experiences because of a misguided adult or adults who continually send the message to the kid that they're special. Special is rare. Special is extremely rare. Special is so rare that, for practical purposes, it doesn't exist. If a kid has to be told he's special, he isn't. Special is so incredibly rare that everyone—including the know-nothing casual spectator—instinctually recognizes and acknowledges it. Variety, in athletics, is truly the spice of life. It's how an athlete develops physically and emotionally into a well-rounded whole.

Too many kids are being steered away from being on real teams with real rules, teaching, real practice sessions, significant and recognized competition while being guided by different coaches who have different philosophies, different managerial styles, and a plethora of important lifelong information to pass on. Why pass this up?

Being on a real team is so important that Corporate America tries hard to convince their work force that it's part of a team. What bunk. They can try having uniforms, team meetings, pep rallies for the sales staff while stressing competition with other corporations, but the truth is much different. Most corporations don't invest in their 'athletes', they abuse them. They use them and spit them out. They outsource the work when the going gets tough, just the opposite of a real team that draws everyone close in troubled times. The worker is but a pawn who is allowed to live a fantasy-of-relevance until a bean counter somewhere thinks differently. Real teams are special organizations, and it's a shame that kids are being steered into profit seeking club organizations where the coach's goal is to boost his own ego as the organizational institution tries to fill their own personal treasury.

Many of our children today are wasting away on the vine of endless activity. Far too many parents have become the problem as they try to avoid letting their children be the devil's plaything as every minute of every day has to be scripted in an attempt to get that rarest of gems—a Division I athletic scholarship. If only the NCAA would just eliminate athletic aid we could reboot some moms and dads and start over with adults who would be good and caring parents, not wannabe coaches or annoying agents.

The economy hums today because kids work too much. Many say that the US economy would suffer a severe drop in production and services if kids were left alone to be kids. Too many business leaders have become the problem for this generation as they fill their bank coffers on the backs of child laborers. In the process the business leaders are propagating the pitiful line that the kids today are learning valuable life skills when, in fact, they are merely being dumped into a situation where school grades deteriorate and some of life's little poisons (alcohol, tobacco and drugs) become part of their daily arsenal.

Children rarely are receiving good guidance today. All too often, today's parent is trying desperately to be their child's friend as they avoid saying "No", as if saying it would confer a lifetime of misfortune on their off-spring. Parents and other essential adults are often too afraid to properly guide kids, afraid to limit the full array of their activities, afraid to help them clear something from their overcrowded plate-of-life, afraid to help them find focus and balance.

What we have today are kids who perceive that the world revolves around them and their instantaneous and endless desires in life as they do the predictable thing by responding to the Madison Avenue hard sell and media USA. Can't blame the kids for wanting to have it all; they're buying the philosophy that corporate leaders are selling. It's what's being taught to them every time a parent or adult makes yet another unnecessary sacrifice to avail the kids of yet another 'essential athletic' or life opportunity.

The kids see their parents willing to forgo virtually any semblance of a private, normal life in their attempts to give everything to their child. No wonder kids are afraid to drop one sport in order to try another; they fear rejecting and offending their parent's efforts. They're so fully invested that the kids can't escape. It's much the same in war, the Mideast war, the War on Terror, the battle to save all of civilization or whatever you want to call it. To the detractors the administration says, "Are you telling us to cut and run and diminish the sacrifices of all those 4000-plus great Americans who have gone and died for this cause?" Well, yes. Let's stop the senseless and needless dying. We've 'invested' over 4000 Americans and tens-of-thousands who have been severely wounded—and squandered hundreds of billions of dollars. Enough! There's one reason to go to war; to save your country. Not one Iraqi bombed anyone in the United States on 9-11. We aren't adhering to the basic tenet of Essential War. It's the Vietnam Tonkin Gulf fake-out all over again. Kids who have been catered to, beginning with, let's say, hockey, basketball or soccer since the age of four, feel guilty for wanting to try something new. So much time and parental sacrifice has been foolishly invested that they just can't switch sports as a mid-teen. They just feel like they're in too deep to climb back to a life of childhood freedom where school and an activity join family time to form the perfect trifecta of life.

Parents will abandon their private life so that Tommy and Susie can simultaneously put in a full day of school replete with accelerated courses that many colleges reject, play in the band or participate in the play, do Mock Trial or Model United Nations, volunteer at the local hospital, get involved in a community religious activity and play a school sport, and make them hold down a weekend or evening job because "it makes them better people". Too many of our best kids don't have a day off to just be a kid. It's child abuse pure and simple.

We have kids who are physically and psychologically breaking. We see them in school and at practice all the time. All the coaches and teachers see them at their school when they sleep at the wrong time of day. This unnecessary disease knows no special socio-economic class but strikes hardest at the lower class that continues to struggle without many positive results. It strikes hard as social and governmental services too often ignore or are too under-funded to deal with the desperate plight of our youth. Kids in America have been abandoned in a shroud of programs that lack the necessary funding and community support. There's more charade in youth services than there is in slight-of-hand magic. These poor kids don't have any idea what a normal life is as our collective national apathy quickly nudges them toward a life of stress, hypertension and premature death.

The over-indulgence that has become an epidemic-of-opportunity in the middle and upper classes oftentimes results in a life that's full-to-overflowing with activity, and we find a generation that has learned to live life without pause and commitment, as they commit to nothing by committing to everything.

While parents and other significant adults do what they feel is best for the children, they are actually teaching them how to shirk responsibility and to avoid fulfilling commitments while partitioning loyalties in multiple ways. The schedule is so full that corners must be cut. They're learning to lie and cheat in order to meet their commitments. Too many are going to drugs that give them energy to get through the day. Coffee? They can't make it to homeroom without it. The lesson we are teaching collectively is this: When a commitment becomes inconvenient, just skip it, cut out early, arrive late, ignore the team, turn your back on your friends, and toss all of your work into the garbage. "After all," claim too many children, "these people are lucky to have even a part of me--because I'm special."

We wonder why kids get into fights. Team turmoil is a new phenomena and parents—crazed fans—are attacking little kids on the playing field. You can look it up. Our failure to peacefully solve problems has become an epidemic in this generation of teens. We wonder why one in ten kids today admits to taking a lethal weapon to school and why many dozens of kids are killed at school by classmates every year. We wonder why so little respect is being shown by the kids to each other and society-at-large.

There is really nothing to wonder at. The cause is well-intentioned parents and other adults who are making virtually every decision on the field instead of letting the kids solve problems for themselves. What we get are young, self-centered prima donnas who are growing up without a social or community soul, without coping skills, without the skill to choose, without the ability to say no, without the tact to diffuse minor incidents, without the ability to make rules, to abide by rules, to care if rules are broken or if rules exist at all. This generation—our kids, our lifeblood, our hopes and dreams, our collective creation—has learned to do many things but to do them poorly, often in ways that are a serious detriment to all of society—the agent of its making. They have not been taught to prioritize and have been encouraged to treat every activity as an equal without regard to importance, self-actualization, accountability to others, realistic future participation, relevance or inherent value, signed contracts or that damnable sense of obligation.

All of these vital life-skills come from seemingly aimless play and myriad adults who help guide and expose kids to a life of responsible behavior, not from an endless array of valueless and commitment-free, adult-led team sporting activities that teach subservience and promise the youth of today endless victories when it's not theirs to give. Losing counts. Losing is real. Losing is okay. Losing is more a part of life than victory. And so is getting back on your feet.

The Syracuse Post-Standard's sports columnist, Bud Poliquin, has bemoaned the paucity of kids tossing a baseball around in the park or playing a pickup game of baseball or football. The reason is simple: The kids have no time for youthful, creative play or aimless, purposeless fun because of the endless menu of adult led club sports, practices, all-star traveling teams and Olympic Development soccer to lure kids and their ever-hopeful parents into the trap, the snare. These kids must, say mom and dad, be division one and professional athletes. Their social standing is at stake within the community.

Sports should be enjoyable while building a foundation for a lifetime of fitness and healthy activity. Coaches, parents and advisers should ensure that sports and activities provide a release from pressure and not be the source of unnatural, destructive pressure.

And what do our kids learn at these adult led games? They walk away with virtually nothing of a positive consequence outside of the well-documented lessons of teamwork. But as the kids quickly rise up the ladder and enter club sports, each teammate is paying an exorbitant entry fee and each has his or her own private agenda. Team considerations are secondary as personal advancement takes on an unnatural, ill-proportioned precedence. In far too many cases, there is inadequate coaching and minimal skill-development taught as playing game after game –sometimes three to four games on a weekend afternoon—remains the philosophy of the day. It's child abuse played out in the open, and we refuse to recognize it. The kids learn to be selfish, to scream at the errors of others, to blame everyone but themselves for bad judgments and errors, to belittle others in public, including the adult refs. The only skills being developed are the dysfunctional, poor and tattered survival skills that are being reinforced and entrenched beyond the point of repair by professionally trained and certified educators with degrees who work within the high school structure.

Need evidence? Just check out the USA basketball team prior to the take-over by Duke University's Mike Krzyzewski, a real coach and real educator. The mighty juggernaut of world basketball, the United States, had players who couldn't shoot, couldn't get along with the coach, couldn't get along with each other, rebuffed the refs, and each one had a separate individual agenda instead of a true team orientation, at least until the educator from Duke took over. And we were getting embarrassed and thumped by lesser talent from Argentina, Puerto Rico and Lithuania. Thank club basketball, AAU ball, insidiously evil, selfish coaches, and parents who got suckered into the pro and me-me-me mentality for that debacle. After a four year learning experience, Krzyzewski and his re-educated pro ballplayers garnered gold in the 2008 Olympics. Me-me-me was no longer the craze as WE was placed on the front burner of athletics.

There is little independent thinking being developed as too many adult coaches—who too often argue with officials and each other and the fans—dictate everything including when to steal second base. What's wrong with just telling a little kid to try to steal if he thinks he can get away with it? He'll learn about himself either through success or failure. Let him give it a try. Victory is paramount in these clubs and biddy-ball leagues. Failure is no longer permitted at the tender age of eight in America. We are teaching our kids to follow orders, to bow to every whim and fancy of the frustrated adult who is applying pathetic professional 'values' to pre-teens and teens alike. And as a consequence we're getting a growing crowd of Americans who think that disagreeing with our government leaders is tantamount to being a traitor. The screamers among us have even forced some leagues to hold "Quiet Sundays" where no adult, coach or spectator is permitted to speak a word during the game. Assaults are not so uncommon anymore. Dueling dads commit murder. Cheerleaders are assaulted by opposing cheerleader's moms. Perspective? It's gone, vanished. The kids hate what they hear while playing their games, and the scars don't easily heal.

There are simply too many adults building kingdoms or getting their frustrated sporting glorification met via the kids as these befuddled youngsters confuse playing in organized adult-led games with having fun.

Parents shell out hundreds or thousands of dollars on sports camps. Sports psychologists are hired. Web site developers are retained because our kids are so athletically special. Recruiting services are paid to help market kids to college coaches who "don't know what they're doing." It's just foolish. A good high school coach will do all of this, plus more, for a deserving kid. The vast majority of these kids aren't getting athletic scholarships because they don't deserve them, and some who do grab the athletic golden ring have spent so much money trying to get a scholarship that they won't break even financially if they do get one. But perhaps that isn't the goal as too many parents get their community social ranking based on their kid's athletic success. And is there any higher 'success' than the university athletic scholarship? Parents need to begin to live with the child they created and love them for who they are, not for what they want them to be or what the kid can do for them socially.

Too many parents are certain that more is better. If one camp a summer is good, then two camps must be better. And it's that philosophy that is dooming their children, cutting short their athletic skill development, social skill development, and prematurely ending their childhood. I can't tell you how many times I've heard kids say that they can't wait to get to college so they can be away from their parents and perform poorly in their sport try-out and get cut. They just want a life and sports should be played because they're FUN.

The bottom line is that the kids are learning little-of-worth playing in the adult-guided and organized leagues. So little is being learned of a positive note that parents would be well-advised to analyze their motives, the activity's demands, and perhaps forgo organized pre-teen sports and simply provide a safe playing environment for their kids. Let them develop their own games. Let them squabble over their rules and work together to ratify new ones. Leave them alone to figure things out for themselves. Let them imagine. There is already too much reality in a child's world today. It's time to let kids be kids and for adults to butt out before it's too late.

A thorough analysis of high school sport teams reveals an ugly truth. The quality of play is down. Kids can't shoot in basketball. Covering the hole in baseball is a lost art. Stealing? Forget it. Injuries? It's an epidemic as kids now get injuries that didn't exist a generation ago. These over-use injuries encountered in the endless pursuit of athletic excellence are happening to under-prepared kids who are trying, or being forced, to do too much, too often. These injuries are occurring to younger and younger kids. And they're injuries incurred by kids who were never just allowed to play in vacant lots or fields.

College stats reveal the same thing. These kids who are starting out so early and are specializing just aren't cutting it. The best kids we've got in high school are the 3-sport athletes who understand lifestyle balance, have whole body development and are growing more adept at entering the cauldron of competition. And, they understand training, understand investing today for a bigger payoff down the road. Many club sport athletes don't really train. They compete sloppily over and over again in a freestyle fashion and that just reinforces sloppy play and the inability to play as a team once under the tutelage of a high school team-oriented coach.

And don't buy for a minute that the 'National Championship' your club squad is competing for is really a national championship. It's just another way to keep your money flowing to someone else. You're being deluded. The impetus for the club-sport trend in America is economic and out-of-control parents who harbor unfilled athletic dreams.

The Soviets knew a thing or two about developing athletes, and they grew to understand that playing a variety of sports beats specialization at a young age. Being good at an early age doesn't statistically correlate to later success. And the burn-out rate for Soviet kids who specialized was off the charts while those who competed in a variety of sports, and specialized later, progressed to greater things as they became the recognized athlete on the national and international stage wearing the famous CCCP (Central Committee of the Communist Party) uniform.

Kids need time to develop, time to explore, a chance to form starry-eyed dreams, a chance to waste time. They need time to unravel the mysteries of their daydreams, opportunities to try different sports, time to find out who they are and to discover their limits. If they are eventually good enough, they need to be on the school teams of their own choosing. That's where the memories originate for latter life when nostalgic thoughts make even a bad day somehow better. Ah, the memories of high school sport. That's the ticket. Zandra Walton attached a P.S. to a letter as she entered her high school junior campaign. "I remember in freshman year you were saying to the older girls that they needed to focus and forget about the unimportant things because this is what they are going to remember later in life. That's so true. This is definitely what I want to remember."

As the season approaches--the summer songbird orchestra fades and is replaced by an endless chorus of crickets--I look forward to the bus rides. The rooster crows early and the team shuffles out of their family cars, bag after bag in hand and slung over their shoulders filled with uniforms, spikes, items of comfort, slogans to read as the nerves grow jittery and food for before and after the battle. Slowly the sun rises fully over the mountains and we're off to a destination that, for the kids, is as unknown as the Americas were for Columbus. On those occasions when we're heading to a familiar venue, excitement or even trepidation will have to be dealt with depending on the runner's previous attempt to traverse the layout of the course.

Once on the dew-covered grounds, Gary's bus sometimes is converted into our home if the wind is too strong for us to put up our ten by twenty foot blue tent. Smells begin to mingle, sweat, juice, food, more sweat, mud, the dirt from the spikes that was not cleaned-up after the previous race, fear, yes, the smell of fear, body gas from trumpeted and silent farts, burps and edgy belches, and the smell of exhaust from the other busses.

The sounds change, grow more intense and lose their melodic melancholy as we go from the quiet of early morning to the pre-race world where words of confidence—sometimes real and sometimes faked—take us to the hectic bustle of warm-up. And then there is the sound of relief, pride, accomplishment or the angst of defeat and failure that fills the air and individual psyches after the race. I have to be careful in the immediacy of the post-race as my emotions oftentimes erupt and overshadow tact. We all need our space, time to register facts and to process what happened.

Going home on the bus is different as hope reappears no matter what transpired during the day. Resplendent in their youth, the specter of another tomorrow appears when the real athlete that they all think themselves to be, will appear and triumph over self, opponents, loss and doubt. Youth are not too constrained by the immediate past as they seem to bounce back by drawing from their reservoir-of-promise that seems the private province of youth.

"Cross Country is a funny sport," said my oldest son, Kirk, who at 27 can look back on his running from a more balanced perspective. "When you're doing it, you can't wait for the agony to end. If you have a bad race, you feel like killing yourself for you realize it was a lack of will that led to the dread feeling of failure. In basketball, you love the training and the games. And you wonder why the quarters are so damn short in high school. But, when you emerge from the woods, like at Jordan-Elbridge, and are willing to sprint to the finish in order to pass just one more opponent, you're on cloud nine. You've won by beating yourself, your doubts and the desire to quit early because it hurts."

Something magical can happen on long bus rides at night as you travel down a deserted stretch of the Thruway with your team. It's almost mystical, spiritually reverent as warriors bond for life after the meet. The camaraderie is different. The bonds that stretch during the race, as one member of the team tries desperately to move up the team ladder by beating another, begin to contract, pulling the team back together in a closer, modern version of the Gordian knot as the warriors form their own Knights of the Roundtable on the bus. The darkness, the fading light of autumn's shortening days, mixes with the smell of decaying leaves that waft through the open windows courtesy of a northerly breeze that will soon bellow incessantly as winter settles in for far too many gloomy months. Head straight into the northerly wind and you soon reach the St. Lawrence River. Shaking your head, you just know that 'The River' is softly quiet as the Seaway traffic slows for winter, the waves rippling slowly to the shore and the camps are locked up for the coming desolate cold. The sounds of silence are different in the autumn, too. It clangs on the ear drums with an ominous hint of weather to come. Sounds, though soft, are clear and distinct, magnified by life's slowing pace and the diminished chatter from a fleeing nature. The cadence of the road hits you while inside the bus like the clop-clop of horse's hooves hitting a paved road. It's soothing, it relaxes you, and it draws down your armor.

Suddenly, the team is closer and vulnerable to truth, to friendship. This is when a coach can capture the true measure of the team, measure their character and watch as the personal, protective or blustery facades fade away. This is when the team decides what it's willing to do together and for each other. This is when bravado is formed and a collective swearing of allegiance—one to another—enables their bravery to come forth.

No, opening day isn't really Christmas, but it's a hopeful day when we all feel that anything is possible, when we feel that we can truly make a difference, when each athlete, young and old, feels alive as the excitement of the season descends upon them and the drudgery of a summer run in the baking heat is behind them. Christmas Day in August, it's my time to dream, and the beginning of my work to make the dreams come true.

Christmas Eve August Style

Some things are a pain, and getting every bit of paperwork completed on time for the first day of the season is a pain in the ass. Historically, Skaneateles has had a dysfunctional athletic paperwork system. Evidence of physicals just disappears. Paperwork, hand delivered by parents, too often goes into a shredder somewhere. It shows up and just vanishes. Fortunately, parents have learned to make copies and that bails us out of some serious legal dilemmas. We've made headway in the system with computerization and new procedures, so now the onus to perform is on me. I need to impress upon our kids the importance of meeting local and state requirements by the first practice or we start without them. And we can't afford that this year because of our limited numbers.

This year brings more importance since missing just one practice will force someone to miss the first meet of the season. I get angry when the little things aren't done. I hate it when someone pushes my buttons by showing up late for practice. But what really sets me off is when someone gives me the shaft on race day. We're all there on the bus, focused on readying for the race, and we find ourselves being sidetracked as we wait for one selfish, inconsiderate person who decided not to show up on time. I should leave with the kids I have, but too often the missing link is someone we need. Do I prove a point by insuring that the team loses? No matter what I do, the message just gets lost on some kid. I've sent home e-mails with the schedule. I've given them a paper copy of the itinerary. We have a parent meeting to go over this but 95% of the parents no longer come. We talk about it ad infinitum the days before the meet. I've given them race brochures with our all-

157

time best performances on the course to offer perspective and history. The brochures have included directions to the meet for their parents, bus loading and departure times, race schedules, and an analysis of the opposition. Nothing seems to work for everyone every day. So this year I'm giving them nothing. We're just going to a race.

I just sent out the first of two mass e-mails to the kids virtually begging that they attend to the details so that we can move forward with everyone in tow. We haven't had a clean paperwork start in my past 60 straight seasons of coaching. I'm sure I'll be disappointed once again this year.

> *Hi...remember that you'll need to have your physical done before you can be allowed to participate in practice beginning on Aug. 21st....also, if you're getting it from your own doctor, the information has to be on file in the school....and it has to be on file prior to the first day of practice. Bringing it in on the first day of practice won't cut it...if you still have to get it, make sure you're hydrated on the day you go....if you run on a hot day, you are unlikely to pass the urine test....man, that'll look real bad on your high school transcript...if you miss even one day, you will not be eligible for the first meet on September 2nd....we will score 7 of 10 runners in the race so we will need everyone.... make no mistakes this year....it's important....clear your schedules.....get rid of the summer jobs...we need you guys to train hard and get your rest the remainder of the day....if you continue to try to do both, you'll send us off in the absolute wrong direction beginning with the first meet....every year we go through this...you aren't Supermen or Superwomen.... you're kids...you'll need plenty of rest during Boot Camp....the training is going to be a challenge for the veterans...for you juniors and seniors, these are the two big years....don't mess them up for a few bucks...the money is NOT going to make a demonstrable difference in your life....put the team first for boot camp....once school starts, school comes first, then the team.... begin striking a good balance in life so that you are healthy and rested EVERY day...there can be no breaks in the chain....we do not want you going through your life wondering 'what if" .... most of you will not be athletes in college...this is your one*

chance in life to accomplish athletic feats....your one chance in life to devote a substantial part of your life, being, psyche and emotions to YOU....take advantage of it....coach

In the past week I've asked kids if they got their free school physical in June and some just couldn't remember. Some had them earlier in the year but they don't know exactly when. Some think they got them over the summer but aren't sure about the paperwork. So another email went home today, a week prior to the season officially kicking off. The distance between today's generation of kids and detail is growing. Perhaps in our collective attempt to make life easy, convenient and deadline-free for America's children, we've accidentally helped foster a sense of entitlement in the next generation of adults. One wonders if the next generation to lead the nation will have too few adults who make the hard, adult choices.

Jonathon Riley

His Olympic trading card says he's from Brookline, Massachusetts. The Greater Boston media, ever since he arrived at Brookline High School in the winter of his junior year, always talks about their hometown kid. When he races at the Falmouth Mile or the Reggie Lewis Center in South Boston, it's always the local kid returning home. Oh, bullshit. Jonathon is a Skaneateles kid who learned how to run right here in the Finger Lakes in Central New York, right here at Skaneateles High School.

Riley took his first steps on the track in 7th grade. Quickly he became a name, but it wasn't as if someone turned a switch and he was off. We all could tell that we had something special, but it would have to be nurtured, for Jonathon, who always had the greatly curved smile on his face, was a tired kid who went home and slept for hours after a day of school and practice. Riley's home-life was a bit unconventional, and I learned a lot from it. There was no mother with them. She stayed behind in Virginia when dad and the three boys moved north and camped out in Rhode Island for a summer. Dad was into the macrobiotic, north-African grain diet, the type that had ying and yang and declared that too much sugar would weaken the ankles. He was incredibly interesting. It was way beyond someone who grew up on Spanish Rice, liver, stews and hot dogs. The Riley's diet was high in energy but Jon and his brothers were low in reserves because of the diet. Couscous was a staple. It was the part of wheat grain that resisted the grinding of the heavy millstone. It's a big food staple in Morocco. And they just happen to produce great distance runners.

I remember sending Jonathon and Jamie home after practice and they'd immediately fall to sleep from exhaustion. They just didn't get all the calories they needed. One day in late summer the father, who was a real-time engineer but was unemployed (everyone in Syracuse is unemployed at one time or another) was augmenting the meals by feeding the boys dandelion greens cut from the yard in their rented house as the daily calorie count had shrunk. The home continues to be called Riley's house. Finally, our running community and the local church food pantry began dropping bags of food on the family front porch of their home to help them eat. I don't know if they ever knew where the food came from. We'd invite them to my home for holiday dinners and birthday celebrations and have the boys over for sleepovers with my boys. Older brother Jamie was great about giving my youngest son baseball cards, good ones. A car was given to them so that dad could go on job interviews arranged by the vice chancellor of Syracuse University. He never showed. In retrospect, we probably weren't giving him what he needed. A job might help, but he was more in need of some understanding and medical help. We could all tell he wasn't himself and that some sort of depression had slithered into his soul. I've heard he's back on his feet in New England at a huge military conglomerate and doing well again. He was a good man, totally devoted to his boys and the team, and he was enormously gracious with his money when he was employed, buying uniforms for our teams. From dandelions to Athens. I miss his friendship to this day.

Back when Jonathon was helping us transform the Skaneateles program, his dad hit a spell of bad luck and the macrobiotic diet would leave Jon's fuel gauge on empty by dinner time. We couldn't rush things. We couldn't overwork him. By the time Jonathon left us with tears in our eyes at Poughkeepsie's Bowdoin Park after the New York State Federation Cross Country Championship, we'd barely begun 400-meter repeats. The secret to Jon's race success was low mileage and a rested mind and body. Jon never went into a race tired. I still can't fathom racing tired. Training through a meet makes me think that someone is coaching by the seat of their pants. How can you tell if the training is working if you don't see a kid run a race fresh? How do you know that your methods are taking the athlete in the right direction? With

Jon, we couldn't risk training through meets or we'd risk his health and diminish his natural talents. And what talents they were.

He had his best races in the Brookline uniform because of what we gave him, and when he stood atop the podium at Boston's Reggie Lewis Center after winning the national indoor mile and then the two mile just two hours and 45 minutes later, Jonathon Riley, our Jonathon, was wearing our old yellow tie-dye cross country shirt, and from the pictures you could tell he was not only wearing it proudly, he was sending a message about his roots that the nation had forgotten in his insanely hot pursuit of the first sub-four mile in nearly a quarter century. In running history, Riley's roots have been forgotten, but we haven't forgotten a thing.

Everyone knows about Jon's quick rise in the mile, from an 8th grade mile of 4:46 to his frosh time of 4:30, his 4:20 sophomore time and his 4:10.89 clocking in his first (junior) season at Brookline. And then the chase was on.

> *In 9th grade I decided I was going to break four minutes my senior year and be the best runner in the country. Now that I think about it, those were pretty lofty goals for a kid that didn't make the state meet in 9th grade but I always believed I could and I'm sure that is why I have achieved all I have, because I believe I can. I'm sure I have raced against people with more talent but I beat them because I thought that I could.*
>
> *That brings me to my senior year of outdoor track. I know that I did not train like a sub-four-minute miler. I'm kicking myself now because I know with a little better training and a better race schedule I could have definitely broken 4. Even the way things were, if I had a few chances between my 3:43 1500 and outdoor nationals, I could have done it. It's tough knowing that I could have put a more definite mark in history and that I never achieved my goal. "*

Once Jonathon resettled across the country at Stanford University, we didn't get to talk much. I was a pure novice with the computer and I felt that Jonathon had moved on. How wrong I was.

It's tough for me to follow the progress of the team because it seems to be mostly new people. That makes it hard because it is difficult to cheer for new names but I care so much about Skaneateles and how the teams do. Those were my glory days of cross country and I wish now more than ever we won a State Championship. It would mean a lot to Skaneateles as a program, if we were state champs. Those were also the best guys (and girls) ever. I had so much fun being on their team. It would have been great to finish up in Skaneateles.

Finishing in Skaneateles just wasn't in the cards. With his father entering his third year without a job, our personal relationship grew testy. Jon's dad would call me two, even three times an evening to talk things over. We got along famously and would routinely have the Riley's over to our house. Neither of us needed a reason. But as his dad grew more challenging and testy—a natural development as he lost more and more of himself, like I did during my extended unemployment, and was watching his sons spend so much quality time with me—we began to snipe at each other. Finally I suggested that he needed to get off his ass and latch onto a job and that he shouldn't badmouth the people who were trying to help him out. The man is brilliant and was on the cutting edge of the computer revolution. Finally, despite all that the running and religious community was offering, he found a place to live in Brookline and left. On one level, I was upset, but on another level, I was happy to see him take action again. I think to this day that the move was to punish me. Life had kicked him around pretty harshly. Perhaps history would have been different if we had been more able to help him out.

Jonathon did break the 4-minute barrier and it was the highlight of his indoor season at Stanford in 1999.

I knew I was in shape so I just went and did it. There wasn't a rabbit but the pace was perfect. Through the half we were at 2:00, the 1200 was 2:59. I was boxed in and people started to move so with 300 to go I just jumped out and blasted into the lead. I was a little premature as Mike Stember (teammate) blew by me with 150 to go. I caught back up and finished 15/100ths behind him in 3:58.72.

Our Skaneateles Laker finished his sophomore year as an All-American in the 3000, Distance Medley Relay and the mile. And it all started here—the drive to break the 4 minute barrier—in his freshman year when he became a known quantity.

In 9th grade the black local headline read, "Jon Riley Mile Champion". The article went on to describe the battle.

> *It was a battle of youth against seniority. It was a battle of early aggression against patience. It was a battle for the title when Sauquoit Valley senior Jason Rende and freshman Jon Riley stood side-by-side on the starting line with Rende disbelieving the credentials of the young Riley.*

My co-coach, Rob Tuttle, a Sauquoit alum, remembers the day well. He was on that Sauquoit team.

"I remember Rende being pissed when Riley beat him in the 1600 at Sectionals in 1994. After the 2 mile, which Rende won in 10:05, Rende started wondering where Riley was. After taking 2nd in the 800 with a clocking of 2:05.2, Rende was getting really pissed. He was walking around saying, "Where the hell is Riley? He must be hiding. Is he trying to come after me fresh?"

Well, yes, that was the plan. We had just competed in our league championship two days before and Riley ran the mile and 800. In a week we wanted to try to get him qualified for the state championship.

As the mile progressed, you can predict what was said in the article.

> *In due course, Rende understood what was happening as he tried repeatedly without success to pull away from Riley. The Laker waited, drafted off the senior, and then exploded down the stretch in front of Rende's hometown crowd to take the lead and the victory in 4:32.9.*

The next week there would be no heroics as Swedish exchange student Kristen Algiers from Watertown High beat Jon 4:27.3 to 4:30.4 to advance to our New York State Championship. Once again, our championships should be for our kids. It's a matter of respect, and someone with good form would withdraw knowing that a kid from New York State would carry a lot more through life if he were crowned the Sectional or New York State champ instead of a kid from Sweden who never had attachments here and would probably never return to North America.

Jonathon was always graceful and magnanimous regardless of the outcome of the race. Perhaps, in my mind, his most gracious moment was when he should have been totally self-absorbed. It was a very special day when he emailed me, a true once-in-a-lifetime moment. The dateline was Athens, Greece on August 25th, 2004 just four hours before he stepped on the track in the Olympic 5000-meter race. He was getting ready to head outside and run for a couple of minutes and do some strides.

Some things never change. In high school he liked to head out for a while on his own and then join the team for warm-ups. And, almost without exception, he'd return with this concerned look on his face and talk about a particular muscle, his breathing, a pain here or there, and I'd always say, "You're ready to go, rookie." It became a comforting habit I think.

After asking about our summer running camp and getting the Skaneateles team in shape he wrote,

> *I'm headed to the track in about 4 hours. It seems like I've been waiting around for a month for race day. I feel good, had a great workout last Wednesday and I think I'm in great shape. Maybe a few pounds over race-weight with the 24-hour dining but I should be all right.*
>
> *It's been pretty fun here in the village although there isn't much to do. There is nothing immediately around the village, and it's quite hot during the day.*
>
> *Opening ceremonies were very exciting, kind of long throughout the middle but things definitely picked up once the torch made its way into the stadium. The track team had a training camp in Crete so athletes could be away from the village if they weren't competing for a while. I spent a week down there. It was an awesome resort right on the beach. Not much for trails, just country type roads but I wasn't running too many miles at*

that time anyway. The last few days I've just been getting some errands done and getting ready to race. Take care coach, I'll write again when it's all done."

Jonathon

Even with the Atlantic Ocean and some continents separating us, he was still sounding like the little Jonathon right before the race. It was the same nervous banter that we engaged in when he was still in the junior high school.

Jon wrote me once he got back to the states. He wasn't happy with his race and he didn't advance to the finals. As time began to separate him from the Olympic experience, he was rapidly gaining perspective and was most proud that his little son, Jon, could be there to watch him. Dad realized that there was no way his namesake could truly register the moments, but physically the child was there by his side.

The highlight of Jonathon's pre-Olympic career happened at Brookline at the indoor national championship.

My son and his best friend James Goss skipped their senior basketball banquet, much to the consternation of the staff and some administrators who questioned me about it, because we all wanted to head to Boston for the high school indoor nationals. We had our girls 4x800 in the meet and we had our Jonathon Riley to cheer for. Jonathon had set the stage with some remarkable indoor moments such as his 8:58 two-mile in the middle of a night when he was racing several events. Nearly 30 years before Jon's date with the sub-9 minute two mile, people like Alberto Salazar and Art Dulong were breaking the barrier with Dulong doing workouts like 32 repeats of 440-meters in 64 seconds or 61 seconds for 12x440s.

On the evening when Riley achieved his 8:58, he started the night by anchoring the Brookline 4x800 as his eased-up 1:54.8 moved the team from 6th to first. Seventy-five minutes later he was on the two-mile starting line with sophomore sensation Andy Powell, and they agreed that Powell would carry the pace over the first mile and after that it would be every man for himself. Riley took the lead with 800-meters remaining and grabbed a quick 5-meter lead but Powell wouldn't give. The 400 split when Riley took the lead was 64.9 but it didn't knock out Powell. The final quarter was Riley's and he closed in 61 with the final 200 a sizzling 28, the times he used to hit in Skaneateles like clockwork in practice before we ever started the 400 workouts. That's muscle memory. Riley's last 800 was 2:06 and his final mile was 4:24. Everyone was sure he could break the 4-minute barrier and re-launch America's sagging distance program, but I heard that he was running over 12 miles on Wednesdays throughout his senior year and, if true, it took just enough spring from his legs to set the stage for Alan Webb's monumental heroics.

Just a week later, on March 10th, 1997, Riley became the stuff of legends.

Called the "Brookline Bullet", Jonathon Riley, who had earlier blitzed the Madison Square Garden 'boards in the Millrose High School mile in an unheard of 4:10.62, walked into the Reggie Lewis Track Facility and ran into history. He won the mile in 4:07.12, surpassing John Trautman's 4:07.61 to become the 3rd fastest indoor miler in national history, passing world record holder Jim Ryun's 4:07.20. I was supposed to be the one to do that according to my first coach, Don Benza, but an energy sapping bleeding ulcer that lingered for years ended that pipedream.

We, Jon's former teammates and his former coach, were yelling as loud as we could as Jon worked those tight banked turns to perfection. We were trackside looking straight into the starting line and resting our elbows on the track fringe on the outermost part of lane six along the first turn. After his astonishing mile, Jon decided to enter the two-mile "just for fun". After two hours and 25 minutes of rest, he was back on the track and his adoptive fans from Greater Boston were going wild.

Riley let the others take out the pace and for the first mile it looked like he'd bitten off too much and was in over his head. He went through the first mile in 4:35 and most people were sure it was over. But we didn't think that way. We knew how Jon ran, how he competed, how he calculated every meter between where he was and the end. We knew he was more patient than anyone we'd ever met. And, we saw something familiar as the race progressed. His legs, his stride, his special bounce was coming back with ever lap that passed. Jonathon Riley had sprung a trap and was ready to spring.

Suddenly the announcer, with his wonderful British accent, noticed what we had already seen. The poor leader, Pennsylvania's Chris Dugan, far, far ahead of Riley and without a Jumbotron TV screen to watch as he clicked off the 200-meter laps, could hear the announcer yelling, "It's Riley moving up. It's Riley cutting into the lead." And finally with one lap remaining and Riley still a good forty meters behind, Dugan was hearing this cockney voice saying, "Here comes Riley." And before the final turn approached the announcer was saying, "It's all over. There goes Riley."

I swear that's the way it was. You could feel the rhythm of Riley as he accelerated and measured his fuel gauge, took account of his mental reserves and counted down the meters until the finish. He had room to spare as he again closed in 28 seconds as his muscle memory that was developed years before in Skaneateles was waiting to be commanded into action. Rushing toward the wire, Riley finished with a 9:03.39. It was the first mile/2-mile double at the Indoor Nationals.

Jonathon Riley, who could have run for Mayor of Boston that day back in 1997, shook hands with everyone, talked to reporters and made his way right over to us. Seven months later when he was at Stanford University we exchanged e-mails and he wrote,

> *My senior year was so exciting and it would have been wonderful to share it with everyone that I started with. It was great to have you, Kirk, James and the girls in Boston at the indoor Nationals. The extra support helped but just that I could share those performances with you guys made them so much more meaningful. That meet was what brought me to another level so I was glad everyone was there with me.*

Jonathon had a presence about him, and his confidence combined with the aura that followed him around helped elevate all of our performances. Tuttle, back when he was running for Sauquoit Valley, remembers a cross country meet in Sandy Creek on October 14th, 1995. Sauquoit was ranked No. 1 in the state in Class C-D while we were mired back in 4th in Class B. We weren't really very far apart in school population, but the state cutoffs were a bit strange—and still are. The Falling Leaves Classic would help sort out the state rankings for everyone as we approached the state meet. Riley, a junior who had moved to Brookline a month earlier but returned, led us that day. But the victory was achieved well before the race. Having a certain swagger and a relaxed demeanor, Riley and the boys were intimidating. Every boy on the team that year was a strong athlete. As Tuttle relates the story,

> *We knew Riley was already tested and was a junior that year. And, believe me, his name was already well known. We were goofing off in the gym and your guys walked in and you were all business. We were looking over because we knew that the meet was going to be tough competition. I'm pretty sure Riley dominated that day.*

Jonathon won in 15:51 with Adam Cross in 2nd in 16:26. Dave Crowther was 8th in 16:42 and Peter Hawley was 12th in 16:55 with Jeff Boden closing us out in 14th in 17:02 on a muddy, humid day with temps in the upper 60s. Sauquoit was loaded that year with talent that went far in college, especially Carl Planty who excelled at Seton Hall. We also beat Canton and they were ranked 5th in C-D in New York.

After less than two weeks in Brookline, Jon returned to Skaneateles just after school opened for his junior year. He'd just had his best summer of training and was growing stronger, more confident and concerned about his legacy. His mileage was up and he dabbled with some two-a-day runs. We were a good team without Jonathon, but with him we became a great team once again.

Before his first race in Auburn, he'd completed a workout of relaxed repeat miles as I wanted to test him to see where we were. His splits were 5:28, 5:21, 5:19 and 5:18, with a minute rest per mile. Against national level competition in Spencer-Van Etten's Andy Carling, Jon had his hands full. They went stride for stride through two miles at Auburn, but Carling broke open the race and won by 22 seconds.

Just a few days later Riley led us in a league dual with Cazenovia at Jordan-Elbridge. "I wanted to see if I could get back into it," said Riley after he broke the course record of 15:52 set by Ron Cox when I coached at Marcellus. Ron Cox, a Mustang for life—tall and angular with shark eyes that caught every movement left or right--was the 7th best cross country runner in New York his senior year. Riley blitzed the course in 15:44 after holding back a bit early. He was racing himself into shape.

Jon really broke into the public eye locally by winning the Onondaga High School League title on a mountainous LeMoyne College course in 16:22 to beat Jeremy Tack, our neighbor from nearby Auburn. Tack finished in 16:50 for 2nd place. We went on win the Section III Championships over John Hohm's Corcoran Cougars from the City of Syracuse 37 to 56 and went to the state meet. Jon was under the weather, I think because he knew his father was ordering him to come live with him in Brookline a week later. Yet, he still placed 2nd behind Michael Fitzula of Cornwall. Not a bad day as he led us to third place behind Warwick and Honeoye Falls-Lima. Sauquoit Valley took 4th in their division.

It was a great final season with Jonathon. He shattered course records all over the place and our girls won their first state championship. Chad Elkovitch, our challenged runner—the result of a birthing problem— who continues to train and compete while working at the Auburn Hospital, was named Harrier Magazine's Sportsman-of-the-Year.

What did I think of Riley with the mop top hair, the ready smile and the darting, alert eyes with the dazzling glint in them?

In 1992 when he was on the modified team, I said that he was the perfect runner, an exquisite blend of Finnish and Irish heritage. He had a super attitude and handled success well. He was a smart runner who had developed his wind while being coached in youth soccer by his father in the highly competitive environs of Virginia. He naturally broke races into four equal components and lived one step at a time, in the moment. Young Jonathon calmly and intuitively could calculate what would be required as he crested the hill, or sprinted down the final 100-meters. He would plan to surge at points that may have been 800-meters down the road. His surge was always a controlled operation. He was reliable, consistent and always trying to get better. I said he was a leader, a conciliator and a charmer, especially with the girls.

I wish that just once in the high school or collegiate nationals, or during a televised professional race, I could have heard, "And hailing from Skaneateles, New York, Olympian Jonathon Riley." Just once I'd like to hear someone say Skaneateles and not Brookline, Massachusetts. Is that asking too much?

Medieval Joust

Most dual meets are, at best, over-hyped productions. In cross country, there tends to be the 'haves' and the 'have-nots', and very little in the middle. My goal has always been to have enough kids to give runners a breather during dull duals. Let them get some needed mid-season mileage and save them for another day when the consequences and opportunities added up to something more than a slow jog in the park. There were years when we'd get 40-50 boys and girls on our team but those days are gone as society softens even the best of kids.

Zandra Walton hated duals against weak teams--where all-out effort was not a requirement for victory--because, "They screw me up. Running slowly just messes with my mind. I hate them!" We often fall into the trap in track where we have our studs run in the legal limit of four events. And our mantra is usually, "Run as slowly as you can to get the points. Save yourself." Some coaches just grind up their kids, and I don't get that. Ah, the desire to win. What we should do is have them race in fewer events and have them run fast, seeking to run negative splits, working on a mid-race surge, working on various aspects of their race, focusing on weaknesses, sharpening strengths. Sometimes we've staged a race among ourselves just to sharpen their competitive edge.

But, when we race a respected rival, sometimes we feel as if we should show our full respect and hold back nothing. Jordan-Elbridge girls' coach, Rob Schemerhorn, who teaches physics just around the corner from my social studies room at JE, always says on the days leading to our match-up, "Don't hold back your guns. Give us some respect." And we do. We've had our three-headed monster hang together, Taylor

Strodel, Taylor Lind and Liz Bevier, and then we try to pack it in with our other girls to ensure the win.

This year the meet will be tough. Jordan-Elbridge returns everyone, including seniors Cate White, Kim Armani and Libby Forward, junior Lindsay Hollis and sophomores Nichole Darling and Nichole Stroud. Somehow I haven't taught any of them. After XC ended for the 2005 campaign, JE was ranked 14th in the state. This year it'll be different, especially after the stunning show of middle-distance prowess they displayed in spring track 2006.

Bill Meylan of www.tullyrunners.com has the top seven girl's teams in Class "C" of Section III separated by a mere 45 points after running his computer race simulations a few hundred thousand times using last year's cross country performances. What JE's ranking in 7th doesn't show is their improvement between last fall and last spring. At the moment, Meylan shows arch rival and defending sectional champ Sauquoit Valley tied with us at 80 points. I think we showed progress over the past winter and fall, and for Sauquoit, I think their spring track season was a season with regression rather than progression. But Sauquoit tends to be more of a cross country team and some years they just don't seem to enjoy running around a 400-meter loop.

As we approach this year's dual with neighboring Jordan-Elbridge, I recall the total absorption and excitement of our famous dual on October 8, 1997. It was boiling hot, 80 degrees. The air was unusually calm but humid as usual. Perhaps it was the humidity that compelled Charles Dickens to label us the "arm-pit of the world." We do suffer through some horrible weather with the predominant color most of the year being gray. During the fall and spring seasons, I'm a madman who constantly checks the radar and long term forecasts, even though I realize that on some days our local weathermen can't predict the afternoon's weather that very morning. My meteorological nirvana is reached when I can find one internet weather site out of about six that I constantly peruse that gives me a forecast that is more positive than negative.

I hate lousy weather in cross country. What I want is speed. I want dazzle. I loved the 2.1 to 2.5-mile distance back in the 50s and 60s. It was a race, not a test of survival like so many meets on ridiculous courses today. And I think to improve the girls' sport we should legislate the

2.5-mile distance in dual meets, thereby reducing the length of the race, which would force the girls into a more congested event where they no longer just form the great-long-line-of-jogging and are compelled to race people. Compressing the distance would make real racing possible for the masses. It would help the sport.

Good weather. I want to reduce the chance of injury and I don't want a race to permanently weaken kids for the championship portion of the season. We did that once in Phoenix at our league championship. It was 40 degrees in 2001. The wind chill was in the low 20s and the heavy rain and snow was driven horizontally into us by a 45 mile-per-hour northwest wind from Lake Ontario. It was child abuse. Our girls won easily, placing 2-4-6-7-8/16-23 for the sixth straight Crossover Title. Those girls were tough, tough as our hardened special forces. Pain? Discomfort? Crying? They would have none of that. Those girls, unyeilding in athletics, continue to be successful and stoic in life; Lia Cross, Julie Lynch, Simone Bras, Cadie Cargile, Emily Everding, Erika Geihe and Kathleen Nyzio. Tenacious they were. They won their 2nd straight OHSL title over large school powers Cicero-North Syracuse and Fayetteville-Manlius 10 days later. They won their 8th straight sectional title a week after that beating Sauquoit 27-130. But by the time they got to the state meet, they were gassed. We still won, just edging Pearl River for the title while East Aurora, coached by the legend from Beaver River, Walt McLaughlin, took a very close third, the scores being 64, 68 and 71. That was one title I didn't really enjoy. East Aurora was coming out of the shadows. Since then, Walt and his wife Martha have been unstoppable.

The mud from Phoenix took the legs from my girls in a slow, insidious manner. It happened quicker in 2004 as we won a squeaker over Canastota at the last invitational of the year at Chittenango. It was a quagmire compounded by a campus-wide construction project. A week later we were stunned by 'Stota as they won the right to advance to the state meet. I just had to squeeze in one more invitational. Damn it! I should have stuck with my original plan. Sometimes I outsmart myself by thinking too much.

Jerry Smith, the legendary coach who pre-dates Fayetteville-Manlius 'professor' Bill Aris, loves the crap. He hates courses that drain quickly. Put Jerry in charge of making a championship course and you're looking at mud, compliments of the local fire department that was once called in to turn good turf into slop. You're looking at mountain climbs, 90 degree turns coming downhill along a cliff, running through swamps, anything except good flat turf. Jerry, who was the captain of his University of North Carolina team decades ago when his mane wasn't white, had his moment at Cornell University with the men's distance team. I think Cornell wasn't used to having someone around with true explosive passion. Jerry ruffled feathers. He's now coaching at Bishop Ludden and has moved an unknown program onto the state stage. His time is coming. Cornell apparently wants more decorum. Sadly, I heard this summer that the Cornell men's coach has not communicated once with Owen Kimple who is a 4:07 blue chip from F-M. . If Cornell blows this opportunity, they'll never get another distance stud, and their AD's goal to win like Stanford will go up in smoke.

On that day back in 1997 in our annual dual competition with our J-E neighbors, the girls, as usual, won easily, beating JE 18-39 and sweeping Marcellus. The three-headed monster split in two, with Bevier and Strodel breaking the course record with a controlled time of 18:03. A seemingly unbeatable Alison Shipps of Cazenovia had the previous record, and that bothered me. It was our home course. The record, with all of our running success, should be held by one of ours—a Laker from Skaneateles. Lind was next to cross in 18:31. We were league champs again and extended the victory skein to 35. We were in the midst of a fabulous run that stood at 79 straight as the 2006 season got under way and we were enjoying being on top of the mountain.

At the JE dual in '97, Bevier was pumped to break the record. After the race, Liz said she felt good surpassing the previous mark and before the race said that she wanted to run the best race "of our lives before leaving Skaneateles." Strodel looked at it differently. She said before the race that the record would be rewarding but kept it in the back of her head. "I didn't set the course record as a goal because it's more fun if it's a surprise," she said. Taylor was not buying fully into the running game. Every summer I wondered if she'd return to us, and I think she did so with great reluctance and a somewhat heavy heart. Why did she come back? I think it was only because she didn't want to hurt my feelings. Taylor is just a loving, trusting, gentle person. She isn't abrasively competitive in the traditional sense of the word, but she'd run you down in a race with personal relish. T-1 as I called Taylor, didn't have that lust for summer training, distance runs, grueling practice sessions, but she put up with them and would lead when it was her turn. Once the season began, together we were able to get her into shape, get her mind focused and get the job done at an All-State level. She also really liked hanging around my son Kirk and James Goss, who she dated well into college. They just dated at the wrong time for it to become permanent.

When Taylor graduated from Skaneateles, she held 16 school records, ranging from a 27.13 for 200-meters to 2:16.31 for the 800. Her 4x800 team was 8th at the indoor national championships in Boston at the Reggie Lewis Center and she even shared the 4x100 record with a time of 52.5. She was named All-State in cross country four straight years and her team never lost a dual meet. I'd say she did okay for someone who found the results of running truly enjoyable and worthwhile, but didn't like the grind, lifestyle alteration and the time commitment that running ceaselessly demanded. She now teaches special education in New York City and remains one of my most special friends.

How good was Liz Bevier? In a span of just 14 days in October of her senior year, she broke four course records. Liz was blonde, buff, confident, brash-with-an-edge and was seemingly always up at around 5 AM to complete the remnants of her homework. She was a perfectionist like many of my girls over the years. We're working on the local desire to create Superwomen out of our girls. I just don't get it. For the final year of Liz's life in high school she lived with Caleb Bender in her parent's building (the Seitz Building) in the heart of Skaneateles on the corner of Jordan Road and Rt. 20 that crosses the state of New York parallel to the Thruway. The Finger Lakes dangle from that cross-state ribbon of highway. Caleb was our opponent from Cazenovia, our Laker rival to the east. Caleb and Liz now have two children with another on the way and are as happy as anyone could imagine; soul mates to the end. I thought there might be something untoward about the relationship in the early days, but it worked and continues to work. Caleb is a big-time computer guy. I should put him on retainer because I'm a mess.

Liz's marks were impressive. At Altmar-Parish-Williamstown in the heart of snowmobile country and salmon fishing up near Watertown, she set the record at 19:08. At the Canastota Classic with rival coach

Andy Pino watching, she traversed a course that ran along the eastern shore of Oneida Lake at Sylvan Beach, Liz hit 18:44. Then there was the 18:03 at our course, and that was followed by a 17:47 at the Phoenix-hosted Crossover Championship that included all ten teams in our two-division split league. Liz won by 14 seconds over teammate Strodel.

A week later we found Bevier with a nasty cold and she missed the Onondaga High School League Championship. We placed a good 3rd behind Fayetteville-Manlius and Jamesville-Dewitt without her. A week after that, Bevier led us to our 4th straight Section III title and sent us to the state meet once again. In the process we once again defeated South Jefferson, which was number 2 in the state while we were, once again, under-ranked at 7th. It took a while for people to understand what we were doing. We were patient but there were times when we railed against the establishment for not letting us into their game. We ended up on Long Island where we placed 3rd behind Queensbury and Pearl River in a storm that looked, on paper—and in person—like the Perfect Storm. Again we beat the odds in horrible weather and finished higher than our state rank.

We advanced to the Federation Final after our showing at New York Tech's fan-unfriendly course but when the meet was "cancelled because of snow, ice and cold", in the words of the meet directors, I sent the girls home for the season and shut down the program. Three days later the meet directors decided that instead of using the word "cancel" they should have used the word "postponed". The true state championship was back on. But we were done. I'd released our girls. I got reprimanded by the organizers and the school for not attending the meet but the English language is precise. The word 'cancelled' means we're done. The definition of 'postponed' is, "we'll do it at a later date". I wouldn't back down and I ended up having to issue a phony apology so that we'd be invited again in the future. No matter what, I wanted to keep my job and I knew how things worked in Skaneateles. I still shake my head over the incompetence of the New York State Federation organizers for their blunder and our school for not fighting for a principle. I'm still disappointed that the school failed to support me. But that's public education.

We also do something very different in New York from every other state. Can you imagine having to pay for your team to attend your state championship? That's the way we do it in New York. If you want to go the Federation Championship against the best of the best because you've earned it over a period of two competitive months, you have to pay for the privilege. In track, the coaches who have kids in the state meet have to pay—both days. Incredible. Is the New York State budget that whacked out?

At the '97 league dual with J-E, it was the boys on that sultry October afternoon that put on the real show when we went man-to-man against our respected opponents. JE's Zach Bennett showed up with a Siberian hat atop his red head and he wore long pants over his uniform shorts. We thought he was nuts. Skaneateles was undefeated for the previous three years and we had a nice 19 meet victory streak to protect. But we were the heavy underdogs.

The times in the meet were amazing on a course that seemed more like the Utah Bonneville Salt Flats than anything else. Many prognosticators had the meet figured as a blowout with JE winning 20-34. But it wasn't to be on a day that started out with the Skaneateles team having a breakfast of buckwheat pancakes at a local eatery and ended up with them destroying a vicious course as four runners went sub-16. Only national champion Jonathon Riley had been able to get under the 16-minute barrier with his course record of 15:18.

Tom Poppe, our talented and tall soph, led our charge with a 15:29 for the three-mile course. He improved a remarkable 1:23 from his frosh time. Poppe was ranked behind the top three from JE in our section, including red-headed race winner Jeremy Cornue who won in 15:24, narrowly missing Riley's mark. "I felt awesome," said Cornue. "This is the race we've been training for all year. We wanted to break their winning streak." Rob Boucheron with the reddish hair, was third in the meet, finishing behind Poppe. 'Bouch' ran 15:41. Bennett was next with a clocking of 15:54 and it looked like JE was going to romp. If JE could win, it would raise Roger Roman's career record to 72-12. We were determined to keep the 'Roman Empire' from expanding any further at our expense. We were the barbarians determined to ravage the Empire.

With Poppe breaking up the JE trio and moving him 50 seconds ahead of Riley's soph time, it was my turn to wait and see if the rest of the boys would rise to the occasion. The crowd on that day was as big as you'd see at any all-day invitational. It was just crazy with parents and fans running around so hard I feared I'd have to perform CPR.

With most of the boys having finished, Roger Roman came running past me fast. He was chugging, breathing heavy as his cheeks puffed quickly. "Damn it Jack, congratulations. You got us." I didn't believe it. I hadn't been spending much time scoring the meet but I knew that we'd made a big move as the meet progressed. I just didn't think it was enough.

Senior Jeff Boden came up big with a 16:17 for 5th place. It was the fastest the Holy Cross-bound Laker had ever traversed the course and it was the 3rd best ever by a Laker senior. Boden took the early challenge and was unrelenting in his quest to get back into top form after struggling during the early season. Senior parties all summer will do that to a kid. There's something about seniors. They will either excel or stumble. It was Boden's job to stay close to the front pack and stay in front of the second pack of runners. He succeeded.

My boys went 2-5-6-7-8 and it was the pack that moved Roman to concede prematurely.

Behind Boden was middle distance runner Steve Alexander (Bucknell) who took 6th in 16:23. Chris Davis, who I really didn't get to know because of his move to the southwest with two weeks remaining in the season, was 7th in 16:24. Sprinter John Scriven finished in 8th in 16:26. I couldn't have been more proud.

At the 1k mark, JE led 25-31. At 1.2 miles it was a ten point margin for JE and things looked bleak. At the red 2-mile flag it was still looking bad at 24-32 and it looked like the rout was on and our winning streak dead.

But, we weren't in a giving mood. We'd talked all about being a man, accepting challenge, carrying deep pain over a course of ten minutes. "Compare what you deal with to someone who is in perpetual pain, a sort of pain that's deep in their body, something that they can't ever run away from, even with heavy duty meds," I said to them. "You can live with this. You've trained for it. There's nothing separating you from victory except your own doubt. And I have no doubt. Remember who we are, what we've done. We're not no-bodies anymore. We're from Skaneateles." Roman is the master of pre-race arousal. He can take a group of kids and make them think that they could safely survive a direct nuclear blast. I'm a novice in his long shadow of success.

"That last mile," said Roman, "was furious. They kicked my team's butts. And I never thought anyone could out-sprint Jeff Whitmore (16:28). But (John) Scriven (Oswego) did. That was unbelievable." Closing the scoring for J-E was 6' 4" Peter Simpson in 16:39. Peter and his identical twin brother James were my computer gurus. When in trouble, they'd come to my house and get me up and running quickly. All I had to do was get my wife to make them a big bowl of pasta and off they went tinkering with my computer's memory.

How fast was the race? The total race time for my top-five runners was 80:59, a full 5:37 faster than a race three weeks earlier. The total time was 5:13 faster than my 1994 team that won the state title. The JV's total time 1-5 was faster than the 1993 team that was the state runners-up to Beaver River.

Alexander, who later won the Bowdoin College Summer Distance Fest 800 in the summer of his junior year (1:58.18) and was seen on ESPN TV hammering down the homestretch at Whittier Field as throngs sitting in Hubbard Grand Stand roared their approval, improved his time by 59 ticks. Davis was 47 seconds faster and Scriven dropped his time by 1:29.

For Davis, we were just glad that he could finish. In his first race we were approaching the finish chute after the first loop of the course at Chenango Valley near Binghamton, and he sprinted, thinking that the race was done. Once he discovered that he had another mile and a half remaining, he continued sprinting to catch someone only to fall back into a jog. He kept repeating the same race 'strategy' over and over until he reached the safety of the finish chute. We assumed we were bearing witness to a Chris Davis death-march. But he learned and improved markedly.

Our pack time against JE on a home course that was deceptive and multi-tiered, with hills that came both sharply and gradually, was just 57 seconds. With freshmen Roger Lind in 12th and Weston Cross in 13th, our pack time 1-7 was only 1:28 but not good enough against the Eagles.

Those boys headed into a modern version of medieval warfare, head-to-head, a personal battle face-to-face with the 'enemy'. Every runner in the race confronted the age old questions, questions that too many shy from today, questions that true warriors must always answer: Can I keep fighting? Can I survive? The boys from both teams were going to a place they'd never visited. It could be heaven or it could be hell and some, once they entered, would vow never to return.

Poppe was that guy as a sophomore running the state 2-mile final in Poughkeepsie. He began waving frantically with three laps remaining and we thought he was having a good time. What we were watching was a young kid begging to be allowed to quit. A lap later, a few guys in front of him caved in to the burn that the pace produced. Suddenly Poppe realized he was in the hunt for a medal and he finished in 9:36. But he was never willing to go there again even after I explained to him that his body wasn't quite ready to do what his mind was willing him to do. His miles and 800s would continue to be things of beauty though.

But in that early October dual between Skaneateles and J-E, and despite charging into the darkness of their own souls where they'd discover something about their core—their true identity—all those boys from Skaneateles and Jordan-Elbridge charged ahead into the unknown, determined to chart their own course and control their own fate.

It was an epic confrontation where sportsmanship and the best in competition stood out for everyone to see. It was a special day with special times and unusually strong humans digging deep into themselves to find courage to continue. In many ways, it was the most superlative performance I've been associated with, overshadowing many a championship. Every kid won that day as fear and doubt melted in the intense heat of confidence.

JE went on to place 5th in the New York State meet that year. Despite not advancing ourselves, we finished the season ranked 11th in New York. Twelve months later Jordan-Elbridge was crowned the 1998 State Champs at Lake Placid. And again, we had a war in the sectional finals. Having chased JE to their crown, the sportswriters ranked the Skaneateles boys 5th in the final state poll without having qualified for the championship meet.

Opening Days

I'm angry because of kids, important kids, who are missing practice for specious reasons. "Christ," I say to Rob Tuttle who somehow just goes with the flow. "It's opening day. How can you miss that? Especially after putting in your time over the summer? I just don't get it." Fuming aloud and erupting like Mt. St. Helens on a bad day is what I do. I want things to be perfect. I want the kids to do this right. And I can't help either the kids or the team when other earthly interests get in my way.

I'm pissed off for what I feel is good reason, but it's always the kids in front of me who get to bear the brunt of my disappointment and see my scowls. And they haven't done anything wrong. And by the 'morrow, I'll have forgotten about whatever ticked me off and the transgressors will get off scott-free. Grudges? I don't have them. No time.

I live in the moment these days. When alumni or former co-coaches see me and bring up memories from long gone days, I rarely remember the specific incident they're talking about. My attention is to those who are currently in my orbit. I don't like to listen to old songs preferring, instead, a new day with new artists, new compositions, anything that might help me march forward in life with the expectation of something new and exciting around the corner. The unknown intrigues me endlessly as it teases like Gypsy Rose Lee, the classic burlesque stripper, as the faintest glimpses of the future are unraveled petal by seductive petal. Needing newness, I grasp at news of scientific or political developments, inventions. I look for construction projects and my ears grow happy with the noise of progress. Getting pulled from an old day to a new one with edgy anticipation, I find myself eager and expectant. The onset

181

of change and a new day gives me a sense of hope for better times, for new medical developments, the discovery of new solar worlds, the unearthing of exotic species of flora and fauna, the development of new and courageous architecture, exciting paintings, and new genres of music.

This team is new. It's never existed and I want to mold this collection of individuals into a formidable group of winners. But, our future is short, lasting only 135 days from the first informal summer run to the Sectional Championships.

Opening day and I'm already bent out of shape. Where is everyone?

The Monarch butterflies float lazily around our gathering area under the scotch pines which are full enough to shield us from all but the heaviest rains, their shadow broad enough to offer coolness at high noon on an oppressive summer day. The air this morning, crisp, 63 degrees, is encased between the twin layers of blue sky above and green grass below, the clover still covered in a whispery-thin layer of dew at 8 AM on a late August morning.

Things are changing. You can feel it. You can see it. You can sense it. Darkness begins to descend and spread its shroud earlier and earlier every night. The sky grows darker and walking out on the dock gets more and more precarious as the contrast between the pitch black sky, the nearly invisible deck planks underfoot and the deep, deep dark of the nighttime water meld into one. The breeze, once carrying enough warmth to relax even the tightest of tense shoulder muscles, now constricts the skin as it begins to blow from the north while the Big Dipper begins to slip behind the giant willow tree that all summer long seemed to be propping it up. The breeze sends signals deep inside where something primal begins to fidget as if a heavy burden has been lifted, as if everything is preparing to change; as if something new is about to erupt.

The Monarch butterflies that I saw so often as a child are rare these days, but they still fly waist high, floating lazily around me at practice as if on an inspection tour, fearless, comfortable, touching the ground lightly and only for the briefest of moments, first here, then there, as we gather around the cinders of the shot put vectors. The Monarch alights and lifts off like a perfectly skipped stone across the smooth daytime lake surface.

The team on opening day, like the monarch, is beginning to feel its potential as it begins to spread its wings, to fly, to take off and return as a baby bird tests itself just moments before taking full flight for the first time. Each runner, like the monarch, moves quickly from here to there, chatting quickly, nervously, as if they are trying to stay one step ahead of any potential threat as they begin the teenage dance-of-uncertainty and embark on the process of learning to place trust in each other, to find truth and purpose in the shared pursuit. Together, yet separate, united yet in competition, they learn to seek individual improvement which, when extrapolated throughout the team, will help construct a monolith of running might. Every move, every word, every step taken in practice, serves to justify the investment that is paid from their soul and withdrawn from their physical being. Then, and only then, can they find peaceful rest for another night where dreams live free and the body reconstitutes itself for another run toward glory on the 'morrow.

One by one they got out of cars dressed in bright colors, shod in new shoes that would soon draw blood from newly blistered heels and toes. Everyone was wondering, despite good summer running, if they'd measure up. They'd be feeling out each other, testing ambitions, challenging legs that are well-muscled and stressing respiration capacity. Some would find themselves rising through the ranks after their summer investment in themselves. Some would grow frustrated and learn to redouble their efforts—or slip away into the fringes where one-shot-wonders live quietly with their few memories and a life-time chorus of "what-if."

There's going to be surprises, some pleasant, some infuriating, and some out of my control. And quickly my perceived ideas about this team will be changed as reality enters my dreams.

Surprisingly, Sam has to pull out of the workout after a mere 5 reps. Running at 3k pace 14 times around the track with a rest period after each 400 equal to 75% of the running time, Sam grew dizzy. I wondered aloud to Rob if Sam was feeling the pressure of freshman Calvin Davis who was not only hitting paces but cutting his times as he progressed through the session. 3k pace is Calvin's physiological domain right now. Sam is more proficient at any pace faster or slower than that.

Perhaps Sam's quick weekend trip to Pittsburgh left his system and energy reserves screwed up. Regardless, I didn't force the issue because Sam was picture perfect all summer. But next time, if there is one, I'll push Sam hard, for a frosh shouldn't have to be pushed by his training partner-dad. It should and must be Sam pulling the kid along.

Beatrice faltered internally as her will broke for no reason at all. Beatrice is a head runner. When her thinking is clear and positive, she's effective. With nine of the 400s completed, she begged to end the session. "It's hurting too much, it's painful, my legs won't go, they hurt terribly," she said with her body swaying from foot to foot as her upper torso bent in fatigue, the exhaustion showing itself in a manner that said she was totally defeated. For the first time in my career I have the team writing down their splits as soon as each track rep is finished. We'll do the same with the distance runs, too. I showed Bea her 400 splits and reinforced the fact that her times were faster by a few seconds than her goal of 92 seconds. The 69-second rest was still effective, but she had entered the realm of the Vulcan mind-meld. "You're right on pace, Bea," I said as I gave her upper arms a confident squeeze. "You haven't even slowed down to hit your pace." I mentioned her negative brain talk and sent her back out on the track. Bea's been squeamish since her two straight bone breaks and we brought her back more slowly than was physically necessary, but her belief in herself, that's something we need to really work on. With a little more help from me, she completed the workout and continued to run well.

Three days later we were running 5x1000 at her 5k pace and after nailing the first four, she lagged behind her group as the final rep was completed. As I read her notebook annotations later that day, I noticed that she'd written, "4:02, 4:00, 4:01, 4:02, felt great." Then she wrote, "ran out of juice, but it wasn't the head. I swear!"

After returning from Aim High summer camp, Bea emailed me, "I run well, I think, when I'm confident…and most of the time I'm not. But most importantly, I need confidence while I'm running so that I don't decide halfway through to quit on myself.

Dave Patruno, co-founder and co-director of Aim High with his wife Jennifer who coached our modified teams last year, was on a roller coaster one Wednesday at camp with Bea. She was in the zone, flying with kids who, based on experience, she shouldn't have been with.

Dave relayed his perceptive thoughts to me about the run that included Homer's sophomore Heather Wilson (2:16.47), CNS's Alicia Finger (10:19.01) and Lindsay Raulli (7:53 2000m steeple), and our own Sofie who stuck with the pace-pushers the whole run.

Hi Jack -

Just a quick observation about Bea.

We did a 44 minute run on Wednesday afternoon. About 2/3 way through the run there was a big mud pit in the middle of the trail. So, some of the kids went in the mud - not sure if Bea did though. Anyway, to the point. When we emerged at the trail head it is about 1.5 miles back to camp. The girls really started to move. There were some good runners in the group. Katie Duerr (Cicero-North Syracuse, 4:58) stands out in my mind as one of them. The pace really started to push and frankly I thought Bea was going to go out the back door. But she didn't. Then the pace really started to move. A lot of times I'd just call the troops back and say, "The goal is the end of October, beginning of November, not August." But I didn't. I didn't because all the girls (there were a few guys with us) were in a zone. Right when I was about to call it off I looked over at Bea and I saw something special. She was in the zone too. So I let it go on. Understand it was 1.5 miles back to camp and the pace was getting progressively faster. Frankly I knew it was probably a pace you wouldn't normally want her to be training at so I was in a quandary. Every 200 meters I would look back and there was Bea right there. They were all breathing to the point where you could hear them. I was so impressed. She was pushing but she was not at an exhausted state at all. She looked so smooth, so comfortable at that pace but she was certainly working.

Later that day I told her how impressed I was. I mean Katie was certainly breathing hard and she has been training well this summer. Bea stayed with her all the way to camp. I really didn't think she could do it and I am glad I didn't call it off. Maybe from a training standpoint it wasn't the smartest thing

185

in the world but I really feel she gained something else. I believe something in her head clicked. I hope she gained confidence from that. I really wish you could have seen it. She impressed me. I told her so later that day. Feel free to mention it to her. She could probably tell you who all was in the group. I believe Lindsay Raulli (CNS) was, too, and maybe Hannah. I just don't remember because I was focused on whether or not Bea could hang on. I hope she has a good season. I did a talk on goal setting. They put their goal in the middle of a sheet of paper then circle it. Off of that circle they draw lines and connect to other circles they make that have in them things they can do or improve upon to help make their goal a reality. So, for example, someone writes they want to win sectionals as a goal. Off of that circle they may write 'recovery.' Off of that circle they may write 'get more sleep' (which aids in recovery). Off of the main goal they may have another circle that says 'nutrition,' etc, etc, etc,.....They are supposed to hang these up in their room and look at it every day so they see their goal and all the things they should be doing to help reach their goals.

I am not privy to Bea's goals but I hope she upped her goals after that run.

Dave

Bea and the girls, four days into Boot Camp, sat down at the picnic table under those soothing and welcoming pines and constructed their chart with all their goals. And, just like every season for the past decade and a half, their goal is simple: "Win Sectionals."

Rachel Vaivoda, who had melted down so thoroughly in an easier 1500 workout with full rest back in July, nailed this one. And, in typical Rach fashion, when she does well, she talks like a chatterbox as the excitement and thrill of success overwhelms her.

Sofie had snot all over the place, compliments of the annual visit from some unspecified allergen. With methodic ease, the senior, like Rach, snorted and snorted and hit her paces perfectly. The two of them crushed their repeat 1000s later in the week, too. I wasn't expecting this from either of them. Did I lose confidence in them over the years? I did. But my confidence in their ability never flagged. Needing to make some slight changes in their training and mental approach, I always knew they could do it.

Hannah, the other brat-pack member from 9th grade, had her first encounter with the team after a long summer at Lake George. I had planned on duplicating her summer training and have her run alone, but she missed her friends more than she realized and asked to be partnered. On our first few runs, she showed why Bill Meylan of Tullyrunners. com is so high on her. Later in the week, the facia that covers the outer portions of her thighs tightened suddenly during sleep. Not being able to lie on her sides at all, she was worried. We went with the workout anyway, after some light stretching. We consulted with the trainer and Hannah was scheduled to see Doctor Petters, our trusty chiropractor. She can get hurt if she doesn't pay attention to her body. Even when healthy she's been advised to do her rehabilitation stretches that came from a physical therapist. I think she slacked off this past summer. Despite the pain that began with each rep and reappeared as soon as each one was finished, she felt that the actual paces were more than comfortable. For some reason the running didn't hurt. I suggested in an email that she put more salt on her food and find a potassium/magnesium supplement. Maybe her electrolytes are out of balance and that's causing the spasms and tightening?

Amanda, the enigma of the team who has a tradition of staying to herself, is different this fall. She's grown up, looks you in the eye and engages in conversation that isn't strained. She's been a lot of fun and has begun trying to tell a few jokes of her own during our downtime when the adults try to lighten the mood and send everyone home in good spirits. I was surprised and pleased with her demeanor as camp opened up and I think she seems happy with her decision to be on the team again. It just might be her safe haven in this world. I found out that her parents split and her little brother who has ADD has moved away with his dad. I think that having him out of her sphere of influence has relieved her of feeling obligated to take care of him. She constantly worried about him and I suspect that Child Services had a file on the family. Such is sisterly love. Last year at the sectional championship at South Jefferson, she was in turmoil because she knew that no adult was at home with her brother. Dad went to Morris's World Famous Bar on his motorcycle at about the time our bus left for the meet and her mom was supposedly at a Tupperware party. Running down the Tug Hill to the flat where the big crowd awaited Amanda's finish—while worrying about her sibling--she was expending mental energy that she couldn't afford to waste on a hilly course riddled with deep, energy sapping mud. Her concern for her brother foiled the day for her.

Karen is heading to Europe and the two days with us have been far less than spectacular after missing the previous two weeks. Feeling discomfort in her heel, there's fear of a stress fracture as rising on her toes brings forth pain. In both the track workout and the 5.88-mile run, she was off her game and never was close enough to see the backs of girls' she had drilled all summer. Perhaps she's done for the year already. I hope it's just a bone bruise. Lexie Mazzeo and Tay Tay Wellington worked hard.

Kristin Roberts, so dynamic in races, continues to do far less in practice than anyone could expect. It's disappointing that she hasn't shown more growth in practice, but Rob is certain she'll slay her teammates in a race. And just days later she hit her marks. Grouping Kristin with Sofie and Beatrice worked perfectly as each was convinced she was as good, or better, than the other two. I think Kristin feels she can run with them so she fought hard and kept hitting her paces. She rose up and we needed to see it.

It was a big morning that first day of practice. Late the night before, I noticed that the big moths that fly around near the porch ceiling--battling defenseless ceiling fixtures like airborne bumper cars knocking into each other--are missing in action. Fall is here. Maple leaves curl on the edges as they descend to the earth, well into the finality of their private death spiral. Nights are cool, while the daily mid-80s still soothe old childhood friends like engineer Ken Levers and his fellow residents of South Jersey. Ken, a blocking back for Billy "White Shoes" Johnson at Widner College in the early '70s, was on his way back home from Maryland's McDaniel College after dropping off his son, Kyle, for pre-season soccer. When he called, he was alone in his car and we caught up on our lives. My mouth talked to him and my eyes watched the rare ceiling battle with the few moths that braved their final day of life.

Our little village swells in the summer with hordes of folks who spend a lot of money. But things are changing. The vacationing crowds that reduced our ability to live simply and spontaneously are leaving, getting back to their normal lives and allowing us to return to ours. The lights along the lakeshore are back to non-summer normal as black replaces the lights that repeatedly dotted our shoreline. It's quiet. The boat traffic and annoying buzz of individual wave runners is gone. And everyone appreciates being able to hear the natural sounds of the lake, the lapping of waves gently on the shore and the relaxed movement of tumbling pebbles against each other, the ducks, the few loons that coo softly, the sea gulls that fly casually overhead, and even the hum of cars moving to and from the village on two-lane lakeshore roads. Echoes of cars and trucks from across the mile-wide lake begin to somehow relax the man who's in a pre-sleep state-of-being. Man and nature are once again in a symbiotic cool state.

I've noticed that it's far easier now to stop and pick-up a USA Today or the NY Times, along with a tasty, fresh-baked cinnamon donut at the re-opened Bakery. Normalcy, that's the goal, and we're on the way to getting it back. Finding a parking spot in front of Riddlers, the candy, newspaper, tobacco, magazine emporium in town, is relatively simple now.

In reflection, opening day was about as good as we could expect, about as good as we've seen over the years, and opening week has reaffirmed that we have potential, that we can dream.

The seniors have fly-paper memories; they seem to remember every workout of Boot Camp that they've ever experienced. Once again I'm reminded that my influence is far greater than I realize.

Dan, whose mom was classically trained at the French Culinary Institute in New York City, has grown out of his pudgy stage and is running well enough to be effective for us this year. Called Dandy by his friends, he's taller, thinner and showing the outline of a rib cage. And we're seeing some whittling of his tree-trunk thick legs as he attacks the workouts. He's pushing like a blade of grass pushes through a cement sidewalk. He's changed. I hope it lasts.

After 3x1000 at 5k pace, Dandy, chest heaving, was on pace in his four-pack training group. The boys, Jeff, Matt, and Dustin, were slicing through the training like Sherman sliced through Atlanta. On that 3rd 1000, slowly, imperceptibly, Dan slipped off pace. Matt, fast becoming the team cheerleader, motivator and respected commander—even by his peers—kept shouting encouragement to 'his' boys. Jeff hates it but appreciates what Matt is doing. With Matt's encouragement, Dandy hit his pace on that 4th 1000 meter repeat.

On rep #5, Dan just didn't have it and he fell nearly 20 meters off pace. I yelled, "Dandy, tuck it in, stay with those guys, you're almost done." Entering the final turn with 100-meters to go, Dan was struggling. He was physically and mentally defeated. Suffering from a tough divorce, Dan has only seen his dad about 7 hours in the last dozen weeks. He's angry, upset, and won't accept his dad's calls. He's carrying an extra weight, a burden kids should not have to shoulder. Matt yelling encouragement got Dan going. The other kids picked up on what was happening. Dan's group was the last one on the track. The more I yelled, the more the team understood what was at stake. This was big. It was important. A teammate was on the edge. He'd either fold his tent and fail or he'd fly and have a chance to advance to greater things.

The kids yelled, screamed and applauded—the clapping sounding like the football team that claps for everything. We're different. We press the flesh when it's real, when it's vital, when someone's life is on the line. Somehow, the team was sending their collective energy to Dandy and he felt it. His black hair was flying atop a tilted head as he received every ounce of help that was sent his way.

Dan rallied and soon those 20-meters were nothing. He'd become a legitimate runner. He was Kip Keino tossing his cap to the infield which signaled his final move to the finish. With arms driving, with a spring to his steps, with Dan standing taller than he's stood for a long time, the gap disappeared. Step by step he eliminated meters. And with a move into lane two, Dandy, he with the sluggish sophomore year and the family life that's breaking his heart, took off, caught everyone and headed for the finish line all alone. Veering from lane 1 to lane 6 and crashing onto the grass between the track and the black chain-link fence, Dandy, on this day and in this challenge, had done it. He'd defeated every demon in his life. For the moment he was free and in full control of his existence like a champion video game player who is the master of his domain in the virtual reality world.

As Dan passed his group, Matt said, "Go Dan!" It was simple, it even might have sounded geeky, but it was effective.

Several years ago it was Steve Corsello who had the insurmountable lead in our last home meet of the season. As the finish was nearing, Steve yielded and allowed senior Patrick Lewis to accept the crowd's applause as the victor of the meet. Steve didn't have to do that. But he did. It's a team-thing. Patrick's time was the course record for two years.

Leaders, true leaders, not only inspire, they know when to step aside and yield to a creature of their own invention. Matt did that today. Not because I asked him to but because he knew it was the right thing to do at the right time for a teammate and friend; a friend in need of a boost.

This boy's team is building spirit, a sense of being in this together. They're beginning to believe in themselves, in each other, in their shared mission to crawl from the bottom toward the top. We're looking like a team, and that means we can afford to hope.

After all the excitement of practice, a practice that goes right, I find myself beginning to have trouble with late summer as Autumn begins to establish a beach head. By the late afternoon, early evening, I'm growing antsy after my morning lift from being with the kids. Football has double sessions to keep the coaches on their athletic high. Soccer has three hour practices that satisfy a coach's need for interaction with his team. But running is different. I believe in one-session practice days, and I don't want to rush things. But by the evening I'm lonely and frustrated by the forced separation from my team. Summer slows me. Boot Camp gets me going again. The best moments are when we travel together and we're 'stuck' with each other 24 hours a day. Those days are the ones that have a big impact on me, and I think, the kids, too.

Alone in my post-practice solitude as my youngest son, KC, has packed his car completely full and left us for his return drive to college in Albany, I watch pre-season NFL on the tube and it seems to exorcise the devil's curse called the slow pace of baseball watched on television. Baseball's pace is sweet in the heat of summer but by fall it's out of whack with the rhythms of life. I need a buzz. Tony Kornheiser is trying to make an impact on Monday Night Football. USA Basketball is vying for TV time while battling the world in Japan. Wasn't Carmello Anthony of Syracuse University, fabulous with his 19 point 3rd quarter in pool-play vs. Italy? The Yankees swept a rare 5-game series in Boston over the Red Sox. Fenway might never be the same as that scar will surely have adhesions that tug painfully for years to come.

Kids return to their college haunts while those who chose a patriotic pursuit--or were shoved into the fighting ranks because of an ugly set of personal economic indices--fight and die in the Middle East. We bear witness to the evils of Hezbollah and Hamas. We watch Israel spiral slowly toward a possible death and we cringe at the destruction of a tolerant Lebanon. The Taliban, that regressive cadre of ignorant, bearded, cave-dwelling thugs, reconstitute and expand their phalanx of hate. Fear flourishes in the world. And here I am, like the rest of America, sitting comfortably in my living room with the TV on, the internet connecting me to the world just three steps from my easy chair and the refrigerator humming and fully stocked not more than 20 feet away. Our local farmers stock their roadside stands bountifully with more culinary magic than anyone should ever expect, and in our leisure we revel in our sports, eagerly seeking and discussing meaningless games as we follow our overpaid and drugged-up professionals like we used to follow our own kids in youth sports. And in the rest of the world babies die, innocent people with a desire for arable earth, breathable air and family safety suffer day and night at the hands of hideous barbarians with nothing positive to contribute to humanity. With wanton and wicked whimsy the soulless sloths of the world view life like a 5 –year old looks at a tower built of wooden blocks. It's just something to knock down. With nothing more to do than destroy anything and everything, dash futures and wipe smiles from the faces of all humanity, the imbeciles of the human race draw us all closer to the day when all out war may have to be fought. We can't long suffer these fools lightly.

Yet, I sit here watching Reggie Bush and wondering if he'll successfully cover the 4 hash marks that separate his New Orleans Saints from a first down in a meaningless pre-season game.

Race Week

We look sharp warming up in our new shirts, workman gray with an arched SKANEATELES on the front, the letters outlined in navy blue, the heart of each letter hollow showing the gray of the shirt. The kids feel important. Everyone is on the same page. And every one of them feels as if they truly are somebody, a part of something bigger than themselves.

These kids aren't stupid. They know what rung they occupy on the national sporting ladder. They know that society has created and continues the propagation of myopic myths about sports, the super-human qualities possessed by and attributed to the athletes of the chosen sports as the laurel wreath is placed on a most select group.

Observant of all this, each of my kids must, of necessity, look askance at reality while giving it a soft but firm back-handed slap, the aggression symbolic of something deeper, something that connotes an urge to be different as they flee the common cultural standards and chart their own life-course. The slap at reality is a quiet, individual acknowledgement that runners are of a different breed, a rare breed that does so much in pure anonymity while reaping deeper internal rewards that accrue to only the long distance runner, rewards that only a chosen few can understand.

Those rewards, revealed in cerebral enlightenment during physical moments of exhaustion, speak of fulfillment, triumph over the self and rewards for going it alone as each runner stretches the limits of their body. The daily ritual is almost spiritual as it raises the human spirit and releases from the soul the secret of liberation.

The reality of the sporting world reveals a spidery web of collective social beliefs and mores that says runners are part of a minor sport. The community standards declare that cross country is not a marquee sport despite its royal origins in Great Britain. The social tenets state that runners are not the equal of athletes involved in more worthy sports like basketball or soccer, or one of the hitting, contact sports like football, hockey and lacrosse. Real athletes who are glorified in those sports on the big stage nationally or worldwide are deemed to be more important, culturally vital, and their activity more indicative of true manhood or a predictor of a woman's overall sexual worth in society.

But on race day all runners pretend that today, for these next few dozen minutes, we're the game, we're the ones who people will marvel at, we're the ones who deserve to be carried through the village square upon the shoulders of the tribal leaders. On race day we each play dumb and hope for numb nerve endings that reach to the upper layer of our thin skin as we're protected from attempts to shame us, to ridicule our sport, to diminish the valiant effort. Today, race day, we won't be bruised by put- downs and ill-intentioned comments meant to cause distress. We won't be hearing the cackles from brutes who don't understand anything outside the realm of their limited and socially sanctified existence. We won't be defensive as we all go on the offensive while in the company of people who appreciate the fine art and the physical and mental struggle that defines distance running.

In our new t-shirts, everyone here at Chittenango, the village that gave the world The Wizard of Oz and the Yellow Brick Road, knows who we are for a change. Today, for our season-opener, we have our act together. We're unified and we present a formidable image to our opponents.

Except for a brief period in the old days when we still had a few bright-yellow banana warm-up suits that were given to the girls as a reward for winning the sectional championship, and a few years in the late 90s when we had a full stockpile of navy-blue sweats, we haven't had school-bought warm-ups.

In the camping areas that imaginatively spring up in the span of mere hours around the starting areas at Saturday invitationals like cities rising from the dirt during the Industrial Revolution in England, spectators are treated to a vast, vibrant sea of color as a grass field is transformed into a highly efficient and functioning tent-city where its inhabitants are well-dressed and members of teams wear the same warm-ups while moving in unison like the Roman Legions. Bright and color- coordinated, the kids who are lean, athletic and lithe move effortlessly with school names, logos and mascots proudly displayed as others in the crowd wonder about the location of some of the lesser known hometowns.

Like an artist holding his completely prepped palette with a special spot for shades of cadmium red, burnt umber, phathalo blue, winsor violet, light blue and titanium white, my crew over the years looked like the palette after the acrylic or oil painting was completed; a mighty mess, a motley mishmash of indistinguishable mud tones. Some of the guys over the years have looked like homeless street people with flannel shirts half buttoned, blue jeans covering skin when GORE-TEX should be the race-day ensemble. We've seen plaid shorts and cut-off sweats, each masquerading as running gear designed to protect against the elements. These new t-shirts, our only protection except for the clothing supplied by parents, have flair but they'll be worthless in a few weeks as cool and then cold arctic air begins to descend upon us as the sun retreats to the southern hemisphere where the rays will touch the Tropic of Capricorn and then amble ever so slowly back to us.

On the back of the shirt that the kids proudly wear, we printed a bold SKAN in block navy blue letters that were outlined in gold. Right under that we reversed the color scheme on a huge XC. We do, indeed, look sharp.

The onset of race-week is a big deal as everything becomes more real. The revelation that we have already spent nearly three months preparing rises into our consciousness and our agenda begins to take on a special urgency felt only by the competitive or serious athlete. With crunch time dawning, we feel an imperative to act with finality as we realize that everything counts from now on.

The week has been spotty with some fine performances in practice. But Sam has been ill after having a summer where he was the master of his own universe. With eyes swollen and darker than normal, with a hunched back instead of the proud stance that he brought to practice all summer, he's become a puker with a 103.5 temperature. He's missing sleep. And his mother has become a part of the equation like most mothers.

Sam showed up for practice Monday with the belief that he couldn't handle the workout, and it was daunting, 10x400 at 1500 pace with a lap of jogging for recovery. Sam not only excelled, he seemed to be healed by the experience. From sullen he turned buoyant. From a state of exhaustion rose a young man who was invigorated. From hitting pace early he dipped down to nearly 60 flat. The scowl became an inviting smile. But that afternoon I was told that his temperature spiked.

Sam's mom was concerned about her son.

What's your opinion about running the race on Sat. if he's better. I don't think that he'll have the strength to perform well. As of now, he's still feverish. Let us know your thoughts.

My private thoughts were that Sam needs to be allowed to grow up. He's a tough kid—brought up in a loving, nurturing home--who I think has been led to believe that he can't overcome obstacles. I was convinced after Monday's success in practice that Sam had learned a valuable life-lesson, a lesson that would give him confidence in his ability to rise above physical impairment. I also thought that mom was looking at just Sam, like all mothers do. He was her baby after all. The truth is simple, without Sam, we're a dead team. Sam at 80% is still 30% better than any replacement we can insert into the varsity line-up. The object of my attention is the team. Sam, somewhat ill, is still able to help his friends. When the illness is above the neck, I say run. When it's below the neck, it's time to see a doctor and hit the bench until cleared. But I won't toy with a big fever.

At 4:30 PM Monday, mom pulled the plug on Tuesday's practice. After the kids had been out on their run for 15 minutes Tuesday, Sam's dad brought him to practice. He said he was fine after throwing up. But with a good summer under his belt, I told him he'd earned a day off. When I got home I read an email that mom had written before practice that suggested Sam wouldn't be whole for Saturday's race. I wrote back that from Tuesday to Saturday was a long time. I followed that with a note about Sam growing up.

Sam's learning that he's capable of doing very good things even when he's not feeling 'normal'......he proved that yesterday.... and, he's been on fire all summer....he's got a lot of fight in him and I think that if we carefully promote his abilities and downplay colds, being tired etc, he'll rise to the occasion.... Christie Ann, he's becoming a man right in front of your eyes.... he's breaking out of his shell...and he leads this team every day....ain't it a thing of beauty?

I think I understand moms since I've lived with the mother of my two boys for 27 years, 32 if you count the years before Kirk's birth. Christie Ann, a sensitive, nourishing and artistic woman who understands that she underestimates Sam like many American mothers today, wrote back that my words made her cry. It's so hard for truly good parents to lose control and influence over their kids, to watch them grow up, to have to begin the process of letting go. I know. I've been there and I still have trouble with the whole process. I called my computer specialist today, Cary Briel, for some help, and he's in the early days of separation from his oldest child who was dropped off at Geneseo College over the weekend. When I told him that I was depressed from September to December after leaving Kirk at Ithaca College, he seemed relieved. He wasn't abnormal after all. He hadn't done something wrong during the process of raising his daughter. He was completely normal, crying was part of the deal, and separation anxiety was the norm for loving parents. Christie Ann has just sent her second child off to college. Sam is next and I think his departure will be rough. We're just poor and caring humans who reproduce and release.

Just as quickly as I finish dealing with Sam, my mind and focus leaves that settled situation behind and I focus on another potential problem. Hannah is in a death spiral and even the other girls have written to me about it. I wrote Hannah a few things to try to inspire her, to help her settle down and to remind her why she loved to run. I closed by saying,

This is what I want for you Hannah....until you feel this again, you're missing the heart and soul of cross country...everything you did yesterday was perfect...find that source of liberation....

> *it's always there for you to use for whatever purposes you want....*
> *coach*

Hannah has struggled for the past two competitive years. At Maine-Endwell High School last April, against state caliber runners who she didn't recognize, in horribly cold air in the 40s with high winds and rain, she broke out and was a dominating runner for the remainder of her junior track campaign. I thought we were in the clear and heading for pay-dirt. I was sure that her senior year would be nothing but success. She has the total package but shies from expectations. And that's what worries me, since life is nothing but expectations that you simply have to meet. Falling short isn't in the cards when it comes to acquiring a business contract, when it comes to staying calm when your child is in danger, when people are counting on your best performance in any number of endeavors in life. Mastering emotions and being able to unleash our abilities on-command is the secret to a successful life. Expectations? It's what drives our culture and separates us from so many other cultures around the world. Grow, change, improve, experiment, become the leader, seek victory. Those are the mindsets that not every culture holds close to their nourishing civic breast. Daring to be different, daring to rise above the norm, eagerly looking forward to challenge, outsmarting and outworking the opposition is what we're culturally bred to do in the United States. Hannah can do all of that. There's no dispute over the facts. Her times are good. But this fall she's decided it's all too much and I don't know why. Just three days separate us from a glorious opening day or ignominious defeat.

Hannah is a handful, eccentric, avant-garde, talented, humorous, 2nd in her class. She's brilliant, creative and fun-loving. On Monday she 'discovered' that a little knee lift, instead of a shuffle, makes running efficient. And with the more efficient stride she found that she could run faster with less effort than at any time in her career. She heard at Aim High running camp that knee lift was a good thing that she should try to incorporate into her running life. Self-discovery is a wonderful thing that all teachers strive to achieve with every student. Hannah discovered all of this by herself Monday despite her Skaneateles coaches telling her about it for years. As I leaned while reading a book about Summerhill, a school that didn't force anyone to learn until they were motivated to learn, Hannah apparently wasn't receptive to the lessons during her sophomore and junior years. On Monday, she was ready to change, to grow and become a better runner. Her excitement was palpable. On Tuesday it was all gone and a dour, defeatist, empty vessel returned to practice. On Monday Hannah was every teacher's dream. On Tuesday she was every teacher's mystery-student. She's conflicted about something and I can't explain it.

We're ready to race. The tenor of practice, the paces, the ability of the kids' to sponge-up the rigors of the training, all point to being race-ready. No more tinkering at this point is necessary. It's time to race, to evaluate the results and to chart our direction. If we're on, powerful Cicero-North Syracuse needs to be concerned. If we freeze-up, CNS eats us up and spits us out.

Game On

Can I do a workout," begged Bea as the sweat and rain mingled on her strained and furrowed face after finishing the first race of her sophomore year, her previous two varsity campaigns having been stained by injuries and unfortunately becoming unforgettable as misery got burned into her memory. It's much like the ignominious red forehead tattoo that distinctively marks a student who fell asleep in class and didn't wake up when the passing bell sounded. It's there. The mark-of-the-flop designates a human who fell to a challenge and the impression is so clear that everyone sees it; the imprint having burrowed deep into personal places that don't forget head-shaking failure. No matter what, you can't will it away and only the passing of time can ease the stigma or, at a later date, redemption is achieved on the same battlefield.

I told Bea that she needed to be able to race-on-command, that there is no way to make up for a blown opportunity by running hard the next day, by smashing a workout on the following Tuesday, or in this case, erasing the impression by doing a workout within minutes of skulking out of the finish chute. Talking to Bea like this has become a routine and I wish I could make it go away for she's a sensitive girl whose deepest fear isn't that she feels inadequate, but that she's more powerful than she knows how to handle.

"I knew this would happen," said Beatrice after falling apart in the last mile of the season opener. "I needed to mess things up so that I could fix it."

"Bea, listen to yourself," I said with a calm but stern voice as my eyes pierced hers. "Listen to yourself, Bea. Say those words to yourself and tell me if that sounds normal. After you study for a test, do you go into the exam and act like this?"

"Well, no."

"Our practice is the same as studying," I suggested. "And our races are the exam. You need to transfer what you learn in school to life."

Bea was a mess after the race and no matter how many times she swiped at a lone tear that rolled down her cheek, it kept coming back as her emotions welled-up but remained more under control than usual. She's trying. Her standards for herself are high. I told her she had to move on. The curse of carrying a completed race into the next week is too heavy. It'll crush anyone who lets it smolder in their psyche because the next race will be run with hindsight, dread and fear instead of looking forward to a new opportunity with hope, lightness and excitement boosting the spirit.

Once I got my soggy old body onto the bus for the trip home, I asked the kids to answer these two questions in their log book. "What did you do right and what do you want to work on at Windsor" the next weekend.

Bea wrote a short book and said all the right things on this day when everyone else was pretty pleased with our showing as both the boys and girls took second to the giant school called Cicero-North Syracuse. We didn't crumble. We came to play.

"I blew it and now I'm paying for it. Why did I blow it? Because I was stupid and let the voice in my head get to me. I panicked for NO reason. I have NO excuse and there isn't any explanation for justifying why I gave up. But it's over and time to move on. Next race I am going to remember how mad I feel right now and use that to help motivate me to not have a repeat of today. I'm going to stick with the people I train with and treat it like a workout."

I kept calling this meet a glorified scrimmage during the week to de-emphasize it because this group of girls seeks to be in total control of everything in their lives. And that's not reality.

We just hired Julie Lynch to coach our modified teams. Before her stints at American University and Wheaton College, she helped us win three state cross country state championships and several state 4x800 titles. She should be starting her junior year of college but she's worn out, fried and in desperate need of some downtime.

Julie, like Erika Geihe at Harvard, was working like hell to be the 2000 version of Superwoman. Both had to be in control of everything. No effort was ever good enough. They competed at everything and despite some heated moments they remain close friends. Julie told me after her interview with our athletic director, "I needed a break. I couldn't keep doing this."

Not wanting to say something that could be construed as poor form, I spoke and hoped everything would come out okay. "Julz, do you remember what I kept saying to you girls? Do you remember the arguments we'd have about AP courses, all the volunteer work, the late nights that stretched into the morning hours, the endless projects, the total lack of play time, the ridiculous attention to taking and retaking those SAT exams? Do you remember me saying that you need to just take the SATs once—maybe twice--and accept who you are, be happy with who you've become? Do you remember me telling you that you need downtime, you need to clear your plate, you need to get some practice at doing nothing, that being a superwoman will eventually send you crashing back to earth?"

Julie nodded and looked me straight in the eyes, her voice as strong and confident as ever, "This tells you how far I've come. I can't go back to college right now. I need a rest. And Erika is feeling it, too." She'd just talked to her at Harvard and Erika is putting in long days at the research lab while trying to get in shape for her new coach, Jason Saretsky, who left Iona for the Crimson. Erika has never seen a coffee break. She wouldn't know what to do with it. Vacation? She's like a third of Americans who just won't take time off from work. I hope she isn't missing the essence of life.

I'm hoping this fall as Julie works with a nice group of 7th and 8th graders that she'll get recharged and begin to see a path through the haze that's making it difficult for her to follow her true course into adulthood. She's a runner and Coach Chris Fox, the exciting new coach at Syracuse University, could do great things with Julz. Julie's mom works at SU so the tuition is covered. Julie needs to meet Coach Fox and it's my new mission to get the two together.

Beatrice, like older sister Zandra-of-Amherst, is a lot like Julie and Erika. All of them strive to do everything at the highest level without exception. There is nothing acceptable except success, nothing except winning—at everything. But right now the damn demon called Fear has a strangle hold on Beatrice and I can't seem to do anything to help. Time will surely be her ally in this battle, but she needs to see the cavalry coming down the hill to her rescue with guns firing away. If I could swat it down I would, but Fear's tentacles are ripping deep into Beatrice while Doubt infects her mind.

There was more trouble on this wintry gray-sky day at Chittenango. Oliver took a header that drew blood from his legs. Stephen, our wrestler, took a plop in the mud. Matt found he has vertical lift after he was forced to hurdle an opponent who fell while crossing a wood plank bridge. It was that sort of day.

Host Harold Muller was on the course at 5 AM setting up for the day's festivities after he and a horde of parent volunteers had spent days readying the course for the first race of the season in New York State. Harold's the head of the science department and he's anal in a good way. He and the volunteers, working with old-fashioned pride on their side, had taken care of everything, and then Tropical Depression Ernesto showed up with the first rainfall of the day just as the first race, the girls' varsity, shot out onto the 2.5-mile course. Sparsely attended on Labor Day weekend, the competition was nonetheless strong with eight teams bussing in.

I was saying to my wife the day before the meet that I wasn't sure I could get the kids to the race in one piece. Sofie, who ended up having a marvelous race, a race that left her with no psychological baggage to take home and rummage through afterwards, was worrying about her father, a State Trooper, who was called Thursday night after two fellow troopers were shot by wanted-man Bucky Phillips.

"They're just shooting troopers all the time," said Sofie. "They're out on patrol and I don't think they have their bullet proof vests on."

She was worrying about her dad who is a gung-ho and successful triathlete. Sofie, on pre-race Friday, had big black rings under her eyes and I wasn't sure she'd be able to pull it together until the massive manhunt got this heinous criminal. Worrying about the big loves in your life will do things like etch tell-tale black marks on the faces of innocents.

Hannah, the gregarious inquisitor, became defiant and contrarian on pre-race Friday and I could see that we wouldn't get her "A" race on Saturday at Chittenango. She takes very little at face value right now. In so many respects she's exactly what I strive to create in my classroom as I try to get kids to push and inquire, to question the authorities in their life. If those in power can't defend their position, I tell the kids to run like hell and get away from them. But sometimes I need the kids to trust, to listen, to be good followers. I've been trying to get the kids to stretch only after a practice or race. And I've been trying to wipe the pre-race spaghetti dinner off their schedule because I've grown convinced over the years that it overloads them with carbs and spikes their insulin levels. And sometimes I think the kids just expend too much energy the night before the performance at these team gatherings. For years I've noticed that we've been flatter at invitationals than we are in mid-week duals or workouts. Some of our state titles, cherished as they are, were an unpleasant experience because of sub-par performances. Those spaghetti dinners have messed up our rhythm, detoured our physiology and played havoc with our energy systems.

"So why did they work in the past and not for us," asked Hannah with a bit of disdain in her voice? I explained that we might have won but we weren't winning in a dominant fashion like we should.

"Well, I don't think you're right," she said with her head looking down at the track.

"You know," interrupted Sofie, "he's been trying to get this through our heads for three years now. Maybe we should begin to listen."

As Hannah was readying to expound once again I said forcefully but calmly, "Hannah, I'm trying to get you where you need to go. It's time to take my hand and let me pull you."

Hannah, not fully buying into the formula yet, took 5th in the meet and was only 37 seconds behind Katie Duerr of C-NS. I know she could have won the race. I have absolutely no doubt about her physical abilities. She started slowly, having fallen behind some of our JV-runners just 400-meters into the race. In an unusual format, each team could run 10 kids and the score would tally the top seven in an attempt to pull more kids into the results while letting coaches conduct a time trial to find their top seven. It wasn't until the final 1200-meters that Hannah got it rolling. She fears success and it's not all that uncommon these days. In order to take some stress off of her before the Chittenango race, I sent her an email.

> *Ok, here's the deal for tomorrow...easy stuff...the goal is to send a message to the other top individuals that they are going to have to deal with HANNAH this year if they want to get to the state meet...that doesn't mean you have to win or anything like that...it simply means that you're willing to fight, and the goal for Saturday is to put up a nice fight...all that entails is using the conditioning you've piled up over the summer and during Boot Camp...so, get a fight song going and carry it with you all morning tomorrow...just go in and do some battling with those C-NS girls who you proved you can run with while at Aim High...don't let them off the hook...YOU'RE FOR REAL HANNAH...enjoy it...so few runners can actually make a decision about how fast to run...most just pray that they can squeak by...the better ones, like you, have gears, willpower, experience, toughness and that simply means you can consciously DECIDE what you are going to go for on any given day...I've seen you go for it...remember the knee lift...'twas a thing of beauty it was...and I know you enjoyed it...so, show them you're ready to fight, show them the spunky knee lift, and show them that no matter the outcome, this is fun for you...coach*

We're making progress. Hannah feels the need to wade into this. She's running from the expectations that people have developed for her while seeking her own intrinsic motivations. She needs to feel her way into the thicket of competition this season. It's just the way it's going to be. Her e-mail back to me shows that I was right.

> *I've never thought about it that way...thinking that I'm lucky because I actually have a choice whether to run well...it's an odd concept but actually rather comforting knowing that I am making the decision to have a good race and not working as hard as I possibly can and just hoping to make it...and it also*

> *makes me more in control...the high knees are amazing and I
> love them...Hannah*

On Friday, Rachel Vaivoda announced that her hip hurt badly. I was beginning to believe that the team was either crumbling from the pressure or that this was just a way for them to blow off steam al-la Jon Riley talking about every little bodily sensation just minutes before every race. Complaints are a lot like cancer. Once it starts publicly, it spreads rapidly and can kill its host seemingly at will.

At the gun, Rachel took off and was our lead girl for most of the race until she was passed by the high knee-running Hannah down the stretch. But for Rach, taking 7th just 42 seconds behind the winner of the race was a great start to her senior season.

Calvin, our top frosh, ran well to take 14th in 14:25. The kid has talent but I still worry about him. After spending about two hours after Friday's pre-race practice picking up the girl's new uniforms, I stopped at the local Byrne Dairy in my wife's Honda Civic on my way home as my intrepid Toyota Echo got its water pump replaced, and there was Calvin dismounting from his bike. I walked up to him in the store and said that he was ready, told him that his training had really taken hold. As he left the store, I rapped him on the shoulder with the folded up NY Times and said that he shouldn't spend time riding his bike the day before the race. Once outside I saw his mom with her bike and mounted over the back wheel was a set of grocery baskets. They had ridden in from their West Lake Road home. Round trip we're talking about 10 miles. On little league game-day back in the early 60s, the coach prohibited swimming and other energy-sapping activities and we all faithfully obeyed. Times have changed. Calvin went out patiently and made a nice move mid-race at Chittenango. But he felt some fatigue over the final 800 and that fatigue's source might be the bike ride.

With his mother celebrating her 50th birthday, Dustin left a bit earlier from Friday's practice than the rest and headed to Watertown's Black River for white water rafting. Turning to no one in particular I mumbled that he'd be tighter than normal after falling into the water and sitting in funny positions while bouncing around in the rapids. And sure enough, Dustin, having probably the best race of his career, got so tight that his stride over the final mile couldn't have been more than two feet long. It's all correctible so I'm not too concerned.

There's so much to worry about and that feeling of total helplessness can sometimes sour a good day. At times I wish that I'd chosen another sport to fall in love with. I envy those coaches who have small, defined areas for practice where every member of the team is within hollering distance from me. I love watching the kids train but wouldn't it be nice to be able to watch every one of them for every moment of practice? I wish I had a custodial staff that would set up the course, staff the press box, do the scoring, the timing and the cleaning up. I love to coach but coaching cross country is much different and so labor-intensive. When we had our campus course it would take me two solid days to get the course lined, marked, and roped off. One day I arrived at Skaneateles from my teaching job at Jordan-Elbridge only to find that some lawn mower had taken every stake from the ground and laid them down. Mad? I went nuts.

We in the cross country coaching profession don't have time-outs to make adjustments. We can't substitute on a hunch. We can't pull a kid aside at the two-mile mark and make use of a teachable moment. We can't bench a starter and use him as a substitute. There's no matter of a technical nature to discuss with the kids once the race begins. We can't delve into mental meltdown matters or work on a tight hamstring once the race begins. I love sports where a coach can make a real difference mid-stream. We who coach cross country just don't have those luxuries. When the gun is shot into the air, the starter standing brave and solitary in the face of a long line of perhaps 250 runners with one thing on their mind—getting position—the coaches yield all control to the kids as we become little more than cheerleaders nervously scratching our asses and running around the course. Everything of importance must be done prior to the race. All instruction, all teaching, all the building-up of confidence, all the lessons about making adjustments, about expecting the unexpected, about positive self-talk, about working with teammates and packing it in against an opponent, must have been done prior to the meet. The lessons must have been internalized by each runner because once the race has begun the coaches are standing there shoulder to shoulder with every other spectator. We hope, we cheer, we implore, but mostly we run from spot to spot and lend verbal assurance to our warriors that they're okay.

On the bus ride home I talked with seniors Sofie and Hannah about having an out of body experience, about trying to place themselves a year down the road into their future. I wanted them to project themselves into the future and look back with more perspective than they have today while in the middle of this thing called high school running. From a distance, from a college dorm room a year from now, today's concerns and problems will seem minor or completely insignificant. The pressure they feel right now? A year from now these three seniors, Hannah, Rach and Sofie will look back and be kicking themselves if we don't get this done right this year. They'll see that feeling pressure at Chittenango—or anyplace else—was just their inner selves playing games with their confidence. They'll see that race days are just another day, a shorter day, an easier day than their toughest practice session. They'll see that we easily misconstrue simple truths while in the middle of living the event, that we miss the easy path too often when it's laid out right before us. In the middle of that big forest, all we need to do is look at one tree at a time. A year from now they'll understand that this is really quite simple. Just put one foot in front of the other until the chalk of the white finish line is crossed. With confidence, with trust, there is no fear. And with no fear, there's only success.

As Julie Lynch said in a note to the kids a few years ago,

> *There is nothing sweeter than crossing that finish line and knowing that you have laid everything out on the course and have united with your teammates in a tremendous effort to add your legacy to the Skaneateles Cross Country history and leave the battleground victorious. Do not deny yourselves the results that you have worked for. I can't believe how quickly the cross country season goes by. Have faith in your training, have faith in yourselves and have faith in your teammates. Trust that you can and will do whatever it takes to achieve that victory which is yours to claim. But above all else, let your heart do the running. When you step to that line, turn off your head and instead let your feet guide you and your heart propel you. Let everything go in that last mile. No thinking involved. No second-guessing. It's just time to fly. When you get to the starting*

line and sing, "We Feel Good," turn off all your thoughts and just go. Run for your teammates, yourselves, and for the glory and joy that comes from doing a job well. Have faith girls.

Lexie Mazzeo, brainy kid with a rare quality of true beauty, understands what's going on. She sees it like Julz.

Overall, I am not very happy with my race. I did a few things wrong but I think it's more productive to use this race and learn from it than to waste the experience in disappointment. I can't settle down like I did in this race. I think I could use my teammates more, whether it's hanging onto them or pulling them. I think I also worry too much about conserving so I won't die later in the race. I need to believe I can pass people. I think if I put in a surge here and there I could get around people. So, this was without question a learning race for me. I know I have a lot more than I showed today and I just have to think during every race, not after.

Numbers don't always tell the story, but we'll take these stats for the first meet on September 2nd. Only 1:03 separated our first girl, Hannah, from our fifth, Amanda whose dark eyes seemed sunken beneath her bushy eyebrows. And going back to 7th we only dropped off to a compression gap of 1:20 as the top five averaged 16:57.

The boy's pack time 1-5 was 1:42 with the top five averaging 14:48. No, we won't rip it up at the tradition-rich VanCortlandt Park course in the Bronx, but we're making progress as this team is proving itself to be different from last year. And that's a good thing.

For Rob Tuttle and me it was a relaxing meet with little running on the nice layout, little yelling, a nice canopy of trees to shelter us from the storm, and a conscious effort to downplay the meet. We shook off some rust, worked out some kinks and swiped away some cobwebs that had collected over the rainy summer. Onward and upward, always forward. School begins in four days, and then it's down Interstate 81 to Binghamton where we'll connect with New York Route 17 East to Windsor for our first Southern Tier appearance of the year on Saturday. Returning from Europe will be Karen, and if she returns with her summer game in tow, we'll add to our arsenal.

We didn't find a superstar in the making at Chittenango like we did in 1994 when Taylor Strodel, just a gangly rookie, won her first race, the Auburn Invitational. The staff and I were behind Cayuga Community College at the transition point where the Nature Trail, covered in cushioning cinders, meets the open field behind venerable Holland Stadium which serves as the home field for the Maroon's football team. Looking up the cinder path we noticed that the leader was a Skaneateles girl. "Who the hell is that?" I asked while narrowing my eyes for a better look. I turned my head left and right. No one knew her. As she got closer I remember saying, "Isn't that the new Strodel girl?" And sure enough, the girl who had shown absolutely nothing in practice was on her way to winning the very first race she ever ran. We didn't find anyone like that at Chittenango, but we found a girl's team that works hard and seems capable of grabbing the golden ring that hangs within reach. And we found a boy's team that could very well turn the corner and be competitive.

The rain soaked everyone and with the whole overheated crew on the bus waiting for me to return with the official results, the windows steamed up white like a cataract cloud turning clear eyesight into a foggy haze. Gary Martin, back with us once again after spending most of his summer on the shores of Lake Ontario near his hometown of Watertown, apologized for having to make us wait for five minutes while the windshield cleared up enough for us to leave the Land of Oz and return to Skaneateles.

With the side windows still foggy enough on our trip home for the kids to finger paint on, Sofie became a bit queasy and came up to the front seat with me. In short order she felt strong again and then it was Hannah's turn to come forward. Curling up on the front seat with her head in Sofie's lap while wearing some God-awful socks and wrapped in her special blanket, we threw the bull and commiserated as once again the bus ride turned magical, the yellow steel vehicle turning into a wondrous pumpkin in fantasy land where fairy tales come true and human foibles fall prey to all the glorious dreams of the greatest dreamers the world ever saw.

We opened the season in L. Frank Baum's world where umbrellas sprouted like trees, where rain flowed off skin like money flows through the hands of an inveterate gambler. It wasn't a win today, but it was definitely a victory.

Labor Day

The lake is different now. At night in early September the black silhouette of the broad willow reflects off the silvery surface of a quiet lake, the tree's shadow oscillating black on silver as it inevitably meets the tar pitch ebony farther off-shore and disappears into its watery infinity. Standing on the end of the dock I mourn the passing of summer and reluctantly honor the coming autumn.

A lone boat motors north to the village as the night's total silence is broken, the waves lapping at the shoreline's velvety smooth stones far longer than logic would expect from a single slow-moving runabout. The Texas family, in the house south of the dock, walks behind closed blinds, their darkened images moving from room to room like mimes silently fighting to get out of an invisible box. Lights flicker on the eastern shore as the first falling of leaves begins. The air, still humid, carries hints of change and even the passing of cars high above the shoreline has diminished noticeably.

The jovial, jocular summer months are about to change as the kids regain focus, purpose and spend time at night doing homework instead of dreaming, socializing, or smiling while life seems endless and beautiful with warm air wafting through their lives. Even walking will take on a different demeanor for the kids as short, sprightly steps taken with a bounce during the vacation months will become stilted, pedantic and louder as shoes slap against hallway floors, the laces untied, the stride sloppy, the shoulders stooped, the eyes drooping Beagle-like from lack of sleep—the smiles turned to frowns for many—as kids go from class to tests ad infinitum, their day dreary, seemingly purposeless and with no evident goal in sight.

But with the final bell reverberating against the tiled, sterile interior school walls, my runners will grow excited and begin to talk in various pitches of maturity as enthusiasm replaces the silence that students are conditioned to embrace in school. Silence, closed mouths, an absence of social intercourse. It all seems so out of place in this age when communication comes in so many different and invigorating forms.

On Labor Day, the village celebrates its rebirth as we release the vacationing public and seize control of our streets, our stores, our freedom to move easily from here to there. On Labor Day weekend we begin our celebration with the Skinny Man Triathlon on Saturday morning as the village is overtaken by hundreds of men and women who seek the ultimate multi-faceted test of endurance. On Sunday we take our largest boat, the Judge Ben Wiles, south a mile from the village landing and let the paying participants jump into the water for a mile swim to shore as an army of kayaks accompanies them on their test of endurance. On Monday we host a five-mile run, the runners leading the annual Labor Day parade through the village streets toward the finish in front of the Sherwood Inn, an authentic lodge like you'd see in Little York, Maine along the Atlantic Coast.

With so many people helping to support high school sports, it's important for us to give something back, so about a dozen kids from the Skaneateles team volunteer to help those great community people who put on the Labor Day event, some of the volunteers working until 10 PM on Friday night and coming back to duty at 3 AM to get the biking course set up along our lakeshore and country roads.

After the race, most of the people head to Austin Park for the last of two days of our Fireman's Fair, an annual fundraiser for the department. With sausage simmering, beer flowing, and live music playing under the rusting steel of the pavilion, the community lets its hair down for the final time of the calendar year. Economic and social classes mix without a hitch. Young and old mingle together. And after the half hour fireworks display explodes above the little village while sending shockwaves south down the lake, we all go home somewhat deflated, cognizant of seven or eight months of dreary weather and endless work separating us from another summer of enchantment and fun in upstate New York.

Things are about to change: It's in the wind, it shows in the sky, you can smell it in the air as fall, aged manure, the fresh harvest and a cooling of the atmosphere all mingle together to tingle the olfactory nerves. Football takes on a disproportionate life and I'm spiritually drawn to college campuses with their brick pathways meandering between tall maple trees with young men and women-of-purpose heading from dorms to classroom buildings with dreams to fulfill, with young men and women running together as the maples surround them with the vibrant colors of autumn that can only be seen in all their special beauty in the northeast. I hear the sounds of marching bands in my head as I stand on the end of the dock where nothing but silence fills my ears.

And in the middle of all this melancholy I feel a need to carry my kids on my back to something greater than they've ever been a part of, something that will transcend the different stages of their lives, that will draw them back even in old age, that will pop up in their minds on a solitary drive home from work when they're in their forty's or fifty's, that will fill their discussion at their ten year reunion and somehow still be relevant at their fiftieth reunion when, nearing their 70s, it will still be relevant, still fulfilling, still important, still a part of their lives and their identity.

Time is fleeting but these kids don't understand that yet, and who could expect them to be cognizant or aware of the impermanence of life, the fleeting nature of our very existence on earth. It's my job to get them to do the things that, many decades from now, they'll be able to clearly see, be able to understand and fully appreciate. For some unexplainable reason, what we do in our teens has an imprint that lasts a lifetime. And I want that imprint to be impermeable, unforgettable and a memory that will soothe these kids even on the darkest day of old age when death is the next and last companion to enter the room.

Sojourn to the Southern Tier

Gary Martin's bus darted in and out of dark tunnels of fog interspersed with crystal clear expanses full of foliage that was fading from green to earth tones as the three senior leaders of the girl's team curled up on the dark green, sticky plastic bus seats and slept under their favorite blankets. Summer was fading as we drove south on Interstate 81 to the 47th Annual Windsor Invitational. The action was heating up from Buffalo to Long Island on this second Saturday of September, and most New Yorkers considered it the official opening day of the season. Other than those three sleeping girls, the bus was as lively as a popular bar in Syracuse's Armory Square during Happy Hour. Clear blue skies provided a pastel backdrop for the rising sun that climbed up and over the deer-filled eastern hills that accompany the interstate on its trip south.

The drive was placid like the waters on East Lake Road as we left Skaneateles. While chugging south along the lake, everything was routine until we saw a green John Deere tractor coming at us with a bucket on the front. Not quite powerful enough to be a front-end loader and not technically designed to be a field-plow tractor, it carried an upside down and hogtied cow, each pair of legs twisted, roped, and attached to the raised bucket. The weighty tan and white carcass swayed as the tractor sped to some off-road pick-up point where a dog food courier would load it for processing. The sight struck us all awkwardly. The only meat we're conditioned to see is red, trimmed and snug inside clear cling-wrap and piled high in the meat market of the local grocery store and ready to toss on the grill. This wasn't neat. It wasn't alive. And it wasn't my Sunday steak.

Arriving with some swagger at this intersectional kickoff meet, we settled into the baseball dugout on the first base side of the field midpoint between the starting line and the finish chute. It was hard to tell where we were. There was just too much fog. As we each entered into a wake-up-and-get-ready hustle after finishing the bus ride that began at 6:45 AM in front of the Skaneateles water tower, the thick Windsor fog slowly lifted as a natural wonder begrudgingly emerged, much like someone scratching off a winning number on a lotto ticket or a large-breasted woman at a Detroit car show seductively pulling a sheet from atop a new sports car model. There before us appeared a scene like you'd see in the rarified altitude of the Swiss Alps. A mountain stood before us with rock formations and flowing fields of grass. The scene was in complete harmony much like the sea and the shore, the young and the beautiful, or baseball's Tinker to Evers to Chance. Bold, strong and lush, stark in its greenness next to the whitish-gray of the fog, the mountain that once lay hidden behind the fog bank rose from the plain of the race course with utter magnificence. Standing in the foreground of the earthly geologic protrusion, we counted ourselves lucky to have been witness to its morning unveiling.

Other things were revealed to us at Windsor. Hannah, who was targeted by the prognosticators as a sure-fire leader in the local running scene, apparently didn't run much the previous summer at her camp on Lake George. She missed out on her opportunity to stand out from the crowd. Still out of shape, she was struggling and trying to convince herself that it wasn't a big deal. At a critical juncture of her career, with her team expecting her to be assertive, to be a leader by example, Hannah switched course, ignored destiny and mostly shut it down for two months. Twelve straight seasons can do that to a kid as the weight of expectations grows heavy. In her mind, the easiest way to deal with expectations was to engage in a policy of self-sabotage. Wandering around in the athletic and cerebral wilderness, I have to find a way to pull Hannah back to the running path, a path not as well-worn as the one that leads to the pop-culture world of mediocrity and failure. I don't want her to be merely normal. She's too good for that. After all this work, she deserves more.

Earlier in the week, Rob and I were sitting side by side, riding around the Skaneateles countryside driving past split rail fences and thick hedge rows that remind me of the lush green football field perimeter inside Tubby Raymond Football Stadium on the University of Delaware campus. We drove past horse stables that are kept neater than a lot of restaurants in the country, whizzed past bikers with the fanny pant-seats that look to me like the butt of a baboon, and joggers of all shapes and sizes. We rode up hills and along lake view overlooks that provide a million dollar panorama of our glistening glacial lake. The community was abuzz on Labor Day ought-six. And just when we were feeling comfortable that everyone was running well, we looked down the road at Sam, who once had an insurmountable lead over everyone. Gliding effortlessly along the road's shoulders, Rob and I were thinking that this boy's team was about to assert itself.

"Are these guys catching Sam? Hell, Hannah's closing in, Rob." I was exasperated but I figured that Sam just grew bored of running by himself. Pushing alone day after day is a daunting mental game and not everyone can master the art of self-flogging. As Rob and I drove down Andrews Road past the Polo Grounds with turf neat, thick, and trim like a putting green, we could look ahead and see the Country Club where President Clinton had played a round of golf just three days earlier without photo-journalists snapping every movement.

"Sam, ya okay man?"

Grabbing his right side he winced and said, "I think it's a cramp or something."

"No problem," I yelled from my open car window. "Just drop and roll up ahead on that grassy patch."

And off we drove down West Lake Street past all the mansions that I'll never get to see from the inside. I don't mix in those social circles and when I'm around the high and mighty, I just don't feel comfortable. They're not my people. I'm the running version of a gym-rat. I'm pretty basic.

The Labor Day 8 AM practice session had gone well, overall, and we totaled seven-point-five miles. Jeff was ready to come up big in the near future, I thought. His footwork is quick, light, and his knee lift and heel kick is so much better than during the summer. Right with him is Matt. He's getting tougher and more confident. We just need to keep his sore knees from pushing him to the bench. It appears that his family has a genetic knee problem.

Dustin and Dan are good but by the end of the week the crew-cut Dan would be gassed, running on empty and looking like a street car without desire and rumbling around a go-cart course after having been in a demolition derby. During his 5-mile run later in the week, every kid who passed me as I stood on the corner of East Street and Onondaga said that Dan was having problems. Much later we saw Dan far down the road. Slowly and painfully, Dan made his way back to the school. Some of the girls had passed him with a mixture of concern and joy for having beaten one of the scoring boys. After pulling Dan aside within 400-meters of the finish, we found out that all the problems were easily correctible: he was dehydrated. He wasn't eating breakfast, and he wasn't eating dinner until nearly three hours after the end of our afternoon practice sessions. We're doing just over 30 miles a week, which is nothing like the Long March the Communist Chinese undertook as they hightailed it away from the U.S. supported Kuomintang, the retreat covering nearly 5000 miles in just over a year. But 30 miles is plenty when someone like Dan is going through a divorce and is in the midst of a growth spurt. He needs food.

I told Dan that he'd gone and done it right the previous week at Chittenango. He'd showed me that he was a runner, a competitive soul who the team was now counting on. So there was no turning back and he'd have to begin paying attention to all the little details. It's the little things that seemingly have nothing to do with running that dictate the course of a runner's career. It's the tightening of the screws, the sanding of the plasterboard, checking for spelling errors in your thesis, zipping your pants before going out. Dan has to be diligent from now on.

"Dan, your kitchen might not be finished, but that's no excuse. You need to get with mom and talk this out. Just walk over to the P&C and grab a few boxes of nutrition bars of some sort and eat a few for breakfast and one right after we finish running. That'll hold you." We can fix Dan, and that's a good thing because he'll be our fifth man at Windsor. But we can't fix Sam.

"I'm sorry, Jack," said Ben, Sam's dad, as we both stood in the hallway outside Rob's engineering classroom a day later. "He's worked so hard, and now this."

Sam's cramps weren't cramps. And they got worse, feeling much like labor cramps on Labor Day. He grew pale as the Labor Day 5-mile race passed the water table that he and his teammates manned in front of Matt's house near where a local kid died by driving his car into a mammoth tree that his friends cut down the next day. Later in the afternoon as they played Ultimate Frisbee, Sam's complexion was more death than life. Finally, Sam told his dad about something that guys never even bring up jokingly with other guys. The pain was in his scrotum. His balls finally busted. Hours later, Sam was in the emergency room. He was going under the knife to untwist his balls.

Sam's out of the line-up but he'll live. He's cured. And he'll have all the body parts for the rest of his life. But it was close, as he was within just a few hours of undergoing an amputation. A team that showed so much promise was now likely to get drilled. We're just not deep enough to compensate for Sam's loss.

Unfortunately we were traveling out of our section and this could doom our goal of achieving a state ranking this year. Strong teams tend to be ranked longer than they deserve, even as they dive like a hawk that's got a rodent in its crosshairs, their reputation serving to protect them and insulate them from a reality check. The up-and-coming teams don't have any gravitas and little street credibility, so the only way they can make it into the rankings is to be 'on' week after week until it's virtually impossible to ignore them. Duke's the same way in the NCAA basketball rankings. No one can blame anyone. It's just the nature of the beast, even with the internet sites proliferating. The rankers are human. They work all week. They train their own teams. They teach. Time is short and they do what they can. Some coaches will pester the hell out of the rankers but I won't. It's not in my nature. I hope people feel we deserve to be ranked but I'm leaving them alone to make that important decision. I'm not big into lobbying. It didn't do Congress—or us—any good. Over the decades, I've rarely been disappointed with the rankings of my teams.

This first week of school presents challenges. It always does. I always hold our hard quality session for the week the day before classes start, and then we relax a bit, go easy, toss in a few 200s and 100s and get some turnover for the legs. And then we go home. There's enough stress for the kids in school as they say good-bye to their summer on the lake. I feel that I have no right to add to the level of stress hormones flooding through their brain and body. Some teachers really over-do it that first week and some seem to relish hammering the kids into abject submission. Anything to feel powerful and superior.

On Thursday before Windsor we got 'thundered-out' by a storm that never quite materialized. We don't mess with thunder or lightning. It's killed people here. Our golf course is wired so that a siren blares if the conditions are ripe for lightning. So we called off the practice. Sometimes it's these unexpected changes in the schedule, dictated by the powerful natural forces all around us, that gives our kids an energy-boost much like a snow day in the winter. They aren't the sort of athletes who hate running, who despise practice, who, day by day, lay slashes on the calendar. They want to be here. It's something that defines them, has molded them, guided them and invigorated their lives. But it's a strenuous sport and an unexpected day off can be a good thing.

We're giving the boys off Friday, but letting Dustin and Dan run around until they feel loose and ready to go. They both understand their enhanced role at Windsor without Sam in the line-up.

The girls, along with most of the boys, have been asked to run 50 minutes on Sunday following the invitational. We can't ask them to meet us for a practice, ever since the new superintendent set up office in the trailers that serve as our district office.

As the first day of school approached, the school custodians could relax after doing their thing. The building's immaculate. And I gave the kids some advice on a few issues as we met under the pine trees on their last day of summer.

"Get to bed. This night (Labor Day) is not your last night to stay up late. It's the first night of your school year. It's the first night to act responsibly. It's the first link in the chain that will form a sensible sleeping pattern that leads to success."

Trying to look each and every one of them in the eye, I said, "If you find yourself staying up late doing your advanced placement homework, one of two things is occurring. Either you're wasting time or you're over-matched. Get together with mom and dad and figure out a solution. This is high school. It isn't that whacked-out tough. So if you're staying up past 10 PM cramming or doing homework or reading, something is wrong and it needs to be fixed. Don't pretend to be someone you aren't. Accept who you are. Fight the good fight but keep yourself from leaning against windmills that are more powerful than you. There's a home football game Friday night against Marcellus, so stay home. There are plenty of games for you to see, but this isn't one of them. Standing around is no good and you know that the crowd will be huge. You'll have dead legs for the race. If you sit in the student section you'll get all riled up and you won't be able to get to sleep when you get home. Remember the bus is leaving around 6:45 AM. That's early."

Based on what I'm seeing this week, my gut tells me that Kristin will have a big race. Same with Lexie Mazzeo. I think that Bea Walton, without the stress of a varsity race, has a chance to run better as she takes small steps in the right direction. She's started speaking about herself in the third person. I've decided to play along and encourage it, thinking that it might reduce some of the angst that she's running with. She's a fighter.

I sit here at home watching Boise State run all over Oregon State's football team on that god-awful blue grass out west. What were they thinking? The windows are open and insects are providing incessant background music. A full orange moon has risen from across the lake, soon to be white as it rises high over my house, and soon to be gone as the cycle begins anew. It's coal black out there despite the moon, the smells of autumn beginning to replace summery romance, flowery sweetness and soft, wispy winds from the south. The gaps of deep darkness are lengthening between the camps on the eastern shoreline as summer residents return home where responsibilities and obligations await. We're alone with our full-time residents, our friends. Life slows down. We have each other, our little community with everyone looking out for each other. The crowds outside on the sidewalk in front of Morris' Grill are all local faces again, reddened from smoking, bloated from drinking too much, hardened by their daily physical labor. The people walking along the sidewalks to the football games are all familiar.

The kids seem ready for Windsor and we're all alone together as the sporting world and local media focus on other sports. We're ready to give it everything. I can feel it. And giving everything for our girls means pissing in our bun huggers. It's what we do. It's a rite of passage. It's a signal to teammates that we're going to lay it on the line every race

221

from now on. It's not something that the girls shy from acknowledging. It's a point of pride.

Each of these kids is in the firm grasp of an idyllic childhood in a resort town that caters to the rich and famous. We want for nothing. That 6 AM alarm is going to sound and awaken us to the reality of a two hour bus ride to a place called Windsor, just north of the Pennsylvania border. We're all raring to go. The expectations are more understood, more internalized now. The sacrifice is good for these kids-of-privilege. Raring to go, eager to win t-shirts, excited about testing ourselves once again with a race already under our belts, we're ready to go, all except Sam, who is healing.

We swept into foreign territory and staked a claim for the rulers from Skaneateles. In conditions akin to a redwood-paneled sauna, the kids ran their hearts out with Matt losing consciousness intermittently over the final hilly mile. The course was slow, with its thick, long grass, its mountain-goat climbs up the wooded hill and its uphill finish. Rachel Vaivoda thrived on the hills and even though others complained, the hills continued to be our friend. We don't do a lick of dedicated hill training. Turnover running, speed training, endurance running on all terrains all combine to make runners good hill climbers.

The girls beat back a field of good teams. Johnson City's Paige Mullins took home the top prize and broke 20 minutes, which I didn't think anyone could do. I like her game. She doesn't consult with the negative voices in her head. She just runs and the game she plays is, "Catch Me If You Can." I'm sure she considers a few of the athletes who are in her race when she's pacing the starting line like a panther-in-heat awaiting the starter's commands. But she knows her capabilities, she trusts her training and she just runs. Our winning low score of 46 edged Johnson City's 67 and Vestal's 75 points in the sixteen-team field. JC and the Golden Bears of Vestal are much larger schools. I'm sure they aren't happy about us. The seniors, the Brat-Pack, again led us and this is not what I expected after two consecutive years of underperforming. Rachel was 5th, Hannah was a second behind in 6th with Sofie in 10th as the additional mileage continues to work its magic on her. Amanda was energized as she was next in 12th and the scoring ended with 13th place Kristin Roberts, who was just 42 seconds from Rachel, our leader. As the race progressed I could see that we were running well. I don't need to compare us to any other teams. I don't need to see the times after the race. I can see, feel and sense when we're good, bad or lackluster. I don't need anyone else to tell me. Instinct is my guide, my foghorn leading me through the haze and the thicket of tortuous information. Tullyrunners.com lambasted us in the speed ratings for the meet, but I know what I saw. We did well. Johnson City will eventually be duly recognized by the state rankers. They're good.

Without Sam, the boys placed 5th and everything they did was positive. Host Windsor, led by seniors, tallied 48 while Vestal totaled 80, Horseheads scored 85, and my alma mater, Chenango Valley, finished with 116. We scored 121.

Sam is walking around like a cowboy who has been in the saddle too long. He's tentative, afraid and acting like a tenderfoot. With Sam we would have finished as a top three team against large schools from the Southern Tier.

Without Sam, frosh Calvin Davis led us in 13th. He was the second frosh to finish. Matt, dizzy, fading from consciousness, took 17th while Jeff nailed 21st place. Dustin took 33rd with legs cramped from the heat, and Dan, nourished for the past two days, took 34th and continues to break down preconceived limitations. Taking 5th place was a victory for us, another step in the right direction.

Beatrice was relegated to her first junior varsity race and she survived. She took 7th, trailing sprinter Carley Billick who took 5th. Bea, bright, Type "A" and too hard on herself, seems to be taking some positive strides. "The only way I'll ever get back to varsity is by taking small steps to improve my racing. Today, I feel like I conquered my mind, but I raced probably way too conservatively because I had more that I could've given on the home stretch at the end. Sometime soon I'm just going to have to prove it. Physically I have so much more." Bea is still fighting to run clear of the fog that enshrouds her. With a clear vision inside her head of what she wants to achieve, she needs to listen to the foghorn and follow its mournful clarion call to the clearing, to the safety of the harbor, past the rocky shoreline and into the grassy flat that leads to home.

Tay Tay pissed her pants. She's one of the girls now.

Looking back at the 'first' day of the season with reports flooding the internet, some suspicions have been confirmed. Sauquoit Valley and Samantha Steadman, defending team and individual champs respectively, who were racing at the twisting and turning Vernon-Verona-Sherrill course in the shadow of the Turning Stone Casino, appear to have washed over the dam after a summer of lethargy. CBA is strong at the top and thin as a wafer thereafter. Canastota is alarmingly awful right now. The Jordan-Elbridge girls could provide a stern test after their showing at Oswego on the shores of Lake Ontario.

The boy's sectional championship race will be won by Tully. Sauquoit looked weak. League rivals Marcellus and Westhill move up to the Class B division for the sectional championship. In my dreams these Skaneateles Laker boys could, after the debacle of 2005, shoot for a top-5 finish at Sectionals. And then, next year, who knows. We just might be back after an unusual year where our boys weren't competitive. Like a phoenix, we're slowly on the rise, maybe.

Hannah 'Banana'

Sweating and panting, the girls stand around me after another run, looking to me for affirmation. They get it. They deserve it. Sam has gotten off his horse and is running with straight legs once again. In his first run since his injury ten days ago on Labor Day, he met up with Pete Davis, who was running home from work at Welch-Allyn. Suddenly Sam realized that they were clipping along at a nice pace. Surprised at both being pain free and running fast again, he just veered off when Pete headed down the west side of the lake and finished his 40 minute run with buoyant spirits.

Once I was home and beginning to get comfortable with the thought that we we're making progress, my computer screen filled up with ten words from Hannah; "Uhhhh, why can't I like running like I used to!?!?"

Nothing has changed for Hannah, yet everything has changed. She acts sullen, her face showing puffiness around her eyes and cheeks. She has only 50 days left to discover what it was about running that drew her to it in the first place as a punk kid. She needs to break out of her self-imposed imprisonment. She needs to relax, enjoy life, to remind herself that this isn't her entire life. Running used to be an outlet for her creativity and it was a time of the day to connect to her core values. Lately she's been on a roller-coaster, feeling connected to us one day and feeling distant the next, complaining of pain one day and seemingly pain-free the next. Sensing this, a few days ago I yelled to a laughing Sofie while she was running with Hannah, and jokingly told her to slap Hannah on the side of the head if she began to have fun on the run.

225

Hannah is looking like someone who is doing the waltz when she needs to shake and bake, do the Peppermint Twist or the Jitterbug, and get funky like the old Hannah.

Week-two of the competitive schedule is in the books as a general feeling of accomplishment has been attained. The boys are nearly whole again and Dustin will begin using his new inhaler in practice. He's redeveloped exercise-induced asthma. Matt's knee is holding up and he seems to be getting a little tougher to boot. I keep suggesting to the kids that when they start to get nicked up, they need to treat it all season. When I asked Matt if he was doing stretches and taking Advil, he responded that they were out. Matt's dad is a doctor. Rob and I got a good laugh from that one.

The girls look to be virtually interchangeable. They're looking quick and strong to me, and I trust my instincts. No one seems to smell success but me. Our collective confidence is growing and I think we're ready to get on a roll. Rob and I are a bit worried that the girls aren't developing any chemistry. The seniors can be found arriving for practice later than everyone else as they saunter to our pine tree meeting place and sometimes they arrive with a bit of arrogance. And at times they remove themselves completely from the team's presence. When Coach Julie approached them one Saturday and suggested that, as team leaders, they should actually be with their teammates, one of them mouthed the forbidden: "We don't actually like them." Quickly reacting to Julie's face as her eyebrows arched skyward, the statement was extended by saying, "Oh, you didn't believe that, did you? We're just kidding." Veteran seniors are expected to lead. Read any newspaper account of a college football team and you'll hear the same old refrain, "We're seniors, this is what we wait for. It's our team now."

Adam Evans, a Skaneateles alum who is at Bentley College in Boston running for Ed Lyons, spent his summer running with teammates, writing e-mails, calling members of his team. We aren't seeing enough of that here and the season is well underway. Chemistry taught me that chemical reactions, Petri dish cultures and experiments of all sorts take time and the patience of a saint. Perhaps the chemistry of this team will just have to take its own sweet time to grow. Patience, Jack, patience I tell myself.

As we experience more success in races and practice sessions, each member of the team is feeling something, and I think it's a sign of some maturity. What we're all feeling isn't at all like the rush of the tide coming in. It's more like the calm that's left after the high tide has been receding for three or four hours. It's a good feeling and speaks well of a team that understands that the early meets are but a prelude, a personal audition for the real show eight weeks hence; the Sectional championship at Long Branch Park. There seems to be a subdued tone caressing the team as it waits patiently, bides its time, works hard and goes about life.

We finally found a hand-drawn map of the Long Branch sectional course and Rob has converted an out of scale 1960-ish course map into a digitized scaled map of the course. We'll be ready.

But we have a bridge to cross. It's disheartening to have so many kids reaching deep inside as they stretch themselves in order to improve, and then to have Hannah struggle mightily to smile and put one foot in front of the other. She has so much ability. The team is doing everything within its power to attain success. It's hard not to notice that some of the hardest-working kids are the ones lacking in one or more of the skills or the natural genetic blessings that serve to produce a great runner. It's heartening to see kids make progress, to improve from last year, but it hurts that one of the gifted ones with vast experience isn't able to carry her fair share of the load right now. She has me shaking my head more and more as I feel increasingly more powerless. She appears on most days to be going through the motions with a frayed psyche. I'm just not confident that I can help extricate her from the spider web that's ensnared her.

Noticing that Hannah hasn't been Hannah isn't something that only a veteran coach could decipher. Tiny, seemingly unrelated bits of information accumulate between coach and runner with the passing of days, weeks, months and years as a knowledge base is developed. Sometimes the pieces fall together and we reach critical mass as we bear witness to 'overnight' growth or a disastrous and sudden meltdown. It's the latter that concerns me. It's there in Hannah's eyes as less light is allowed to enter her being, and blank, hollow eyes stare too often outward toward a world that has grown less comforting, less hospitable, less fun. It shows in the way her facial skin seems cosmetic, plastic, a façade that somehow provides shelter and sanctuary from the world. Hannah has grown up a lot while I've watched these past four years. From an innocent little girl she's grown into a performer, a singer who writes and performs with big Linus Walton, the sectional discus champ. Neither has any fear of the stage.

As she seems to fade right before my eyes, it's the absence of her laugh that's more noticeable than anything else. It's been missing and it's as distinctive as Howard Cosell's nasal voice as he enunciated each syllable of every 5 dollar word on ABC's Monday Night Football, or John Madden's corny euphemisms that seem to clarify everything in the plainest of terms. The laugh is Hannah, it's the barometer that releases her from high pressure and moderates her emotions. It defines her exuberance, her bounce, her whimsy, that special innocence and altruistic outlook on life. The laugh can be seen in her eyes which are usually wide open and in search of the next great thing to do as she pirouettes 180 degrees and goes off with her knees knocking and her feet flailing like propeller blades, not behind her but out to her side; not exactly what you desire from a runner. It's those legs that have been causing her problems. Hannah is mechanically a mess and it's started to cause problems with her Ilio-tibial band. Hannah's is irritated and we need to find the exact cause, perhaps in this case a misaligned pelvis. I wrote Hannah an e-mail that spoke of my concern for her IT band. But that wasn't why I was writing. I needed to get her to open up, to coax her from her burrow.

> *hey, Hannah…are you still doing those exercises that the physical therapist gave you a year or two ago? your mechanics are slipping and I think that's why your IT band fascia is hurting….you're not running the same as you were last spring (mechanically) ….I've been looking at pics of you and it's obvious that things have changed which means, I think, that you're out of muscle balance again….I'd start doing those things and I'd keep doing them or I fear you'll seize up…be careful about this…I'm also moving you back up to the paces you should be hitting by now…. you may find yourself training more individually, too….you need it…we need to get the old Hannah back…she's missing in action and has been missing since the second day of Boot Camp….I'm not going to be a sissy toward you 'Banana'….*

you and I have only 53 total days between now and the end of our mutual cross country 'affair'...we don't EVER get to do this again....last chance to get it right....last April you were on the cusp of high school greatness....you were on your way to being a Laker Legend...I'm not sure what's happened over the summer but I suspect you didn't get the training you needed and I think you're still a bit out of shape....I'm not ready to give up...you're still doing fine....but you and I both know that we're not racing and training and acting like Hannah-the-madcap-competitor....I still want to get 'there' with you so if that's no longer your goal, you need to tell me so I can back off....I'll go as far in this running game as you want....I don't want to try to pull you to a place that you no longer want to go to....so, get back to those exercises and let's get you physically healthy again....coach

Hannah's response is telling, and it's as much information as a child psychologist could get from a kid in a year of intimate sessions.

well...it is true that I'm not the same as I was at the end of last season, but I think that it's been hard for me. I think that track is good for me because every time I get on the line it's me and only me, meaning that I don't have other teammates to gauge myself against, ie: I've always run with Rachel in cross country so when I am in a race with Rachel I run with Rachel, but in track I always run races by myself, so I run with myself. After last track season I kinda lost a little of my love for running, I'm not really sure why but I think it was just because I had accomplished really what I had set out to accomplish as a high school runner; have a really great season and make States. So I was just like, all right, I've done what I'm gonna do, what is there to look forward to now? And I know that is a horrible attitude because I still have three more seasons and with the proper training I could get a lot better, but I just kinda fell into a "I'm happy with where I have been so what is there to look forward to now?" attitude. And I know that you're probably not gonna be happy with me for saying this, but I'm only saying this in hopes that you can say things to me that will convince me that I do have more places to go and more things to accomplish in running, and I know that I am still a little out of shape. I didn't do the best job running this summer and I'm only telling you this so that you can help me get into shape when it counts. And I know you're not happy with me for not putting in the most amount of effort I could, but I need to look forward at what I can do to make it work from where I am right now. I just need to have one really great race, where I prove to myself that it means something to me, because I know, and you know that I am a much better runner than anything I've ever done. I've never really been as good as I could be, but as of right now it's not the same mental block I've struggled with in the past, it's a "do I really love running enough to wanna put in the time and effort it takes?, or would I rather just do a half-ass job, not work as hard, and still be all right?" And I know that it will be a happier year and our team will do much better if I do go to the extra mile, and I think that I feel more like that now than I did two weeks ago, but I'm just now getting back into the "I like running and I wanna be trying and doing well" feeling, whereas in past years, I've been like that right from the start. I think that I still need some base work, some time for me to realize again that I want this. I want to win sectionals, I want to win all the dual meets, I want to be beating Rachel, I know that sounds horrible but I know that I should be so it's something I gauge on even if that's a bad thing. And I want to want to run again, and I want to want to race hard, and I think that part of my attitude is coming from the fact that I'm not in the best shape I could be, or should be, but that's something that is fixable. I think that it's unfortunate that I had to have this relapse after having a great, successful outdoor season that made me think I'd accomplished everything I wanted to, but I think that is also good for me to realize this and to work toward getting back the swagger that I want, and the will to be really good, and have people worry about seeing me on the line. Well that was an insane email, and I probably just told you more things that will make you mad than happy, but I feel like not telling you things is not the

*way for you to help me, and even if they will make you upset,
I'd rather have you know so that you can make the proper steps
to help me want to run again, and want to race again, and
want to be competitive again....let's try to get this sorted out is
all I'm saying...Hannah*

That was intense for me to read, and I had to read it several times
to really understand it. But in the re-reading I found Hannah. She's in
there. All I have to do is figure out which buttons to push and in what
sequence and she'll be okay by the championship. My fear is that if she
isn't on her game soon enough that either Jordan-Elbridge or CBA will
end our dual meet win streak. If Hannah isn't right, CBA could go 1-2-3
on us and we'd take the next seven places—and lose. Jordan-Elbridge is
a greater threat to beat us at Sectionals if they don't fall apart, but CBA
is the immediate threat, the dual threat. We don't have much time to
get Hannah going again. And then the pressure is just going to grow
exponentially.

The lucky athlete is the one who can retire on his own terms as
instinct tells him that his time has come and gone while he cognitively
recognizes the birth of a new passion that is directing him to new
challenges. With George Washington, it was the return to a Mount
Vernon that was falling apart. Thomas Jefferson, when leaving the
presidency, felt like he was leaving prison and couldn't wait to get back
to his beloved Monticello to study Greek literature. Resigned to his
realities, the lucky athlete calls it quits while feeling freer and more
excited than he has in years. The unluckiest athlete of all is the one who
is forced to quit because of injury while the passion still burns fiercely.
Some just lose the love for the game. Hannah has lost the passion.
I've seen this before back in high school and college with friends who
played football. Even with a winning season the routine got tiresome,
and with more than a few weeks left to go they began counting down
the days until they regained their freedom. Hannah's counting days
way too soon.

*very interesting banana....it's what I expected and what I
suspected....being the big girl on the team is very different than
just following the leaders and absorbing their goals.... after I
saw how poorly Samantha Stedman ran yesterday I thought*

that with a normal summer from you that this would be your game, but you said it right....we have to go forward from here.... my suggestion is this....life isn't real flexible...you need to be ready and prepared to take advantage of a competitor when they slip because you know that everyone out there is waiting to take advantage of Hannah if and when she slips...Minale from CBA for instance...you know that you're in her crosshairs...so, our goal is to make sure that you get back to the top, get that internal drummer hammering nice and hard....there's still time and we'll get the base up for you this week....but I'm concerned about your ability to take this....as I mentioned, your mechanics have devolved dangerously....if you're not careful... very careful...you could cripple up real bad....you need to want this enough to stretch, to do your drills and exercises like you used to.....becoming an adult means accepting responsibility.... other people are counting on you and I know that's not what you want to hear....your teammates are busting their humps and it's harder for them to be good than it is for you...it's more painful for them than it is for you....you've been blessed more than them.... I see it on your face and it looks like a who-cares face....it's not what I want to see...you need to remember, need to know—just like I did and everyone else has—that as a high school first semester senior, you ain't done squat yet....there's no reason to be complacent, no reason to lay down the sword...no reason to feel as if you're better than high school...and I fully understand when kids get to that point...it gets routine and routine can be stupefying....Erika, Julie, they bot felt that way at some point in their senior year but you have to remain the master of your fate...you have to control your life and keep it going in the right direction....waste is, well, wasteful....that's a deep one...stay productive, stay responsible, make sure that others can count on you.....it'll be more important in the future and habits cemented now will serve you well later besides making life easier.......this year is important just like all other years....your situation is no different than when you perform on stage...people who pay to hear you are expecting you to meet their expectations...so this shouldn't be a big deal....as for

*running with Rach in XC.....I'm not buying that.....we don't
attach a rope between you guys....there's no reason for you NOT
to be 40-60 seconds ahead of her based on your comparative
3000 times last spring.... she's middle distance, you're distance
through and through...you know that....she's doing great for us
right now but she isn't you...now, what I've told you is exactly
what I tell my students, it's what I told my two boys....so, don't
think I'm coming down on you...I'm not...it's the teacher in
me giving the Reality 101 lecture...that's all...everyone needs a
reality check at times....so take this with the right attitude...you
really aren't any different than any other kid Hannah....you fit
the mould pretty neatly....that's a good thing...the important
thing is how you deal with all of this....straight ahead is usually
the best way to go so it's good that we're clearing the air about
this...you're exactly right, we can't help each other unless we
each have the facts straight....so, let's see how we feel after
this coming week...it's designed for you by the way....I don't
give up on kids, and I don't stop working with the good ones
just because they hit a dip in the road....we all hit them....I
do wish we'd been able to work together over the summer on
this because it might have helped out...but, as you said, this is
where we are so this is where we begin anew.....I'm with ya
girl.....I'll feel better when I start to hear the laugh again....
keep plowing ahead....this semester is a big one for you...after
that? who cares...haha....coach*

I need to help Hannah see that running helps her create a big
umbrella that's capable of shielding her from a lot of life's foibles and
disasters. Endurance running, unlike most other sporting activities,
builds an interwoven Teflon web that helps us fight illness and disease,
helps maintain healthy emotions, guides us to the right foods, motivates
us to get enough sleep, and makes us understand the importance of
proper hydration. The rigors of distance running make us hard, from
calves bulging to our long sinewy thigh muscles, taut abs, squared
shoulders and undersized but strong biceps. Hidden from view, our
respiratory muscles are as strong as a locomotive and our heart pounds
with power, volume and ease. Running makes us resilient and tough.

Running on a team makes us dependable. It makes us trustworthy as much of what we do is done in solitude, in the shadows and along the back roads of our hometowns. Coaches and teammates need to have confidence that everyone is covering the workout properly. Competition in the distance realm teaches us to respect the efforts of others, to understand that we can't control the actions of opponents so we need to take care of our personal lives first, foremost and always. We learn that we can't look a lap ahead; that we must remain in the moment, living each step for all it's worth, driving, pushing and propelling ourselves with purpose, with intent, with honor and desire. These connections help us draw strength for the workday demands as we meander through life working in our careers, getting up in the middle of the night to change diapers, dealing with life and all the pitfalls that permeate it.

Hannah is flipping the calendar, looking ahead and living for tomorrow instead of living and enjoying a sure thing called today. She's planning, scheming, looking ahead, wasting today by using it like a crowbar to leverage her way into tomorrow. Hannah, deep thinking, sensitive and a combative fighter, is overlooking the simple things in life that give it meaning and purpose. She's not absorbing every airy scent, the cacophony of sound that surrounds her, chuckling with those who laugh and welling up with emotion for those who cry. Forgoing the present, she's gambling that the promise of tomorrow will trump today, that the gift that's exposed by open door number one will be overwhelmed by what lies behind closed door number two, or three—if her key pulls the pins and rotates the plug in the door lock. People seem to focus on the big events that mark a life while it's the little things that happen every day that actually make up, mark and fill our lives with meaning.

The bolts on Hannah's rudder need tightening before she drifts so far beyond the horizon that I can't get her back safely to shore.

I asked modified coach and Skaneateles alum, Julie Lynch, to give me her take on Hannah. As usual, she was incredibly perceptive. Julie thinks that, among other things, Hannah is afraid to let me down, to disappoint me, to not live up to my expectations. And Hannah needs to know that her worth as a person is not wrapped up in her performance as a runner.

Our success for so many years was because of Julie, a five-time state champ. She was simply a powerful person who scared and willed teammates into performing. Much like she stated about Hannah, her teammates did not want to disappoint her. She had enormous faith in each and every member of the team and she let them know it. Julie's heart beats for more than just herself. She feels the pain of others, she senses their insecurities and as she gets older she has begun to feel that it's her mission in life, for God and for herself, to try to help those whose lives are in jeopardy.

With Julie in our inner circle just two years after being on our team herself, she's going to see me from a completely different perspective, and as the layers of my character are slowly peeled away, I worry that Julz will see me in a thoroughly different light. I worry that she'll understand that I don't have the answers and that sometimes I don't even have the right questions. Julie grew up, matured and was transformed from a little girl to a woman under my watch as her coach. I worry that Julie's discoveries about me will disappoint her much like Hannah fears that she may disappoint me.

Frustration, Perverts, Trucks and the Grind

Because of a pile of road kill and narrow road shoulders--that slope like the Dow Jones graph after the Dot-com bubble burst that swiped billions of dollars from unaware American investors as their agents sat on their hands and stuffed their phones up their asses--we can't run on East Lake Road. Because of bus driver concerns we can't run on Rt. 321 that stretches north toward the fish hatchery. And now because we have some demented pervert running around in Skaneateles Falls, we have to be careful when we run north of the village toward Mottville. He's 6'6", 172 pounds and with a heavy dose of sarcasm after looking at the police printout, Rob said, "He doesn't look anything like a sexual offender." Man, he had the look. Police have been hanging out in the Rec Center swimming pool because the creep has been hanging out there. At practice we passed around the dossier and picture of the predator who spent just a year in a local prison. When Rachel Hosie saw that he sexually assaulted someone under 14 years old she tossed the paper to the track and said, "As far as anyone here knows, I'm 15 and too old for this guy."

Virtually every road in the village is a main thoroughfare and we seem to be a magnet for trucks of all sorts: trucks driving north to get tarvia for roads and driveways, trucks driving north for stone fill, 100 trucks a day driving west hauling the waste from New York City, trucks using our village roads instead of paying Thruway tolls, trucks, trucks, trucks. It makes you yearn for some peace and quiet. There isn't a safe place for us to run in this country town. Our little warm-up run from the school north to the 'point' on East Street used to be as uneventful as a Syracuse University football game in 2004: Nothing ever happened. But now we have to constantly yell for the teams to hug the shoulders as cars roar past incessantly.

With all the distractions surrounding us, I'm attempting, like all coaches early in the season, to judge my team. But it's a frustrating and elusive practice at best as it rests more on subjective observations and art than objective reasoning free of emotion. Sometimes we see things that aren't there and other times we can't see the elephant in the middle of the room. Maybe my judgment is flawed this year, but I don't think so. I think we're hitting on all cylinders. I like this team. I think we're fast in practice and in meets. I trust my senses and my institutional memory of past teams. We compare well. But others are seeing us differently. Bill Meylan feels that his speed ratings on www. tullyrunners.com are actually inflated for our first two meets but he left them as listed because he didn't have time to change them. He's a busy environmental research scientist. But, I'm just not seeing this fatal flaw in our team. I'm watching some of these kids run better than they've ever run. But several savvy opposing coaches are also dubious. I think they're wearing blinders and are looking through rose colored glasses. One put the crux of the issue on the seniors.

> *Well, after a few beers tonight I'll give you my take on your team. Your seniors have ridden their freshman state title and never stepped up to the plate. They were good but never seem to be leaders. It sucks when out of three no one steps up. I expect your girls will still have good seasons, but none will be unbelievable. They just don't have it which is probably the group thing.*

The three seniors are racing surprisingly pretty well but we've hit a few rocks in the road. Hannah at times has lost her composure as her confidence just can't seem to break through and regain mastery of her thoughts and movement. And I know she's frustrated. As practice started, Rob and I were hit upside the head as Hannah made a series of statements that were out of character. "Jack," said Rob, "she's just saying stuff. There's no truth to any of it. Hannah says things just to say them.

Don't worry about it." But I worry. I worry about everything including whether a block of granite can withstand a rainstorm. I'm frustrated. I no longer understand Hannah. But I'm not giving up. And neither is she as her internal struggle begins to reach a boiling point. We'll work it out. I hope. As Hannah goes, so goes Rachel and Sofie. They gauge their paces off of Hannah. When Hannah hits a rough patch, it hurts the other two seniors. Have the three been consistent? Have they improved as much as I anticipated? No. But what I'm seeing from Rachel and Sofie this year is good stuff, their best stuff. Sofie has upped her game the most. And if we can get Hannah back to her game, everything will fall into place. But where is the Hannah I've known all these years? Hannah's on-again, off-again season was in peak form the past two days. Acting like a champion after clipping off mile repeats of 6:15, 6:15 and 6:06 with two minutes of rest per mile, I thought we'd finally turned the corner. She was bouncy, determined, tough and knocking down the miles with precision. The next two days were lackluster efforts that found her running with our lone frosh who is nursing sore quads. Physically she's beginning to hit her stride. I think her time is coming. She just needs to nail one good race. And she needs it now.

On the boys side, Sam is Hannah's double. As Sam goes, so goes the team. Sam has stepped off his horse but it's obvious that he's taken a severe hit from ten days of being sent out to pasture after his emergency testicle surgery. He grinded and grunted as his arms, chin and jaw tensed severely on a workout that a few weeks ago wouldn't have dented his armor. Doing 3 x 1200 reps at 10k pace with a minute rest per rep, I figured he'd fly. Following a 15 minute break we scheduled 2x1000 at 5k race pace with the rest equaling the duration of the run. And after a nice 10 minute rest was the final piece of the sandwich: 2x800 at 10k pace. With the other boys choosing to do 6 x 1000 at threshold pace, roughly 3:38 per 1000, I could easily tell that they were having a much easier time of it as the foursome of Dustin, Dan, Jeff and Matt ran in a tight and formidable unit around the track. Meanwhile, Sam and Calvin were struggling. My conclusion was that neither boy has any mechanical or chemical efficiency at the 10k pace. The quicker pace of the 2x1000 at 5k speed got the two of them going in the right mental and physical direction. Rob suggested that we cut them some slack and give Sam and Calvin what they crave, some speed in order to leave their neurons feeling quick and their heads feeling successful as the workout ended. Closing the workout with a quick 64 for his 2 x 400, Sam ended the day upbeat. Calvin closed down with a pair of 70s as his freshman body continues to adapt to varsity training with speed being the last arrow to be placed into his quiver.

We'll play the wait-and-see game before deciding if Sam is healthy enough for next week's meet at Long Branch Park versus a weak Solvay team on Tuesday. Fellow league foe Cazenovia with three front runners will also await us. And then we close the week at the Auburn Invitational on Saturday, a short 10 minute drive for Gary Martin who will be presented with a nice golfing jacket with "Track and Cross Country" embroidered on the left breast. His name will be written underneath.

Athletic Directors at the high school level love league competition. Most cross country coaches hate league duals. For the next month we'll be in the dual meet portion of the season so we won't be training much which is another source of frustration. With a dual meet each Wednesday and an invitational on two of the Saturdays, we can't afford to train. Our goal is to keep our mileage over 30 miles a week. We've never been able to do that but this team needs it.

The New York Sportswriters ranked the girls 3rd in the first ranking of the season, but six of the top 12 teams are from Section III and only one of us is going to States.

Sauquoit Valley looks horrible. It seems they've exploded like the Hindenberg airship. The defending champs just don't look to be a threat.

Canastota looks like a good-normal team but Theresa Trudell's CBA looks daunting. A rival, they haven't really held a candle to us in the past. But now it's almost like we're Butch Cassidy and the Sundance Kid up on the rocks of a hardscrabble bluff looking out on the prairie as the cloud of dust from the stampeding posse approaches with all due diligence. "Who are those guys?" we say incredulously." That posse is CBA right now. I don't like the way the guys went down in the movie. They died.

With just a day remaining before we enter the grind of the dual meet portion of the schedule, Rob and I had a meeting with the senior girls. We need to build a bridge between the older girls and the younger ones. I never thought we'd have to do anything like this with a mere dozen girls on the team and with three great vets at the helm. But we can't run from reality and that was Sofie's message during our discussion. "Each team is different and we have to stop looking back at our experience and do something to move us in the right direction." Sofie's gonna make it. Her head is screwed on right. Rach was thinking in a similar vein. "We did it right all summer." Hannah, with tears in her eyes again, said, "I can't take care of myself. How am I going to motivate someone like Hosie?"

Hannah just seems to be spiraling out of control despite some good days that are thankfully becoming more frequent. She remarked that she's never once raced hard. Rob and I both know it. I offered her the chance to leave the team with her head up but she said that not being on the team would make her more miserable than being on it. Something's going on and it's doing more than just simmering. Something is going to happen, one way or the other. Something will break the logjam and I hope it's something we can all deal with. She's a good, zany kid who should be enjoying her senior year instead of dealing with a mountain of frustration.

Hannah is still admitting that she runs from reality. Her dad sees it and has been talking to her about it. He sees that Hannah can do just about everything half-ass and get away with it and still end up on top. The girl has talent and brains, that's for sure. Hannah's dad knows running and he still runs fluidly when he gets the chance while traveling the country for his literacy group. Even Hannah's 81 year old grandfather still runs on rugged terrain around Lake George. It's what the family does.

For days I've been wondering if I could approach the girls about our challenges and goals. Last year they just freaked out when we had the typical pre-race talks about opponent's strengths and weaknesses, about the strategies we might use in the meet. So, I took the leap and mentioned how good CBA would be in our dual a few weeks up the road. Our 79 dual meet win streak is on the line, and so is our string of 13-straight league championship crowns. And then there's our goal of winning the sectional title again after a two year stint as the runner-up. CBA could destroy everything with their three up front and an improving fourth girl. It's the three up front that can do the ultimate damage by taking the top three spots in the dual and clinching the title before we've even sent one girl into the chute. That's not the way we want this streak to conclude. We want to have a chance. We want to fight to the last 'man' like Butch Cassidy (Paul Newman) and the Sundance Kid (Robert Redford).

My point in talking about CBA was to let the senior Brat Pack know that their team goals would never materialize unless the other girls felt that they had a connection with the seniors. No underclassmen, I said, will ever squeeze the final ounce of juice from their body unless they feel an attachment and an obligation to athletically perform for the older girls. A bridge needed to be built so we all could connect on a personal level. Just talk, I said. Just be with them before practice instead of being the last three to show up.

I had provided enough fodder for Hannah to stage a revolt, and she did. She's been pretty defiant so far this fall. Her body language was reminiscent of someone recoiling from the strike of a rattlesnake. Her eyes showed true fear. There was flight, but no fight. "I hate it when you tell us about a race and how good someone else is. I can't deal with it."

Rob, a generation younger than me and not quite as patient yet, was so frustrated that he'd left our meeting and returned just in time to deal with this. "So, you're saying you can't deal with reality?" Hannah meekly said, "I guess so," as she shuffled her feet on the pebbly red track.

Hannah looked back in history to find instances where past groups of Skaneateles seniors didn't do as I was asking them to do with the underclassmen. Rachel, throughout most of our talk, stood off to the side reflectively, weighing the issues and the information. Rachel was suspending judgment as she sifted through the information in order to find the truth.

What I don't want from these girls is a Herculean effort that will detract from their running. It could be something as simple as leaving the senior dining room at lunch on race day Wednesdays and going to sit with the team at their cafeteria lunch table. When Karen led an LAT rep in the cemetery the other day, all one of the girls needed to do was give her a rap on the shoulder or rump and tell her that we expect that every time—and just say "nice job". It's taking the time to tell a younger kid about our streak, telling her that we don't lose—ever. Soon the younger kids will get it. They'll understand that they're a part of something greater than themselves, something that goes back to the year of their birth. Being a part of living history can be an enlightening and invigorating thing. The streak doesn't breathe, but it's our job to breathe life into it. It's what we do.

I can't tell them this. I can't be the sis-boom-bah every day in every way. Try as a coach may, kids eventually tune out the rah-rah rants. The Knute Rockne speech has to be held in abeyance and used in special circumstances. Hannah claims she runs to make us happy and that there's absolutely nothing internally driving her. She's afraid to lose, afraid to disappoint, afraid to succeed and she's stuck in neutral. She needs a kick-start, a blazing fast and successful race to get her going again. And she needs it now. I've gotta do something.

Since 1992, when frosh Carly Brown was a mere one year old and just thinking about standing up, we haven't lost a dual meet. Like a tsunami pushing aside everything in its path, we've vanquished every foe that's lined up with us. There was never contempt, disdain or a lack of respect involved. It was almost professional, just normal business, like having to slaughter an animal because you knew you had to eat—or perish.

Taking apart Cazenovia and Solvay for our 80th and 81st straight wins involved a battle with ourselves. Caz and Solvay were mere props on a day when lake effect clouds collected over the course and threatened to fill the sunless sky with rain drops. Our shared concern was selfishly centered on just us. Were we going to be the masters of our own race for a change? Were we going to take control of our emotions and let the natural power just flow? The power I knew we possessed came from practice after practice, in some cases over a period of six years?

It was only September 19th and early in the school year, but we had a real test to pass. This one was personal.

As the girls took off to check the course that hugged tight to the Seneca River as it passed the Syracuse University crew boathouse on its way toward the port city of Oswego and Lake Ontario, I pulled Hannah aside, reached out to take hold of her hand and turned it palm side up. Grabbing two little pieces of rubbery magnets, I carefully placed them into the little concave cradle formed by her palm. The little magnets said, "I Care."

I could see right away that she was a bit thrown back and taken by surprise. She smiled like only Hannah can smile with her puffy lips joyful and reminding me of a young Goldie Hawn. The other girls were wondering immediately what I had just done with Hannah. Energy-filled giggles soon followed as they descended down the hill and rounded the bend toward the flat next to the river.

A half hour later I pulled the non-seniors aside and continued the process of teaching them about our history to give them a sense of who we are—who they are--and to give them an understanding of the work and pride that many, many girls have put into building this program. Like it or not, the girls have found themselves a part of something historical, something emotional, something great. They've become a part of the dual meet streak. I talked about our goals, OUR goals, not their individual goals. Impressed? I hoped not. This needs to be a slow process that builds and builds like the tsunami roiling from some tremendous underwater upheaval as it gains strength covering hundreds of miles of vast ocean expanse. I continue to plant the seeds and the growth will have to take its natural course. I need to keep watering it and hope that the seeds are strong, the food nutritious and the soil a good medium for growth. Something needs to be growing by the time we face CBA. The local Post-Standard is already hyping the meet. Ace high school reporter Neil Kerr doesn't miss a beat.

The girls were excited, even giddy with laughter while watching the mod squad in their first meet. Kids walked. They even stopped and stretched mid-race. I think having the varsity watch the little kids was a good thing. It seemed to bring perspective while easing tensions. The little ones were going to help us I thought.

While standing with Rob in a clearing near the finish line as the damn mosquitoes feasted on us, Hannah rushed over in a mood that I hadn't seen this season. "Coach, get me going. Get me started." She was bouncing all around like a prize fighter standing in his corner before the bell gonged to start the pugilism. "Tell me what to do, I'm ready today."

I wrapped my arm around her shoulders and steadied her. Twisting her body toward me until her face was looking into mine, I put a hand on each shoulder and calmly said, "I'm giving you permission to fail, to utterly fail—fall flat on your face fail. Do what you want the first

800, but coming down the hill let it go and let's see where the wall is for you." Off she went.

Hannah never saw the wall. Trailing in 4th and a fair distance behind the leader as she came down the hill and disappeared into a riverside loop, she reappeared later all alone. No one was in sight. She'd made a move that was remarkable. She was doing it for the first time in cross country. Four years and I'd never seen this. She was free, unfettered and unburdened for the first time. There was no doubt, no fear of failure and no shying from success.

At the finish she had covered the 3.0625-mile course in 19:03, faster than any of my first team All-State girls. Her pace was 6:13 per mile which fits right in with her mile splits last week of 6:15, 6:15 and 6:06. The girl can do it when she's clear-headed and calm. Hannah was re-emerging from the darkness.

All the girls ran well. Rachel Vaivoda crossed in 20-flat. Sofie was 20:11. Kristin Roberts was done in 20:20. Rachel Hosie was three seconds back and Alexis Mazzeo nine seconds behind her. Our pack time was a good 1:20 on a day when our leader ran a first team All-State time.

Standing around the chute, Hannah just smiled. There was no end-zone in-your-face celebration. There was a calm that comes only to those who have sat with the gods and know the truth. Hannah had learned something important. She'd learned about herself.

Rachel V. said it was the magnets. "It's our new motto: We care," she said.

Hannah, feeling no IT band pain, said she kept the "I Care" rubber magnets in her shoes. And off they all went to spend 30 minutes jogging the sectional course that they'd see in seven short weeks.

Journeys

She wears blonde hair that hangs cheaply and looks older than her 12 years, and if you figured she was from a long forgotten trailer park, you'd have the right picture in your mind. There's just a wisp of self-confidence in her as life has repeatedly kicked the adopted girl in the gut. Like her legs, her character lacks definition. She smiles. She seems genuine. But there's an air about her that says she could go either way in the blink of an eye. You don't see any in-between when you look at her hanging out at practice. She's lucky to have Coach Julie on her side for Julie's heart is big enough to take her in and give her a place to call home. Julie will listen for a long time. My attention span is shorter.

We don't all get to the starting line by walking and running the same path. This tall, skinny 7th grade girl, who looks like a runner, just recently joined our team. But she's up against the odds. She's trying to dig a foundation with a plastic spoon. She's not one to be confused with some of the pampered silvery spoon-fed prima donnas from the good side of town. Her phone number isn't even in our area code at her home far down the east side of the lake past Spafford and near Homer. The landmarks in her life are in Cortland, a good 30 minute drive south from here.

At practice last Friday before our spectacularly unspectacular performance at the Auburn Invitational where the girls won (2-4-5-6-7-8-9) with JV-like times in an uncontested race while the boys fell four points short of first as more problems developed, our little girl was enveloped in Julie's arms, crying, as a tale emerged.

It seems that her family is in the midst of an ugly divorce. They're all ugly at some level aren't they? Julie's bear hug was tight and reassuring. The girl just wanted to run and from what I've seen she probably has scant chance of success despite a body that looks like it belongs to an aggressive lightning-bolt-of-a -runner. She's dreaming and a part of our professional duty is to help nurture the dream. It's also part of our humanity to offer help to those who can benefit from us. Mom won't pay for a sport physical and dad, if he had his way, wouldn't let her run at all. It looks like the little girl is the pawn being kicked around in the dissolution of this family. Divorce acts on kids like a meat grinder acts on chunks of meat as red chunks go from an identifiable entity into some unidentifiable sausage.

Long after practice was over and the kids were heading home to get ready for Friday Night Football under the lights, the wafer thin, perpetually underdressed blonde told us that she had to be at school until 9:30 because no one would come pick her up. With just a dollar clutched in her child-like little fingers--long, thin and vulnerable like a little girl's--I put my arms around both Julie and the little one and marched them up to my car where I put a few dollars into her hand and told her to eat something warm from the concession stand like a Hoffman's hot dog. I couldn't believe that I endorsed eating a hot dog, but I couldn't take her home like a lost dog that I'd found on the side of the road.

I can imagine what mom looks and acts like and I know I'll never see her at a meet. I've seen the type at every parent open house since I became a teacher. Would she reek of smoke that fills the old jalopy that she drives? Would the smell of booze accompany her to open house? Would she look sporting with visible tattoos, stringy, unwashed hair and leather clothing? Would the white of her teeth be blackened by years of abject neglect like the pure soul of her daughter in a few years?

No money, no one at home who cares enough to give a daughter more than a buck for food as she embarks on a 15 hour workday alone. And she wants to run. She cries because she can't run. Wanting to run tipped my scales. I'm used to the crying. She had me in her camp. What 12 year old wants to run so much that she cries when she can't?

Rob thinks I'm being played. I hope not. But he's right more times than not when it comes to unraveling the truth about some kids.

The next day at Auburn with the skies threatening all morning, Julie told me that our little girl had gotten up from sleeping at 3 AM to catch a ride to her 30 year old sister's place of work. There was a lot of sitting around at work until her sister's boss granted a short coffee break for the two of them to drive to the school for the 8:00 bus. And she wasn't running. There could be something about her character, her willingness to suffer, to make sacrifices that just might help her as a runner, if we can get her a physical. I brought up her situation at the meet with a wealthy doctor but he didn't seem interested in helping out. Maybe I wasn't direct enough. She might be a tough kid mentally. Physically? We'll see.

I wonder what it's like for her and millions of other little kids as she lies in bed at night staring at the ceiling. Is the girl's mattress high-off the floor and on bed springs or is it a tossed away mattress that has a spot in a corner of a dirty floor? One of our top runners had a mattress like that, and the father loved him. What goes through her mind as she stares into the darkened ceiling alone in bed at night? Are there dolls to hug, stuffed animals in bed to cuddle with? Has anyone read a bedtime story to her, helped her memorize dorky little poems or sung her a silly song at a joyous family party? Are her cheeks softly rubbed at night, her lips kissed lovingly, her blankets tucked in reassuringly as someone turns off the bare, lonely ceiling light and says, "I love you?" It's easy to guess that Christmas morning is a lot like a balloon with a hole in it as the day just disintegrates into one argument after another as disappointment mingles with booze.

The girl's eyes plead for some sort of help that she can't yet understand, though they're still bright, hopeful and full of promise. But you can see doubt beginning to cross her face and I wonder how tough she'll really be as life begins to conspire against her. With innocence meeting reality, I wonder how much hammering she'll take before she gives.

The day of the Auburn Invitational was the Skaneateles Homecoming and the concern of the day was lip gloss, cool shirts, how much skin and breast to reveal, who would ask who to dance and would the DJ play danceable music.

Sam hasn't quite been himself as we enter a tough and important week. It seems that his delicate operation has left him unable to sleep in his usual position and he's been routinely waking up at 3 AM. I should have noticed. All summer his eyes were quick, relaxed, clear and thoroughly confident. Lately they've looked out from someone who is quite different, and it shows in his racing. The eyes are darker, slower, showing less life and energy. He's been run down twice in a week over the final 100-meters and the final sprint has always been a ready weapon for Sam. His journey back isn't complete but he seems to be moving in the right direction. If he isn't hit with anything else this fall his final meet could be States. I just hope the annual Skaneateles virus passes him by.

The boys aren't going to States this year as we take a step back for every two steps forward. I keep hearing from their parents that the boys are staying up late. Dan missed the bus to Auburn and he didn't eat breakfast again. And he didn't race well at all. Dustin was standing on the starting line as the starter made his approach when he realized that he'd forgotten to take his inhaler. With the bus about 300-meters away I figured that he'd miss the race. Off he went while a few teams did some last minute stride-outs and stayed out there talking, praying or telling dirty jokes for all I knew. It gave Dustin enough time to get back but it didn't matter. The puffer didn't have enough time to open up his lungs and bronchial tubes. And he didn't race well either. Jeff couldn't find his stride whether he was running fast or slow. But he got it moving over the final 1200-meters and waged a furious duel with a Weedsport runner that had the crowd in venerable Holland Stadium roaring. He won the head-to-head sprint on the old cinder track.

Karen is dead last on the team after a summer of dominance. Her trip to Europe during the first two weeks of the season wiped out her dreams. When her dad said to me that he couldn't understand it, I should have set the record straight and said it was the trip stupid. I've never had anyone return from a long vacation to some exotic place and do well.

Beatrice just can't get it moving at all. She convinced herself early that she would hang on to the girls that she routinely and easily runs with in practice. Running in 9th, she succumbed to her negative talk once again and finished in 23rd and next to last for the team in the small school race.

Coach Reed, I feel like it's necessary, even though I don't want to hear it from you, to hear the hard cold facts. What do I need to do? What do you think: am I just not trying hard enough in races? Am I out of shape? Have I over-trained? Is it just mental? I don't know what to do anymore. I feel pretty helpless. This all makes me so upset. Racing how I have makes me so upset. I want to change things. I want to do better. I want to do what I know I can. Just tell me whatever it is that I need to do and I'm going to try my best to do it. Z thinks maybe I've over-trained in recent weeks because my legs are chronically fatigued and because in practices after races I always run hard when I'm not happy with how the race went. This summer, this season, I've put in so much, invested so much, that it's hard for me to just throw it all away. I've worked so hard; every day in Ireland up running at 6 am, running camp, the ten mile run, Boot Camp, etc etc. I want to make a change for the better. I want to know what to do. I want to finish out the season strong. I know I can, I just don't know how I'm going to get there. My parents think I should be 'sidelined' in practices and not allowed to run hard until I realize how much I miss it and realize why I want to be running. Just a thought because I don't know.

Beatrice and I have had many tearful heart-to-heart discussions about her mental block. Nothing I've said has worked. Not so surprisingly, she's not the first to have FOR, Fear- of-Racing. It's something the boys used to say to tease a teammate when they'd become a practice wonder and a racing bust. The boys even named a banquet award for it, The Davis Cup. And, after due deliberation, they'd choose the annual winner who would accept the award and display it proudly at home for the following year. Steve White, who sells antiques to movie stars and anyone else with enough money to buy his exquisite stuff on Genesee Street in the heart of the village, gave us the cup. Though he travels the country buying and selling, he does everything in his power to follow us around the state for our meets. Before his knee surgeries, morning commuters would see him with white shorts and bare-chest running the roads in the winter. He was one tough guy and has a horde of skiing and other trophies stored in his house.

Adam Evans, one of the primary figures behind the Davis Cup, was on the receiving end of one of my 'get off your ass' e-mails last week after running a disappointing time at Franklin Park in Boston, the racing hub of New England college cross country. Adam never quite turned the corner in high school and despite a season-ending injury in his college frosh year at Bentley, he's been pounding the miles, getting stronger and fitter, and still he couldn't turn in a respectable time. Writing to him last week, I said he understood everything and wanted to do it right but there was a fear of failure, a fear of disappointing and a fear of succeeding and it had him spinning his wheels on race day. All of that stuff is heavy baggage and he has to toss it aside and just run. "Running is what you do Adam. Toss the baggage, forget about Ed (Coach Ed Lyons), forget about failure, forget about succeeding and just run. Don't THINK! The race will take care of itself when you do it like this." Adam, if he turns off his mind, can be physically and mentally light, able to float like a butterfly and sting like a bee, and I reminded him that it's all an incredible head game, like playing chess with himself. "Adam, your chances to do this right are slipping away so don't focus on the number of times remaining in your senior year, but take it one race at a time, one step at a time, one split at a time, and live entirely in the moment that you've been given by some greater force. Use it wisely, don't fritter it away, start with purpose and redouble it at the three-mile mark where your mind begins to turn negative. Remind yourself what you're doing because going home having done it right is so much more fun. Just think about the huge breakthrough workout you had the other day, remind yourself what the alumni have been saying after seeing your workouts. Remember how you felt afterwards. Every race should feel like that. Just run, don't think. Good luck and let me know how it went."

We talked for an hour a week later after he ran a 27:06 on the same course as the recent debacle. He ran nearly 40 seconds faster on a day that delivered wind, rain and cold air. Somehow I have to get the same message into Bea's head, but by my calculations, we're at the Three Mile Island stage of the meltdown and it's going to take time to put her back together. What's the half-life of a runner suffering from a lack of confidence?

Beatrice, it's obvious that running is important to you, being injured showed you how much you missed identifying with it. It's all mental. If there's some real mysterious underlying physical reason I'd be real surprised since you're just fine in practice. You aren't over-trained. Running with mental stress is a real burden, it weighs on you and crushes you. It ain't healthy either. You will either gain control over yourself or this is all you'll be able to expect. The more you press, the greater the problem grows. There really isn't much I can say that we haven't already discussed. We each are in charge of ourselves and nearly everyone who runs feels exactly what you're feeling. You have chosen to respond in a negative way to the sensations of racing and no one can change that except you. I've told you that it's just an evolutionary remnant that's trying to protect you and you're so fit that you don't need protecting. Your success in practice should be more than enough evidence of that. You're a bright person who is probably in control of your homework and classes. This is different, you can't control the variables or the other people. You can only react to them. Perhaps thinking about the variables isn't worth it since it isn't working. Your focus should be on positive self-talk. No more excuses. No more searching for excuses because there are none, Bea...Your mind is the problem and only you can change it....the only other way is to get with a sports shrink but that means big bucks and a lot of time-consuming driving. You shouldn't need one anyway. Positive talk and trusting yourself is all you need. With all the mileage and workouts, I don't know why you aren't willing to believe in yourself. Everyone you talk to builds you up. Negative thoughts are a self-fulfilling prophecy. It's the same with positive ones. Luck is preparation and you've prepared well so stop tripping yourself. Don't look for reasons to fail. Look inward for that's the source of the racing problem. It's you and just you and you can fix it at any given moment—— IF YOU REALLY WANT TO. Some people seek attention through negative actions and I don't think that's you... So, get positive, stop stressing. It's just running. It's no big deal, just one foot following the other. The heart, lungs, muscles, tendons and ligaments are all doing the work without you having to direct a thing. Just think positive thoughts, stop worrying about other people. Yesterday you were fine until your mind got you again. You run a long part of your distance runs faster than you race, so what's that tell you? You're racing fit...just let the race come to you...don't force it...See ya Monday. No more running alone. You can't do that in a race. Just run. You were fine in camp and everyone saw it so just take things a day at a time. Wanting to get to the next meet to make up for the last one won't get you there faster, and it'll slow you down because you're already stressing. Live each day and stop thinking ahead, run each step and stop thinking ahead. Stop thinking of the last step, you can't change it. Just think of the step you're in the midst of because that's all you can control. You're not a failure by the way, you're just experiencing some temporary problems and your day will surely come.....coach

Our girls are on the cusp of what could be the end of a long journey of success, 14 consecutive years without a league loss in a part of the country that is hot for cross country. The coaching in these parts is good. They're devoted, knowledgeable and competitive. They're mostly career coaches. This is who they are and what they do. Our collective success in the state meet for a state that routinely leads the national rankings and does well at qualifying kids for the Footlocker Nationals and the Nike Team Nationals is remarkable. We're in the heart of New York, central New York. And our small schools are tough.

We meet Jordan-Elbridge in just three days and if they come out ready and willing they could be on the threshold of a dream. Coach Rob Schemerhorn has endured many meets with us where he's found himself frustrated, stomping off and talking to himself, "Why can't I get these girls to run faster?" It isn't the girls, it's the culture of the school and community. It's one of too little belief, scant confidence and of thinking of themselves as losers, or at least they don't see themselves as winners. As a teacher at J-E, I'm like all the teachers as we try to get them to dream, to dig deeper and try harder. We tell them that they can be winners by copying the winners and doing what they do and not sticking tightly to the loser pop culture like big-knuckled hands wrapped around a pine tarred Louisville Slugger. These J-E girls are talented, perhaps the most gifted bunch in the section, but they don't know it, they don't know how to live with it, know how to nurture and water it so that it blooms. If they're 'on' and running like a top-10 team in the state, and if we run like we did at Auburn, our streak dies at 81. The journey, long, successful and full of momentous triumphs, could fade away as it enters the curled pages of so many history books. Forgotten? Perhaps it will be quickly forgotten by most, including the team as it devotes more time to real-life worries. But for a 14-year span, we were the game, and nothing can wipe that from my memory banks.

82 & 83

Squatting down in front of the white chalked starting line that was hiding beneath long grass on the JV practice gridiron, Hannah was clawing at the ground like an ancient ancestor foraging for roots. Clutching clumps of long grass in each hand, she twisted and yanked it out of the ground over and over while mumbling to herself.

"She's so afraid to disappoint you," said Julie.

I pulled Hannah aside earlier and told her that the race against arch rival JE was already over. No competition. "Hannah, this is no big deal today. I can't tell you anything but we're fine, okay? I know things I can't tell you. It's our secret." I was lying but her dad told me that she's become immobilized by pressure. We need to give her an out.

My lie hadn't stemmed the tide of fear that was welling up inside her. I tried again. "It's all individual today Hannah. No team, just you."

"What? No team? Do you mean I can come in last and you'd be alright with that?"

I nodded, smiled and gave her a one arm shoulder hug from the side. She just needs to know that no matter what, we aren't bailing out on her. She needs to know that she's more than a runner to us.

She stopped clutching clumps of grass but she started in about 15th place on a course we see so often I refer to it as our home course.

I could only imagine her thoughts based on all the time I've spent with her. Her tongue can spit out a few salty words before she realizes it.

254

"Oh shit. Why do I do this? I hate running. I can't stand the pressure. Why do I go through with this week after week? Everyone expects more of me than I want to give. This hurts. Look at all the kids in front of me. This is embarrassing. I'm the best one here and everyone knows it. But I hate it. The grass is so freaking long it's messing me up. Stop bumping into me bitch. Oh, I've still got 2 ½ miles to go. There's the hill. Fuck this. I hate it. Oh, this isn't too bad. I'm feeling better. Where'd that come from? I think I can move now. Going down that hill I'm leaving this crowd behind. I've got to get moving. The sooner I finish, the sooner I'm done. Nice try girls. But I'm out of here."

"Rob, look at her go," I said. "What's gotten into her? She was dogging it terribly at the start. Man, when she gets her mo-jo going she's gone. I wish we could bottle whatever it is that she's got going right now."

"Oh, this is glorious. No effort. I'm free. No one around. No team to worry about. It's just me up front and alone. I'm pulling away hon. This is what I was born to do. This is me. But I hate it sometimes. Ah, that's just the crazy me. It takes me a while to move but I'm moving now. Oh, there's coach with the camera again."

"There's the 'Banana' I like to see," I yelled encouragingly. "Are ya gonna smile for the camera?" I clicked with the Kodak.

That one came out nice. It'll be a keeper I thought.

"Oh-oh. Ok, it's not a big deal. Just a rib. What the hell is up with my rib? A frigin rib? Oh, it'll be ok. Maybe I'll settle down a bit and take it easy. No one can catch me anyway. Nice crowd ahead. I should put on a show but it's hurting. Sorry guys. I'm on cruise control, saving it for the next race. Oh shit, another race coming up. I'll have to do this all over again? I hate it. There's the last hill. Gotta get up. There. Not so bad. Down the hill and into the woods and coach will be there with the camera again I bet when I come out. Out of the woods and into the chute. Done. Finally. Wow. The crowd is big. Okay. I'll kick it in. Nice and tall. Lousy form but it's all I got today. There's coach. And the camera. Okay. He likes what I did today. Guess I'm okay since he's smiling." And then she smiles proudly.

"I wish we could have given you more of a fight," said Rob Schemerhorn after the final tally came in. Skaneateles girls 21, J-E 40. The state's 3rd ranked squad beat the 9th ranked team. I didn't expect this. Rob Tuttle and I figured it could go either way. We thought we'd win but we wouldn't have been surprised if it was close or worse. I guess we aren't quite believing what we're seeing right now. I see good competitive running, much better than last year, but when I compare some race times to past years on similar days on the same courses, we aren't in the game at all. I've never been so mystified. I wonder who we really are.

The day was perfect for a race, for our 82nd and 83rd straight league wins. 1992, the year the streak was born, is virtually ancient history to these kids. The air was warm over J-E, a nice 73 degrees with a thin white veil of clouds muting a baby-blue sky. The weather didn't seem to bring any harm to anyone. The girls moved up all race long after a lethargic start. And the boys are beginning to surge mid-race. Sam is well enough post-surgery to break free now. He's gaining confidence and beating people who he's never defeated. After Sam crossed the line in 18:04 to win his first race, it was Calvin beating J-E's number-2 runner, Donato Direnzo, by twenty seconds. Calvin is looking more determined and athletic than I've ever seen him and he's probably a big race just waiting to happen if he dares to go for it.

Jeff was an empty vessel the day before the race with symptoms of a nasty cold sapping his energy reserves. I sent him home run-free for the day. Thinking he would have trouble surviving this rugged course, we gave him no directives as we walked toward the starting line. Sometimes kids run better when they're sick. It gives them something to focus on besides the running. Placing 5th, he led an ill Dustin and a recovering Dan to the chute and the scoring was done with each boy passing their counterpart over the final mile. Matt's head was spinning and he had trouble with his eyesight again. He's just not in shape. He was so toned and strong over the summer and then his knee got the best of him. With the missed practices he is still looking good but something is missing. He shouldn't be struggling at this juncture of the season.

Rachel Vaivoda had it going before the race. She felt it and I sensed it. With J-E's Nicole Darling and Cate White taking the pace out fast, it looked like Rachel might be overmatched. Wrong. She worked hard, stayed consistent, and after pulling even she pulled well ahead to grab second.

Sofie's legs were heavy and sore and I have to decide if she needs a blow after a heavy mileage summer or if she's feeling funny because our mileage has dropped ever since the dual meet portion of the schedule started. Two more weeks and we'll be done with it. After our trip to the home of the Soccer Hall of Fame in Oneonta this weekend we'll skip next Saturday, let the kids sleep a bit, and get in a good workout.

The pack came through today. Just seven seconds behind Sofie was Amanda and it's good to see her begin to come out of her shell. Sixteen seconds back was Kristin Roberts who gained strength as the race wore on. Another ten seconds back was Lexie who reported to me via e-mail after the meet that she "regretted to inform" me that her foot began hurting in warm-ups and hurt enough afterwards to make it difficult to walk. With no apparent accident or misstep, I can only think stress fracture. The same foot hurt over the summer but as suddenly as it became a problem, it vanished. It looks like round-two is upon us.

With Rachel Hosie back at almost 25 minutes, I'm beginning to think that she's not going to replicate her late-season charge of last year when she emerged as our number one runner. She's young and growing. Maybe that's it? It looks like her horses and her annual September illness may take her out of the loop. I hope I'm wrong. She may be an athlete who underperforms until the final race of the year. She did it last year. Just ten seconds behind Mazzeo was Carley Billick, so we shouldn't lose too much if someone goes down for the weekend.

One more prelim at Oneonta against an unknown field on an unknown course and we're almost through the grind. Then it's on to CBA and Bishop Ludden at Green Lakes State Park, a state championship site in the near past. Theresa Trudell won't have the course finalized until Monday because the park ranger wants to keep us off the main road. She has to jigger the course after she returns from her trip to Warwick, the site of the state meet. Rachel Vaivoda has taken great offence at CBA going to Warwick. She's taking it personally. "How dare they think they're good enough to go there to look at the state meet course. They haven't beaten us yet."

After our race, Hannah said, "We'll kick CBA's ass." If the old Hannah shows up, we will.

Phone Calls

"It's Lou," said my wife. "He called last night, too." Lou and I coached together for the better part of a decade. Now he's at West Genesee. Lou is 'The Man.' He's big, gruff and won't take any shit from anyone. And the kids know it. They also know he's on their side unequivocally. If there's anyone in the kids' lives who will tell them the truth, it's Lou. Kids need that. Too many of us are afraid to unveil the Goddess of Truth for the kids. Self-esteem? Law-suits? Parental problems? Lou doesn't really give a damn. Hidden behind his dark glasses and secreted behind his basement-deep voice is a soft interior that few are allowed to see. He's a softy and the smart, talented, hardworking kids know it. Lou is the most loyal person alive. He shows more faith and trust in his kids than anyone. And they respond in kind despite the greatest odds. There were a few campaigns when all wasn't going well but we still won. Lou would often say after the wins continued to pile up, "You're doing it with smoke and mirrors, Jack." Coming from Lou, I took it as the highest of praises.

"How ya doing?" said the deep voice. "Did you go anywhere this weekend?"

"Hey Lou. We found a rinky dinky meet. I'm getting good at that this year; small races, good finishes, big confidence builder. But the kids are responding. They're starting to believe. I'm not sure if what I'm doing will help us this year, but it should help the boys for their senior year. They're learning to win, beginning to expect to be up front. And that's the goal."

"How'd it go?" The voice was so low and modulated that almost anyone would think that he didn't give a damn about anything. But he does.

"The girls won. Beat a tough Maine-Endwell team that's 10th in the state in class "B". The boys won, too. Can you believe that after my moaning and bitching last year? How'd you guys do?"

"McMahon won, about four seconds ahead of F-M's MacKenzie Carter. But F-M's girls may be better than the boys. And the boys went 1-2 in the meet. Liz Deir of Honeoye Falls-Lima set a course record, almost broke 17 minutes."

"Give me a break. Shit, Sam had the second fastest time of the day at Unatego and he barely broke 18. McQuaid can be fast. By the way, they have a monument in your honor down there in your old stomping grounds."

"What's it called," he said, "Louie-Land?" Lou knew where I was going with this.

Lou has a history with women. There's the national-team volleyball player who he met at the state track meet in Poughkeepsie. There's the Caribbean cruise. There's the abandoned beach in Central America. Yeah, you get the idea. The guy's a magnet for women. And then there's the navy tales from Asia. For a guy who started out in the Culinary Institute of America and who later became a phys-ed teacher, he's left his mark in all quadrants of the globe. He's married now to a great, pretty, professional woman. It took a multi-dimensional lady to tame the beast. Louie-land is closed.

Head coach Jim Vermeulen's West Genesee girl's team is on target to tie for the league crown after running well at McQuaid in Rochester. Cicero-North Syracuse is formidable. Even though Vermeulen has a good one-two punch, I don't think he has the depth to beat C-NS. If they do win, it's because assistant coach Lou got under their skin. Lou favors speed over anything else. He bought into our system and he's exported it to West Genessee. He's gradually making Jim a convert. These things take time. Motivating the girls is what he does best. He connects with them, and they with him. A major part of our success at Skaneateles was the playful Lou, almost always hidden behind those dark, dark glasses. We each brought something to the table. I know what he brought and it's something I don't possess.

Harold called while on his way to pick up his daughters. Harold-of-Chittenango. He knows how to make a wimp tough. It's called miles, lots of hard miles on the hills at Green Lakes State Park. The park's lake offers up pink water from its dead lower depths. Nothing but a strange bacteria lives there. The lake's bottom waters replicate the lack of life back in the Permian Age when there were no flowering plants and no animals with fur as volcanic activity made the air thick with soot. Carbon and sulfur dioxide bubbled into the atmosphere from beneath bodies of water just like those at Green Lakes. Life was almost extinct as nearly everything on the planet had suffocated. Harold runs his kids at Green Lakes all the time. I don't think he's risking their lives running mile loops along the tree-shaded lakeshores. Michelle "Shorty" Brandt, his gallant female senior bound for college in a year, took third at McQuaid which is one of the largest meets in the nation. Mt. Sac might be bigger, and the Manhattan Invitational can probably claim more runners. McQuaid, which used to make us wait until December for the complete results, now gets the results on-line within just a few hours of the finish of the final race of the day-long format.

Harold, whose daughters go to Fayetteville-Manlius and have been confronted with ridiculous amounts of homework—enough for Harold to reduce his homework load in his Chittenango science courses—has a funny team. They perform one day and collapse the next. But somehow they manage to pull off the upset. Jamesville-Dewitt awaits this Wednesday, the same day that we face the daunting challenge of CBA, a team that looks to have lost its 3rd runner, Katie Webster, at the Pre-State Meet at Warwick. Rob Tuttle and I have been trying to figure out what CBA's coach, Theresa Trudell, meant when she sent me an e-mail about cancelling the dual meet. Laying low? Playing possum? Admitting that the game is over due to injury? She's thin. If one girl goes down they're done, especially after the way we've been running. The 14-year long streak just might live.

I usually get a phone call from Julian Corsello, the father of jailed Steve Corsello who killed Matt Angelillo in the devastating car crash. Julian has the scoop on everyone in Skaneateles, from the adulterous husband to the guy who seems wealthy but is skating on thin ice, to the big-time developer whose house is built by shoddy carpenters from New Jersey. And he's always seeing things sunny-side up. He always wants to know how the team is doing and he's seemed surprised when the recent reports have been good. He knows what we've been dealing with and it's as much of a surprise to him as it is to me when we pull off something. I'm still not trusting the kids like I should and I'm not sure exactly why.

Neill Kerr of the Post-Standard has been a faithful caller looking for a scoop or asking about the behind-the-scenes truth about Steve Corsello. Neil never writes anything negative about anyone. His calls come late at night and he seems as gentle as the waves in a lap pool at an aquatics center. "We don't want to hurt these kids," he often says. And he's right. There's no good reason for the Terrell Owens atmosphere to drip down upon the lives of teenagers. For the most part, the majority of the kids in high school sports are involved because their friends are involved. It's really pretty simple. The studs and studdettes are few and far between.

There were no phone calls at our Hampton Inn near Oneonta, New York for the Unatego Invitational-near Lou Delsole's hometown . The cell towers propped atop the mountains along the Susquehanna River just weren't up to the challenge. I like being cut off from the world.

The thick white fog lifted slowly from the valley along the Susquehanna, that deadly ribbon of moving brown liquid that periodically destroys lives and property. Slowly, the landscape was revealed. I couldn't see the course until right before the gun was shot into the crisp air that was calm and invigorating. It was just like Windsor.

Earlier, at breakfast, the only thing being lifted was the covers of the steamy pots at the food alcove in the Hampton Inn. We had to compete for breakfast with college volleyball teams that were in Oneonta for tournaments at Hartwick College and the State University of New York at Oneonta. They were tall, well-muscled, learned, quiet and reflective as they hunched over their plates and bowls of food. We saw a former Skaneateles basketball player, Hillary Pundt, who had joined the Utica IT team after a summer working at the Patisserie Bakery behind the Sherwood Inn. She looked good in her new colors.

Baruch and Utica IT were the primary college players we were going against in the breakfast nook. We competed well. Lightly toasted English Muffins came out doughy instead of browned and crispy. Miniature boxes of Rice Crispies and Cocoa Puffs were ripped open. Travel bags piled up on the floor between the tables, stuffed to overflowing with text books and notebooks, oversized towels, spikes, various lucky charms and stuffed animals.

The kids were well-behaved at the hotel. In earlier years, we'd gather to watch the Friday night showing of X-Files and then some of the older kids would tune in to a body piercing expose' on HBO. It seemed that every part of the female body was getting pierced. We quickly had the front desk restrict the viewing of HBO. We'd always enjoy watching the Saratoga team walking around in front of the hotel with their coach and his dog. They weren't left alone much and if we talked to them in the breakfast line, the female half of the coaching staff would step right between us and the talking would cease as her facial expression said "Don't mess with my girls. Don't even think it or I'll hurt ya."

Our kids used utensils at the Neptune Diner the night before the Unatego race. It was filled with a lot of stainless steel panels. It was bright. It looked like the 1950s but the kids couldn't appreciate the history. But, they were polite. Sitting near the middle table with driver Gary Martin manning the father's position at the head of the table, I harkened back to the Fonz and his Happy Days friends. It was that sort of place. A woman made a special trip to tap Gary on the shoulder and told him that we should be proud of our kids for their exemplary behavior. "You'd better tell Jack," said Gary, pointing to me. "They're his kids and he's responsible." She repeated the message while placing a wizened hand on my shoulder and I appreciated it. Most people look to find fault with kids but this earnest, wrinkled woman who'd seen a lot in her lifetime, looked to see the good in our smooth-faced kids.

The kids were civilized, most having plenty of opportunities in their lives to eat at elegant restaurants, some having routinely done so around the nation and world. Josh Youle just got back from a summer of hiking around Europe. To this gang, going out to eat is no big deal. Not too many years ago a trip like this would be a very special occasion with the kids really looking forward to a night in a hotel and a few meals at a restaurant. They'd dress to the Ts, the girls all made up and wearing skirts while the boys sometimes dressed in ties and proper slacks. Today the boys wear cut-off shirts, dirty dark jeans and Allen Iverson basketball shorts. Some of the girls were adorned in shirts opened at the neck and showing some skin and nice jewelry. There were all sorts and varieties of fashion at our tables, some formal and others informal. Overall, the girls' attire seemed more appropriate for a restaurant than the threads the boys wore. Things have quickly changed.

At breakfast the following morning, the Utica IT and Baruch kids looked great in their team sweats. We looked like a bunch of good kids who had picked up some clothes at the Rescue Mission. Only the innocence on their faces betrayed the gruffness that was their clothes.

Breakfast is thought to be an intricate and important part of a runner's life. Once at the state championships we stayed in the same Marriott as Tully's Dominic Luka and Olympian Lopez Lemong. Piled high on their Syracuse China breakfast plates was bacon, a big old slab of pure fat. And Lopez went out and won the state title with Dominic just behind him. We thought about what we'd learned about nutrition from the Sudanese runners but decided to stick to our own methods. Later in November 2006, after our high school state championships had been run, Lemong placed 4th in the D-I XC National Championships just 15 seconds behind the winner.

Hannah keeps talking about beating CBA this coming Wednesday. Talking with more confidence, she said that whatever place Sam finishes at Unatego, she'll duplicate it. She does.

Together in the lobby of the Hampton where the desk clerks were wonderfully helpful, Rachel Hosie, who is quickly recovering from her chest cold and destined to show remarkable improvement in the race, started the counting process by spouting "1" as we took attendance and readied to depart the hotel. All 24 responded in the usual kid-manner. "You're number two, dumb shit," as an elbow digs into the ribs of someone who'd forgotten their assigned number.

At 8:45 we drove off into the fog bank toward Unatego High School between Otego and Unadilla. Unatego, our destination, really doesn't exist outside of the brick high school building. It's not on any map.

We quickly knew that we were in a portion of the state that had no idea who we were and what we've meant to the sport for nearly two decades. We used that to our advantage. One after another asked us how to say the name printed on the front of our t-shirts that we wear pre-race. It's not all that uncommon for us to have to pronounce our name. During our first trip to Lehigh University for the annual Paul Short Invitational before they switched to a Friday race schedule in 2006, the good professors, athletic department workers and the always-doting alumni who work the meet no matter their advanced age, repeatedly asked about our school's name and its proper pronunciation. Having given up, a young black woman said with a welcoming smile, "We've decided to nick-name you Skittles. Every time we confront the fan who stares at our name, we bring up the Skittles episode once we've gotten out of ear-shot of the inquisitive cross country groupie.

Carly Brown, the lone frosh on the team, was excited after showing a little more growth and trust in her training. Chatting away excitedly after racing well, the blonde with the strong physical attributes said, "Did you hear everyone talking about us? They kept pointing at us and you could hear them asking their friends who we were, the team with the big "S". I love that. They couldn't believe how good we were. I like it when I can hear one of my teammates tell them that it's pronounced Skan-e-atlas." Carly is beginning to buy into the whole system. She's feeling pride and is thriving on our success. I hope we can hold on to her but I don't think we will. They're other voices calling from off in the distance.

After the awards ceremony had concluded, meet host and local legend Lee Schaeffer made a point of coming over to Rob and me with his hand outstretched. Shaking our hands he said, "In all my 35 years hosting this meet, I've never had every member of a team thank me when I gave them their individual plaque." Twice in 24 hours our kids had been praised. I'll have to make sure the athletic director hears about this. He usually hears silly things about the girls wearing jog bras in public or more relevant things like the girls running three abreast down a side road. He doesn't ever hear good news.

Despite winning the girl's and boy's races, the kids stayed humble as they warmed down on the well-manicured campus, slowly doing the old man shuffle, tossing the Frisbee and gathering for the awards presentations. The grass was thick and long in the natural setting of the Unatego amphitheater that sloped down to the three arched openings that led to a courtyard of sorts. It was obvious that many of my kids had not often received public acclamation for a real accomplishment. As their names were spoken loudly on the public address system and everyone's eyes were pointed toward them, they initially looked up and then sheepishly hung their heads, some temporarily immobilized and unable to move their feet. After receiving their plaques, they moved up the hill to their teammates, trying desperately to shrivel to a size that was unable to be seen as they worked hard to blend in with the crowd. They were definitely unlike one boy who looked as if he'd practiced his two-step dance of celebration.

We hadn't run on travel day, Friday. Did that help us perform? Did the day off help Lexie's foot feel better? Did the extra day of rest help Hosie stick with the pace longer? Should we try it again this coming Tuesday before the match-up with CBA? Rob and I would be hashing over all this and more on the ride home.

On the bus trip back north, Gary found the Syracuse University versus Wyoming football game from the Carrier Dome on the radio. The game was tied 10-up at the half. After getting our subs at Subway in Sidney, and after leaving the two-girl staff frazzled and worn out, we settled into our drive and listened as SU pulled out the win in the second overtime period.

As we readied to cross the Chenango River on our way home, I saw that every square inch of the Chenango Valley High School campus was taken by cars. The football game was huge, pitting rival Chenango Forks from just over the hill, against my Chenango Valley Warriors. The railroad trestle, a blackened vestige of the industrial revolution era that preceded me by at least a half century, still sported the white paint that said, "CV 68". It sent me back decades and my mind was reeling. The bridge we were driving over as we connected from Rt. 88 to Rt. 81 was a replacement for the one we tossed notebooks from on the last day of school on those hot June days that signaled the start of slow times and summer romances. Getting to second base was the big thing back then. It's probably not much different than today. Our actions weren't exactly something to be proud of—though there was plenty of bragging, and lying—but the natural forces of nature did their thing. We were just typical guys. We justified it by using our limited knowledge of Biology. Nature made us do it. In Italy, the men simply aren't doing it. They're sticking around with mom well into their 40s instead of marrying and propagating the species. As a consequence they aren't even reproducing at the replacement rate and have to rely on immigrants to do their work which ticks them off. Maybe they'd be more inspired to leave mom after walking across our bridge in Chenango Bridge in June and July. Maybe they'd start looking to get past second base.

I remember one day riding with two-mile state champ Dave Brinsco, he of Emporia State and me just a CV frosh-to-be. He somehow managed to go through all four gears on the bridge while we listened to the original version of "Let the Good-Times Roll." Ah, the days of my youth.

The kids bonded well on the trip, unlike Coach Julie's trip to Fabius-Pompey east from Skaneateles on hilly Rt. 20 with her modified team. "I think I did the right thing," she said after telling me the next day that she had to stop some real bickering among some of the girls. "They ran well and placed 4th against some big schools. And James Blonde, a nick name we gave to a tiny little blonde girl, had run well. In two days we'd find out that some of the other little girls had mooned and flashed their breasts to passing motorists. Things keep changing. It's time for me to begin walking toward the door.

We'll know in just a few days if the trip worked. Against CBA the girls will have to spit out their guts or the streak will end. They know it. If the trip worked, they'll do everything to uphold their end of the bargain, to fight, to not give in to pangs of doubt, mid-race sorrow and sharp physical pain. It's a chance for each of them to reconnect to our glory days when challenge was ably met by strong girls with an undeniable will to win. Will they fight for each other? I think so. In the past, they'd be on the phone with each other to boost each other's spirits in this challenging time. Today? They'll be text messaging and emailing. It's all the same.

The Day Before

I was a part of the end of a great winning streak back in 1968 while running as a junior at Chenango Valley for Coach Bob McDaniel. The school had not lost a single dual meet since the sport's inception at our school that was built into the side of a mountain along the unpredictable Chenango River near Chenango Bridge. Starting in the late 1950s, CV was training on the railroad tracks that split our mountain into an upper and lower loop. Running on the cinder bed along the railroad tracks was love, love of the symmetry provided by the evenly placed telegraph poles; love of the crunching sound that emanated from beneath your churning feet; love of the smell as foliage, cinders, industrial air and fresh air mingled together in a perfect mix. The sound of shoes striking loose cinders is exquisite, much like a winter boot with deep treads gripping into freshly fallen snow on a sub-zero morning. Steep trails took us up to the top of the mountain behind the school and into the province of wildlife and flora. Moss, slick and plentiful, made the trails treacherous, dangerous. But we ran on unfazed, guarded and guided by some mysterious force that scripted our every step.

No matter who was on the team, from State Champs Dick Lapman (1960) and Ray Smith (1964) to Bud Sweet, Al Whieldon, Tom Woods and all the rest, not one of our teams had ever lost. The Pennsylvania border wasn't too far south of us and we traveled there on occasion for invitationals.

It was a bright day when we raced for the title in 1968. We left gloomy. The winners of the two divisions in the Southern Tier Athletic Conference (STAC) met at Broome Community College. It was us against the Little Red from Ithaca and it wasn't even close. We didn't have any game that day. Chris Roser, one of our leaders, who is now a principal at Hornell High School, was so disgusted that he walked back to school. He simply refused to ride the bus. He wasn't worthy. I rode the bus. I was coming down with the runs and I wasn't going to take any chances. A year later at the IBM sectional course the runs did me in once again, and my little freshman brother Hugh beat me as I deferred to him and pushed him into the chute in front of me. It took a while to figure it out. In the end the link was cider. I drank too much of the freshly produced caramel colored liquid that was bottled in abundance locally. I mean, I drank way too much. The gallon jugs were just about the right size and I only weighed about 118 at the time. I alternated long guzzles from the plastic jug with manly bites of Spaulding donuts all powdered white with thick layers of sugar. It was heaven. And then I was in the bathroom losing ten pounds in the two days leading to the sectional championships for three straight years. It was a streak I wasn't proud of and it put a real damper on my career. In college I switched to pitchers of beer and manly bites of pizza.

We lost to Binghamton Central my senior year in a similarly embarrassing manner. We'd started a new streak as Central High went 1-2-3-4 behind Henry Shuford, the first great black distance runner I'd ever seen, Steve Banker, Jim Dickerson and, in a surprise, Bill Serbonich. I'll never forget their names. The 2.4-mile IBM Homestead Golf Course was 'soggy' according to reports in the Binghamton Press. I was 5th. Hannah's mindset was mine that day and I'm desperate to get her to succeed where I failed. As her coach, I owe her that.

It isn't often that teams enter the hunt for a championship. Winning is rare. Most kids who choose to run cross country are more than likely forced to seek smaller tokens of achievement as they reach for personal glory and individual improvement while pretending that their team is in the hunt every time they line up behind the starting line on some muddy flat somewhere.

Championships are a time to prove superiority, superiority of one runner over another, superiority of one group of seven over another, superiority of one training methodology over another, superiority of one coach and his relationship and motivational abilities over another. In the heat of the moment, that's what we believe. But luck has a lot to do with it, too, luck in the form of being ready if something unfortunate happens to the other team. Luck, in the form of being able to fire on all cylinders on the right day. Luck, in the form of being healthy and rested with a boy or girlfriend who isn't messing you up with little mind-games.

Proving superiority through athletics is a step up from what we as a species have routinely done. When some group of white guys, drunk on some form of southern moonshine, killed Emmitt Till and mangled his body beyond recognition, did they prove racial and individual superiority? When a white employer hires a lesser qualified white because he can't stand the sight of a black or Asian man, is he proving his mental and professional superiority, professional judgment? When a male supervisor tells a female applicant that he doesn't hire women with children because they miss too much work, has he proven gender superiority? When a minority application for a housing loan is rejected because they've dared seek to purchase a home in a neighborhood that rejects 'their' kind, is that proving superiority? In the grand scheme of all things human, taking it to each other on an athletic field is a civilized and equalitarian step forward. Our games are open to all.

Losing is something that I don't intend to do this week. I've seen a monument, a streak, go bust under my watch twice in my life. The first was back in 1968 and the other was a few years ago when our decade-long sectional streak went bust. I won't let it happen again. This league streak, that sort of snuck up on us, is all we have left. We need to protect it from extinction.

I've pushed these kids through some pounding practices after having agonized at home in my easy chair while planning their macro and micro cycles. I've tried to really get to know them, to goof with them, to keep them relaxed, to give them a safe haven while at practice. They won't lose this week. I guarantee it.

I spent my Sunday afternoon sending pictures to the team through the wonder of e-mail. Good pictures, pictures of them in full stride coming down mountain trails or leaning into a turn through a field of wild flowers. The pictures showed them resplendent in their uniforms with sweat glistening on the flesh of their necks and upper chests. They were running tall, running with pride, carrying on our tradition, running with power, with purposeful steps as eyes looked bravely and confidently toward the future, toward the next step and around the next bend while always thinking about crossing the finish line.

The match-up of state powers puts the 3rd ranked Skaneateles girls against the 8th ranked Lady Brothers from Syracuse Christian Brothers Academy. It's our 15th ranked Skaneateles boys against the 8th ranked boys from Bishop Ludden, guided by the legendary Jerry Smith, who was hired by my former Marcellus runner, lanky Athletic Director Pete Cass. Our boys, who were used to being highly ranked in the state for over a decade, are back in the hunt after a two-year hiatus. At practice they were already aware of the statewide acknowledgement. There wasn't any chest thumping or public celebration. They actually took it in stride even when they realized that they'd climbed over 100 spots in the last year as they rose from the bottom and emerged top-side with their pride intact. They'd done it right by training over the summer. Their efforts were being rewarded and I hope it'll take them through their senior year. But you never know about seniors. It's boom or bust with the boys and just as I think I understand what I'm dealing with, there's a Sandy Koufax curve ball coming straight at my head. We're going out into the world together in a year and I have a real need to get it right—for them, and me.

On the eve of the meet, Harold Muller of Chittenango called to see if we were ready. He knew that on paper that CBA's girls were better than us. He also said that our boys should beat the higher ranked Bishop Ludden boys. Harold's a considerate soul, and like me, he's a coaching geek. We live for this stuff. "Harold," I said into my General Electric phone, "how long have you been winning this league thing?"

Responding matter-of-factly he said, "Ever since the Freedom Division was formed." Harold's a rigorous scientist. There aren't a lot of adjectives or adverbs in him. He's Joe Friday-direct and a hell of a coach. Our league adopted patriotic division names after 9-11. He continued, "But when was the last time your girls lost?"

"1992," I said matter-of-factly.

"Well, you've got more on the line than I do with Jamesville-Dewitt's boys."

"Jack," he said, "Any great speeches I can borrow from you? Short of a miracle, J-D's 3-4-5 have us put away."

Laughing, I said that I can't even talk to the girls about CBA. It freaks them out. "In fact, Harold, we talked about taking Hannah and Rachel Hosie to Tully this weekend and Hannah was surprised that she was excited about it. That's more than unusual for us. All I've been doing is having Gary pick them up in the bus, drive them to the meet, and we send them off to race. That's my secret with this crew. Great coaching, huh? Ignorance is bliss."

CBA coach Theresa Trudell told me last night that we'll be using the same course as last year when our girls rallied behind a late surge by eventual winner Rachel Vaivoda 27-32 for our 13th consecutive league title. CBA went 2-3-4 and we took 1-5-6-7-8-9. This year we need to exploit their lack of depth like last year but we need to get Hannah and Rachel to break up their terrific top three. The first girl to finish will wear CBA purple. We have to break up the next two. It's imperative.

Originally we were going to use the course that Harold uses when he wants a home course advantage. Harold likes hills. He times hill workouts at Chittenango and keeps a record book of each hill session. A depth chart actually exists for each hill attack and the kids fight hard to run a time that will propel them to the head of the chart. Harold's course at Green Lakes is all hills and anyone who goes out too fast will wilt and soon die. One hill is a solid 800 meters long and it's steep. Just as you think you're at the peak, another peak appears, and then another, and another. The CBA girls voted down that course yesterday. We'll use the not-so-hilly hill layout at Green Lakes. Our girls are great hill runners but we can't run down 'em. And that hurts.

The boys had a rally of their own last year, winning 27-32 over CBA as recent-grad, Carson Sio, a strong 400 intermediate hurdler who was running XC for the first time, cranked it up a notch at the finish to pass a trio of runners to sew up the meet.

I'm not a ritualistic or superstitious man. I'm doing nothing unusual tonight, though I spend most waking moments thinking of the race, the season, the kids and our challenges against both CBA and Tully for the sectional title. Back in my senior year of high school I got into a routine of listening to Tommy James and the Shondells' raucous "Mony Mony" before I left my bedroom inner sanctum for school across the valley floor. Some Friday nights I'd jog down Calgary Lane to Wisconsin Drive to River Road. Some pre-race nights I'd run far too fast. I knew

I wouldn't sleep well the night before a race. I was too wired. I think I quickly realized that today's big craze called visualization didn't work before it ever came into vogue. I always won my Friday night races. By the end of my frosh year, I wasn't winning anymore and I knew that I'd never escape the long shadows cast by my Chenango Valley predecessors, the Legends of the Valley.

Today? There's no specific number of beers to drink as I pretend to watch TV. I roam the web sites looking for a reason to be optimistic about the end of the season. I go over my scouting reports. I look back at the workouts to see if I'm on the right track. I eat whatever my wife and I plan on as we walk out the door in the morning. And I fall asleep easily while briefly carrying on a slew of conversations with my pretend reporters, my kids and the voices that romp freely in my mind as awareness begins to fade into dreams.

Bob McDaniels, my high school coach, believed that if he could pull off some preconceived run the day before the big meet, we'd win. It took us a while to figure him out. We'd be running up on the mountain behind the school expecting deer or other animals to dart across our path, but the most startling intervention was seeing coach up ahead leaning on a tree or squatting as he watched us move up the mountain. He knew every shortcut on that damn mount and he used them judiciously, effectively. He'd chug and grunt even as he approached retirement, his thick, muscled body clad in cotton gray sweats moving fluidly. He didn't like to lose. His marine crew-cut spoke volumes. He was gruff yet friendly. And we always got a Christmas card from him. Back in the 60s that was a big deal because adults, led by the ever-misguided Doctor Spock, were a hands-off generation when it came to child rearing and teaching.

For years, the results of Coach's romps on the mount proved that his superstitions worked until that afternoon when Ithaca beat us, led by Ron Redfield-Lyon.

The only superstition I had involved turning left after standing up from the lone locker room toilet and spitting back into the bowl. For a few weeks my senior year I let the nail grow on my little finger but I quickly bit it off as I continually failed to meet my God-given promise on the wooded trails.

My goal is to ensure that Hannah doesn't fail. She stumbled early but she's beginning to look forward to racing. Inside is where I have to reach. There's always an ember of fire within the runner waiting patiently, sometimes valiantly, to be fanned, to be turned into a flickering flame and, in time, into a roaring fire of faith, persistence and dreamy confidence. It's like the tinkling of the ivory piano keys, struck randomly one finger on one key time after time until a beat, a rhythm develops. Slowly, as one moment of time passes and is joined by another, a song rises in the soul, a song that sends flutters where the human spirit lives as sleeping muscles deep behind rippling abs begin to twitch in excitement. Muscles that were once loose, relaxed, flaccid and useless are transformed into entities that have form, substance and purpose. The simple little song that began with a flutter, with a flicker, roars and no more is the runner waiting to fail, to fall, to disappoint. He's risen from the dark, from the ashes, having risen from the dead in so many ways as he prepares to fly while a concert, a full-blown concerto, plays confidently in his head.

The day of the race with CBA and Bishop Ludden dawned dark and rainy. And the bad stuff was yet to come. On my drive from classes at J-E to the serenity and lush landscape of Green Lakes, I play with the radio dial in defiance of every bit of logic I possess. I know that Syracuse radio is about as good as a promise from some politicians to protect and nurture congressional pages. As soon as I'm out of range of WICB, the Ithaca College student-run station, I quickly hit the AM button and catch up on the sporting news of the day. It doesn't take long before I'm hearing the same old thing. Those talk show guys have figured out how to fill a lot of hours of talk. They say the same thing over and over and come back to the same thing and repeat it over and over. Rare is the minute when something new, insightful or groundbreaking is offered to the AM listener. I can listen at 10 AM on one program and hear the same dribble at 2PM, at 5PM, at 8PM. It doesn't take me long to hit the CD button on the console as I play my pump-up music to get ready to meet the kids. Getting the music just right is important to kids, especially athletes who are on deck or kids who leave home and venture to a far away college. Every truly hip kid when I was a teenager, listened to WENE, the Triple Cities' only rock AM radio station in the mid-1960s. As we trekked from Chenango Valley to our meets we'd bob and weave in our bus seats while listening to WENE and chant our fight songs. We were sure that the songs got us ready to rumble. It was on one of those trips when I first heard a song played back-to-back. Man that was a breakthrough day when we thought that anything was possible. We all knew that local history was being made as Del Shannon's *Runaway* filled the cozy confines of the CV team bus as we drove north on Interstate 81 to our next race. At CBA, we were the runaway winners.

The Day After

We'd been pounding the mountain trails and slogging through mud and long grass for the better part of a month and it was time to just let them go. Turnover had suffered and without foot-speed no one was going anywhere at the end of the season. Rob and I were convinced that the kids needed a healthy dose of dedicated speed. *"Hey girl, just let yourself go."* Sometimes the lyricists of good rock songs have a few things to say, and O.A.R. in *Hey Girl* struck a nerve. These girls and boys just need to get going, to get back into the flow. "I need 200s," said Rachel Hosie. They need to fly again. Like nested baby birds being well-mothered, the neurons that have developed over endless eons sense the need to fly, and off they go as the patterns of nature continue to unfold in a seamless cadence. At practice Rob and I did our best to convince the kids that they could handle the workout and they did so with confidence and poise. With the pain from our meet at heavily forested Green Lakes settling into their sinew and muscles, the kids believed and proved to themselves that they can do anything.

We hammered the workout on the track and the crowd was the biggest we'd ever had for a practice. The modified football team was hosting rival Marcellus who showed up in their Christmas colors of red, green and white. They killed us, so the future of the Skaneateles football team is bleak. It could be the same for our girls cross country team despite some talent at the lower level. Coach Julie had the mod squad on a run and two of her girls got into a fight that was severe enough for passing motorists to stop and intervene. The pugilists are gone for a week as we applied the same rules that apply in the classroom. Fight and you're gone for five. When Harold-of-Chittenango called and I mentioned it, he didn't have a comeback. When we commiserate on the phone we're just bellowing, bitching, complaining and trying to top each other. I got him on this one, unfortunately.

My fear for the speed work training session was that the kids would be gassed, tight, empty. I was wrong. "This is the best workout we've had all year," said Rob as we talked the kids into standing tall, true and tough between intervals. "You're as tough as you want to be. Fake it. Cross the line and walk away. Put your hands on your hips, spit, act street-tough. Eventually you'll begin to believe it and that's when you can enact some revenge on the course. You saw Bishop Ludden's kids. Sure, they have a crazy man for a coach who preaches two things; tough and tougher. But I think we're smarter than that. We just need to know that we're tough. You heard the top CBA girls breathing. They were bellowing. They were maxed and you could tell. So no slouches or pantywaists from now on. Are ya with me?" They're good kids. The boys immediately think I'm dissing them and I can see it in their eyes, in their posture. I didn't see it last year. I have to be careful to attach some love when I talk to the boys. They need to know that I'm on their side and believe in them. The chastisement is clearly there in the message but they also need to hear that we're in this together, that they've been doing a good job, and that I know they're better than what they recently showed because they've done it right on many occasions this season. The girls just take it in stride and I'm not sure if I have any real impact on them like I used to.

Rachel Vaivoda had a knot in her quad that drove her to visit her chiropractor. She ran her fastest paces of the season for sets of 200, 200, 400. Sofie ran 6 x 600 at 3k pace with a mere 1:43 rest after doing a 30 minute run to warm-up. Then she did a 400 by slamming a 200, resting for 15 seconds and slamming another 200. After practice The Citizen, our Auburn newspaper, interviewed her for next week's feature in something they call "The Zone." The strawberry blonde with the freckles was beaming afterwards. Hannah and Rachel Hosie, who are racing Saturday, did a 30 minute run and two sets of 200, 200, 400 and felt great. The pack hit consistent 80s for their 400s and ran with purpose, passion and determination. I think we've finally gotten the training groups right. The boys looked like they did earlier in the season and that's a good thing after letting Bishop Ludden beat them up yesterday.

The day before, as Rob and I walked toward the finish line at Green Lakes State Park after we were certain that we'd turned-back CBA's challenge, we wondered what the girls would say. We weren't exactly sure how they ran, but a brief analysis would show that they ripped off a good one. I went right up to Hannah and fortunately very few parents were in attendance so we could talk freely. "I know I can beat them. They're not that good. On a flat course they can't beat me. I mean it." I'm seeing something different in Hannah. Maybe she's like my students. In October they can't fathom the relevance of their lessons for a state exam way down the road in late June. Hannah is beginning to see the end and the time remaining is something she can begin to deal with. In four weeks she can begin to lead a more artistic life which is something she's spurned for us. She loves music and is thinking of making a non-teaching career of it. Hannah's talking about upcoming meets. She's excited. She's ready to rip one. Hannah was so excited that she was invading my space, moving toward me even as I stepped back. In America, we tend to move apart. In Latin America, they move toward each other when they speak. I swear I could see her medulla oblongata moving. She looked good. The green snot was hanging out of her nose as it wrapped back toward her cheek bone. The sweat was profuse and her proclamations were said with conviction. "Just ask Rach. They pulled away from me on every uphill and then I'd catch right back up on the flat. But going down they'd pull away again. It kept breaking up my rhythm." I responded that the rest of the season was flat and she loved the sectional course. "I'll break 19 there coach." When I responded that we should hold off on predictions because the weather will play a part, she said that it didn't matter. We're growing up. We're getting ready even though CBA put race winner Kristen Fekete and Francesca Minale in front of our team. We took 3-4-5-6-7-8-10 to finish them off with ease. For days thereafter we received compliments from custodians, other coaches, and people in the checkout line at the store.

"Jack, it's Harold," yelled my wife from the kitchen. "You sandbagged it Jack. They gave you no fight at all, he said." Earlier, several cyclists who were easily taking the hill up Andrews Road yelled, "Great win over CBA yesterday, Jack." Always involved in the Auburn Great Race that's held in August, the guys knew me from past encounters.

The raw score of 25-35 did look impressive against a state-ranked team. There's two ways to look at it. With injured frosh Katie Webster unable to do anything except help score the meet, we beat up on their pack and walked away with the win. The flip side is that with the freshman in the line-up we'd probably have suffered the ignominious fate of losing the meet and breaking the streak because a team finishing 1-2-3 gets an automatic win. The flip side of that is this: Our girls ran out of their minds. As a team we averaged 20:42 on a course that ripped us apart from the inside as lactate piled up like cars on a California highway as a fog rolled landward off San Francisco Bay. Last year with the same team on a day that was actually a bit better because it was cooler, we averaged 21:08. Each girl up and down the line-up was about 30 seconds faster. And they looked it. Kristin Roberts might have had her best day ever with an improvement of 1:04. And she kept it going today in the speed workout. The girl is coming on at the right time of the year. I'm still waiting for Rachel Hosie.

As I told Neil Kerr of the Post-Standard, when you've done nothing but win for 14 years, a lot of luck plays a part in your fortunes. We got lucky a while back when Westhill had that one-year-wonder team that no one could beat. The year that Westhill was heading our way like Haley's comet making its rounds, their school population grew just enough and it forced them to be moved to a division for larger schools. Luck. Pure and simple, we'd never have beaten them. But we can't determine who lines up against us. All we can do is show up and try to run faster than the opponents that the league, section and state send against us. And we've done it 85 straight times now in the league.

I just realized last night, as the filter in my mind sifted through the constant bombardment of facts, anecdotal evidence and hunches that incessantly bounce around in my head, that I might have a chance to retire without ever having come home to deal with defeat. The girls have been that good, that consistent, that driven to succeed, that willing to lay it on the line for me, that willing to pee and shit in their bun huggers. I know that a lot of their sacrifice is willingly suffered because they want to do it for me. And that means the world to me as I approach their careers, their seasons and practices with the same seriousness of a surgeon planning for the next day's operation. The impact of their sacrifice is immeasurable as it strikes deep inside my conscious being. I carry with me every moment of every day the impact that my words and workouts will have on their lives. Each step needs purpose. Each pang of pain must be principled and justified. Each moment with me must trump the time they could be spending with friends wandering around the brick sidewalks in the village or undertaking a lead role in the school play. And their lives are so complicated--so convoluted and as layered as a sweet onion grown in the black earth in Oswego--that I sometimes think we're trying to talk to each other while we jump chaotically together on a trampoline, the chance of us meeting and moving in unison rare enough that I think that Republicans and Democrats might have a better chance of agreeing on abortion.

No matter what, we can't deny that we're connected quietly and intricately in this delicate and daring dance of preparation and competition. We live and die with each other as every step in our weekly march toward racing perfection is called forth for judgment at week's end. It's a morality play that plays out every day as the kids urgently plead to get better and I try with utmost sincerity to match my plans to their needs. And I suspect that it's one of the final purposeful thoughts that zip unconsciously through a coach's mind as he lays prostrate on his death bed, the sheets tight and stained with family holding hands, praying and mourning the impending loss of a treasured soul. The hand that once gripped the stopwatch is wrinkled and the face that smiled and revealed every soulful feeling is shallow. But the little bit of life remaining is still noble, full and valiant. Coaches make a difference in kids' lives and that means something. Our time together is valuable and it's worth taking with us to the grave six feet under the land we once ran upon with disdain and indifference. Like finishing a long run with some speed so that the quick turnover is the final message the muscles receive, I wonder if the final thoughts in a dying person's mind are what they carry with them into eternity.

Off to the side of the Green Lakes course in the dewy mist stood a deer that was slightly amused and obviously confident in being able to carry out its mission in life. It foraged without a hint of fear of us. The doe appeared as the girls started their race and it reappeared at the end of the meet. As the girls stripped just before doing their final strides, the deer was in no hurry to leave. In contrast to the deer, Fekete and Minale were quick to leave the starting line when the foghorn forlornly sounded its distinctive, musty signal. We dropped behind quickly but by the 800 meter mark we were right with them and the meet was essentially over. Our pack was out and fighting to the finish. Just 47 seconds separated Hannah from a sullen Amanda. I think it has something to do with an issue that she's suffering quietly. Her mother and father have never come to see her race. She has a heart of gold but it's surrounded by a silent sorrow. I wonder how she'd have raced if her dad was bellowing faithfully all over the desolate course that rose mightily from the earth just south of the Erie Canal.

The battle wasn't exactly like Yamamoto and Nimitz at the Battle of Midway, but it was a serious race with a lot on the line.

The boys left for home with a split decision. With Gary driving the bus we reflected on our throttling of CBA as well as getting humbled by the 8th ranked Gaelic Knights of Bishop Ludden. I hate losing to Jerry Smith like he used to hate losing to me when he was at Fayetteville-Manlius with Bill Aris in their earlier glory days.

The boys looked more like we did last year than we've looked all this season. Only Sam and Calvin were able to beat the time that was run last year by Patrick who prematurely retired after his sophomore year. And that's a problem that we talked about before we started the track workout today. With all their summer mileage, all their speed, stamina, endurance, growth and success this year, there was no reason except for a mental letdown for this to happen. As Rob says, "If you can't get up for the private schools, what can you get up for?" Rob and I are both public school advocates. I hate that private schools even exist. They just seem anathema to the core values of America. Join the team. Learn to deal in the cauldron of society, to share ideas, to learn to mesh with those who are different, poorer, less wise, less fortunate, less able to call a friend to get something cleared up or to get a high paying job. I hate the separation because it goes against what we stand for in this nation. We're all in this together, one for all and all for one. We dig the trenches together, we face hurricanes side by side—rich and poor—and we play on the fields with one another with a common goal that can only be achieved if we forgo individual thoughts of glory and forge a union. The thought that some people feel they are so much better, morally or otherwise, than the rest of us that they have to distance themselves from the reality of our nation just grinds my gourd.

The day wasn't just about us. Former coach Lou Delsole with Jim Vermeulen at the helm led their West Genesee girls into a league title battle against Cicero-North Syracuse and fell just short, losing by two because their third girl repeated her lackluster sectional performance of last November. Finishing 6th on the team after everyone else had stepped up just ripped into Lou's inner being. He'd kept the pre-race pep talk simple as most of his work is done in practice. That's when he earns their trust and begins to hone their confidence.

Harold's undermanned Chittenango boy's team, which is probably the worst of his career, out-dueled host Jamesville-Dewitt by a few points. I'm sure that it was probably his best job of coaching. And I think he agrees.

Rachel Hosie is the key to our success for the rest of the season. She's just had her yearly cold so from now on she should be healthy. Last year at this time she was in a similar position and I didn't think she'd be helping us much. But then she took off. After the CBA victory yesterday she said, "I'll be back Saturday." I hope she is because it'll be like the Triple Entente in WWI being joined in the trenches by the American Doughboys. She tips the scales.

Looking at the kids who I've coached and who I've coached against— and looking at my students over the decades—it's amazing that some kids get nothing but shit at birth--and then it gets worse. Some get the perfect parents, the perfect body and the inquisitive brain that has all the neurons twisting around each other so the sunshine of education enters their lives and some see life as a series of unsolvable problems. Some get globetrotting parents while others get gutter-rolling alcoholics. Some are eager to explore while others have no desire to leave the trailer park or slum. Some get private clubs and some get private horrors.

Katie Webster, the tall CBA runner who was sidelined, has the distinctive and attractive features that go perfectly with her effusive confidence and her gift of gab. She's gregarious, entertaining and able to take a jab as well as she's able to deliver one with the appropriate dose of sophisticated humor. The stubborn, purple scoring tent that refused to open fully was more appropriate for a hobbit. Bent perpetually at the waist and shoulders, she collected and tabulated the results and looked at ease with herself despite knowing that she was the one who could have turned the tide against us and ended the streak.

As Francesca Minale walked off the grassy course with her proud and smiling mother in tow, I congratulated the senior who would love to go to Cornell and run for Lou Duesing who's a spectacular coach and human being. "Thank you sir," she said with a broad smile cracking her pretty Asian face.

Winner Fekete congratulated my team after I mentioned how strong she looked in the race as she pulled away from us.

The Post-Standard will say that CBA lost the meet, but they won a new fan who happened to be an opposing coach. I hate liking the kids from private schools.

Disappointment

"Jack, if the kids think they're going to catch those seagulls, they've got a lot to learn." Turning from Marty Cregg who shares in the ownership of the Skaneateles Polo Grounds with his generous mother-in-law, I turned to the massive, manicured lawn that serves as a place for the high-priced horses to romp and saw the team taking off from the starting line for next Wednesday's final dual meet of the season against Marcellus and Westhill. With the seas gulls startled into unplanned flight on a cloudless day high atop Andrews Road on the west side of the lake, it did indeed look as if the kids were in hot but futile pursuit. The lawns, 44 acres in total and mowed by Cliff Smith to ¾ inch length in a process that takes two days of his attention, will serve as our home course for the first time. Our legendary course on the Skaneateles campus was closed by construction and our temporary home in Austin Park in the middle of the village has footing that feels, in spots, like you're running on the smoldering black and red embers of uneven, jagged, ankle-turning terrain near Kileuea, Hawaii's sputtering volcano.

Dick Sterling is a state trooper who works drug cases for the government while also doing some things that he can't talk about. He's joined forces with fellow Ironman Michael Parker, our ear, nose and throat specialist, to design the Polo Grounds course. Sterling, who has seen Coach Rob at an annual northern New York State outdoor rock-fest while working undercover during the Labor Day holiday, said, "Parker and I are putting the final touches on the X-C course at the Polo Field. We have run it several times and done it with the GPS and have it pretty much tweaked. I think the team and the coaching staff will find it a fun and classic course." The course is a simple figure-8 and has everything, including a horse-shit mound to cross when leaving a mowed field path that bobs and weaves around all sorts of flowering trees and bushes before entering a twisting wooded trail with a hard-packed dirt floor. If we wanted, we could have the kids run through a horse barn besides running on the polo field, crossing a stream and running up and down gradual slopes that total 150 feet in elevation during the course of the race. The course flows past the home of John Walsh, the founder and marquee star of "America's Most Wanted".

Everything on the course is being handled with the care and precision that befits Marty's personality and background. You'd expect nothing less from a University of Notre Dame alum who moves his polo horses to South Carolina in early fall as they transition to wintering and playing in Florida.

Dick Sterling is excited because his daughter, Sofie, received a call from Division-I University of Binghamton who said that they have an interest in her. "I am not her coach but I feel she needs to lean out a little more to step it up to the next level where she needs to be," he stated. "The coach will be at Sectionals to look at her. Sofie needs to understand that to take it to that next level she has to eat, sleep and live running… period." The irony of that statement would dramatically play out in a most disappointing and head-shaking manner in the next 24 hours.

Dick's right. And what he's talking about needs to occur in the summer. Fortunately, Sofie has never balked at her summer assignments. She loves cross country. By the time indoor is flowing she's already talking about the fall. When outdoor track begins to heat up she's positively yearning for cross country. She's made a big commitment this year and it shows in her body, her stride, the ability to maintain pace mid-race and her ability to kick. We've made positive progress with Hannah, too. She's been consistently in the front of her races and her demeanor, posture and choice of words show that she's ready to take on challenges without faltering.

While Sofie and the rest of the gang worked out on the new course at the Polo Grounds Saturday morning to prepare for the Westhill challenge to 'The Streak', parentless-Hannah, who has been farmed out to the Sterling family while dad was away on business and mom was at Lake George closing up the camps, spent the night at Sofie's and slept well past early morning. She had a race to run at Tully at noon with our 6th runner Rachel Hosie. The rest of the girls had been racing well for themselves but Hannah and Rachel needed more racing to sharpen their game.

The plan worked well. The majority of the team got to run the new course twice for a total workout of six miles on a beautiful day while two of their teammates, who serve as barometers of our success, raced head-to-head with Tully, our top rival for the sectional crown. With Rachel taking the early lead like always, and with Hannah initially dropping back like always, the earth seemed to be in perfect balance. Rachel dropped back to finish 25th in the race. "I just missed my teammates. It's not the same without them." Hannah worked her way up to third, the position-of-choice this year based on her place of finish in most meets. But this time something happened. She moved. And it was because her self-talk was different.

> *It's like when you're on the couch watching TV and your mother tells you to clean your room and you definitely don't want to do it. I felt good behind Kelly Coyne (Tully's top runner). My breathing was good and my legs were fine. But I just didn't want to make the effort to pass her. I knew if I did I'd feel good about it, just like getting off the couch to clean my room. So I did it. I wanted to feel good. You know? I should have just kept going and gotten the lead but I passed her and settled back down. If I had just kept moving I would have caught her, Kelseigh Groth from Lafayette and won. Did you know she was a freshman?*

Hannah is coming on, she's growing and learning how to run up front. Most of us aren't born with that specific DNA. It's a learned behavior and that's why, at times, I've left 9th grade boys on the modified team. I wanted them to learn how to win, how to compete, how to take the full measure of themselves and their opponents. Hannah's time, just six seconds short of winning, was 19:48 and it moved her into the second slot on our Laker Leader Board behind Lia Cross (Colgate) and above many D-I runners. She'd done well and based on what my two 'barometers' had done, I figure that we can have five girls with Tully's 3rd. No one else knows that but me. I devised five different models to set up a comparison of our teams and this is the one that I think fits reality the best. I wonder if anyone is noticing. So far I seem to be leaning against strong windmills.

So, what's so disappointing about all of this? Nothing. My Sunday dawned late as I behaved like a thorough bum. I was totally determined to remain in bed until the digital clock read 10:00. I accomplished my mission. Getting up, I stretched my back while using the big blue ball and doing my new pretzel stretch while leaning against the sofa and watching "Meet the Press" host Tim Russert skewer the candidates for the Missouri Senate seat. After reading about Syracuse University's gridiron loss to Pitt, I hit the track and logged 8 solid laps, completed a lap of 100s, walked one lap as I did push-ups every 100 meters, cooled down a lap and hit the village for my Sunday ritual: stopping at Riddler's for a New York Times and 10 pieces of bubble gum, crossing Jordan Road and standing in line at The Bakery for a warm cinnamon donut, stopping in the Patisserie for a loaf of fresh chiabotto bread, and driving home along the lake shore while listening to the Ithaca College radio station and carefully eating my donut.

Then came the phone call and everything changed.

Hi!

I couldn't figure out who it was.

We just wanted to talk to you about something.

The voice was meek, weak, scared and fragile, even fearful.

It's Sofie. And Hannah.

There was some fumbling as objects hit together. There was some noise and a low-level of commotion. Then I could hear Hannah's voice. It was initially strong and upbeat like usual. And then it changed quickly and choked up.

Coach, we have something to talk about and it's real hard.

I thought there was some intra-squad turmoil involved. That's all that popped into my head. The shit was about to hit the fan and the blades were whirling rapidly.

There had been a party that was attended by plenty of student-athletes, but other than Hannah and Sofie, no one else would stand tall and take responsibility for their actions. Only my two seniors would face the consequences. Another girl who is beautiful, but had been troubled with booze since she was a frosh, blew a .325 on the blood-alcohol gizmo. She was closer to dead than alive when they got her to the hospital. Sofie and Hannah knew that the girl was in big trouble and they, along with a few others, decided that the girl's parents should be called with the bleak news that no parent ever wants to hear. The police followed up and the story began to unravel.

> *We tried to make the right decision. We know we're in trouble but the police told our parents that we were good girls and that we did the right thing to call for help.*

"Girls, you know you did something wrong though. You know the school rules. So, let me ask you the big question. Did you drink?"

Yeah, we did but not much.

The 14-year streak was in full jeopardy and I hoped that this was the first time the girls had gone out to party.

When prodded, it sounded to me like they'd had a beer but it turned out to be vodka that the inebriated one had brought with her from home. Sofie's mom, when I talked to her, said she was surprised that they'd held off this long. Skaneateles kids drink and there's pressure to follow suit. With our team history of Steve Corsello drinking and driving and killing his friend, I should be the most upset and the one to bring down the hammer on the girls. But I'm concerned about keeping them talking to me, trusting me. If they clam up, Rob and I won't know anything and we'll be useless as teachers. First and foremost, we're educators dealing with something that grad school doesn't address. It's our job to instruct, to help them learn to make good choices, to hold them accountable on many levels. The girls understand that drinking was a poor choice, but when crunch time came, they stepped up and in a selfless act sought help. And then they called me to confess.

Shouldn't we get a lesser punishment? We tried to do right.

They knew that they'd made the right moral choice, though it was a hard decision in retrospect. They knew they couldn't leave the girl to die. The cop saying that he was proud of them helped to soothe some pangs of doubt and worry. Sofie's mom thought that they weren't intoxicated at all by the time she saw them. I don't know where the truth rests since the girls were deemed drunk by the officer so he didn't even breathalyze them.

The girls understand that it's their first athletic code offense. They were emotional and cried for six hours that evening. It took them a full four hours to get up the courage to call me. And frankly they've put me in a bad spot. If the word gets out in the coming week or two and the athletic director asks me if I knew, what am I supposed to say? Of course I knew, they told me. So here's the dilemma. Without Hannah and Sofie, we could lose Wednesday and there goes 14 years of work by a lot of great kids, and me, and all the other coaches who've been involved. But there's Rob's and my credibility. The other kids on the team will surely hear about the incident. One set of parents has demanded an investigation and it sounded to me like they were trying to deflect their daughter's continued reckless behavior onto Hannah as if Hannah forced their daughter's fingers to grip the bottle and force the booze into her stomach. I have a few kids who, being kids, might use this and they'll own Rob and me in short order if we don't bench Hannah and Sofie.

So, what to do? Rob and I decided today to enact a two meet suspension and then we'd call the athletic director. At a minimum Hannah and Sofie will miss our final dual meet of the year—the one that counts—and their last opportunity to race at their beloved twin loop Phoenix Firebird Invitational. They'll miss their only senior home meet. They'll pay, not for doing what was right, but for making a damn stupid decision, a decision to go to a party where they knew booze would flow just four days before they'd be called upon to lead us into the competitive arena.

Sofie's mother and father will be seeing a lot more of her. Grounded. But they also understand that Sofie has been bored to tears by sitting home on the couch every Friday and Saturday doing what her teammates expected of her. "It's been boring," said mom. "She's been really good about all this." There's pressure in this town. And it isn't good pressure.

My e-mail was filled all night by Kristin Roberts who has suddenly developed a sore back and an upper leg problem. I advised her to see Dave Petters, our local chiropractor, before the problem gets worse. We need her Wednesday. Without her we can't possibly win. Taylor Wellington, who worked hard over the summer but isn't yet a factor in the varsity races, is on a week-long trip to Las Vegas, so she isn't going to be available. We'll be on a razor thin edge for this meet. If the girls run well, we can carry over the streak to next year. I hope Rachel Vaivoda can handle the pressure. Historically she's melted down when the pressure rose significantly. But I have a hunch she'll rise up in this instance and beat Westhill's top girl. Marcellus will most likely take the top two spots, but after that they're as weak as a lake trout that's been played on the line for a half hour. From the promise of Tully we traveled to the bitter depths of disappointment in just 24 hours. Cross Country is just a game but it's really a whole lot more. I don't look forward to telling Sofie and Hannah at practice on Columbus Day that they're benched.

On Monday I was able to let Hannah know about the potential for a season-ending sentence at practice. She showed up vital, energetic and light-hearted. She was faking it. Her feet barely rested on the ground. But she's socially fragile and I knew she was into her cover-up act as her defense mechanisms were working all-out.

Sofie was on college visits so all of this will have to wait until she returns to school and gets bombarded. I ended up talking to the police while at practice as an officer cruised behind the school on his hourly check. Later I spoke to the officer who was in charge of the case in a mid-afternoon visit with him at the police headquarters. It looks like Hannah could be arrested and booked for providing a place for the party if push comes to shove. She's incredulous. She never hangs out with that crowd. Hannah stayed with Sofie while her dad was on business in Alabama and her mom was closing the summer camp at Lake George.

Shortly after my wife and I had dinner at the Bluewater Grill along the east side of the outlet at the north end of the lake, I got a call from Hannah's mom and I drove into the village to see them. Hannah was crumpled up on the stairs in a fetal position but we coaxed her into a chair in the living room that looked to be trimmed in mahogany. Hannah was sobbing and she had trouble understanding that her mom was dealing with emotions of her own. We decided to get it all out and called the police and in no time the investigating officer was pulling into the driveway. We talked. Hannah opened up and either confirmed information or enlightened the officer with new information that filled in some gaps. Hannah rarely stopped sobbing and the skin underneath her eyes puffed up and reddened. I think in the officer's 12 years on the force he had rarely seen such contrition. Suddenly he offered a deal. Instead of criminal court he would recommend youth court and Hannah jumped at the chance. She was so embarrassed.

We exchanged e-mails after she went to the police station to help lay out a time-line and render her official statement.

> *Well, time for bed girl....I wrote the letter that the officer wanted so I'll drop it off tomorrow at the police station....you need to help your body handle the stress and that means taking vitamins, getting to bed, eating healthy....it's very important.... the stress can break you down and after we survive this we want you strong so that you can come back with a vengeance....that's the goal 'banana....back with a vengeance....self-preservation.... relax....I think things will only get better from now on....sleep well....coach*

I hadn't wanted to call Rick Pound, the athletic director, but I did. And he called the Vice-Principal who had forged a strong bond with Hannah. I truly have no insight into how this will turn out. The standard rule is to bench the first offender for 25% of the contests. It looks like she and Sofie may be back to run the sectional championship. As I got ready to watch the new episode of "Heroes" on NBC, I got Hannah's e-mail.

> *Thank you so much coach…it's good to hear that from someone, because while I know my parents still love me and they tell me*

*they'll never abandon me and I know that is true, it's still hard
for them because they're so upset...I'm just really frustrated that
the one time that I decide to come to my house, and not even
plan on coming here because I was just SOOO uncomfortable
with being at Justin's and scared of not having a ride home,
I have to get caught when all those other girls have done it a
million times....but maybe things happen for a reason, and
in this case I really hope that something good comes out of it
and I know it will, but thank you very much for everything
you've done. You've done so much to help with the police and
my parents and just making all the right decisions, only one
more stop to go, Mr. Major, and I'm just gonna tell him exactly
what happened, and that it was a unique situation, very out
of the ordinary and that it doesn't happen often. I just felt
socially awkward...well thanks again for everything...I'll see
you tomorrow at practice and give you a report...hopefully
without tears again...thanks Hannah*

When she saw the boy drinking who was going to take her home, she
freaked out. And that's when her small group left for the safe confines
of her house. Hannah, like other good kids, hates to lose control. And
everything from now on will be completely out of her hands. Like other
good kids, Hannah wasn't able to stand the inertia and the slow pace
of justice so I was enormously pleased that the officer took the time to
visit with Hannah and take her full statement. Hannah is still headed
toward a rugged time but at least she's seeing progress, and movement
means the world when you have no control over your own life.

The officer asked me to write a letter on Hannah's behalf.

To The Skaneateles Police Department,

*I write to you on behalf of Hannah whose recent actions have
brought her to your attention. I have worked closely with
Hannah all year long for the better part of six years. She's a
good kid. We spend a lot of quiet time together on school busses
as we travel the state. There's really very little I don't know
about her because she's always felt at ease with me and has
confided in me for years.*

She doesn't drink. Of that I'm sure. With her parents holding the hammer-of-parental-justice over her, with her parents constantly--except this past weekend--calling ahead to confirm that a parent is in the house that she is going to, with her training with me six days a week year 'round, there's really no time or place that isn't accounted for in Hannah's life. Based on the past 61 seasons that I've coached, I can state that there is no way an athlete can compete at Hannah's level if he or she were spending weekends in a drunken stupor.

I also have big ears. I hear everything and I haven't once gotten a shred of evidence that Hannah partakes in illegal activity.

Hannah is full of life. She's maturing gracefully with periodic pitfalls like most good kids. She possesses a very logical mind and she doesn't have to be hit in the head with a hammer to get a message across. I can tell you that Hannah is enormously embarrassed by this whole affair. She knows that she's let everyone down, that she's risked our 14-year unbeaten streak, that she's compromised the zero tolerance that we preach within our team. When Hannah says that she'd never do anything like this again, I believe her. Hannah's heart is in the right place. She hates to disappoint people. She hates to lose control of her life. She wants to be looked up to as a good person more than as a good runner. It's going to take quite some time for her to deal properly with this whole situation, that I know for certain.

Hannah takes full responsibility for her stupid decision this past weekend. She was out of character while staying with a friend who had a different circle of friends who, for the most part, are normal, good kids. She knows that she mishandled her decision-making and has vowed to never stray from her much quieter, more sedate group of friends who do not drink. Some kids need to be punished repeatedly before they change their behavior and get the message. Others only need to suffer consequences once. Hannah is a member of a group that mends their ways when those who she holds in high regard express disappointment in her. Hannah knows the path she should return to and I'm enormously confident that she will, indeed, not stray again. She hates booze and looks down at the kids who drink weekly, disdains their lack of dedication-to-a-cause outside of their own instant gratification, and despises all the bad that drinking brings into a life. She knows her core values and I'm sure they will prevail.

My charge now is to get the remaining nine girls to believe that they can win. The situation sends me right back to the sectional race against Canastota when we'd lost Julie Lynch to a broken thigh bone. Without their consent, next year's team has been handed the torch. It's theirs to carry now. Somehow I have to convince them that destiny has chosen them for a reason and it's their responsibility to carry the torch proudly, to keep it burning, to do everything in their power to not let it flame-out. Three weeks from now, if the school doesn't grind the girls into a pitiless pulp, we'll do everything we can to return with a vengeance. We'll show 'em. God knows we'll show 'em at sectionals.

Benched and Chagrined

I was tired, damn tired, tired enough to nap through a call from my oldest son Kirk, my oldest pal in the universe. That's what I've called him since the moment of his birth when the two of us just sat behind a hospital curtain and talked about all the things that life was going to bring to him. He had no neurons that could make sense of my one-man diatribe, but he looked into my eyes nonetheless. I guess my voice must have been familiar since I used to talk to him when he was still in his mom's belly. The nurses were quite taken by our talk, I later learned. But as far as I was concerned, we needed to talk and we've not stopped, until tonight. The girls are wearing me down. I just needed some 'me' time, to get off my feet, shut the eyes and shed some emotional baggage like Ali letting potentially crunching punches slide off his pretty face while he rope-a-doped. My kids in school are wearing me down. They couldn't pass a simple map test on Western Europe that we've worked on for five weeks. They just don't care. North Korea can starve their people for two decades or more and still develop and blow up a nuclear device. We can't pass a map test when the answers are the only thing on the blackboard in front of them. I'm worn out.

I do my best work in the morning and late at night. In between I'm about as effective as a street hooker at high noon in front of the Cathedral on Good Friday. Sometimes I'm just ashamed of myself but when Kirk called I needed a rest and the phone had been ringing incessantly. I hate its intrusion into my life without my consent. It rang all night long as it ignored my wishes.

"Jack, Neil Kerr's on the phone," said my wife reluctantly. I had just started to pop a Hoffman hotdog onto the grill. She knows I hate phone calls, especially at dinner. I had just asked her to tell whoever was calling that I wasn't home but she knows which calls to screen. And she knows that I take most of them despite my bitching. I got home late from practice and the sun was already making its final slide down the pink sky into oblivion, leaving us dark far too early in the day. It's that time of the year when we have a Harvest Moon. As the sun sets the moon rises in the east. Each morning when the sun rises, the moon is still high in the northwestern sky, just a faded whitish remnant of its brilliant night-time self.

"Jack, it's Neil. I scheduled a picture for your girls at 3:30 Thursday. Is that okay?" Damn, I've got to keep this drinking thing quiet, I thought to myself. "Sure, Neil. We appreciate it. You've always been good to us and I'll never forget it. We'll be on the track for the photographer." Neil asked where we were going this coming Saturday and I said that we're taking a partial team to the Phoenix Firebird Invitational hosted by longtime coach Bill Lonis. "What are ya up to Jack? Why just a partial team?" Well, I hemmed and hawed and said that we're doing everything we can to get ready for Sectionals and some girls will be training and not racing. I don't know if he was buying it but that was my story and I stuck with it.

Damn, the day after we could lose the 14-year unbeaten streak, the Post wants to take our picture. How am I going to explain it once the expected loss is public knowledge? Rob's certain that we can't beat Westhill. I'm still hopeful but I have my doubts. We talked to the team just a little today and only about half the girls knew about the drinking and the two meet suspension that was handed down to Hannah and Sofie. It was a fair punishment and left them room for redemption. Too often school administrators forget about that part of education. Maybe the new athletic director, Rick Pound, will be doing things right. He seems good at this. He doesn't punish, dump the bodies and walk away like those barbarians in Iraq who capture, torture, disembowel, dismember and then dump the bodies of their fellow God-loving citizens in the sewage-filled streets of Baghdad. Pound, 6'4 and nearly 300 pounds of football and lacrosse player, counsels, talks, teaches. Our kids respond to that personal, one-on-one time-consuming relationship.

The sky was bright the next afternoon as Rob and I lined the course, sprayed yellow arrows on the Polo Ground's green carpet and set up the finish chute lined with our blue and yellow-flagged rope. What a course. Clint, the groundskeeper, mowed and rolled the course and she's lightning fast, fast like I've never seen. We decided to leave the horseshit pile to give the course some additional character. Running between the tall fences that parallel each other on each side of the running paths, the kids will feel special on this league championship day.

Sofie received her two-meet-suspension while on a road workout of 3 x mile repeats with two minutes of recovery. She hit some good times even though she was exhausted by a college trip to Marist and Quinnipiac and the strain and stress of the drinking episode. And just as she was being told of her punishment, the Skaneateles Journal was delivering the weekly edition with a beautifully written feature about Sofie as Athlete-of-the-Week.

Confused and lacking direction in the midst of turmoil that looks to a teenager like everything must look to a toddler who's rug crawling and looking up at everything, Sofie e-mailed her thoughts, worries, dreams and concerns.

hey coach,

the miles were good today... 5:58, 6:02, 6:05... not to mention I haven't slept much the past few nights. I just got off the phone with Mrs. Amboy and talked to Tiffany a little while ago. She seems to be doing better, besides the fact that she's going straight to rehab tomorrow when she gets out of the hospital and apparently has permanent internal damages. It's upsetting that it takes something like this for a handful of people to realize how dangerous drinking is. I'm not going to lie to you, my friends (girls and guys... yes I have guy friends) are a group of partiers, and I've been struggling with it for so long now... finally I gave in. I don't know why. I'm having the best season of my life, I had an amazing run saturday morning, I'm Athlete of the Week, I spent my entire summer working towards sectionals... and I jeopardized everything. That is the worst feeling in the whole world. I know things will eventually get better, it just absolutely sucks right now. And the worst part is, I don't even know where to go from here. I had a talk with Julie Lynch today about the whole situation. Why do you coaches always know what to say?

On a better note, I really, really liked both Quinnipiac and Marist. I'm kind of struggling with the whole question of whether to run in college-thing and they're both DI which makes it even worse. My only thought after this whole situation is maybe I want to concentrate on running in college. After all this, I've definitely come to the conclusion that running and my team is far more important than going out. I know why I was racing better at the beginning of the season... I wasn't tired. Over the summer I worked and ran, I didn't have a life... I made my priority running. So I just don't know... I'm confused... some days I definitely want to run in college and others I think I'd rather be lazy on Saturday afternoons. Who knows what will happen... but I have to go eat dinner... and maybe do a little something for the team. Let's hope they don't all hate me too much. But anyways thank you so much for being there for me no matter what. You have no idea how much that means to me. see you tomorrow.

Hannah missed practice but did a run on her own alternating 15 seconds hard, 15 slow, 30 hard, 30 slow and a minute hard, a minute slow. She's drained. I've seen more potential in a dried up well with tumbleweed blowing past it. She'll be fine in a few days but right now she's cried out all her energy and she's bereft of substance. She's just hanging on but as Rick Pound said, she'll come back with a lot of anger. You never know what a team can do when they are thrust into a challenge. The girls responded in the way that any coach would be proud of today. Rachel Vaivoda, the lone senior remaining, and Rachel Hosie, the hope of the sophomore class, both vowed to take charge. The girls said that Amanda is really up for the race. With luck, her diabetes won't show its snarling face. I know Lexie Mazzeo and Kristin Roberts are ready. And Taylor Wellington, back early from her Las Vegas vacation, appears rested and prepared to challenge her opponents.

One-for-all and all-for-one. Mod coach Julie Lynch understands how big this is since she and her gang were the link between the early streak and the current crop of winners. Winning, it's what we do.

Corsello

After our first practice on the Polo Grounds and before the phone call from Sofie and Hannah, I was asked to write a letter to the Syracuse University Admissions Office on behalf of Steve. It looks like they'll admit him in the fall of 2007 if the state parole board will back off a bit and actually look at his case, his prison record, and compare his sentence to every other teenager who has made the same grievous, deadly error in judgment. Steve is rapidly becoming the marquee for drunk driving and it isn't having any effect on kids here in Skaneateles. I wonder if people really thought that nailing him to the cross would bring anyone back, resurrect the simpler times of the 50s, or sway anyone's behavior. If I could just get Steve cleared to run for their new coach, Chris Fox, I'd be thrilled. Steve needs to get on a productive path and Fox is producing and producing quickly. He has good runners but I'd say they were only good in high school on the regional scene. They aren't blue-chip runners but they're looking like it now. Being young men and women who most consider second tier athletes, it's remarkable that they're winning invitationals. Fox is on to something and he's working fast. My letter to the college was, I think, truthful, honest and hopeful. Steve's parents concurred.

Dear SU Admissions Counselor:

I write to you on behalf of Skaneateles graduate Steve Corsello regarding his application for admission to Syracuse University.

I have worked with Steve since he was in eighth grade when he rushed onto the New York State track scene.

Steve is a very honorable young man who has grown immeasurably over the years and his growth has been intensified many times over because of a deadly mistake that resulted in two years of incarceration in the state penal system. He's learned. Steve made a mistake that an untold number of teenagers make when alcohol is involved. His letters to me from prison reveal an enlightenment that can only come from endless reflection and loss of freedom. He's engaging and can readily converse with adults and peers alike. His breadth of knowledge seems to know no bounds.

Entering his junior year, Steve began to grow-up noticeably. He became a leader who led by example. Steve's work ethic has never been questioned. He's one tough kid who is unquestionably toughest on himself, sometimes too tough. He expected an awful lot of his teammates but he expected more from himself. Steve pushed his teammates hard but he pushed himself more. Steve was always there for his teammates and always gave 100% to the activity before him whether it was academics, music, athletics or deciding to read every word of Dickens and Hemingway while in prison.

Steve was a young man who strived to excel at everything. I found that Steve seemed to need to excel, and he worked to achieve goals, whether it was athletic, accelerated course work, his religious activities, his many jobs, or his involvement in the school's musical productions. The amount of hours Steve devoted to making other people look good was incredible. Certainly he must have received something personally gratifying from all of that hard work, but I sometimes wonder if he was the great beneficiary or if the many adults in his life were the greater beneficiary. I have found Steve to be willing to make the necessary sacrifices in order to succeed. Steve developed good time management skills and somehow he was able to keep many balls in the air at once. He's truly a remarkable, strong and persevering young man. I don't know how he goes on living with his recent past haunting him every waking moment.

Steve's code of honor runs deep. He took a team loss personally even if he won his events. Steve always showed a true, lasting loyalty to those around him. Once you're in Steve's inner circle, you'll always be in Steve's inner circle. He will never turn his back on a friend, and he'll never break a promise. His word is gold.

Toward the end of the spring season during his junior year, Steve seemed to have emerged from the doldrums of his teenage years. He was walking tall. He was lighter on his feet. His speech cadence quickened. He was thinking quicker on his feet. He had grown truly confident and knew what he wanted to do with his life. He was deciding whether to attend an Ivy League school or a military academy. College coaches found him to be very engaging. After taking weekend courses to enhance his SAT scores, he emerged with a point tally that made him proud of himself. The heavy judgmental hand that he had been hitting himself with, for so many years, seemed to relax its grip. He seemed happy, content, and assured. And when you saw him on the track, you saw someone who had worked to make his athletic gifts emerge. He finished third in the state 800-meter final and topped that by claiming 2nd in his senior year while carrying the burden-of-knowledge that goes with knowing that your sentencing date is just a few weeks away.

Steve is fully aware of the world he has been sentenced to and the free world that he yearns to return to. He is conversant on topics that should be far removed from his life right now. He isn't afraid to convey his feelings, philosophy or attitude toward a subject. He's confident about what he knows and eager to learn about the unknown. When he looks you in the eye, you know you're talking to someone different from the norm.

Haltingly, like every kid I've met, Steve is maturing. He can take more licks than anyone I know. Knock him down and he'll get right back up. His honor is beyond dispute. In the best of interpretations, Steve is a man's man. He's among the best of his generation in spite of the black mark next to his name that will follow him every day of his life. He isn't your typical frosh candidate but I'd suggest taking a long hard look at his candidacy because he'll one day be a man-of-merit.

I have no answers for students who choose to drink, the pop culture being such a formidable opponent. I hope circumstances in the future don't necessitate the writing of another letter like this. I'm just not sure what action I could take that would alter the course of the future. All Rob and I can do is try--again and again.

I Believe

I awoke to the drumbeat of falling black walnuts hitting the soggy ground, the drumsticks pounding out a beat that alerted me to the day ahead. It was race day, the showdown with nearby Marcellus but more ominously, Westhill, the 5th ranked Class B team in New York. Dan Reid knows his business and I know he'll have the Warrior girls up for the meet.

We've come through a lot this season and we're still coping with the latest round of news involving seniors Hannah and freckle-faced Sofie who is beside herself, having said, "I won't be able to live with myself if we don't win. We've just got to." Telling me about her teammates, who haven't said a torpedoing word about either girl, Sofie said, "They're real nervous. We just have to stay positive for them. What should I be saying, Coach?"

Trying to think quickly as I layered blackened carbon paper between three scoring sheets like we all used to back in the stone ages, I said to Sofie that everyone has a chance to be a hero. There are few moments when an individual human can stand as a lone pillar bearing some enormous weight. With the fewest of exceptions, rare is the moment in our ephemeral existence when we can truly make a difference, when we can sway the course of history. Championships fall into that rare realm where one person-on-a-mission, a single soul who won't be deterred, can make a difference and alter the results. "Sofie," I said as I stapled the scoring packets together in my front seat at the Polo Grounds, "All we can do is keep 'em relaxed and positive. We'll all live, even you, no matter what happens."

Hannah has been a challenge both before the drinking experimentation and now, but together we continue to take vicious swipes at the dragons in her dreams. Running is a strange and defiant animal that seems tamed one moment while ripping its fangs deep into your flesh the next. You don't merely need heart to run: a racer needs to feel immortal. Every competitor needs to discover their soulful self, the childish yet mature self that takes measured risks and believes that impossible is nothing. Triumphant runners know that getting too close to the flame can burn, but it can also enlighten. Pushing the envelope is worth the risk and with willpower, effort and a blinding focus, any obstacle in the way of success can be obliterated.

In the absence of the meaningful soulful encounter that clears your vision and sets your compass like Moses cleared the way across the Red Sea, many runners plod forward tortured, conflicted by an agonized and twisted psychology, half in the game and half out. Without the artful connection successfully linking the brain, the spirit and the will, the runner hangs in limbo, one foot in heaven and the other testing the bounds of hell. The suffering is not quite hellish torture for the disengaged runner but they're also cognizant that those fleeting moments of divine bliss on the trails are not eternal. And he knows why. Tasting the Gods' nectar intermittently and infrequently during training and racing, the runner who is neither fully committed nor aimless keeps hoping, keeps pulling up the dolphin-split running shorts with the elasticized waistband, continues visiting shoe stores to look at, pick up and try on the newest incantation of running shoe, keeps scouting the opposition and continues to review the running log, but does so with a black veil flapping over his heart as reluctance keeps entering his consciousness. The final step that requires the runner to bite the bullet--and just do it--is a tough one. Stuck in neutral astride a deep, dark chasm, the hellish oscillation repeats itself day after day with hourly fluctuations that eventually leave the runner deflated, confused and talking to himself.

That's been Hannah, though recently she's rectified and resurrected her career as clarity and a measure of passion begins to well-up in her. It isn't just food energy stored in the cellular structure of the body that leads to success. It's the passion that gets stored within the soul that also nourishes the dream. The committed-Hannah runs up front, rallies over the final 800, glares and spits snot. The limbo-Hannah jogs with our slowest girl, does repeats with her and openly spouts off about not running in college as she unintentionally infects the spirits of those around her who harbor that dream for themselves. Wanting to be the best one moment and running from herself the next, we all do our best to rein her in because we're a stronger team with a happy Hannah. I'm positive she'll figure all of this out, but my timeline is a lot shorter than hers right now.

The wind at the Polo Grounds was vicious as it began the slow process of bending trees in an artful and entertaining manner. Up on the St. Lawrence River every tree leans in a southeast direction and all can claim to be victims of the constant rush of Canadian-borne winter winds. The whole Polo Grounds scene reminded me of the Scottish golf courses at the British Open with gray skies sucking the blue out of the water and the curl out of a girl's hair. It was 60 degrees when the gun sounded as the time to think was replaced by a time to run, to roar, to cheer, to watch some kid become a hero.

We went out hard, harder than any of my recent teams. A pack of gold was up front as they made their first turn at the far end of the polo field some four football fields into the race. Coming out of the woods in the distance they looked different and I realized that this race wasn't going to follow a script. The hunt was on. There was a title on the line. The pace was furious but the race didn't string out like usual. Up front was a swollen pack of gold that looked like a snake after eating something too big and I wondered if we'd bitten off more than we could chew. The pack bulged even though we only lined up ten girls. Reappearing at the top of a long descent that dropped 150 feet over 1200 meters was a pack of five with junior Kristin Roberts leading the way. In rapid order came Amanda, Rachel Hosie, Rachel Vaivoda and Alexis Mazzeo. The front-four would hold together until only 17 seconds separated them at the finish. And Mazzeo would be a mere 17 seconds farther back in 10th place.

On the second loop of the figure-8 that was groomed for speed, Carrie Carlton of Marcellus bolted for the lead just before the Westhill pack made their move. Earlier, while talking to Westhill coaches Robin Wheeless and Dan Reid, I got the impression they would have their runners surge on the second lap as they started the gradual downhill.

When they made their move I was ready for it. And so were my girls. We covered every one of their accelerations and moved up ourselves at the end, winning 22-33 with Kristin Roberts running like she's never run, seeking the front and never faltering in her desire to lead the team and keep the streak alive. "I will always remember this meet because I figured out that I can do a lot more than I think. You can really do anything, but you have to want it. You have to know it," she said several hours after the meet.

There was no huge celebration afterwards. No one had to tell the girls anything after finishing 2-3-4-5-8 against Westhill. When it clicks there is no need for external affirmation. When it clicks, when the body, mind and soul have acted as one as life both slows and becomes clear while also traveling forward at warp speed in a blur, the celebration is calm, it's quiet, it's as satisfying as an ice-cold lemonade sipped from a chilled glass on a maple tree-shaded front porch on a hot afternoon while the World Series is played on an old-fashioned transistor radio. It just makes you smack your lips with satisfaction.

The race was tough for both Hannah and Sofie. For Rachel Vaivoda it looked as if someone had just told her that she'd never have to take another standardized test in her life. As I walked back toward the starting line where the girls had gathered after the race, I heard Rachel Hosie proclaim "That was next year's team. We proved we can win." Some high fives were exchanged and smiles were worn all around as sweats covered the stressed muscles and dry trainers replaced the ¼ inch spiked racing shoes that propelled us to our 14th straight league title. Rachel Vaivoda, that special smile plastered all over her face, had her arms stretched out to her side for 30 feet before she wrapped them around me in an embrace that grew tighter by the second and lasted, and lasted and lasted. She dug her face into my shoulder and kept saying, "We did it, coach. We did it."

The meet was important to a lot of people besides us. Jordan-Elbridge pulled off an enormous upset over CBA. The next day at school as I stood in front of Erin Bariteau's Earth Science lab, Kim Armani, a beautiful and vibrant J-E senior approached and got the question off her chest, "How'd you do yesterday?" She was pensive, hoping for an answer that would promote them to a tie for the league title. She hadn't yet read the paper.

"Kim, we won."

"Damn," she shouted in personal agony. She immediately grew red-faced. Kim says that she only wants to play lacrosse in college and that she hates cross country. There's more love for cross country than she's admitting to herself. She asked how much we won by.

"The girls really did it up, Kim. We won 22-33."

Blasting out again, she roared with a sheepish grin on her face, "You always do that." And then she thundered, "You crush everyone even when you're worried."

I was, indeed, worried before the race. The team was slow to arrive at the Polo Grounds about three miles from the school. Some took the bus but most drove or rode with friends, stopping down the road at Taylor Wellington's house to get ready for the meet.

The wind blew hard from the southeast in advance of a snow-packed arctic weather system that was pin-wheeling around a low to the west as it drifted up into Canada. My team staged its own version of the Diaspora, scattered here and there as if blown around to the corners of the expansive Polo Fields by the wind. Some wandered off toward the bus. Some went toward the horse barn, a couple sat in the middle of the parking lot. A few paired up and others just walked through the swaying fields and woods. I kept thinking, "Where's my TEAM?" In time the girls got back together as if some powerful surge of gravity had overpowered them and drawn them to the back of a pick-up truck where some leaned against the black steel side panels and some sat with their feet hanging and swinging from the downturned tailgate. They laughed raucously like they didn't have a care in the world, but burning deep inside was a fire as each in their own way and in their own time had decided that they would be the one to step up and keep the torch burning. You never know when a hero is born. They each had a secret and that secret would be told when the gun sounded.

We kept the benching of Hannah and Sofie secret until about five seconds into the race. That's when Westhill coach Dan Reid noticed. Warming up with the team, doing some brief loosening up movements and completing some strides like they'd normally do, no one knew that Hannah and Sofie were not going to head across the Polo Grounds with the rest of the kids at the sound of the gun. Our plan worked. Dan Reid of Westhill came right up to me after the race had started and asked about Hannah. "Isn't she running?" he asked with a quizzical and concerned look on his face. I answered by saying that Sofie wasn't racing either.

Wondering why, I told Dan a little about their Saturday night and he was as disappointed in them as I had been. "They're such great kids," he said. "Can I talk about this with my girls, Jack? Every chance I get I talk to them about this. I've got great kids and I don't want to lose any of them. I won't use names." I trust Dan's judgment. He's an educator. He teaches our kids.

"Dan, your girls will figure it out real quickly," I said, "but go ahead. If something positive can come from this, let's make it happen. But you know, we had our school lobby filled all last week with the road show for all the kids who have been killed by drunk drivers around here, and it didn't make a damn bit of difference. Maybe it's just human DNA and we'll always be dealing with the problem and the human losses," I said as I wondered if kids would just have to keep dying needlessly and so tragically.

With no coattails to ride on, the girls had shown mastery over their emotions. Bea, with racing that doesn't match-up with her training, continues to struggle and it's important for her to know that I haven't given up on her. Taylor Wellington was far off the mark early but flew over the final stretches of the course to become a contender. After the race she said that she'll remember the day as a moment when her team ran with the confidence to keep the winning streak alive. "We learned that the team doesn't rely on one or two individuals, we are all strong and we will fight for what we deserve and have worked to have. We kicked ass." Rachel Hosie improved about as much in one race as anyone I've ever seen. Carley Billick overcame a slow start and moved up. It was the same with Carly Brown. Summer training phenom Karen has just lost whatever was motivating her this summer.

Sam out-legged Marcellus 4th man Jake Bolewski for 7th place in 17:28 as he convulsed and held back the vomit that was erupting up his esophagus like molten lava exploding out of Mt. Vesuvius. Calvin Davis continued to stake his claim as one of the most talented frosh runners in Section III as he finished in 10th with a time of 17:58 against an impressive field of All-State runners. Jeff, who was spurred on by the home crowd that had gathered on his side lawn, used every inch of the home stretch to pick up two spots. Dan was galloping through the corrals west of the horse barn and had one of his better races. Matt staged his late-race resurgence after faltering badly mid-race. Finishing the league season 4-4 shows that the boys are moving in the right direction and the task is to get them to the next level. We have one more chance next year to get to the top and we'll need more than the usual incremental improvement. We'll need a summer like no other.

With the wind still blowing, the gray clouds hustling toward the north and the course gradually being broken down, we had time to think, to reflect and ponder just what had happened. The hurried atmosphere that had earlier swept through the vast expanse of green fields overlooking the lake was suddenly transformed into a quiet, prairie-like scene with the sounds of silence soothing the soul as the lungs exhaled fully for the first time in hours. The streak, that thing that hangs around our necks like a soldier's dog tags, that thing that now identifies us all, that thing that began in 1992, still has legs. It lives. The torch still burns.

Dan Reid of Westhill wrote that we'd done a good job against his girls. "Please pass my hearty congratulations on to them," he commented. "I really think the streak is an amazing accomplishment. So many things can happen over the course of a span of years like that and your girls just keep getting it done. You and they should be very proud."

Clothing styles have changed. Hit TV shows have come and gone. Governmental administrations have been replaced and replaced yet again. Instead of talking about an impending ice age we're talking about Global Warming. We're still talking about the Yankees and not the Red Sox, and the Cubs are still living on fumes and dreams and hoping that Lou Piniella can make a difference. For us, it's on to our final goal of winning back the sectional title. With just 23 days between us and the Sectional Championship, anything can happen. But I like who we've become. I like the way we handle adversity. I like how we're racing, clinging together and confidently placing one foot in front of another with impunity. Barring the Bird Flu, we're going back to the front.

Surprise

Rob and I found the footing sloppy, slippery, exactly what I didn't expect. Phoenix, up north of Syracuse, is well-known for being a mudder's paradise. When Harold-of-Chittenango and I talk about our teams, we inevitably talk about our best boys teams going head-to-head in the most Armageddon-like conditions at Phoenix. The battles have been memorable. He's had guys run with pneumonia and beat us, and I made sure that my top-gun Weston Cross in the 2000 race heard about it during the race. I've had guys run with a ready-to-explode appendix and a broken ankle. The battles have been legendary, first-rate, uplifting and civil, above all else, civil. When Steve Corsello got into trouble, it was Harold's top guy, Ozzie Myers and his family who drove west toward the mayhem in Skaneateles to lend support to the Corsello family.

Harold knows what he likes and he was going to hire Weston for a science opening at his school based solely on Weston's commitment and work ethic. Harold loved Weston and he especially loved watching Weston race at Manley Field House and go right from the finish line to the bright orange garbage cans to puke.

Making our way up to the plateau that served as the gathering place for the spectators around the Phoenix start-finish lines, Rob and I walked over to our rival coaches, Michelle Franklin-Rauber of Tully and Theresa Trudell of CBA. Earlier in the week I'd suggested to Theresa that she talk to her great friend from Tully and tell her that the mantle of favorite had been officially passed to her Tully team after their great showing last week at their invitational. As we approached with a little sun brightening a soon-to-be-gloomy sky, we yelled "Hi" and Theresa shot back, "I'm just telling her that she's the queen now." In the background was a long line of colorful tents stretching to the starting line 100 meters to the east.

After the meet Michelle and I walked to the cafeteria scoring room and she said that everything had changed and my Skaneateles team was once again the gorilla-in-the-midst.

The season was changing and the green bloom of summer had quickly changed to low-flying lake effect clouds that the day before had swept off Lake Erie and dumped 1-2 feet of snow on our Buffalo running friends. I've always wanted to know what East Aurora's Walt McLaughlin did to take ordinary kids to the absolute pinnacle of running. Walt coaches a stone's throw from Buffalo proper. He'd done so much for the Beaver River runners north of Syracuse and then he was railroaded out of the isolated Mennonite community by a jealous athletic director who coached a losing football team here in Section III. Walt and his wife know how to coach. They'd taken the Beaver River girls to the top in NYS for years and the boys earned one state title after another. Late in his Beaver River days they'd earned the distinction of being the top small school in the nation. The barren gym walls were transformed into a memorial as, over the years, the walls were wallpapered with state championship banners. After leaving Beaver River it took him barely three years to take an unknown East Aurora team to regional and national attention. The snow in Beaver River routinely totaled over 300 inches in a typical winter. Walt now lives south of Buffalo where it just snowed 2 feet before we'd reached the mid-point of October. I wondered how he dealt with Mother Nature so successfully.

Everything about Mother Nature was changing. When the sun is low on the horizon on a late afternoon during a mid-October practice, the road appears silvery and slick as it winds between thinning hedge rows as ground hogs prop themselves up on their hind legs to watch us power past. The cornfields change from a healthy green to a light brown that's somehow refreshing and comforting as it rustles in the breeze. The road appears narrower like an old English byway as the colorful and freshly fallen leaves collect in brilliant heaps along the drooping shoulders like snow that's windblown and drifted to the roadsides.

With the leaves having fallen, some striking architectural features are suddenly revealed, features that once were the private domain of their home owners and neighbors. Birds dart through the denuded thickets in playful flight while grey squirrels and diminutive chipmunks wander around the maze of trails that are provided by house-bordering yews where they grab the red berries and stuff them into their puffy cheeks.

The look of life has changed as the remnants of summer linger one day at a time as the northern world prepares for the impending whitening layer of snow.

Looking happier is a blossoming Amanda Golden, her acne giving way to silky smooth facial skin. The heavy dark eye brows that give her a moody look have gotten a recent plucking and it's opened up her face. I've really grown to like the girl who is now a junior. There has been no growth spurt but she's growing up and now looks you in the eyes when talking with you. She's also developed the habit of slyly fluttering her eyes when a smile crosses her face and sometimes she tips her head downward and to the side in a move that will one day make guys swoon and follow her anywhere. She isn't a rabble rouser or a look-at-me sort of girl, and she isn't one to shout and lead the team anywhere. But, she's a hard worker and week by week she's beginning to show the cards that will make her a successful adult. I've often been disappointed that her parents wouldn't drive her to our voluntary summer practices, but it's hardly her fault. But she's growing on me as she emerges from her shell and learns to live with her physical and family ailments.

As the race at Phoenix progressed it was obvious that one of the ruling triumvirate up front would wear the Queen's crown, and we had two-thirds of the ruling body with Rachel Vaivoda and Amanda fighting and changing positions with Weedsport's top girl, Sarah Wignall, who was coached by a sensitive John Lawler who loves to hunt and fish to the point that none of his marriage plans have ever worked out.

Rob and I were betting on Rachel to win but just seeing her run with Wignall was a positive sign because Rachel had trailed Wignall every step of the way at the Auburn Invitational a few weeks earlier.

Phoenix is a wonderful double loop course and it's high on our kids' list of favorites. Maybe it's the memories or the fast times on those rare dry days at Phoenix but I think maybe it's the atmosphere that's created by host Bill Lonis. It's just laid back, relaxed yet competitive. It's a down-home feeling and it starts with Bill who wears a white shirt with a tie yanked up high on his Adams Apple. He looks out of place, more like a teacher in the 50s and 60s than someone who has to connect to the hippest kids the world has ever produced. And that's why I like him. He's different in a different way than everyone else. Everyone today is different in the same way. They're either jocks, academics, gothic devotees or nerds. Even the most daring are daring in exactly the same way with weird body piercings, tattoos and black lipstick just like their fellow conforming non-conformists. Bill is true to his origins. He is who he is and I respect that in a man. And I think the kids know that he's the real deal and that's part of the magic and charm of the Firebird Invitational.

On a two loop course there's pretty much nothing but predictable observations on the first loop. It's the second loop when the surprises occur and that's when the race is won or lost.

After circling the school and surviving the mud pit that was rapidly becoming the repository of lost running shoes, the racers entered the woods for the final time. As they went in Rachel had dropped back a bit and it was all Sarah and a confident looking Amanda. When they emerged from the wooded trail and crossed a soccer field before descending into the muddiest mud-pit on earth, it was the blue bun huggers and the gold jersey with the blue "S" on the front that had broken away from the Weedsport girl outfitted in a top that was green on the top half with a white lower panel and green shorts. Amanda had a chance to be an invitational winner. She would be our 10th in the past 15 years.

Amanda likes to be cold, so she decided not to wear the white long sleeved wicking shirt that most of the girls wore under their jerseys. Plodding through mud that covered the shoes in the driest portions of the course, Amanda and her size 10 feet led her tiny body to victory in 20:24. I never saw this coming. On my personal score sheet I had her listed 4th with Kristin Roberts, the hero and team leader three days earlier against Westhill, on top. Kristin ended up getting beaten by two of her JV teammates. You just never know.

Amanda ended up going to the hospital after the Phoenix Invitational her freshman year. She'd melted down, the victim of eating too much of her favorite breakfast Fruit Loops and no protein or fat to help balance the blood sugars. It's been an ongoing battle but on this day Amanda, the Phoenix Firebird race-winner, ate well and got it right.

We rolled to the win with Rachel Hosie coming from far, far back in the pack to take 3rd. "Guess I'm a late closer," the horse riding champion said. Rachel Vaivoda, running again without her senior friends and teammates was a bit off as she placed 5th. Lexie Mazzeo went out strong again but held on longer as she took 8th and, again, finished one place from winning a t-shirt. Roberts got a late start on her warm-up and didn't get any strides prior to the gun and she cramped terribly, placing 14th.

Our spread from 1-5 was a good 1:19 but just as impressive was Carly Brown winning the JV race in a walk with a time that would have put her in the 13th spot in the varsity race. She can be a notable success in running with her fluid and dreamy mechanics but it has to be her dream. I hope she begins her REM sleep phase soon but I'm not hopeful of seeing her in her junior and senior years. It's just a hunch.

We've always gone to Phoenix and skipped the Manhattan race at Vanny, VanCortlandt Park. It isn't the thought of gangs, syringes on the playing field or bus drivers getting killed that deters us. It has nothing to do with the lack of parking, the lousy and historically inaccurate scoring or the expense that continues to keep us out of New York. We just like Phoenix and its course is better than a VanCortlandt Park course that's simply far from being fan and media-friendly.

The lone great thing about Vanny is the history. The course just doesn't change and today's runners can compare their time to the legends that ran Vanny. The newest member of the club is Fayetteville-Manlius runner Tommy Gruenewald, who is coached by the pied piper of Central New York running, Bill Aris. Tommy went out and broke Colts Neck's Craig Fory's record by 1/10th of a second, running 12:10.6 at the Mecca of Cross Country. Fory's record didn't last 20 minutes.

Bill Aris took on a kid who had bad mechanics--mechanics that were slow and plodding--and turned him into one of the fastest distance runners in American cross country history. It's like Gruenewald came in playing a two-fingered chopsticks, then, with a lot of work was playing like Jerry Lee Lewis with his fingers, knees and toes, and finally, after the whole training program came together, assumed the identity of

Vladimir Horowitz. The kid has come a long way and he's going where no man has gone before, no American Olympic runner, no American Olympic medalist, no one who has ever run on the fabled Vanny course. Brad Hudson was gracious as his record was erased, a record that had stood for 33 years.

After Rob studied our results at Phoenix and reflected on the VanCortlandt Park results that were quickly posted on Bill Meylan's Tullyrunners web site, he wrote to me and said, "I think West Virginia's football team had more rushing yards than our boy's team today." Yeah, the Mountaineers clobbered the Syracuse Orange football team, again. The good news is that SU basketball has begun practice.

After the Phoenix race, Sam, upset with his 4th place finish, said that he was quite frankly tired of being just mediocre. "I want to be up there with all the rest," he said. Sam is beginning to dream and it's a good sign that he wants more out of himself. Jeff has been frozen in time in my photos of him. If I could get the kid to run indoor track and spring track we'd be able to make him as immortal as he looks when caught in digital mid-stride with that cocky Prefontaine "I-dare-you-to-go-stride-for-stride-with-me" look. Even his body posture smells of destiny-in-the-making. Dan is feeling his oats and he's running with a defiance that is forcefully submerging his fears. Dustin just can't breathe as his asthma meds are beginning to fail on a weekly basis. Matt seems to have fully recovered from the early season knee problems. The longer we don't talk about it the better they seem to get. He's a Minnesota Fats-hustler on the track but he's still learning to deal with the vagaries of running on soft, muddy and hilly terrain as it tosses him around like the Andrea Gail from Gloucester on the high seas in the Perfect Storm.

The rest of the guys are on different wave lengths with some seeming to run until they twist their stomach and muscles in a hundred different ways as they extend themselves to the bitter end. Others appear to be happy jogging until they meet the final stretch and are forced to man-up as they duel to the chute in front of large and observant crowds. I know the crowd loves those balls-to-the-wall finishing kicks, but I have a different take on them and would prefer that the runners actually try to compete in the races instead of just going with the comfortable flow.

We're all beginning to show our true colors and the surprise appears to be that our girls are looking like gold.

Riding the Wave

"You know there's a title in our future," wrote Rachel Vaivoda. "A title. DEFINITELY!" With each team victory Rachel is one step closer to her personal Nirvana which is much like Superman's Fortress of Solitude, a place where mere shards of glass are much more than they seem as they collectively serve to bring wisdom where once confusion reigned supreme.

Rachel is beginning to come into her own and I'm not speaking about anything physical since she possesses all the tools. I'm talking about the mental and emotional Rachel, the one that consists of spirit, karma, feelings, anxiety, uncertainty, faith, poise and presence. She's beginning to see a bigger and clearer picture of life and her part in it instead of seeing her future as a kaleidoscopic, chaotic entanglement of steel rebar and chunks of cement piled high after the implosion of a city high rise. Rachel is beginning to understand that putting seemingly non-related pieces of life and experiences into blank spaces in a puzzle-of-life helps to flesh out her visions. With each oddly shaped piece inserted into its proper place, color, shape and meaning rise from a blackened canvas as if revelation itself had been imparted, by God, to her heart directly and personally. It's like the ah-ha moment, the epiphany that comes when you finally understand Algebra. The more she is inserting life's little pieces into her personal mural-of-life the more she understands challenges, the more she comprehends how the karma of past, present and future are intertwined in the same seamless thread that not only led her to this specific point in life, but will lead her to the next junction and through the next adventure.

She was an absolute wreck last winter and spring but I think she's maturing and has gotten a tight clench around the neck of uncertainty and fear, the twin demons of every athlete.

> *There is no way anyone can touch us. And you know why? It's because we all want this more than anything. And we are not out there because we have to be. We are out there because we want to be. We want it. And that is what has changed. We are confident and we all know we are able.*

Rachel's perception of the team is the same as Rob's and mine. The tide has turned for this team that inhabits a beautiful part of the Finger Lakes, that geologic marvel left behind by the last glacial retreat in North America. The team is a lot like the lake. Just when you think the water is going to be warm for the rest of the summer, it turns over, the cold water that's been hiding far below the swimming layer rises to the top as the warm water suddenly sinks. It happens almost every year. For our team, the turnover just didn't happen the past two years. This year we saw the turnover and I think it has a lot to do with the team running without Hannah and Sofie as their absence has forced the team to step-up, to mature, to grow up, and for those two it had a lot to do with being deprived of a modicum of dignity and the honor that comes from running for a distinguished, well-known team. It had a lot to do with embarrassment, too. Everyone is being held responsible, Hannah and Sofie for a single action that ran counter to the code of athletic conduct, and the team that learned to be accountable in their own right when so much was on the line.

> *I'm not pleased with my past two personal races, but I think not having Sofie and Hannah took out more than two scoring positions for me. They have always been a support system and it's hard for me when I don't have that. But, I mean, you can really look at this as a positive. When we had Hannah and Sofie, no girls ever felt the need to step up. But when we didn't have them, they did something great and they now know that they are supposed to be like that all the time. Like Rachel Hosie and Amanda know that they should be at least up with me and that is going to help us so much. We want it. I want it.*

Rachel is even looking lighter, more bouncy in practice. Rob and I just look at each other and wonder where it came from. Her mood is lighter and she's shed whatever shackles have been binding her. Today, the opening day of the week for training, she showed up and was excited for practice. "I bombed a physics exam and you all know that when I do miserably on an exam, I'm on a mission in practice. So look out."

Rachel isn't counting down the final days of her high school cross country career like so many around the country. She's cherishing every final moment.

> *I just need to get it through my head that I have only 3 more high school XC races. Ever! And I want to do it. I know we can. Get excited Coach.*

Rachel and the girls knocked down a workout today like they haven't ever in the past. They did another set of 10 x 400 at 3k pace with only a minute of rest per rep after they concluded a nice 30 minute run. Another group, the Hannah, Sofie and Rachel Hosie group, did 5x800s at threshold pace with just 30 seconds of rest. Both groups dropped all the negatives that they could have thrown around during the session. They all stood tall, hands on hips and spitting after ever rep. They walked, they reassured each other. They ran with aplomb, with composure, patience and swagger.

Sam and Hannah went on long Sunday runs the day before, with Sam covering 9 miles in 6:40 pace and Hannah finishing a slightly shorter run and feeling great.

Hannah seems to have turned a corner and she's excited to reach graduation day so that people can see that she isn't who she was on that Saturday night a week ago.

> *I've learned so much from this and I'm just anxious for the next six months to come along so that everyone else can see that as well. Thanks again.*

Hannah's mom and I have kept in touch and she's seeing the same thing I'm seeing. We're both watching growth as a teenager gains some perspective and pulls herself up after getting knocked down.

I'm seeing a bit of a different girl myself — some of that being "a bit too big for her breeches" attitude seems to have dissipated. I'm hoping it lasts — and I think it will. What I most hope at this point is that Hannah can parlay some of her hard lesson to good and meaningful advice for others who might think that they, too, are too smart to get caught or are clever enough to avoid the vortex that bad decisions can sometimes open. I hope this climb out of the deep pit Hannah dug just a week ago stays smooth and ever moving up! Thanks for your attention. I know your support means EVERYTHING to Hannah.

I took Hannah home today after the team vanished about as fast as a mid-summer rain on a humped and hot blacktop road. This is the one thing that I think the kids are missing and I hope it doesn't come back to bite us in the ass. The teams used to hang out for a long time after practice, lounging in the sun or just sitting in a cramped hallway that would turn stuffy by their mere sweaty presence, the boys and girls mingling and acting as one unit, as friends who were more than runners, more than teammates, more than mere social acquaintances. There was something different. It was more meaningful, more robust and more real than the realist thing in life, like the difference between a hamburger and a filet mignon. They were simpatico. They didn't need to go home to see their family. They were family.

Going home wasn't the same back in the 60s. Parents smoked, and they smoked indoors. It was putrid. It was choking and nauseating to wake up to the smell of smoke rising from the kitchen to the second floor bedrooms like a bullet from an assault rifle penetrates cement walls. There was no cable, no VCR machines, no TiVo, no computers, no internet, no video games. We didn't have satellite radios in our cars or homes. We were lucky to have a hi-fi stereo in the house that was as big as a small meat freezer. Transistor radios stood as entertaining companions on the bed stand. iPods? Not a chance. We had 45s and 33 1/3 plastic records that we cherished as much for their music as for their cardboard album art. We had books that we mostly stayed away from as if they were girls and we were 5th grade boys. We had 6 inch TVs that were black and white. Pizza? We hardly had that. The only thing we had was each other and an old beat-up pale green Chevy with the stick shift on the column.

After tough runs as the weather got colder we'd hang out in the showers, sitting under 12 shower heads that seemed at the time like Niagara Falls at about 120 degrees. It was heaven. I'm surprised none of our asses got athlete's foot because we just sat on the cement shower floor with steam filling the area like a foggy morning in the Finger Lakes. On warm weather days in the spring we'd lay around on the foam high jump landing pit that was a slight step up from the sawdust pit. The foam pieces were wrapped up in a mesh sheathing like black-mesh stockings that leave just a little to the imagination, and after rainfalls the small, angular foam pieces were as despicable as you can imagine, with pieces of the foam sticking to you like clumps of wet sawdust. On other days in the fall we'd lie on our backs under the sparse canopy of trees that separated our baseball field—where we started and ended our home cross country meets—from the military storage depot that stretched for a mile while storing things that no one ever dared talk about.

There were days when we'd catch a ride home, but usually we'd walk the two miles across the bustling Tow Path that has since been transformed into Interstate 88, courtesy of Senator Warren Anderson who wanted a faster way to travel from his district in Binghamton to the state capital. The bridge that crossed the Chenango River was stoic by modern standards with simple green railings that were a minimalist's masterpiece. There was no class, beauty or aesthetics to the bridge, only function. On the west side of the bridge we'd look at the black iron railroad trestle that some brave soon-to-be graduates would scale as they used a broad brush and white paint to inscribe their year of graduation on its side.

We'd walk past the old little league fields that were turned into a driving range. At the corner of Kattelville Road and River Road we'd stop at the Red and White and pick up a huge bottle of Royal Crown Cola filled with caffeine that would get us the final mile to the dinner table. Once in-a-while Don Benza, our junior high coach, would pick us up and take us to his home half way up River Road.

My kids aren't experiencing any of this. As devoted as they are, they are still rushing from here to there in a mad-cap manner. There's always someplace to be both before and after practice. On race-day this Saturday at the Pre-Sectionals at Liverpool, the PSATs are going to compete with the race for our attention since Skaneateles insists on committing the kids to a six-day week. Most schools have the PSATs on a weekday.

On our walk home we'd all be carrying an oversized white sports bag with a black ADIDAS emblazoned on the side. Inside was anything but text books. Today the kids have backpacks filled with notebooks and textbooks that are super-sized. Some kids have two backpacks to help them carry home the nightly avalanche of homework. Recent studies indicate that a lot of the homework assignments are counter-productive. But too many educators aren't receptive to scientific research as past pedagogical dogma paralyzes them.

After assessing our results this season, we've decided to change our season-long plans. We have sensed that we are in a flow and Rob and I decided to ride the crest of the wave straight through to the sectional championship. The past few years we seem to have peaked at the Phoenix Invitational and then fizzled. We think it's due to the long racing layoff that we've given the kids after the thrill of Phoenix. So, we're eliminating the layoff and keeping our rhythm. We entered the Liverpool Invitational. I've been telling all my fellow coaches that there was no way we'd go there and now I'm going back on my word. I've always believed that less is best and no matter what the physiologists say, teenagers can benefit not only from a lot of sleep and scientific-based training, but rhythm. We're in a groove and it's important that we keep it flowing. Sauquoit Valley has been charging lately so we'll be able to compare our times with the times that they record in an earlier race this Saturday. Tully is staying home. Andy Pino's Canastota team will be at Liverpool, too, and it seems to be imploding as Sauquoit has owned them for the past three weeks with more and more convincing victory margins. Sauquoit always starts out slowly and comes on, but this time they don't seem to be getting all the boats rising with the tide and I think our depth will swamp them.

Hannah said in a personal handwritten note to me, "I can't wait for November 2nd when I can be racing and we can tear up the rest of the section." The August and September Hannah would never have said that. The tide has indeed turned. Hannah is back!

Targeting Baldwinsville and Seeing Red

We're carrying a load into Saturday's pre-sectional race at Liverpool along the shores of the rapidly rising Seneca River. I'm eerily reminded of the 1996 debacle at the St. Lawrence University state championship when the river rose after days of incessant rain and flooded the course. For nearly 36 hours, the sky has dumped on Central New York more than the media cranks up the laughs at Paris Hilton's expense. With nearly 3-4 inches of rain turning the dirt to mud and then the mud to liquid, I suspect there won't be a step of sure-footing on race-day and I think that we'll be greeted by standing water that will be most unwelcome in the cold arctic air that's breaking through into America like rushing water breaching a busted dam.

Three of the girls are spending a sixth day in school this week in order to take the PSATs. I hope they'll be OK. I'd completely forgotten about it since I hadn't originally scheduled a meet on October 21st but the need to keep the girls in a fighting flow convinced me to make an amendment to the schedule that was published months ago.

On pre-race Friday, the message to the Skaneateles-7 was simple after their 20 minute run in wind chills hovering near the freezing mark as rain poured from the skies like tears from the collective eyes of Red Sox fans after Bill Buckner made like a croquet wicket and allowed that little red-stitched white ball to roll between his legs. "Take down Baldwinsville". The B'ville Bees placed 4th in race "A" at last week's Manhattan Invitational under perfect conditions. We'll see how this double-A classified team does against a bunch of class "C" mudders from Skaneateles.

The girls were absolutely clear-eyed when they stepped into the bus and that's what I look for when assessing our chances. They're healthy, rested and fresh after a mid-week lightning storm forced the cancellation of practice for the second time this fall. That's rare, but rare seems the norm this year as global warming messes with all my plans, courtesy of a Greenland block that's changing the flow of the air currents in the northern hemisphere. As a result everything shitty seems to flow through us.

I reminded the five girls who learned to race without Hannah and Sofie that their job is to go out like they did both times last week. And I told the twin seniors that their job is to just go and not worry about the other five. We've got to get the team to learn how to race together with underclassmen now souped-up.

Early in the week I had my second colonoscopy. No cancer, no polyps. I was foggy afterwards when my wife dropped me off at practice as the Gastroenterologists at Community General Hospital sent me home with a perfectly clean bill of health. The day before at J-E I made a point to talk about the procedure in all my classes and told the kids to encourage their parents to have the procedure done if they're getting close to 50 years old. Walking down the hall at the end of the day, several teachers said that my class was the buzz and talk all day. Maybe someone will have their life saved. Kids love body fluid talks.

Despite my foggy thinking at practice after the procedure, things went well as we adapted our plans to fit the kids who showed up to train. Socrates said that to succeed we need to meet the audience at their level and I've never forgotten that lesson. With the sun peeking out from behind a sky filled with puffy white clouds moving southeast in our typical pattern, the ears were treated to the familiar honks of Canadian Geese heading south in their trademark V-formation. Not one goose strayed from the group. The pack was tight, efficient, moving in unison toward the agreed upon but invisible goal.

We split into two groups with the boys doing 5x800 at threshold pace with 30 seconds of rest while the girls and Rob ran the mile and a quarter through the village to the cemetery on Rt. 20 for their lactic acid training (LATs). When the girls do the reps properly along the cemetery trails, we get maximum benefit with the least physical stress and a miniscule amount of damage to their body. They feel fast, successful and come out of the session ready to accept another weekend challenge. This time Baldwinsville, the 21st ranked large school team in the state, is the challenge.

The girls, with Rob overseeing everything as he ran from one cemetery monument to another--up and down the rolling hills beneath the giant pine trees--did two sets of LATs, the first consisting of undefined 'hard' runs of :30, :30, :60, :30, :30, :60 with a 25 second rest per :30 rep and a :50 rest per minute rep. After a ten minute break we reversed the second set and had them run :60, :30, :30, :60, :30, :30 reps. The girls understand the meaning of 'hard' runs in the cemetery that's filled with fading white tombstones dating back to the early 1800s. It's our community's historical treasure that's guarded 24 hours a day by a Civil War cannon. The routes we've flown for the last 15 years are seemingly genetically encoded into their brains. The packs are tight and no one veers off on their own. Pride dictates that we all 'girl-up' and get the job done.

The girls want to win. It's what they're used to. Winning is like sliding a wet finger tip around the metal bottom of a nearly empty Planters Salted Peanut can as a conglomeration of brown husks, salt and small peanut chunks stick to the finger and send the salivary glands into a tizzy. Winning is exactly like that finger that goes from the salty bottom of the can straight into your lips. Once you start, you want even more.

At the Liverpool Invitational, I watched kids of all stripes, shapes and sizes prepare for their race, and I got to wondering. If our athletic potential is revealed through the repetitive grind and tedium of endless practices, and if competition reveals the truth about who we actually are, what does race preparation tell us? Anything?

After the boys and the non-racing girls ran a great 7-miler on a picture-perfect fall Saturday that covered the north and south side of County Line road, the varsity girls headed to Onondaga Lake. We arrived about 90 minutes before our 2:25PM race-time at the Liverpool Invitational which was actually the pre-Sectionals minus a few teams. All of our competitors except Tully were there. Sauquoit Valley and CBA lined-up in the race prior to ours while Canastota would race an hour after us. We hadn't seen Sauquoit or Canastota at all this year as our plan to stay away from our rivals was beginning to show some merit with the girls running to the front in every race.

We tossed a blue plastic tarp on the dry grounds on the leeward side of the deep bright orange tent that was the home of the East Syracuse-Minoa Spartans. The wind wasn't much on a day that was raging good compared to the previous 48 hours that saw 4 inches of rain finally fall as winter-like winds blew tree branches onto power-lines leaving too many people stranded in the dark. Somehow the Long Branch park trails were dry and fast for racing. The times would be stellar despite three or four juicy mud puddles.

We were all ready to wear the gold jerseys emblazoned on the front with the superwoman "S". Most of the Skaneateles-seven were still struggling with the memorization of the course so Rob and I kept repeating that they were just going to be following people along a path that was already visibly well-worn.

"Coach," came the desperate shriek. "I can't find my uniform." Rachel Hosie was in a funk and I could see that the panic was already devouring an unhealthy dose of adrenalin as her adrenal glands supplied an antidote to the fear that was running rampant in her body. "I know I had it in my hand," she said as she held up her navy bun-huggers. The sophomore was running back and forth like a filly with knobby-kneed legs too unwieldy to handle.

Without thinking I looked at the completely distressed Rachel and said, "How could you be so stupid?" As soon as I said it I regretted it. Most coaches wouldn't think twice when telling the rock-solid truth but I hate to make bad matters worse. And that's what I did when I should have just collected myself and figured out a solution. We usually carry a spare uniform in the med kit and when I didn't find one there, the med kit suddenly found itself upside down with safety pins and spikes flying all over the place. That's me. I don't like surprises on race day.

Rob was quick to suggest that we see if the kids all had the t-shirts we bought them at the beginning of the season. That didn't fly. We then tried to see if everyone had their white long-sleeved moisture wicking shirts. That didn't work, but Rob had carried the last three from our supply in his pick-up truck. With some switching to get the sizes right, we got all the kids into the white cool-weather tops with no printing on them. The girls liked it. They liked the tight fit. They liked the look. They liked the feel. What started as a potentially tumultuous calamity that would have forced Rachel to the bench, in violation of the Federation uniform rules, turned into a propeller that would help move us forward in a tough field that included the red and white clad Baldwinsville Bees.

With the girls late getting into uniform, our warm-up also got off to a tardy start. Of the bunch only Rachel Vaivoda seemed to have her total act together. "I'm ready coach. Just jogging around made me want the race to start. I'm ready. In fact, I think the team is ready. We want it today." Rachel has quickly turned into a woman this fall. From a frazzled girl last spring who let nearly everything in life matter more than her running, she's become a good juggler who realizes that more success can be achieved if one of the six bowling pins is tossed from the juggling act. Efficient, confident, well-rested and valuing the rare opportunity to be competitive, she's taken charge of her emotions.

Somehow we got to the line early. The previous weekend at Phoenix we showed up with a minute to spare and were still taking off extraneous clothing as Jim Engle, the starter who rides his bike around the course to officiate, was giving his final commands. I made it my purpose to lighten up the atmosphere and somehow we started talking about the Pity Clap. I've been kidding Hannah about starting slowly and I asked her if she liked the applause that is reservedly given by the crowd for the final finisher. She unleashed her trademark laugh and I knew all was well. We were relearning how to work together and we were getting good at it.

The girls sang their song, did their cheer and all looked ready. Earlier, back on the blue tarp as the girls put on their spikes, I saw Amanda drinking something and the taste made her face wrinkle-up like an old white-haired lady in a dowdy light blue and white dress as she gingerly sipped a piping hot bowl of soup. After she won the Phoenix Invitational, I figured she had this all figured out. Who knows what it was.

Sofie, back from her two-meet suspension, crouched on the ground and said, "I don't know why I'm so nervous." I gave her a little nudge with my shoe and said that if she wanted to be nervous, she needed to get away from the team and be nervous alone. Rob and I were also worried about Hannah who seemed more unsettled than we'd seen her in a while. Without the two seniors in the line-up the previous two races, we noticed that the kids were calm, unfazed, relaxed and having a good time in the days and hours leading up to the races. It was different with the two seniors and I think that their outward fear or apprehension prior to racing was being picked up by the younger girls.

While losing the past two Sectionals with second place finishes, we lost to fear itself prior to losing to the winners from Canastota in '04 and Sauquoit Valley in '05. This year is different as composure seems to have replaced wide-eyed doubt and trepidation. Sofie came out of her funk in quick order as the positive nature of the other girls took charge. Kristin Roberts is ready. Alexis Mazzeo is always ready. Even the PSATs that lasted from 7:30 to 11 AM couldn't put a damper on us. We were staying positive. Rob had been watching the runners approach the finish in earlier races and we decided to go straight through the mud puddle instead of around it coming into the final 100 meters of the race. The girls liked that idea. No pantywaists today.

At the gun the team took off. By the time they made the first gradual turn to the left we were all up front and setting up residency in the top ten.

By the mile mark, Hannah had decided to run for the lead. She had decided not to follow anyone. As she passed, I kidded her and asked if she had the right end of the race. It seems to help her when I say before every race that it's okay to be last. Her mother was really worried when she saw her senior and last of three children take the lead coming off the starting line in complete contrast to virtually an entire career of running that consisted of holding back early. Coming down the one hill on the first of two loops, Hannah had slipped to third and I was just hoping she'd hold on to that spot. We were in good shape. The B'ville girls had a few up front with us but seemed to lack the depth to stay with us. Out of sight they went on a little loop near the Seneca River that was flowing fast from the rainstorm and suddenly out popped Hannah all alone. She made her move in the same place as her winning effort on the same course against Solvay and Cazenovia earlier in the season. Our girls have decided that they like Long Branch Park.

Hannah pulled away for the win as she joins our Hall-of-Fame. She's the 11th Laker to claim an invite victory and the second in the last eight days. We won our fifth invitational of the season and our gamble to maintain rhythm while forgoing rest seemed to pay off. We are definitely race-sharp.

Hannah's 19:13 was the sixth fastest on the day as the team placed 2nd out of all 37 teams that raced in three different sections. Only Cicero-North Syracuse got past us and we'd closed the gap significantly from our first meet of the season at Chittenango. More importantly, we'd put our cards on the table. Sometimes that's the best way to get what you want. We'd played coy and played hide-and-seek all season so coming into the open at Liverpool was a gamble. If we ran well we'd make a statement of our intent. If we'd done poorly we'd have opened the door for Sauquoit, CBA, Canastota and Tully. We shut the door with a definite thud.

Our average time for the top five girls was 19:53 while Sauquoit, having their best race of the year, put up an average time of 20:29. We put four girls in front of Sauquoit's second. Canastota's average was 20:36 and we put four girls in front of their first. CBA was once again missing one of their fabulous trio but today we put Hannah far in front of the remaining dynamic duo while their 4th and 5th are still so far back that each will add 40 to 50 points to the team's total at Sectionals.

B'ville, the 4th place finisher at the Manhattan Invite in Race "A" a week earlier, tallied 63 points to our 42. And we didn't get a lot from Rachel Hosie who was emotionally gassed from the jersey incident, and Amanda, who gave herself an injection to counter the low numbers that a pin prick revealed.

Behind Hannah's 19:13 was Rachel Vaivoda's 19:51 and Sofie's 19:55 and Kristin Roberts' 19:59. That pack is what will pull us through any local challenge. And when we get Amanda and Rachel Hosie back on the right page, we'll be tough to keep out of the state championship after our two year hiatus. Hosie crossed the line in 20:25 and two seconds back with a furious kick was Alexis. Amanda struggled but never gave in.

The three senior girls were tired but excited to have a night out with their mothers. "It's mother-daughter bonding night," said Rachel. They were heading out together to see the hit movie *Marie Antoinette*. If the boys had a male bonding night with their fathers, they'd go see the Texas Chainsaw Massacre: The Beginning.

As Gary was driving us back to Skaneateles as the thin cloud cover once again took the heat from the 50- degree day around 4 PM, there rose a voice from far back of the empty 70-seater bus. "Hey coach," yelled Hannah, "are we staying overnight for 'states?"

It's the Weather, Stupid

Any illusion I had about the girls running 30 seconds faster than last season at the Tully race course just east of Rt. 81 has been wiped away by the weather forecast and the effect on me is akin to slipping while punting a football and landing so hard on your back that the wind gets knocked from your lungs. I'm deflated and worrying. With only five days between tomorrow's OHSL Championship meet and the Sectional Championship at Long Branch, we have no room for lousy weather-induced illness, injury or dampened psyche. I know they're a half minute faster but I don't see how they can show it.

From the National Weather Service.

Tonight: Periods of rain. Low around 41. South wind between 11 and 16 mph, with gusts as high as 28 mph. Chance of precipitation is 100%. New rainfall amounts between a half and three quarters of an inch possible.

Saturday: Periods of rain. The rain could be heavy at times. High near 51. Breezy, with a southeast wind 14 to 24 mph becoming west. Winds could gust as high as 36 mph. Chance of precipitation is 100%. New rainfall amounts between three quarters and one inch possible.

We've maintained a high level of training and positive spirits despite the past week's weather that would qualify as a series of good mid-winter days with highs peaking at 40 as the steady 30 MPH winds topped the trees in my front yard. Like someone being born ugly and stupid and then having a black cloud hanging over their head every day for the rest of their life, the driving rain that is bred and repeatedly propagated by the Great Lakes to our immediate north and west hung around our collective necks like so many jewels hanging around Mr. T's neck. You could bitch, yell, juke, shake or dress with four layers between the elements and your skin, but nothing you did could change anything. When it comes to our weather, every action is reactionary; the only pro-active thing about all this is having the time, money and wherewithal to purchase foul-weather gear that insulates you from scalp to toe. Despite repeatedly being buffeted by a blustery Mother Nature, we survived the week unscathed and our goals remain intact as the season draws to a quick close.

It was cold enough for me to inflict pain upon myself as I warmed up with the kids. Touching my wet tongue to the teeth and gums on the upper right side of my mouth sent a twinge of pain through me as the cold immediately irritated my receding gum line. And it's still October. We're really going to suffer this winter.

Today is our pre-race day as we begin the countdown to the OHSL meet. We ran a mere 20 minutes and clipped off a few 100s on the track while we enjoyed the mid-40 temperatures. A week from today we'll either be celebrating our sectional victory, and advancement to the State Championship, or we'll be done, the season ending with a suddenness that leaves you feeling as helpless and useless as a faith healer in a crowd of atheists.

Waiting for the rest of the boys and girls to return from their individual runs, Hannah blared out that we'd changed in the past year. "Coach, do you remember what we were like last year at this time?" The memory isn't good and I'm glad that the 2005 episode is behind us. "I was so nervous, so scared. We all were." I told Hannah that the team needed professional help last year and I just wasn't man enough for the task. "I'm excited now," she continued. "I can't wait for tomorrow. I wish tomorrow was Sectionals, not in a bad way. It isn't that I can't wait for a week. I'm just ready for it this year. We're not worried at all."

While I digested Hannah's confident statement, I waited for the others to return, and I realized that they no longer had to cling together for sustenance, for support, for life. They'd grown, both the boys and girls. We'd succeeded at some level in getting them a step closer to being independent and doing what they sensed they needed in order to end the training week feeling right about the upcoming race.

Rachel Hosie, like the rest of my Lakers, was reminded to bring her jersey, her white moisture-wicking long-sleeved shirt, and to clean her spikes so that we could get some nice sharp ones cranked in on a day that was sure to be muddy. Rachel has also realized that she races well with a pre-race dinner—the night before—of chicken from Doug's Fish Fry. On her short run she stopped in at Doug's and picked up an extra container of Ranch Dressing for her poultry. Sofie is convinced that she races well off of Taco Bell. Others down a nice hamburger and I think we've broken the back of the Friday night pre-race Pasta Dinner. A month ago the girls started getting together mid-week and the correlation to good Saturday racing is dramatic and unmistakable. There's no more insulin spiking and crashing. We're on with a rush from the sound of the gun and we never look back. This Friday the girls all showed up at school with homemade green t-shirts that said "Lean Mean Running Machine." The team just looks and acts different. Sofie even looks taller and I noticed that Lexie's calves are much more defined. Only Beatrice has fallen short of her potential and I'm not even sure she'll run at OHSLs as concern about her hip has her near the point of crying, not from the pain, but from emotional uncertainty and more disappointment. She fears ending another season feeling disgruntled and with an injury that will keep her on the sidelines for indoor track like in past years. She's over-thinking but it's understandable. Losing your mobility for the better part of six months is a daunting experience that twists shut the valve of confidence. The doctor has detected no problems except a tight back. The chances of her bones breaking again are slim, especially in light of a clean bone density scan that showed her to be normal and, thankfully, healthy.

Rachel Vaivoda didn't do well on a physics exam and that's good news for her racing tomorrow. "This isn't good, Coach, since I'm planning on majoring in the sciences in college." Rachel has learned how to motivate herself. Her biggest motivation is doing poorly on a physics exam. It turns this placid and lovely girl into an angry racing-bitch. "Don't worry, Coach. I'll be ready tomorrow." When she heard that Hannah and Sofie had done well on the test, the blood pressure was kicked up a notch and that's usually bad news for the opponents.

Hannah is carrying a double burden heading into the OHSL meet at Tully. She arranged to take her ACT exam at Tully and then catch a nap while waiting for us to arrive in the yellow limousine around 12:30 for the 2:00 kick-off. Hannah's beginning to think about running at Middlebury College. We're making solid progress getting her back on her game and her feet grounded. If she decides not to compete in college, I want her to make the decision from a position of strength and success, not frustration and failure. Tully is a good 30 minute drive east from Skaneateles and we all have to travel through some of the greatest apple growing country in the nation. We'll pass by orchards with trees loaded with Red Delicious, Empire, Cortland and Macoun apples. The bus will travel past Beak & Skiff, McLusky Orchards and Navarino Orchards and so many others that lost hundreds of thousands of dollars during the fall harvest season because about a third of the immigrant apple-pickers didn't return for the harvest. Thank the Republicans for their xenophobic fear.

Hannah, who bragged about getting to bed at 9:30 on her Thursday 'sleep night' will hear the rooster well before the sun is scheduled to rise as she eats and drives to Tully so that she can claim her exam seat by 8 AM. She can handle that task. What concerns me is the effect on Hannah from the legal delay that took place on Wednesday night. At practice Thursday afternoon she was venting a plume of steam about a situation that would have engulfed almost anyone else in a similar position where control had been completely lost as the law continued its ever so slow grind toward resolution and hopefully justice. I think there's a plot to drag this out and keep her on her toes and in line.

Today, after our 20 minute run and 2x100, we talked while on the track about drinking, about driving while drunk. It's an epidemic in Central New York and it's as prevalent as gutter balls in a bowling tournament-without-bumpers for 8 year olds.

The girls all agreed that displays like we had a few weeks ago in the high school lobby—called the Commons--of kids killed in drinking and driving accidents didn't quite achieve the results that so many adults expected. "What we need is to see the life of the driver who lived and see how it changed," said Hannah. Sofie and the others agreed that death is too big an issue to really wrap their arms around. "We can't really digest it, Coach. What we need to see is a picture of Steve Corsello with his friends, with Matt Angelillo, and then see Matt's grave and Steve in his jail cell." I'd never been presented with that side of the argument, the kid's side. It makes sense. Seeing what's changed in the lives of the survivors is something that might make a bigger impact than a heart-felt display of the deceased's life and death no matter how justified, logical and necessary for many of the adult survivors. Hannah said she could completely understand the crying of the accused North Syracuse girl when she appeared in court for the drinking and driving incident that killed her friend. Her life had been ruined. "Everything changed because of a decision, a simple choice, and it changed everything not only for the dead, but the living. And there's nothing anyone can do to unwind time," said a philosopher calling herself Hannah.

Hannah said that her legal ordeal might do more to reach kids than the deadly accidents. "They all know me and they'll all see how it messes up my life. That's what might convince some that it isn't worth it," Hannah proclaimed as if she suddenly saw that something good might come out of her legal troubles and her suspension from racing. The whole case will become even more real on November 15th when she is scheduled for another appearance at the police station. All hope of having Hannah entered in the Youth Court experience was dashed quickly. Officer Lukens said that the program was completely full and she'd have to appear before an adult criminal court if something else wasn't worked out. With her hopes fading fast, seemingly as quickly as a college freshman's bank account, Hannah seemed strong. "It'll work out. I think I'll get something like six months without getting in trouble and everything will go away." It's called Adjournment in Contemplation of Dismissal.

I'm not sure what team will show up at Tully for the OHSLs where we line up 40-something teams on one starting line for one race. The start is long and last year we shut down our engines about 10 seconds too early and got engulfed by those on the right and left wings. We never recovered. I'm not a big fan of the meet because if anything goes wrong we have no time to resurrect ourselves, to mend broken bones, to loosen tight tendons, to liberate ligaments from the turmoil of tightness and strain. We've placed in the top-five every year over the last eleven, winning four times and setting the low score record of 40 on one occasion. I fear that Fayetteville-Manlius could shatter our mark and I'd be disappointed in that. Being the only small school to ever win the meet, having the record low score is a bonus that just serves to irritate the big school coaches. I like that.

My eye-glasses are scratched to a cloudy, foggy haze and they're rapidly becoming useless. The heat at the Windsor Invitational sent profuse amounts of sweat from my furrowed brow to my lenses and I promptly—and stupidly—cleaned them with my cotton shirt, the salt crunching scuff marks across each lens as I furiously worked the lens between my thumb and forefinger. Since then I've liked what I've seen from both the girl's and boy's teams. I wonder how they'll look tomorrow at the OHSL meet as I watch them in the rain, cold and wind through the lenses of my new lineless bifocals?

Fool's Gold

Maybe Rob's right about the OHSL meet. Sure, it's a championship but there's nothing to gain. It's just something you do whether you like it or not, like sending a thank-you note to your aunt for a pair of socks that look strikingly like the pair you've gotten for your birthday the past six years.

"They're just not into it, Jack. They actually did okay and they'll be tough next week at Sectionals," Rob reassured me as I walked around huddled against the forces of Mother Nature, forces more understood by people in Hurricane-prone areas of coastal America.

Until I saw the water-soaked results hanging on a rough hewn board like pictures of the missing after 9/11, I was feeling okay about our girl's showing. "Sixth!" I was incredulous. We wanted to beat West Genesee and Baldwinsville, but if they'd beaten us, I'd have been all right with that. They're good. They did beat us, but not by much. It was Liverpool getting past us that put me over the top. We'd beaten them by over 100 points a week earlier at their invitational. That's two years in a row that I've been shaking my head and pursing my lips after the mighty OHSL Championship meet.

We were the top small school to finish and our three seniors, Hannah, Rachel and Sofie led us once again, yet I was disappointed with the underclassmen who had stepped up so bravely while Hannah and Sofie were suspended. As before the suspension, the four girls decided to ride the seniors' collective coattails. And it cost us. We'd been in the top five every year for the past 11 years. Now that streak is broken. But like Rob said, the OHSL meet just doesn't mean anything unless you have a chance to win. We've been in the pole position many times in the past and each time that we were a legitimate favorite we ran the course as if we just knew that we couldn't be defeated. We owned the course and we knew that we'd win. It wasn't false bravado. It wasn't an in-your-face display of arrogance. It was just a firm understanding of what we could and would do. The meet had meaning.

I think the girls harbor a goal that's much more important than anything we've chased all season and the overwhelming passion that it involves has set up full-time residency in their brains and their hearts as virtually everything, including the state meet, has been overshadowed. It's Sectionals and in their collective mind the OHSL Championship is nothing more than Fool's Gold.

Getting to talk to West Genesee's Jim Vermeulen and Lou Delsole is a gas. They're both firmly in the old school ranks. Lou was dressed to the nines, four layers worth, and he wasn't a bit cold like the rest of us. "I look like those little kids in a huge winter coat that mothers put on a bus, all stiff with their arms stuck out and unbendable," said Lou.

Jim was pleased with his girls and he thinks that he has a male stud in his 11th place frosh, Steve Houghmaster. Speaking of his girls, Jim said,

> Our girls have pulled themselves up a bit these past weeks. I shouldn't be complaining, but my problem is I always see potential—and this group hasn't achieved theirs yet—so I was unhappy with their performance. Yeah, I know that sounds piggy, but I just want 'the perfect race' from them once this season, and now we're down to Sectionals with little chance of making Feds as was their team goal. I can go right from race winner Margaret to our #5 Gwen and describe what kind of mental mojo each was operating on—or not operating on—at OHSL: first mile psych-out; fear of fatigue; backing off pain; over-thinking. And it sounds crazy talking about a repeating OHSL champion like this, but I think Margaret knows she only ran to win yesterday. She could have buried runner-up Mackenzie after the two mile mark, but she decided to play counter-punch instead. And why not, it's worked for her all year. Unfortunately, that kind of conservative strategy seeps

> *into the brain and then you get eaten up by the big dogs at*
> *States and Feds.*

Jim continues to pen great newspaper articles about the merits of high school athletics, about the virtues of hard work, sacrifice, yielding to a group goal, about countering the pop-culture and how it's the non-winning teams that truly define the heart and meaning of high school sports. He's much more than a coach and his kids are lucky to have him and Lou on their side.

"He has mud in his eyes," was the constant refrain said in a haughty and humorous tone by those fans who lined the approach to the finish line at Tully's wonderful course that was turned into a mud-pit. It was a down-home meet with parents spooning bowl after bowl of their homemade chili for the shivering throngs, the brave-hearts who just don't let lousy weather drive them away from something they love.

Mud was layered on my not-so-water proof Gore-Tex pant-leg-zipper like flattened caulk on a seam. I had mud up near my waist and I hadn't done anything but stuff my hands under my armpits or into the waistband of my pants as I slowly lost small motor control. If we'd had to fill out finish line cards like in the old days, I couldn't have done it in legible form. Thank God for Pat Leone's timing system which is the best in the nation.

As the races progressed, the uniforms became mere background for the mud while the school colors served as nothing more than a canvas for Mother Nature's modernist mess. I remember watching one guy approach the finish and he was layered in fresh, dark mud from head to toe. As he passed me I saw that his backside was the same. "Rob, that guy belly flopped and did an ass-splash." I couldn't imagine how cold and uncomfortable he must have been. As I later found out, Tully's custodian let the kids use the school showers. He was a brave and considerate man.

Tully is a plateau between song Mountain and Labrador ski centers but I could have sworn that I heard the PA system announce to the crowd the approach of the 2 PM high tide.

According to Jared Lindsay, a Skaneateles running alum who is now my pizza and calzone chef, the Rainbow Trout are feasting all along the shore of Skaneateles Lake but I firmly believe that there were parts of the Tully course where I could have tossed out a perch-colored Rapala and pulled in a nice Rainbow.

Next Friday the winner of the Class C race gets to celebrate a summer and fall of sacrifice and hard work after hooking and landing their quarry. There's no turning back the clock. We are what we are and I think we have enough good cards to sweep the chips off the table. What we need now is luck, pure and simple. No sickness. No injuries.

Sauquoit's top girl, Samantha Steadman, seems to have regressed since her good race a week earlier at Liverpool. She was a good half minute off her expected finish in relation to comparable runners, and her team still lacks depth.

Canastota is a bit of a dark horse but they showed in the recent past that they are capable of taking a big leap after a peaking sequence has been applied by Coach Andy Pino.

CBA's top three are probably going to place in the top-10 but their 4th and 5th are just too far back for Theresa Trudell to have any real hopes. Francesca Minale has been working a job on school and pre-race nights to get some cash and it's taken the starch from her legs. Kristen Fekete says she doesn't know why she's not running fast but Theresa says it's the group she runs with that is determining her running fate. Running with slower kids isn't moving her in the right direction. Katie Webster, who got hurt at the pre-state meet, took off about three weeks and she isn't running like normal. Running three months a year just doesn't give you the sponge necessary to absorb lay-offs necessitated by injury or illness.

Tully's Becky Bloom seems to have imploded and her coach can't explain why, except that when younger girls on her team became threats Becky seemed to have lost her fight. It's not all that uncommon. Kelly Coyne, their lead girl, is slipping back but if both Bloom and Coyne re-engage we could be in trouble. You can't ever count a kid out.

Hannah is doing great. By the time we left Tully, she had been there almost ten hours. Hannah earned All-OSHL first team honors with a brutal finish that moved her into 10th in a superlative individual performance. Rachel Vaivoda continues to be a positive force as she missed All-OHSL honors by six-tenths of a second while placing 31st. Sofie grabbed 50th but I think she was already looking ahead to Sectionals. This was a race she had to run but her heart wasn't into it at all. I'm beginning to think that all roads lead to the Sectional race for the seniors. I'm not sure the State Meet is even on their radar screen right now. They really want to atone for and reclaim that Sectional Championship title. I think I've underestimated its importance for these three former state champions.

The underclassmen lagged far back for most of the race and then closed to make it look better. Kristin Roberts has far, far too much talent to hold back like that. Alexis Mazzeo just doesn't seem to like the mud. Rachel Hosie continues to yield to discomfort until the end of the race when she shucks the pain and just goes. Amanda went out too fast as she's fallen into her destructive freshman habit. Before much of the course has been covered she's gassed and holding on for dear life. She knows that extreme physical moves will have extreme consequences on her blood. We keep preaching 'steady' but she's got that youthful impulsiveness that leads to trouble at times.

Inside Tully's lobby that doubles as a cafeteria and academic hall of fame, I addressed all these issues with the girls who will return next year and I don't think anyone was surprised to hear me bring up the various topics. "If you ride the seniors next week, our season is done. It's that simple. You're too good to let other kids do the work for you. I'll never forget how you all stepped up when two of them were out of the line-up. Once you step into that front-running arena, there's no turning back. The Rubicon has been crossed." They all looked at me with eyes wide open and I could see that my words penetrated their brains and souls. They understood. I think we'll be fine at Sectionals.

The pit of my stomach is already letting me know that something is about to happen. I can feel muscles where I usually feel nothing. I test myself more and more as I try to hold a pace longer on my runs, hold my breath longer as I work the abs while drawing my stomach back towards my spine when I'm driving to and from school. Like Bob McDaniel, my high school coach, I think that if I can do these stupid things that have no relation to Friday's race, we'll win.

When I return from Long Branch late Friday afternoon I want to be able to enjoy my pizza, my beer, and I want to spend a few miserable hours trying to find a hotel for the kids.

Too many hopeful coaches who have scant chance of moving on to the state meet lock up all the rooms during the summer. In order to get rooms once you qualify for the state meet you have to time it just right so that your call is preceded, by mere minutes, a defeated coach's call cancelling their block of rooms. Some years you get lucky and it's just a half dozen calls. Other years it might take a few days of dialing and bitching.

Let the bitching begin. I want to win.

The Waiting Game

Waiting, we're playing the waiting game now. I can't sit for long in my plaid chair that mixes soft hues of brown and gray-blue, its old cushion beginning to look like a swayback horse ridden hard and long. The nation is glued to the TV as Louisville and West Virginia knock each other around in an exciting football game that has national implications. I walk into the living room to see my wife as she sits and stares at the TV watching her favorite show, Grey's Anatomy. I don't stick around long as she grabs handful after handful of popcorn from the Act II popcorn microwave bag. It produces the most God-awful smell in the world and I get to live with it every night of her life. I scan last Sunday's New York Times Magazine but can't get through any of the articles that are printed on slick and great smelling paper stock before I'm up and wandering around once more.

Passing time isn't easy. These are the helpless hours, the final hours of existence between the last training run and the gun. Last year I spent my time the night before Sectionals trying to figure out how to beat Sauquoit Valley. Try as I might I couldn't produce a single scenario for success. That told me something. But I kept trying to be the super-sleuth and unravel some mysteriously hidden set of clues that would point me to a victory that ultimately proved to be elusive and unachievable.

This year I'm different. I'm anxious, not nervous. We're ready, more mature, better prepared, more relaxed and carrying a bigger wad of mileage that should help us avoid getting stuck in the belly of the snake, that portion of the long line of runners that looks bloated and out of proportion to the rest of the sleek and fast moving line of finely-tuned and dedicated athletes; the best among us in society. I think the torch will still burn when our final runner enters the sanctified realm of the finish chute where the living body is allowed to catch up with itself. It'll be 12:21 PM on Friday November 3rd when a victor is crowned on a day when forecasters say snow could stick to the ground for the first time as the cold wind picks up the warm Great Lake waters from Lake Ontario like a favorite sweater picks up lint.

The night's sleep won't be easy but I won't roll around like a tumbled tile being readied for a high-roller's bathroom in a walled, gated and guarded community somewhere in snobby America. This will be no long and lonely night. I'm confident. I'll sleep, but when my wife gets up early for school I'll still have time to dream and the dreams will be wild as I slumber half awake and half in la-la land. Getting up will be easy, far easier than on any school day. We've got some celebrating to do—I hope.

When there are forced lulls in the action, there's time to think, to reflect, to sit and try to collect the moments of the season that frame it forever in my mind.

Gone is the heat of summer with tar boils popping under the whitened waffle soles of Rachel Vaivoda's Adidas, Carly Brown's Nike Frees and Alexis Mazzeo's Sauconys. The kids logged their miles in open expanses where withering heat from the sun engulfed their senses with Amazon Rain-Forest impact. No matter where they turned they couldn't escape the suffocating heat while on their runs. With the heat now replaced by arctic air the kids have adapted like a chameleon changing color to go with the environmental dictates. The early morning summer runs with well-rested, clear-eyed bouncy kids have been replaced by a relentless and energy-draining diet of afternoon practices with puffy-eyed runners who ache to sleep 'til noon. The kids are filled with an urgent, passionate immediacy now as tomorrow has become today. Their actions and thoughts matter and they intuitively sense it. The new awareness isn't palpable or accompanied by obvious signs of nervousness or fear. More seasoned and weathered after two straight second place finishes in the sectional title-fest, there's an air of confidence and assuredness in this team of Skaneateles girls but not a drop of self-righteousness or hubris.

During the dullness and drill of summer training, the unspoken words softly reverberating in their heads questioned the point of all this. What's the purpose of living tired, of looking at the sunny day as a time to run instead of an opportunity to lounge by the lake? What's the benefit of having aching muscles that throb incessantly like the surf ceaselessly pounding the beach? Running constantly rules and overtakes one's consciousness as it intrudes like a butcher knife into life, controlling the simple things that other people never have to think about, things like eating, sleeping or drinking water. With our feet and asses comfortably cooled by the lake's waters as we sit in a beach chair in the same position for hours without flexing the muscles, we worry about cramps and muscles that could conceivably grow dangerously stiff. We have to take leave of a Yankee game on Sunday afternoon as we grudgingly get up off the couch in an air-conditioned room to go log our summer miles. The first perfect fall Friday night can't be enjoyed at the school football stadium because we race the next morning and preserving adrenalin and protecting the legs is of utmost importance. Everything adds up for a runner and the last thing you want is to miss a trip to the state meet like Eric Leonard of Chittenango who was out-leaned at the wire, Pat Leone's timing team having to go to a photo-finish to end Leonard's dream of making 'states. Three-tenths of a second, less than a tenth of a second per mile was the impassable barrier that Leonard will co-exist with for the remaining decades of his life. Why do we do all this? We conduct ourselves in this regimented and sometimes forlorn manner to eliminate the "what if" from our future vocabulary. It's as simple as that.

We're all here for one primary and overriding reason. It isn't for self-esteem and it isn't to merely participate. We want to win. The seniors, the Brat Pack, want to prove that their frosh state championship year wasn't a case of being carried on the skirt tails of their older All-State teammates. Those younger girls who are now due to graduate in a mere eight months want to prove that they belong and that they're the equal of past generations of Skaneateles champions. Winning, the desire to be on top, to carve a name for yourself, that's the purpose. It drives people. Winning, it's the logical goal that pushes or pulls and drives average people to become successful athletes. We don't do it just to do it. We do it to win, to be the best and somewhere along the sometimes muddied, excruciating, blistering and frigid paths we learn to have fun alone and in communion with each other.

Each of us in our own time and in our own way has learned to accept the razor sharp edge of truth. And here's what we've all learned repeatedly. Our whole is greater than the sum of our individual parts. As a team we matter. As individuals we cover the spectrum of what it means to be average, indistinct from the hordes of humanity that are walking past each other on city sidewalks without even an acknowledging glance from one to another. As individuals we're each the wallflower that goes through the school dance unnoticed more times than we want to admit. We're all vanilla and wanting to be the rainbow sherbet. We're the straight legged khaki pants looking for pleats and cuffs, the starched white shirt looking for diamond studded cufflinks. Alone in solitary pursuit of some goal, each and every one of us is but a single seashell hoping beyond hope to be noticed on the shores of Sanibel Island—the world shelling capital that calls itself 'shellacious.' But, banding together in singular pursuit, this random group of dreamers from different school and community cliques who wear the same uniform emerge from Superman's telephone booth special, distinct, noticeable and different, far different from our daily mundane selves. The anonymous life we live day after day changes when we don our Superman "S" gold uniforms. We're not running away from our daily problems, we're creating problems for others to solve as we express ourselves in an eminently splendid and human way. Through our flight-by-foot we don't flee life, we create it anew. And we give it purpose, meaning and vibrancy. When we wear the jersey we shed our cloak of invisibility and become something special. Our senses quicken. We see people pointing at us as our leader and then our wolf-pack race past. We hear, with sensitive ears, people talking about us as our swollen phalanx slices through the course with precision. As individuals we're ordinary. Together, we're a hell of a force.

Becoming more than just the typical kid who's confused and searching for meaning in life while wandering aimlessly and lethargically from activity to activity, over time—as drop by drop the salty sweat falls from our brow scraping open a new awareness—we understand that reality compels us to be more than mere friends and to step out of shadows cast by those who dream too little and dance too cautiously.

Taking a step up the evolutionary ladder we become teammates locked together until the collective quest has been achieved. Day by day the truth creeps up on us like the chill of a late fall football afternoon as the sun slowly descends to the horizon and then sinks behind the denuded western hills. The seconds tick away and the seconds become minutes like so many small steps become miles. Without any purposeful intentions, an enlightening and magical metamorphosis takes place. No longer just slimy worms lacking vision and hell-bent on making an isolating cocoon, and no longer riddled with paltry potential, we discover that we're stunning butterflies that can fly and go anywhere upon nature's winds. No longer individuals without a clear path, we're teammates and the bond formed will always link one to another as each name is forever forged onto the pages of local history.

Rising above the peasantry, soaring over fields of mud and shattering arbitrary socio-economic barriers, limitations no longer seem insurmountable and dreams are no longer privately sheltered or discussed with no one out of fear of being ridiculed. When you can run, you feel that you can do anything. Physically and emotionally intoxicating, running is incredibly empowering as it unleashes energy we didn't know we possessed.

I'm dreading the end of the season. I want the butterflies to make it all the way home instead of running out of gas and becoming fodder for some unthinking glutinous creature. Being on the top end of the food chain is the goal.

I continue to tell myself that we're ready. I point to an early week conversation with Rachel Hosie and Carly Brown. Both were tired on Monday and they looked like the wet noodle that little league kids claim the opposing pitcher's arm looks like while on the mound. "Coach, what are we doing today? We're tired." Standing next to them I held my tongue as I tried to assess what their words meant after a Sunday of rest. Were they ill? Were they drifting away from our collective goal? Were they melting down or were they just tired because of the changing of the clocks as fall's brightness became winter's darkness? Rachel told a short story about coy-dogs in her yard on Sunday night that howled and kept her awake from two to six that morning. Carly, the team's only frosh, wasn't sure why she was tired. I sent them along with the rest of their team on a nice long run and they returned looking and feeling better than any of television's extreme made-over woman. They were bouncing around like newborn fillies.

Hannah said on Thursday that she had gotten up on her own all week without the aid of an alarm clock. Lexie was in bed by 9:30 every night this week and it showed on her face. Rachel Vaivoda is jumping around excitedly like a little girl who got exactly what she wanted on Christmas morning. "I haven't had a good sectional race yet," said Rachel. "I've been awful but I'm ready this year." And I believe her. She's been steady and has been master of her mind all season. Kristin Roberts is prepared and I know she'll lay it out. Amanda Golden worries me a bit. I can't read her like the others. At Phoenix when she won the invitational, I was probably the last person in the place who saw it coming. To me she's like a book by Shakespeare. I never could read the old English bard. And I can't read Amanda. Taylor Wellington's dad fell from a roof while at work and will probably have to have a series of operations to put his spine and arm back together. There's talk of a cast and Taylor, like most teens, doesn't show any cognizance of the severity of the injuries—or she's the master of the emotional cover-up. I have no idea how she'll run. Carley Billick looks good but I'm not sure that she fully understands that she has an immense amount of talent. This sectional race is her audition for next fall. Sofie is working with Rachel Vaivoda on some t-shirts and I think she's ready, based on early week runs that revealed a more forward-leaning posture and quicker feet.

The boys have been somewhat lethargic the past few weeks. Some of them seem to have chalked-up this season to history before the final curtain has been drawn as we try to stretch them into a newer physical universe. Sam is shooting for a top-10 finish and hopes to hang with the top-five kids who are not on Tully's team . On his bedroom wall was a note that read "Top Five." That's significant because it's showing that Sam's getting into this. The top five individuals who are not on Tully's probable winning squad will move on to the state championship. Sam's close but probably on the outside looking in. Calvin seems content to repeat what he's been doing because he's edging closer to Sam over the second half of the race and by the finish is close enough to touch Sam's long shadow. Both must come to understand that racing is personal. Either you own them or they own you. It's man vs. man and balls to the wall. Hang on or get dropped.

The need to win is the thread that binds us all together. Victory doesn't strike blindly like love, nor does it strike randomly like lightning. Victory is earned with a little luck like river rafters who somehow make it through the whitewater rapids without slamming into some sharp-edged submerged boulder.

Victory isn't happenstance; it's earned, not necessarily in the immediacy of the championship moment, but over the span of summer months and years spent on the country and lakeside roads with each week seeing the corn growing taller until it's harvested. As the fall deepens, we see leaves fill the gutters of our roads and we watch the summer crowd retreat to the hinterlands of some far off oasis that can't compare to Skaneateles.

We've summered well. We've battled the pop-culture, eschewed most temptations and stuck to our collective goals. Getting back to the front is what sends the stomach butterflies into full flight. We're on our toes, healthy and ready to soar.

Survive or Perish

The roads are not midnight black now as the sun spends scant time shining down upon us. Having lost their fresh mascara of early summer tar, the roads now look like a grand but weathered charcoal boulevard that's lost her charms and curves; the local lanes now seemingly stretching straight and true and appearing abandoned as the early winter scene is set for the loneliness of the long distance runner.

Sectionals kicked the stuffing out of runner after runner and left the remains looking like the Thanksgiving table after everyone has pushed away and headed for the davenport. Discarded after the ravenous chomping of family and friends, the turkey carcass and trappings soon stink and disintegrate like so many runners' year-long dreams have wilted and rotted like neglected grape vines or the rabbit that's been smashed flat and mangled by a ten-wheeler-without-a- conscience. With the sectional championship in the history books and logged permanently onto so many internet web pages, new dreams have already been born and new shoes have begun taking runners-with-goals down roads that look like wide expressways instead of narrow by-ways that are hemmed in all summer by lush hedgerows tightly woven and seemingly impenetrable.

Wooded lots that were once made thick and robust by growing leaves that chattered excitedly in the summer breeze are different now, somehow looking despondent, deserted, and on a bright Saturday afternoon the blue sky can be clearly seen through the sticks that were once proud woods tempting lumber jacks, kids at play and uncountable legions of small creatures.

Running along late-Autumn's roads reacquaints you with the small sounds of nature that are drowned out in the summer by the car engines of thousands of vacationing families, sounds like critters leaping around in the roadside ditches as you jog by, the chatter of squirrels tight-roping across the wires high above the road and the background sounds of children playing somewhere off in the unseen distance. Even the sound of lawn mowers and leaf blowers now calms and reassures instead of annoying the road running legion of joggers who privately harbor illusions-of-future-greatness.

The Sectional trails remained dry as threatening skies were kept at bay by nature's competing high and low pressure systems. Combined with some great athletic competition, Championship Friday was sure to be stirring and memorable. Large and vocal crowds intently announced, with roaring yells, the approach of lead runners all day long as splendid athletes carved their names into history along the fan-crowded trails at Long Branch. Voices carried easily along the shores of the Seneca River and through the trails that cut in and out of the woods. Echoes added to the excitement as deceptive sounds bounced here and there as determined runners finished their races spent and exhausted. Some were on cloud nine and some were in hell, the smiles of the joyous victors blunting the physical and mental pains that buried the losers' dreams like tar and feathers smothered the lives of escaped slaves in an earlier, uglier American age.

Hannah was slow to get into her warm-up, beginning at 11:25 with the race to begin at high noon. As I studied her I thought that maybe she didn't want the end to begin. She was calm, resigned to the coming completion of her career within the borders of her competitive home, Section III in central New York. Amanda was calm and confident—almost serene—as she looked for Purell after taking a piss in the busy public bathrooms in the park. Her mind wasn't exactly on the race but I could understand. Rachel Vaivoda was ready to go, eager to get into her warm-up and ready to dispel the ghosts that have haunted her dreams for two years.

We didn't race like some withering vine depleted of its fruit and standing abandoned and useless in a neglected field. During the half-hour of warming up we did our own thing individually and finished as a group tightly tied to a uniform goal. We aren't a drum-line where every note, step and dip of the head is scripted. We're deeply into freelance. We're artists painting a blank canvas, sculpting by chiseling pieces of marble to form permanent shape. We were intent on surviving.

At the sound of the gun I was standing 100 meters out and looking back at the long line of emotion-filled and dreamy-eyed runners charging off the starting line with honor and grace. For a brief moment when the starter said 'runners set' a few excitable kids darted out and moved back in line like perch surface-feeding on mayflies in June. Within moments I was talking to myself. 'Damn it!' Tully was employing the same tactics as us. Michelle Franklin-Rauber knew that their only chance to beat us was to stay with us from the gun and hang as long as possible. Despite studying each other's team and coming to the same conclusions and forming the same strategy, only one of us would survive.

Running hard from the gun that was shot by Jim Engle, Tully actually outflanked us as they came out of the 19th starting spot far from us in box five. Once again I told the kids that it was the best spot on the line. By mile marker one I could tell that we were prepared for the long haul and by mile two we were in the lead and the lead was insurmountable. Bill Meylan of Tullyrunners.com had us predicted to win 75-90 over his second pick, Tully, if all five of our top runners performed well. Not wanting to irritate or offend the competitive Michelle, who he works with every day as an unpaid volunteer at his Tully alma mater, Meylan hid the truth according to the computer simulations, simulations that nailed the scores all day long. "You actually graded out to 55 points, Jack," he told me after the meet. After the 3.1 miles of running had been completed, the pack had done their job tallying 46 points to easily defeat runner-up CBA with 94. Tully's third girl got trampled at the start and never recovered. We finished 3-8-9-12-14 as we defeated the next six teams, all of which were ranked in New York State's top echelon.

Bill's comments on his web site tell the story.

POST-Race Comments ... Skaneateles won with an impressive team performance ... Jen Pernisi (APW) finished strongly over the final 800 meters to win the individual title. Pre-Race Analysis ... Skaneateles is the favorite ... but that's the only consensus the computer simulation could determine ... All of the contending teams have a high degree of variability in their performance records and that opens this race up more than might be expected ... If the top five Skaneateles runners perform well, then Skaneateles should win ... If not, the race is up for grabs.

Reporters crowded around me and I stated that I wasn't surprised by the results. I expected it. I knew the girls were ready. The vibes were right. It's like being on a date and knowing that tonight is the night. We'd gotten lucky and our health was impeccable for the race. I think our opponents were all healthy, too, so that made the victory sweeter. No one wants to win by default due to illness or injury. Coaches Franklin of Tully and Theresa Trudell of CBA asked when I was retiring so that they'd have a chance at winning. Those women know how to flatter a gray-haired man at the end of his career. I appreciated it. Michelle asked what magic dust I sprinkled on my girls and I told her that I don't ever talk about the race with them. "It's boring," I said, "because I like to do chalk talk with the teams, but I can't do it with this group. It took me a while to figure it out but we're better off if I just act dumb and say stupid stuff, crack lousy jokes and try to keep them loose." I think Michelle really gets too into her runners. In high school at Homer, she was the energizer bunny and would never relent. Coach Jerry Frare taught her that. At college she became a national champion for Jack Daniels at Cortland State. She's as knowledgeable as anyone but she doesn't yet understand giving in--and coaching means giving in sometimes. "I'd run through a wall before I'd let you beat me," she said after the race as we analyzed our teams' performances. She's well into building a family of her own and these subtle child-rearing tricks will soon become a valuable part of her arsenal. When her quiver is full, look out. Being a mom or dad changes so much about how you see and deal with kids.

Times and kids have changed since Michelle was a competitor. Kids today are different, creations of a far more diverse and self-indulgent society, one that provides options to every obstacle. That doesn't create competitive kids. Sometimes you just have to give in and pick another battle to fight.

At our local meets, I look for both Theresa and Michelle. I like them. I respect them and I enjoy shooting the shit with both.

Hannah didn't have her best day but she understood early on that the pack behind her was tight and doing the job. Despite her late surge I think she was content to take 4th overall. Rachel Vaivoda and Sofie both erased their demons and took 8th and 9th in the team scoring as Kristin Roberts, who hung tough with them most of the race, finished in 12th just eight seconds back. Rachel Hosie promised that she'd take 10th but did well by taking 14th as she duplicated her 2005 sectional finish. Lexie Mazzeo ran well and upon my urging unleashed her furious finishing kick to place 22rd. Poor Amanda Golden's blood sugar levels just dived during the race and I have no insight into why she could win the Phoenix Invitational after eating well but was unable to smell the same level of success thereafter. I know she's frustrated and angry with her body.

Carley Billick was our 8th girl and was disqualified for wearing ear rings. When I told her of the infraction she was crushed and sobbed to me, "I ran for nothing." Holding her tight amongst the frenzied teammates, family and fans eager to congratulate us, I told her that she'd run a great race and didn't hurt our effort. Being a kid, the team effort temporarily took on a secondary importance. In need of an alternate for the state meet, I told Carley that she'll travel with us to Warwick for the slug-fest with Bronxville and Greenwich. Realistically, we're gunning for third.

Sam tried to move on to States but continued to have trouble dealing comfortably with discomfort. As the race progressed he faded from an early position where he was in line to qualify and finished 18th. Try as he might, he was never the same after his Labor Day emergency operation as his confidence and sense of youthful infallibility was constantly questioned. He'll rebound with the start of a new season.

Calvin Davis did well as he again closed hard to take 23rd, just 18 seconds behind Sam. Matt did well for himself and Jeff again held back too long but seems more than capable of moving up dramatically if he would only follow the laws of physiology and train straight through to his senior year. Dan ran well and Dustin again failed to defeat the plague called asthma. Stephen King, the wrestler, took it out hard early and probably had his best race.

Rob and I shooed the girls from our 10 x 20 foot blue tent after the race and talked to the six returning boys. They show promise but few really have chosen to take the well-worn path of dedicated runners. Matt, Jeff and Calvin are dabbling with competitive running and none of them have intentions of continuing to build on their summer and fall of development by doing indoor track. I think in quick order Calvin will be a full-time, year 'round distance runner and it'll pay off. Matt belatedly decided to wrestle again, and I can't be disappointed in that as long as he returns to track in March. Based on a newspaper story, he seems intent on directing an Ultimate Frisbee team instead. I don't get it. The paper was detailing his rise in running and the family history of athletic success.

Calvin will fall under the tutelage of his father for the winter and I fear that the experience will slow his development, much like Steve Corsello, who was pulled back from his 8th grade success by his well-meaning father who fell prey to the ideas of fast-talking outsiders who were but a flash in the pan as coaching prowess and a single individual talent were thought to be a cause and effect phenomena. Long runs will be Calvin's menu all winter when a diet that includes healthy portions of speed is what his young body requires. It's too early for all the mileage in my book. Jeff snowboards all winter and just chooses to skip spring track while bailing hay in the summer, a sure formula for a runner who has to try like hell to regain his previous year's form.

We told them that if they wanted to take the steps to get to the next level we'd take the trip with them, but that we were okay with them continuing to mingle running with their lives in the same format as they have up to this date. We can't guarantee victory over Jim Paccia's Tully squad and I doubt any team has that illusion right now after Tully's Black Knights decimated the field by taking the top three spots. But without us taking further steps in the right direction we have no chance of moving up from our 8th place finish. Maybe I'm spitting in the wind because I'm not sure these guys have an athlete's mental make-up or the necessary physical gifts. That's no slap at them. They're gifted, well-adjusted and great all-around kids who will be solid as adults. You never know what can happen when you tempt dame fortune and lady luck by dotting your i's and crossing your t's. Sometimes good kids, without all the talent, but on a mission, win.

The CBA girls ran well with Francesca Minale taking first in the team scoring behind the lone APW girl, Jen Pernisi. Katie Webster, the tall talented frosh who sat out our dual meet after suffering a knee injury at the pre-states at Warrick—and who will now unfortunately head to the basketball court—took 5th and moves on to the state championship as one of our section's five individual entrants. Missing out on the trip to the state meet for the first time in her career is senior Kristen Fekete who Webster beat out for the final spot. Despite that incredible rush of three purple-clad runners up front, we were able to defeat CBA comfortably, thanks to our pack. The tough lone wolf howls at the moon by himself demanding respect, but the cries of the pack shatter the quiet of the night as fear sets in.

Sauquoit Valley failed to defend their title and their whole season seems to have been one problem or injury after another. Samantha Stedman, the two-time defending champion, atoned for a sluggish season with a 3rd place finish. She has so much talent but, like a Hollywood starlet blinded by the bright lights, can't seem to steer clear of every hurdle.

Tully saw the wheels come off once again but Kelly Coyne in 4th place moves her on to the state meet. She's a talent and Michelle knows it. She could ascend to the upper reaches in an instant. She's always just one race away from arriving in the big-time but I think she lacks the total passion required to reach the very top. Her teammate, Becky Bloom, fully atoned for her string of recent poor performances by finishing as the third girl on Tully's team. Redemption must feel good for her.

Canastota--the squad that ended our 10-year sectional winning streak in '04--competed with nearly the same team that beat us up two years ago, but they fell to sixth and look to have been over-ranked all year. The ease with which we dispelled them shows how much our girls grew over the past two years.

Rachel Vaivoda vanquished her demons. Later in life as she's bouncing her own tiny daughter on her lap, and even later when her precious little one begins to dabble in sports, Rachel-the-mom will be able to offer a personal story of redemption, a story of success triumphing over failure, a story of a teenage girl with paralyzing fears who later learned how to stand tall. Rachel will be able to tell her daughter how she learned to win. Years from now in moments she can't possibly anticipate or comprehend, Rachel will be holding a fearful child whose wide-open eyes will be looking up at mom's in lost-wonderment. Rachel, looking into her daughter's soul will speak with a voice she's never used, a voice that's choking-up yet wise, confident, strong, convincing and reassuring. Powerful memories will gush from the deepest recesses of her mind into wide open consciousness, her throat muscles clenching and going into spasm as she says to her baby, "You can be a champion, honey. You can be just like your mommy. In fact, I bet you'll be better no matter what you want to do. And no matter what, you know I will always love you." With an incredible bear hug Rachel will stand her little girl on the ground, grab her shoulders firmly, steady her a bit, pat her on the bottom and send her little girl out into the world to begin charting her own winning path. Tears will well-up in Rachel's eyes as she watches herself run away and she'll understand that learning to love means learning to let go. The genesis will have been Long Branch and the day when the Skaneateles girls, when Rachel, went back to the front.

To States & Beyond

The place was lit up like opening night on Hollywood and Vine in an otherwise dark strip mall along a street filled with other open air plazas, chain restaurants and stores that you'd recognize in any city in America. Inside the Bella Vita were murals of New York City streetscapes and the noise from a little kid's soccer league banquet that gave us the feeling of being on those city streets on a day hot enough to open the fire hydrants.

Leaning toward the middle of the pushed-together tables I said, "Whose parents are coming down?" Hannah immediately spilled her lemonade with a flurry of active arms that reminded me of the whirling arm action of pitchers from a long gone major league era.

Hannah's parents are staying with her dad's college roommate who is lucky to be alive. On the bright sunny morning of September 11th a few years ago, his roommate ignored the public address orders to stay off the elevators after the terrorists slammed their planes into the Twin Trade Center Towers. "He did the exact wrong thing and he lived," said Hannah, as if justifying her sometimes contrarian approach to life and her dealings with authority. Other parents are staying with family or friends. Some are in motels, and Sofie's parents made the four hour bus trip to Middletown by car in a mere 150 minutes. Her dad is a state trooper and along with Doc Parker and Pete Davis, a team photojournalist. A few sets of parents were on the road well before sunrise in order to devote another day to their daughter.

Dinner was good but it caused me concern. The dishes were saucy, creamy, rich and full of delicious fatty substances. Lexie's calzone would make a stoned college kid with the munchies happy as hell with all the cheese and liquid fat floating on every stringy bite. I told Rob about my worries and he said that if Lopez Lemong—the Tully great by way of the disemboweled nation of Sudan—can eat a plate piled high with bacon we can survive this dinner. In my mind it was a glorified pasta dinner and I feared a collapse for the state meet the next day.

It was our last pre-race meal together, the final time to sit as one in public with piles of food before us. The pitchers of water were evenly placed on the tables as our time together as a team was rapidly drawing to a close. We'd come so far, surprised so many pundits with our resounding Sectional victory, and there we were laughing it up, convivial and connected, without a care in the world a mere 15 hours away from the big one, the state championship. Not just any state meet, New York's race of champions. This one means something. We're good here in New York and there's an unending slew of talent running around the cities, villages and rural roads across the aptly named Empire State. Winning the New York State title is like getting an Oscar. It's a label you carry proudly all your life and it's an accomplishment worthy of extraordinary effort. The label, "State Champion" will headline your final newspaper appearance as loved ones will list the triumph high up in the obituary. We've won this esteemed title five times in cross country and five more in track. It takes talent, sacrifice and luck. We arrived at this season-ending event uninjured and healthy. We were peaked perfectly. But the dinner? I feared an ill-timed insulin spike. I'm really worried about a busted race in our immediate future. There's a lot to be said for peanut butter and jelly sandwiches.

All week long Rob and I had to hold back the girls while keeping them loose. The time for work had passed while the time to rest was upon us. There was no talk of the race but the unspoken words were clearly felt, and I didn't see anything but anticipation and excitement. They were positively bubbly all week as we ran the final few miles of a season that started back in June. For a few of them, Hannah, Rachel Vaivoda and Sofie, their journey and their date with destiny began six full years earlier. "We have one more race, one more chapter to write," yelled Hannah after the sectional triumph. If only Hannah will follow through, I thought to myself. And why should Hannah and the team fully expect anything other than to finish with a bang instead of a meek and feeble whimper? They were not winners by a freak accident at Sectionals. They won with style, with panache, with grandiose dreams leading the way as pride helped them finish the job and recapture a title that had rested proudly in Skaneateles for a full decade without challenge. With deep intent, the girls set a goal of winning the Sectional title. With thorough follow-through, they did it. Maybe their emotional gas tank was empty, I thought.

The girls were realistic about the challenge that awaited them at the Warwick course that reminds me of the British Open with the drumlins, rolling hills, fields with long grass and hordes of humanity running from one side to another to get a better look at their favorite sport. With the 64 degrees and bright blue skies that greeted us on Saturday, November the 11th, I was positive that we'd get good results but I worried about the forecast that called for heat unlike anything we'd seen in a month. We did everything right and I felt we were destined to run well with a few kids earning All-State accolades and being called to the stage to receive their medals at the post-championship awards ceremony.

We've grown accustomed to watching other team's dreams die under our feet. Year after year stretching into several decades when all roads led through Skaneateles, an unending string of high school student-athletes have graduated without seeing their labor of love yielding the one award that they'd sweated and dreamed of achieving; beating Skaneateles to win the league or sectional title. Hundreds of the area's greatest kids have faltered at the time of greatest opportunity as we've risen to the heights of unchallenged masters of our own fate. From college and through adulthood our focused and worthy opponents carry that ugly and itching scar with them as fate decrees that the frustration of losing will forever be attached to the runners like a barnacle to the underside of a sea-going ship. As time passes, the scar grows less visible, but on days when the air smells of molding leaves or the wind carries the smell of an old cinder track, their minds become supercharged with memories of their days spent on cross country trails, the flat of railroad beds and the hard, unforgiving tarmac of roadways leading like spidery fingers everywhere while always leading back to the school. And the first memory, the initial recollection that pops into the head's of all those runners is the stinging memory of losing—and losing again and again—to Skaneateles.

Every year we hear the opposing coach's refrain, "This is our year. And if it isn't this year we'll beat Skaneateles next year." But when the final league standings and the sectional winners are posted, it's inevitably Skaneateles on top. Winning Sectionals 11 of the past 13 years hasn't grown tiring or boring. Laying claim to the league title 14 straight years is still a thrilling occasion. Winning never grows old. The thrill remains as vivid and important as the first time many years and many kids ago. Losing is an abrupt conclusion that initially lays waste to honorable and healthy dreams along with so many collective efforts of so many honest, good and hardworking kids. But like Darwin hypothesized, win or go home, survive or perish, kill and eat or starve and die. Winning feeds more than the soul as it makes you king of the hill until the next challenger takes his best shot at you and the crown.

Rachel Hosie and Rachel Vaivoda were jumping out of their skin all week and it peaked during our jog/walk around the three-loop Warwick course that cleverly hid some deceptively long and gradual hills that did the same thing to your legs that taking a spark plug out of a slant-six car engine would do to the speed and mileage of your 1960s-era car. Our local runners are masters of big, steep hills while the course with the severe downhill descents leave many of us watching as other runners walk away from us. The predictions about the early leaders faltering on the long and slightly uphill homestretch would prove to be prescient on a hot day that would be more expected in early September than mid-way through November. With our peaking process working better than it has in at least three years, I was confident that the course, which seemed designed for us, would keep our feet moving fast as our bellowing hearts pushed oxygen into the deepest recesses of our cells. With rolling hills, short sightlines and lots of gradual twists and turns, the course seemed perfect for us.

Sofie is convinced that we're a talented team, as talented as the 2003 team that heralded four All-State runners. That was the year that the Brat Pack thrust itself with utter confidence onto the big stage and helped us win a state title as freshmen. They were unafraid, gung-ho, eager and willing to lay it out without giving it a second thought. Sometimes ignorance is bliss.

After a few hours in the Holiday Inn I was worried that the hotel would suck every drop of water from the girls' bodies. After showering before we went out to dinner, I splashed some water on the mirror and within 20 seconds the mirror was dry. When I saw the girls boarding the bus for dinner with Gary at the helm, I noticed a hollow look on their faces. They were already drying out so we instructed them to run the showers long and hot before hitting the sack in order to fill the air with moisture. And we begged them to steadily hydrate.

The 10:00 curfew was easily met by the girls as a comedian had a small crowd roaring in the bar. Because the club cost fifteen dollars to enter, we all went our separate ways. Rob fell asleep around 9, which forced me to make the final bed checks alone. The Comedy Club would have to go on without us. As I walked past each door and put an ear to it, I wondered if someone farther down the hall would think I was some screwy Peeping Tom. The rooms the girls slept in were unusually big with good beds. We were in the lap of luxury as the school sprung for two kids to a room. We'd never experienced such high-living on a trip. A few rooms had no windows and I was feeling a little closed in, but once I walked to the lobby around 4:45 PM and saw nothing but black through the front doors, I figured the windows were useless as the unrelenting onset of darkness greeted the final surrender of the sun on a day that we seldom see in central New York from mid-October to sometime in April when the cloud factory known as Lake Ontario shuts down for repairs.

On the bus ride down Route 17 toward New York City, the girls read a front page article in the Post-Standard about Tommy Gruenewald, the record-setting runner who shattered the VanCortlandt course record for Fayetteville-Manlius coach Bill Aris. The article must have inspired the girls to pull the covers up to their chins early. Tommy hits the hay at 8:45 every night like clockwork even with an academic load that includes three AP courses. He shops for himself, cooks for himself and is up before school for his first run of the day. The kid's a Spartan in the best sense of the word and just maybe the girls learned something by reading about him. Gruenewald, the kid who worked himself into mythical, God-like shape and raced himself into the American history books, is a kid just like my girls. I was hoping that my sleeping girls were dreaming and thinking that if Tommy G. could do it, maybe they could do it, too.

Hannah wanted to know how many kids receive awards at the ceremony. I was hearing Hannah talk like she's never talked about racing. She seemed to have firm, realistic goals, goals that would reward her and help her team. I was convinced that I'd see her standing proudly on stage with the best in the state after the race.

As I sat in my musty hotel room alone and in the quiet as the muted TV sent waves of intermittent flashes of light into my darkness, I realized that we'd left an abandoned school Friday morning while every other Skaneateles student was home in honor of the fallen, the mutilated, those willing to give up their normal lives to serve some greater cause, the cause of defending freedom. Friday was the day before Veteran's Day.

My school, Jordan Elbridge High School, remained open. For my teaching community, there would be no Veteran's Day observance. Steve Reynolds, who I used to call the Secretary of Defense when he was a bright, precocious, inquisitive and blindly patriotic 10th grade student in my class, was killed in Iraq not long ago. He was blown up by a roadside bomb. It hurt like hell to see his name and portrait scrolled on the TV screen by PBS and other network news magazines.

The Auburn National Guard has been activated and will soon arrive in Iraq in hot pursuit of those engaging in a bloody civil war. In all reality, we don't know who we're pursuing. Some of our grads are in that company and will probably be forever scarred as our befuddled leaders mess around in another nation's national chaos. Some of those who will soon set foot in a God-forsaken nation are 50 year-old fathers of our students. The others are just scared kids who were scared shitless just thinking, as high school seniors, about going off to college or heading to military boot camp. When we talked, as their senior year was drawing to a close, eyes shifted nervously as their body's weight shifted from the right foot to the left as hands were thrust into pockets that couldn't hide them. You could see my student's fear. Their verbal and non-verbal expressions of fear made us all sad. And we could offer nothing of comfort in return. And we at J-E stayed open on the day before Veteran's Day.

It was as if life went on as usual. People played, some worked, television ads continued their putrid campaigns to sell us things we don't need in buffoonish displays of sophomoric behavior. Life went on as if there was nothing out of the ordinary occurring and affecting us, our national dialogue and collective psyche, and our planet's well-being. I guess that's what President Bush meant when he told us to go shopping after nearly 3,000 good people were slaughtered on 9/11. With nearly 3,000 Americans now in graves in scattered locales around our nation, it seems that the war-without-any-visible-dead in Iraq will continue until the legions of angry Americans reaches a critical mass and we all understand that it wasn't Iraq who invaded and destroyed our beautifully complacent lives. How many will die in pursuit of a guy who didn't threaten us at all?

When we heard that Steve was coming home in a closed casket with a military escort, we looked out our windows at a flag that was flying high, flying proud. Roger Roman, our social studies department chair and the coach of JE's cross country team, tried repeatedly to get the flag lowered to half-staff. What he received as an answer was a faxed package of flag regulations totaling almost 30 pages from someone. Protocol, formalities, decorum. "Fuck it," I yelled to Roger in his empty room. "He's ours, he died for us and we hear nothing but shit about protocol? Did anyone think about that when we elected these spineless, cowardly chicken-hawks who sent our kids over there under false pretenses? Where's the outrage in this nation? Do we stand for anything anymore?" Roger is persistent, and finally we saw the flag lowered. I love this school but on this one we initially blew it. The community soon came together and former principal Noel Hotchkiss delivered a teary, choke-filled tribute to Steve. But he was still dead.

I find it difficult to blame the administrators who, without exception, are relatively new and have no ties to Steve Reynolds. He was from a different era and didn't touch any of them. When leadership experiences a changing of the guard, history dies. It's just the way it is and maybe it's good for it allows us to move forward without the heaviness that comes from inherited emotional trauma. Maybe it frees us to be new again. I just don't know.

Surrounded by darkness in my windowless room, I thought back to our trip down, a trip that was chartered by Gary Martin, a trip where, mile by mile we left behind the sunless skies of central New York and entered a treasured downstate land where the sun lives and blue skies boost moods upon awakening from a night's sleep. Trees still clung to some of their leaves and the air held a soothing warmth that we'd not seen in three weeks as 40 degree air prematurely settled over our upstate homeland. Heat. Damn heat. Would it hurt us in the race? I was worried about that, too.

Driving back home late Saturday afternoon after the state championship, we approached Central New York and I said to Gary and Rob, "What horrible fucking weather. I'm sure glad we're home and leaving all that sun behind us." After a few more moments watching the rain splashing on the bus windshield, I said that I'm coming home with a sun burn and I'll be telling my wife I had a disappointing day. She'll think I'm crazy after she spent the dank, dark day in a constant cold drizzle that hangs around like a nasty sinus infection that eats penicillin for breakfast.

On Sunday morning I made my pilgrimage to the high school track in the village for my 10-lap run. The sky was low and moving fast from north to south. Gray replaced the pacific blue that shone down on us at Warwick a day earlier. The air was 25 degrees colder than it was for the championship run at 10:20 on championship Saturday. My mood was sullen. I slowed my steps, put on the brakes and then stopped; a personal no-no. My hands rested on my hips while I thrust my head back and reached for a breath of cool air—and some answers from above.

We'd placed third in the state championship with our worst performance of the year. We weren't just off our game. We got throttled by two better teams. And I watched our girls suffer from the slow pace that made them painfully inefficient.

Just a week earlier we'd had our best race, I thought as I stood there in lane one of the first passing zone and tried once again to come to grips with the apparent failure. I learned at the meet that some girls had stayed up studying well past 11:30 all week. I just didn't beg enough I guess. With college coaches operating with meager recruiting budgets, the state meets around the nation often serve as the only real scouting report. Screw it up and there goes an important introduction to many, many coaches who can help defray the $50,000 annual costs for good student-athletes. If running in college is really important to the high school runner, getting to the state meet and performing on command is the way to get noticed and recruited. We blew that this year after doing everything right to get the chance to perform on the big stage where notoriety is achieved the old fashioned way; by producing when it counts.

The team seemed more interested in the trip than the destination upon first reflections. It seemed more interested in trimming the tree at Christmas than reveling in the true meaning of the holiday. T-shirts were made, dinners were eaten, big decisions about what to wear to school were duly deliberated, but no one really seemed to think about the race which was the purpose of the summer, the fall, and our trip downstate. Somewhere along the path to the state championship we lost track of the goal. I heard from a parent that some of the girls, right after the sectional championship victory, said that we couldn't possibly beat Greenwich and Bronxville, so our season was over. She was right. We couldn't beat those two teams. But a good third place showing would yield individual awards and All-State honors for all the hard work we've each put into the season. The team thought that we were just going on a trip.

In our State Meet post-race talk I kept hearing about the letdown after winning Sectionals. My response was that the Sectional race was, indeed, our primary goal for the year; the only goal really. We wanted to get back to the front. But, I said, with such a resounding victory and a win that made the predictions of a close race look utterly foolish, why didn't that serve as a springboard for more success? Boys are different. They eat up stuff like that and a good group of them can be persuaded to do absolutely anything. An improbable victory would send them into a warlike frenzy and they'd ride the emotional wave all the way to the beach with sabers held high. Perhaps that's one reason we send 18 year-old boys into combat. They can get fired up! All the things that the girls were focused on are important aspects of getting 'up' for a race. But they missed the point. Frills on a dress don't get the handsome, smart and athletic boy. It's substance that truly works the magic. Yet, I did, indeed, understand. The over-riding goal was recapturing the sectional title which was an accomplishment that the girls were truly proud of and it would forever serve as the link to our proud past. It all actually made sense once I got my wits about me. They'd given absolutely everything in that sectional effort. There were no physical or emotional bullets left.

Rachel, Hannah and Sofie are going to be proud of placing first as ninth graders and third as seniors at the state meet. They'll smile at the memory of preserving the OHSL league winning streak, recapturing the sectional title and putting us back on the map. But I wonder if the passing of time and the onset of adulthood maturity will awaken in them the "what if"question? It never really goes away. The mark is indelible no matter what they think now. I told them about my final cross country race as I dealt with a terrible case of diarrhea. I pushed my little brother Hugh into the chute ahead of me. I was nowhere near the front. It's still my first memory whenever I think about cross country. I can't shake it and it's been 39 years as the ghost of that failure floats around me and haunts me at the oddest and most random times.

Kelly Coyne, the blonde talent from Tully, placed 6th in the best race of her career. Bubbly Jen Pernisi from APW, who's bound for Lynchburg College, was 11th as she just nipped Sauquoit's amazing big-race runner Samantha Stedman in 12th. CBA's Francesca Minale and Katie Webster, obviously recovered from her mid-season injury, took 15th and 29th. I guess we were truly intent on beating them at the Sectional meet. At States, we weren't near any of them.

It wasn't the fact that Greenwich and Bronxville beat us that had me in a hissy-fit. It's the way that we placed third. We did it ugly. We did it in a manner that didn't meet our standards or the girls' abilities. We weren't good and college coaches wrote to me wondering what had happened. We weren't fast. We weren't determined or vigilant in pursuit of our goal. Deep down, we were content with the Sectional title. I get it. As the state meet approached I'm not even sure we had a goal as I heard more and more about their private lives during the week leading up to the event. Each of the girls had made quantum changes in their lives leading up to the Sectional slug-fest. They'd done everything right. They were living like Tommy Gruenewald. It was different leading into the state meet. Cognitively I can understand and accept it. But my competitive nature cries out in the still-of-the- night like a 3 AM fire siren echoing across the lake valley and rallying all able hands to the conflagration.

I was initially disappointed in these good girls whom I loved, so I purposely stayed away from them for a good half hour after everyone had been cleared from the finish chute. I needed to cool down. I could see the parents looking our way as the girls leaned against a fence talking to their loyal fans. I feared saying something that I'd regret so I kept my distance and talked to Rob and other coaches who wondered what had gone wrong.

When I did talk to the girls I said that they missed the target. "Making a baby isn't the goal, raising it so it can safely enter life happy and able to be self-reliant, caring, loving, hardworking and diligent is the goal," I said while standing in the front of the bus as the girls huddled mid-way toward the back. I don't think they really understood what they'd done and how much they let themselves down. I told them that "Getting the contract isn't the goal—as important as it is. Fulfilling the terms of the contract is the main idea, carrying out your pledge is the responsibility you agreed to." I'm not sure if that sunk in. Probably not in hindsight. They're too young yet. I wasn't trying to be critical. I could have easily just chalked it up to hot weather, given each of them a hug and said, "Good job". But I thought it was important for a reality check and for us to talk about real life. The race itself wasn't the issue. Stepping up, meeting a challenge, standing tall, being true to yourself and doing the job right the first time and doing it for the others on the team is the path we all need to learn to take. Someone had to take charge of their peers but no one did in a positive and constructive manner. We need to be responsible for not only ourselves but each other. And on this state championship day we all failed, including me. I didn't have them emotionally ready.

We didn't help each other succeed. Instead we helped each other secede from their ultimate racing challenge. And always at their beck and call were loving parents with wide open arms eager to lay on an unconditional and emotionally reassuring hug no matter what. And that's as it should be. But the goal, having been recently reached a week earlier at the Sectional showdown was felt to be fulfillment enough. I was having trouble buying that. The cry of 'great race" directed to the Skaneateles girls dug deeply into me, the phoniness sending the exact wrong message to the kids. It was like being at a little league game where every strike out is applauded as a nice effort. Sometimes it's okay to be disappointed and to know that you didn't do well. It wasn't a good race and I felt the girls needed to own up to it, accept it and move on to another day when they would be able to accept all the expectations of a task and give it a Winston Churchill thumb- in-the-eye in order to survive rather than perish.

In an e-mail, Rob wrote a great suggestion for the coming fall: "I think we need to have a theme for next season...something like 'we stick together', or something similar...stress that they should want to run for each other." He's exactly right. We need to put blinders on them and herd them into a corral that will lead them in the direction we want them to go. I thought we'd done that this year and for the most part we did. The success at Sectionals was all the evidence I needed to suspect that we'd be ready to roll at the state meet.

Being such a good team made the day seem much worse than it really was. Hannah was right as she covered up the scores on the final tally sheet and said, "All anyone will ever remember about this day is that we took third. They won't know anything about how we ran."

Just as I was at my lowest point and questioning my coaching ability while walking with Rob toward the top of the huge, rounded drumlin that stood in the middle of the first loop, I heard a voice from behind me say, "Hi Coach Reed." It was the moment that would soothe me, remind me of my mission and bring me back to earth. The angels were watching over me I thought. Out of the clear blue sky that seemed to go on forever like a high Montana sky deep in the summer, she came to me. The grass, tall and light-brown was bent from thousands of feet trampling on it as fans, parents, brothers and sisters ran from side to side while their running prodigy chased their personal dream of running glory. She was 35 years old, fair and pretty and far, far removed from my life, and just like I was there, back in 1987, to pull her from the despair that was the discus circle, she was here at the state meet to pull me from my deep well of self-doubt. Debbie Snyder was still blonde with thin lips and a perky, impish, shy smile. Her skin had lost just a sliver of the smooth and sleek look that all teens carry with them while thinking that the blessings of youth will last forever. The tiniest of tiny crow's feet, nature's tattoos that speak of wisdom and of having lived well, had started to etch themselves into her face like a barely visible hairline fracture of a metatarsal. She looked full of life and exhibited the effervescence that I remembered from her youth. God, I thought, she was getting more beautiful with age.

Yes, I knew her instantly but doubted my memory. Thankfully she introduced herself by name to eliminate putting me in a bad spot as I searched my brain for a name to match her face and my memories of her. Seeing her took me back to 1987 and our championship track season at Marcellus when I was ending my first year of coaching. I started my 62nd season two days after this state meet at Warwick.

"Coach, I can't tell you what you meant to me," she said in a voice that made me weak in the knees. "Many of us weren't taken seriously and you rescued me from the discus circle and told me that I was a distance runner. I'm still racing and training for a marathon," she said to me with pride and gratitude. It's funny how some people can thank you for something and not really mean it. It's perfunctory at best and all the parties know it. This wasn't like that. I felt every single word she uttered with a heavy conviction. I shivered and shook and she wanted me to feel like that, to feel the gratitude that she had carried with her for decades. I'd changed her life and here she was 20 years later hunting me down in an open field with perhaps 5,000 people running around like a bunch of college kids rushing the arena gates to see their favorite band. In this case, the crowd was high on life and reveling in the dreams of hundreds of kids who were chasing and seeking a place where pain would engulf them. I know I've changed over the decades but she still recognized me and that flattered me. It had been a long time since our orbits had crossed. I didn't think we'd ever grown that close despite really liking her, and perhaps too many coaches and teachers think like that as we underestimate our impact on kids. My dedicated kids today will be with me for years and we really grow on each other. Back in Marcellus it wasn't like that. I'd just started teaching global studies but during the six months leading up to the outdoor track season I'd done enough recruiting to put together a team that totaled nearly 70 girls. We were tough, deep and talented and we'd just wear down other teams as wave after wave of fresh and proud Mustang athletes toed the line or got set to run down a runway or prepared to step into a throwing circle. Marion Smith was the head coach. I assisted and learned a lot in our three track years together. Most of the girls played soccer in the fall.

Rob, who was by my somber side, was stunned that Debbie and her sister—who I also remembered--would stay with us for nearly 20 minutes and he was talking about it two days later as I still wore the mask of sorrow. "What you do, Jack, has an impact on these kids. You can't be too hard on yourself."

Debbie was at the meet to watch her son run, an 8th grader named Otis from Burnt Hills north of Albany in that incredibly running rich part of New York State. He ran great and placed 30th for coach Chip Button as he served notice that he's going to be around for a few years.

As Debbie and her sister took their leave and got back to their lives, we hugged. I wanted to hold her for a long time but I didn't. I wondered if I'd ever see her again. She remembered having to go to the bathroom while on a slow bus heading home from some far off place in Vermont with a bunch of her teammates. Somehow they persuaded me to stop at a house. Luckily the lady let in the Marcellus hordes—all with the bursting bladders—to relieve themselves. You never know what the kids will take with them as they say good-bye to high school and head out into the larger world where sanity dictates we cheer the future while quietly pocketing the past.

Getting back to my reality and my current spot in the vast unknown of the universe, I watched my girls the following Monday at the indoor track sign-up meeting as they and a bunch of sprinters, hurdlers and throwers huddled around Coach Tuttle's long engineering tables. They were excited, the third place finish having no luck with affecting a perpetual death upon them. Smiles were all over their faces and slowly my frown turned into a smile. They acted proud, self-assured and happy. All of them wore their yellow state championship t-shirts. Above all else, they were reminding me that they were just kids who dared to dream, who sometimes succeeded and sometimes tripped, who would dare to tempt fate and play tag with the twin companions of all runners, fatigue and pain. Taking third at the state meet in what I thought was a severe letdown hadn't dampened their lust for life. We'd actually accomplished all our goals. Being resilient is a healthy character trait and one that will help each of them survive in a world that sometimes forgets the need for compassion and forgiveness. No, they weren't a wrecking machine. But I love 'em nonetheless.

The cross country team had been officially disbanded and as we transitioned to the indoor season and its challenges, a pounding rain, cold air and an invigorating northerly wind helped us make a clear separation between the summery November state meet and the coming six months in Central New York that seem to be greeted with hearty cheers by the few people who drive snowmobiles in their spare time. Each of us already knew that the space-time continuum had forever changed. Sofie knew it and said as much to me after the meeting. Hannah looked at me after the meeting and said, "You're looking different Coach. The wheels are turning aren't they?" as she smiled and we made yet another connection. We understood each other like never before. Her instincts were right. I wasn't thinking about the indoor season at all. I was mourning the end of something difficult, something special, something that fate decreed and we dutifully obeyed. I was mourning something that was forever gone. I had feelings to work out as separation anxiety began to enter my life.

Time continued to move forever forward and at the end of the first week of indoor practice, as we stood freezing on the track, Sofie sidled up to me and said that she'd missed me. Her voice was soft but matter –of-fact. This year I've been assigned to coach the boys. Finishing her statement she said that we needed to bond—it had been a long time since we'd had a soul to soul talk. We'd had our moments together in the sun, the rain, the mud, slop, snow, heat and cold and we'd done it together, for our school and for those who came before us. We'd preserved a winning streak, recaptured the sectional crown and made our mark on the state scene with a good 3rd place finish.

Life is going to close in soon as the winter settles in with a vengeance and the remaining years of my life dwindle to a precious healthy few. The right music sounding from my computer seems to bubble in my veins like it used to when I stood in the middle of my school gym at Chenango Valley Jr. Sr. High School in front of live kid-bands like The Malfunctions and The 2nd Edition, the drums shaking my inners and enlivening my soul. With the right music or the right team you think that life is endless and that everything that will happen will be good. Traveling with my team is easy and worry-free, unlike my other travels when old-age-induced anxiety overwhelms me.

Life has begun to grow long and the trip tiresome at times but when I'm with my team I'm feeling young, I'm a believer, I'm hip, robust and cocky and I understand that the kids are good for me. When I'm with them I'm in the moment swaying with the rhythms of life as the universe seems to exist for me and only me. When I'm with my team I'm as alive as I've ever been. Hills seem less steep, distance is nothing but a relative thing, high knees are the norm and friendships are personal, deep and forever as a glue-like bond attaches us to each other for all of eternity, an eternity that will see us all thriving, successful, happy, healthy, safe and wise. That's my wish for each of my boys and girls.

Running and coaching have made me who I am and everything in my core is generated from those magical experiences on the well-treed mountains and the roads with the desert-like waves of heat that lure me deeper and deeper into a long run. Smells, sounds and friends all serve to get me in-a-lather as past and present mix in exotic ways that mimic a drug induced trance. It's a lot like getting a shot of Demerol and in an instant everything is right, everything is possible, and tomorrow will be better than today.

My days are growing fewer and fewer as the end is beginning to close in faster and faster. It's just time to move on and carry all my Debbie Snyders with me into a more solitary, uneventful life, a life of retirement. It's time for fate to release me and set me on the final course where entering the finish chute will have an entirely different meaning. Having been defined by running for my entire life, I wonder about the future, try to picture what's around the next corner and hope that I'll be more filled with anticipation than apprehension as I stride toward the turn and enter the unknown.

Life is like launching a kite into a blustery sky. You never know where the winds of fate will take you, who will enter your life at some random, unpredictable moment or pull your strings the right way.

At the end of that final bus ride together as a cross country team, darkness began playing games with us as an enchanted closeness again was felt by everyone. Arms were wrapped around bodies, heads got snug against shoulders, high-pitched screams and laughter filled the air and spells of utter quiet roared in my ears.

The contemplative Hannah readied to speak on the bus ride back north after her last state meet. Cloistered in the enclosed catacomb of the bus, that was filled with the steady hum of the powerful diesel engine while the rain pattered on its tin skin, Hannah's thoughts wandered wildly. Her unconscious mind had been unleashed and it took a strange turn. She said, "I don't know a single person who will bury me. I mean, I don't know anyone, yet, who will be with me at the end of my life."

A lot of life remains for us all I hoped as I walked across the dark parking lot on the east side of Skaneateles High School somewhere between Syracuse and Auburn, New York. I looked back at the bus and waved to Gary one last time with the rain making my glasses useless. With a firm two-fisted thrust I stuffed and zipped my blue-trimmed canvas bag that has traveled with me to practices and meets for decades and tossed it into the back seat of my car, the journey fulfilling and close to its inevitable end. And then I exhaled. A single tear fell from the corner of my left eye and a contented smile creased my face as I settled into my little car for the five mile drive home all alone.

Perhaps, I thought, it was time to fly a new kite.

Cool Down

The drum beat that drove me so endlessly all summer and fall has finally slowed down as some of my edgier emotions begin to hibernate until the coming spring like so many of earth's favored and furry creatures. It's now the time of year when different emotions are allowed to unfold expansively, when gratitude holds sway over vice and greed, and when the more humble side of man's nature is released to express itself. With the approaching holidays providing opportunities to adjust our attitudes, our foibles are more easily overlooked while we more readily recognize each other's favorable human traits.

On this 16th day of December just six years removed from the millennium, I grow reflective and can more easily accept what fate has decreed. And I smile while being forever hopeful in the thought that good can prevail in this world, a world that oftentimes seems much more wicked than decent like the fairy tales tell us as young children. It's the time of year when we can dream holy, when the town squares, community meeting halls and living rooms become wonderlands where dreams are born and an inner calm inhabits our flesh and being. It's a time for soul-searching when our cheery dreams surmount our gripes as hope drops its cynical masquerade and greets life as a wondrous miracle. Holding a light and trusting heart in our chest, we like to think that in the midst of someone's terrible grief that a compassionate God will reach out and lay a healing hand upon slumped shoulders that heave and sob under the crushing weight of despair. People with hearts hope that some teary-eyed child, sitting expectantly on Santa's expansive lap asking for his help in making another person's life better, had their wish granted. We believe in belief and believe in the wholesome goodness of people's intentions. We see the best of our collective traits in each other instead of focusing on the fainter traits that serve to twist us into tormented twits. In December with the cold and snow playing with strings of brilliant lights that are carefully wrapped around so many pine trees, the complexities of life can be easily answered if we just listen to the prayers of little children.

The mind works differently and more slowly this time of the year and with each day that further separates me from the heat of the past season I gain favor with my recently stored memories. It's been 35 days since we walked off the Warwick state meet course with a 3ʳᵈ place finish that would amount to a temple of success for most coaches and teams.

Suddenly, today, the neurons finally twisted and formed a connection that I could deal with as clarity entered my thoughts. Warming up in my post-run shower after clipping along at a nice pace for two solitary miles on the track as the morning's drizzle stopped and the slight breeze grew still, I realized what had happened at States. For weeks I just couldn't postulate a theory that made any sense. We'd hit such a peak, such a striking series of confident strides while winning the Sectional title that I just couldn't fathom what had happened to make the wheels all fall off simultaneously at the state meet.

As the shower stall warmed up and my lower back muscles began to yield to the constant assault of a hot, powerful spray, my mind suddenly snapped as I experienced my cross country epiphany for 2006.

Saturday, December 16th was a big day. I finally had it all figured out. For the better part of the past 15 years, the girls of Skaneateles have been in the enviable position of making it to the state meet several times a year, some years making it all three seasons. That taught us something as the constant exposure to powerful teams from around the state made the competition personal. What really made the state meet personal for us was our ongoing rivalry with downstate power Pearl River. It seems we couldn't live without their presence. We were good for each other despite the competitive nature of our athletic relationship, much like Ruth and Gehrig, Shaq and Kobe, the *Beatles* and the *Rolling Stones* were all made better despite competitive differences, jealousies and the heated battles to be proclaimed the best. Winning the sectional banner in 2006 was important to the Skaneateles girls because it was a personal battle. We knew everyone. We'd seen our opponents and read the words published about them in the local papers. We'd listened to the gossip and read the cross country internet forums filled with spirited information, rumors and tales of team's ongoing growth. But it was Pearl's repeated presence at the state meet that made us a powerhouse on the big stage where the ultimate titles were waiting to be plucked.

Pearl was personal for the girls of Skaneateles. It was healthy. It riveted us. It drove us. And it pulled us through the barrage of sectional emotions to the bigger stage where we were in constant pursuit of state titles. With Pearl constantly out there waiting and preparing for us like the dark lays in wait for the light, the challenge was readily taken up every season and handed down from one generation of runners to another in a tradition that was easily carried forth in every step we took in summer, fall, winter and spring. Pearl was our shadow, our dog tags reminding us who we were—and where we wanted to go. Maybe we were their shadow. Who knows.

When we were separated by a new state class alignment, one nail was put into our coffin. When our cross country sectional streak was stopped in 2004, more nails were hammered into our team's coffin. Losing again in 2005 sealed the coffin lid shut and severed our relationship with state championships. We were forced to chase a new goal, a goal that was still personal and important, but different—the league and sectional crowns. The goals were all local now and all the connections to the state meet and any chance of it being personal had been removed, leaving the new girls from Skaneateles with only the cold ghost of yesteryears to lead them.

Going into the state meet in November of 2006 meant little to my Skaneateles girls. It was a reward, not the ultimate destination. It's taken me some time to get that. The girls had read little to nothing about the teams. We had no connection to them, no intertwined recent history, no personal, previous head-to-head races, no face-to-face smack-downs that serve to help us all invest just a bit more of our sinewy selves into the tug-of-war for supremacy. The end result was that we showed up and ran, but didn't race. We didn't lean out and grab for the gold ring. We stood in the shadows of the gym during the dance and watched emotionless as the prom king and queen from Greenwich and Bronxville swirled together around the polished gym floor, alone in the glare of spotlights.

There were no tears for there were no emotions harnessing us to the pulse of the challenge. We'd already won the Sectional title.

Rob Tuttle thinks he's figured out what we need to teach these kids and it's something that our championship teams of the past had in their DNA. Christina Rolleri, Vanessa Everding, Erika "Never Quit" Geihe, Julie Lynch, Zandra Walton, Jessica O'Neill and the rest not only drove the knife into their opponents, they gave it a vicious twist at just the right moment to ensure the demise of every team's lofty dreams. The girls on the 2006 Skaneateles team weren't merciless killers. They didn't have the cut-throat killer instinct. They weren't willing to take the wind from their opponents like my teams from the past–until it became personal, and the sectional race was personal for them in every way. I'm sure, now, that's why they rose up and stomped the field. It was never a lack of ability in my eyes. They just didn't have that incredible thirst for victory-at-all-costs when confronted by anonymous opponents. With a shrug of the shoulders, they ran in the state meet instead of letting the vinegar flow through their veins. We're not all the same competitive creatures and that's just a function of human nature. It's what makes this world gnarly, cool, and interesting. It's also a coach's job to engage that competitive spirit that resides in each of us.

Today, this Saturday that was dark and gloomy like most winter Saturdays in Central New York, was a big day for Hannah. She received her acceptance e-mail from Middlebury at 8 AM. She's in and she's happy. Last night she told her dad that she's considering joining the Middlebury Panthers team for 2007. Joining the reigning national D-III champs isn't some pipe dream for her. But she needs to jump in with both feet and stop straddling the line-of-commitment. As time wore on, Hannah decided to remain a civilian but she did join an Ultimate-Frisbee team. And she's incredibly happy.

The local giant-killing girls from Fayetteville-Manlius harbored a secret all summer and fall of 2006. And at just the right time they battled the best of the best in New York and moved on to race the best in the nation. Using every bit of their competitive spirit, the Hornets from F-M emerged as the national champions for 2006 after pummeling the field at the Nike Team Nationals by a 50-point margin. Bill Aris—who coaches the team with his son, John--fought a harsh bout of bronchitis in the week leading up to the cross-country flight and one can only wonder how fulfilling the return flight must have been with his victors in tight and merry tow. Once on the west coast they were warmly greeted by F-M alum Kathy Mills—adorned in F-M regalia—and the F-M Hornets felt right at home. The pioneering Mills, a 1975 State of New York cross country champion, is married to Nike CEO Mark Parker. I suggested to Aris that he approach the Parkers about constructing the nation's first Nike Center in our home of Syracuse. With Syracuse University Athletic Director Daryl Gross closing Manley Field House to all but the football team, we need a place to compete. Congratulations Mackenzie Carter (4th), Kathryn Buchan (5th), Jessica Hauser (29th), Hilary Hooley (44th), Courtney Chapman (46th), Molly Malone (48th) and Catie Caputo (76th). As time wore on, F-M would repeat as national champion in 2007 and would be favored again as the 2008 season kicked-off. And they won that one, too. The improbable three-peat had been completed. And we used to take their best shot and emerge triumphant.

F-M's capturing of the national title simply solidifies New York's grip on the national cross country scene after Hilton's victory in 2005 and Saratoga's win in 2004. Cross Country in New York State rules. The F-M boys have taken a second and third in the past three years while Saratoga ran home with the title in 2005. That's dominance.

Julie Lynch, Skaneateles alum and my 2006 modified coach, never joined forces with the Syracuse Orange woman's cross country team. I had made it my mission to get Julie and SU coach Chris Fox together. I think they're made for each other. My first call to Coach Fox's office was met with a rather abrupt rebuff, I thought. The call was quick and after telling Fox that I had a recruit for him he said he was busy and that I should call back or he'd call me back. Several days passed so I got on the phone in my J-E classroom and tried again. Getting the answering machine I said that Julie ran for American University's Matt Centrowitz, was a 5-time New York State Champion, and her mother worked for SU so tuition would be free. Julie received a call that afternoon and they met the following day. She'd look good in orange but it won't ever happen. She's a photo-journalist major in the S. I. Newhouse School of Public Communications.

In November, Julie traveled east on route 20 to Colgate University where she cheered on her former American University teammates at the

Patriot League Conference Championship. They got rolled. But Julie and Matt Centrowitz conversed on friendly terms as a degree of healing had occurred between a coach and his former runner. SU's Fox said that he was great friends with Centrowitz but that they had vastly different philosophies regarding training. At the time, I thought that if Julie could hit the roads during her spring internship in Washington D.C. and over the summer on the Jersey shore where she held down three waitressing jobs, she'd be ready to benefit from some of Fox's magic. I wonder if she'll ever experience her moment of "What if?"

Alum Simone Bras recently wrote me and said that she spent her first post-college fall coaching the Greenhill High School cross country team in Texas. She's a mother now and after a risky operation, healthier than ever.

Harold-of-Chittenango got his top runner, Michelle "Shorty" Brandt, past the public school's state meet and into the Federation Championships where she finished 53rd in the toughest 250 runner field in New York history. The dynamic junior who doesn't know the word 'quit', has a lot more to give. She'll be a contender her senior year for the Bears.

The wisdom of my father and my sons continues to bless me; one voice is weak, the voice old and the body force-fed oxygen through a 20 foot clear plastic tube that remains coiled on the floor by his unmoving side. His spoken words are serene, understanding and reflective while the other voice—Kirk's voice—is young and ever hopeful while never seeing the dark laying-in-wait. Dying but still saying, "Life is good," my dad, William Church Reed, lives a proud and uncomplaining life, an honorable life with memories of World War Two on Saipan in the Pacific Theater as fresh in his mind as yesterday's memories for a teenager. Kirkendall Church Reed, my oldest of two sons, was happily married to Melissa Zurita on December 2nd, 2006 just a week before our team's banquet. For him the crowd is always cheering and the game is never over until you've won. My youngest son, KC, has but one semester remaining to earn his undergraduate degree as he perseveres in his chase for the perfect girl. Loyalty is his most endearing quality as he sails through life on an even plane, an even keel. Though I try mightily every day to emulate him, I fail. Through all of this my wife, Patricia, financially wise and strong, counsels me to be patient. Sensing that I'm more easily lived with if I continue down this coaching road, she allows me to spend my life playing at this game called running. While I've been away and busy, she has trained herself to run nearly five miles a day. She's putting me to shame and says that I should keep coaching cross country in my retirement. Perhaps she wants me out of the house. Time will tell.

The team banquet in December was my 61st and I tried to make it a vital component in my runner's lives. Over the years, I've said everything that could possibly be said, yet, I still try to make it meaningful though the process has grown personally tedious. I'm not proud of that but it's the simple truth.

Rachel Vaivoda was named the team MVP while Beatrice Walton won the Workhorse Award for her constant fight to master her mental demons. Rachel got mono during her senior track season and never got to finish. She's now a steeplechaser at Bates College in Maine. Bea steadily turned things around. By the end of her junior year, the demons were all dead and she seemed completely different as her senior cross country season began. In an early indoor meet during her senior year in 2009, she PRd with a 2:28 800 meter run. Kristin Roberts was named Most Improved while Carly Brown was the Rookie-of-the-Year. She quit running at the beginning of her junior year. Alexis Mazzeo was the winner of the distinguished Eric Roschick/Harrier award while Vaivoda also carried home the Gus Roberts Coach's trophy. Amanda Golden was named the Christina Rolleri Most Outstanding Runner for her invitational victory at Phoenix. She's now at Marquette University but runs for fun and health. I was personally suffering because I knew that we just couldn't give team awards to Hannah and Sofie. They deserved them but the drinking incident had to have consequences. I think they understood and I was proud of their behavior at the banquet when they gave their presentation speeches for their teammates. I don't present the awards in cross country. After my opening spiel that brings out the stopwatches of those in attendance, I turn the celebration over to the team. Teams of kids have been chosen by Rob and me to present the awards to teammates and it's the highlight of the festivities. The parents love to hear their kids honor teammates.

For the boys it was Sam winning both the MVP award and the Eric Roschick/Harrier award. In his senior XC season, he was on a roll and heading to the state meet. But at sectionals, he faltered, never got into the flow and faded out of contention. His mind let him down. It was his only blemish for the entire fall. During his senior track season, Sam PRd in the 800 with a time of 1:58.98 and then he spent the entire frustrating summer trying to get in touch with his Rochester Institute of Technology coach. Unable to contact him, he trained himself all summer and took third in the frosh tryouts. And, at that point, he grew concerned because his college coach paid him absolutely no attention. It was never fun so he quit. But he's doing indoor as of November 2008 and already thinking of transferring. Jeff was presented with the Most Improved award. After not running a single step coming into his senior XC year he got mono and was unable to finish. He's now moved on to Notre Dame but he's also thinking of transferring. Winning the Jonathon Riley Most Outstanding award for his rousing finish at the Jordan-Elbridge dual meet was Dan, who was caught with a bottle of whiskey at a school dance in mid-December. He realized, after imbibing two sips while sneaking around in the lavatory, that he was doing something "incredibly stupid". Though he stuffed the tightly closed bottle back into his coat pocket, he got caught and immediately, like the stand-up young man that he is, confessed and accepted his two-meet indoor track suspension. He's a bright, upbeat boy and I hoped he would get past this but in his senior year things began to come apart. Grades began to suffer, the wrong crowd became his friends and he quit running completely. He's not headed to the Air Force Academy as planned and I've lost contact with him. Calvin Davis was the overwhelming choice of the Rookie-of-the-Year award. He continues to work incredibly hard. He's loyal and absolutely trustworthy and almost broke the 2-minute barrier in the 800 during his sophomore season. And his dad is beginning to take a new look at speed-oriented training. Hardworking Luke Edson was the logical winner of the Workhorse award and Matt earned the Gus Robert's Coach's award.

The banquet edified and reinforced my understanding of the season. Hannah spoke of her physical clumsiness in her senior good-bye speech in front of the large banquet crowd in the church. Referring to her first state meet, Hannah said,

> *Typical of my freshman year, I found my two companions and we ran together like naïve little freshman do. Coming to the*

close of the race, however, I, as is my custom, fell full out on my face. Much to the dismay of the coaches, Sofie and Rachel slowed almost to a halt in order to make sure I was up and running once again. And when we reached the finish and knew that our team had won the state title, we laughed about my clumsiness and stumble. While this may seem like an isolated incident, it is not. I can recall more times of falling than I can count on both my hands and feet. My years of running have been about stumbling and falling, and learning how to get up again. Sometimes I trip and with my arms flailing manage to stay on my feet, and at other times I fall into a steeple chase pit and get completely submerged in water.

But regardless of the intensity of the fall, I have learned to pull myself up again, and, with the help of my teammates, who stop and wait for me along the way, work to move on. From the falls also comes the greatness. After the worst of races often comes the best of races. The embarrassment of falling, and the shock of adrenaline, can push a runner to new heights. As I began to fall more and more, my friends gradually stopped waiting for me but I still knew that they were there for me. And through the toughest of falls, it has been my teammates that have helped me get back up once again.

Later in her emotionally-filled speech, Hannah mentioned that racing brings her a euphoria that she has not found in anything else she does, apparently—and surprisingly—not even her music. From the outside looking in, I think running is a bigger piece of the puzzle for Hannah than she has yet admitted. It's the keystone of her character that supports everything else. Her spirit is only free if running is a steady portion of her diet. Perhaps, in time, she'll realize it and take up recreational running.

One has to salute the uniqueness of the human spirit. It makes us believe in possibilities just when cold logic and an avalanche of data should make us fold our tent and go home. It makes soldiers sing going into battle behind the raspy and musty sounds of the Scottish bagpipers. The Spirit of '76 pushes can-do Americans who follow a brave trumpeter leading warriors into an earthly battlefield hell. It helps us to be magnanimous after a trouncing victory and congratulatory after utter defeat. The human spirit always simmers as the will to win waits to be stoked.

Our special human spirit presents itself ever so boldly in the actions and lifestyles of those who dare to be cross country runners. It uplifts me, makes me proud, gives me hope and makes me bow before those special people who call themselves Harriers.

Where Are They Now?

Yesterday, July the 8th, 2008, after a three month reprieve from death, I wept again. First, it was my mother, Avis Arlene Kirkendall Reed, who entered the hospital on her 83rd birthday. It was January the first. She died alone on the sixth. We hauled my dad into the hospital to say good-bye. How the hell do you do that when good-bye means forever? Next was my father, William Church Reed, Sergeant, 879th Bombardment Squadron—499th Bombardment Group, World War II, who died with my brother Hugh by his side on February 13th half way through his 86th year. He refused to go through a Valentine's Day without his bride of 59 years. On St. Patrick's Day in March, it was my 16 year old furry friend, my dog Peppy, who was put down by a veterinarian who was certain it was the only decision to make. I was devastated as 2007 seemed to be a year right from hell.

And the shroud of death continued when I heard that John Kelly, a former runner and proud protector of the people of Richmond, Virginia, was killed by a drunk boater at 2:40 AM while John sucked the life out of one of the best days of his life—his final day on Earth and a day he didn't want to end. Moving forward so slowly in his boat with his girl friend, Heather Wilkins, by his side, it took an hour to putter and drift a mile south from the Village of Skaneateles to the dock at his parent's house. Within 100 meters of docking, a speeding and out of control boat hit the passenger side of his craft and went airborne, killing John while Heather fought until being declared dead at University Hospital a few hours later. The drunken men from Westhill High School left the scene and their only call to 911 was to see if anyone had reported the accident.

An hour and a half had passed by then and John was dead from neglect as cowards once again carved a scar into the heart of civilized people everywhere. When the personnel at the command center questioned the caller, the phone was hung up as the chicken-shit men conferred, trying to decide how to answer the inevitable questioning by police. The noose closed quickly.

On the last day of his two week yearly family reunion at his parent's home, John had played tennis in the morning, driven the family boat for an afternoon of tubing on the beautiful lake, met friends on the south end of the lake at the Glen Haven Restaurant for a four-hour dinner, and convened with still more friends at Morris' Grill in the heart of the village. A bit earlier, he'd been brought to tears as his best childhood friend, David Abbott, had chosen him to be the Godfather of his 3-year old son. John called his 17-year old nephew and told him the exciting news. It was the last time they ever talked.

John was predeceased by Eric Roschick, his 1991 Skaneateles teammate who was killed in a car accident in Los Angeles on his way to the law boards.

That night of John's death, both my sons, Kirk and KC, spoke with him at the crowded Morris' World Famous Bar and Grill. My boys were there for the final stage of James Goss' and MacKenzie Reed's wedding. James is one of my former runners and Kenzie, my niece, ran for nearby Tully. All my boys have said is that John talked about me endlessly. His experience with Skaneateles cross country came up again at his eulogy on Wednesday, July 11th as hundreds of people who loved him waited outside the stuffed church on Jordan Road. John coached the Benedictine varsity lacrosse team in Virginia and on July 9th was scheduled to close on his first house. The amazing thing about John was that he always left you feeling great about yourself. He had a gift and he was only 32 years old with a whole life ahead of him. Who will drive patrol car 9304 now? Who will try to fill his shoes?

On June 28th, 2007 at 9 AM, Steve Corsello walked away from the state pen a free man. No longer a boy, he's trying valiantly to move forward with his life as a ceaseless smile has crossed his face. Steve never smiled when he ran in high school, approaching every race like a boxer entering the squared ring. But now he's different and more appreciative. And the smile-of-freedom radiates the happiness of a stress-free life without bars. He loves the freedom that comes from his runs. He sees hope. He sees a future. Former teammates are joining him on his morning runs. Soon he would be entering his freshman year at Syracuse University. On August 2nd, just five days removed from receiving his acceptance in the mail, Steve and his parents met with several deans and lawyers from Syracuse who told Steve that he would not be permitted to compete on their cross country or track teams. They were afraid there might be too much 'temptation'. When confronted with Steve's legalities that mandated a parole officer hearing every week, membership in AA, a weekly therapist session and a weekly counseling session, the college did not budge. Steve's father roared that all their athletes should be like Steve Corsello—and as clean. Letting the news slide off his back without even a deep sigh, Steve moved on, apparently not keen about representing an institution that lacked so much character and feared media attention. Moving on and planning to race through the fall on his own, he never would forget what was, what could have been, what is, what still could be and what's forever gone. On June 28th, 2008, Steve had fulfilled every requirement imposed by New York State. His marks at SU were within a few tenths of a 4.0 and by the end of the summer he had already completed four courses in Calculus. At the end of August, he walked onto the campus of Amherst where the President welcomed him with a smile and open arms and coach Erik "Ned" Nedeau began working his magic to see if Steve could fulfill his strongly stated goals of going sub-50, sub 1:50 and sub-4.

Just a 17-year old at the time of the accident, he's 21 now and still thin, impressively strong and seeking knowledge at every opportunity. Inside the state pen he read 40 weighty books. When interviewed by an esteemed member of the SU English Department who expected very little, Steve was asked about any recent book he may have read. After listing every one of those 40 books, the professor smiled sheepishly and said," I haven't even read most of those." The system made Steve pay, but it seems not to have changed his basic make-up. He's one tough young man. Entering SU, he was excited to begin class, thrilled at the prospect of sitting in a classroom instead of studying in the state pen, and competitively super-charged as he said, "I have something to prove."

On May 24th, 2007 Debbie Snyder's son, Otis Ubriaco, set the New York State 8th grade record in the mile with a sizzling 4:30.61 while proudly wearing the Burnt Hills uniform. Debbie, my former discus thrower from Marcellus and a long distance runner in her own right now, must be proud. I wonder what Otis and I could have done if he'd been a Skaneateles runner? He sounds like an amazing kid from a good family and a successful running program. Maybe one day I'll meet him—or watch him on TV. In early November 2008, Otis, a soph, was the state XC runner-up.

Hannah was never arrested but completed the 25 hours of community service that we asked of her. She never complained or said, "Why just me?" She bravely spoke alone with the Assistant District Attorney despite the advice of attorneys who have all learned to play the game one way—warily and defensively. One attorney, Linus Walton with the Einstein head of hair, supported her decision to go it alone. He was right. The DA was impressed. Hannah is an incredibly articulate and bright young woman who is as impish and precocious as they come. She's atoned for her transgression and moved on with her life. As 2006 turned to 2007, Hannah organized a New Year's Eve Party for 25 friends. She rented a bus, they skated at downtown Syracuse's Clinton Square and went out to dinner. Unfortunately, and despite great efforts, Hannah 'Banana' continued to struggle during the indoor season and finally was felled by a hip injury that took 'forever' to come back into the running version of Feng Shui. Somewhere along the way and sometime in the spring, Hannah's love of racing simply slipped away like so many pebbles pushed asunder by a rushing stream. Trying as hard as she could, Hannah could not rekindle her love for running. But for a few races in the fall of her senior year, she roared with the local legends. We chatted briefly during the 2008 Boot Camp—yes, I continued coaching XC after retiring from teaching—and she seems perfectly happy and content with her life at Middlebury.

Rachel Vaivoda saw her senior year fall apart, thanks to mono that went undetected for months. By the time we had it diagnosed, we were well into the spring track season and she was unable to finish what she'd started many years ago. At least we found the reason for racing times that were grossly uncharacteristic and sub-par. Building up steadily from 17 miles a week to nearly 40 by the end of summer

2007, Rachel seemed ready for action. Missing college Boot Camp for a several-day-long surfing trip with the freshman class, Rachel tried to make an impact on a Bates College XC team that I knew nothing about. It didn't go well. But, by the track season she was a different girl, a confident girl once again, and a girl who contributed to her track team as an effective steeplechaser.

Sofie seemed to drift during the indoor season of her senior year and was conflicted by the decision of whether to run in college. By the spring track season it became apparent that she hadn't been well for quite some time. With iron levels low and her immune system unable to fight off anything, she was out of the line-up down the stretch as her high school career concluded meekly. Still not 100%, she trained well over the summer of 2007 and was excited to join the Hornets of Lynchburg College as hope rose from the ashes of dreams deferred. Opening up her training at a camp with her team on August 18th 2007, Sofie was ready to embark on a fresh start. The weekend before her conference championship, she broke a bone in her foot. She opened the 2008 XC season on a much higher note.

Josey Witter attended Lynchburg College, too. He was designated as the best senior athlete at the Skaneateles Senior Awards Dinner, the same honor bestowed upon his college coach, James Goss. Josey went over 21 feet during the indoor season and cleared 6'6" in outdoor track. He joined the cross country team his senior year because I said it would help him. And it did. After a rough start in college, Josey got it together in his second semester but he never competed at the college level after an awful first meet. He never returned for his sophomore year and is now a guard at a local factory with plans to join the Coast Guard.

The lanky and brilliant Tom Poppe has caught on as a French chef at the amazingly popular Joelle's French Bistro north of the Village of Skaneateles. Seemingly the recipient of backhanded compliments whenever anyone with a historical knowledge of running sees him after a prolonged absence, ('You could have been a great one, 'Pop) he's remained on an even keel, remained happy and confident, survived the unexpected death of his father, and parlayed years of learning to cook into a career as a respected chef at a restaurant that's garnered regional and national acclaim far quicker than anyone could have imagined. Pop has always been able to 'cook'. He continues to call me for long conversations as he drives around Greater Syracuse to see his many friends, and on occasion, he drops by the track to get a report on his successors.

Zandra Walton summered at the Mayo Clinic in 2007 as her running proved problematic until the track season of her junior year—and even that year ended up strangely with a foot problem and disagreement with her coach. Her entire college career has been haltingly successful, the result of untimely illness and injuries. She'll be a hero some day in the medical or research field. Zandra discovered some differences between her native east coast and the Mid-American culture during her stay in Rochester, Minnesota. Wearing scruffy running shoes back east, doctors at the Mayo are permitted to wear only black or brown shoes. Running everywhere in a jog bra in central New York, Zandra was in violation of the strict Mayo Dress Code when she finished her runs and sat to stretch in the gym wearing just shorts and her jog bra. Having exposed her bare shoulders, she was cited. She was even 'accosted' by a motorist while on a run and wearing a smaller jog bra as the annoyed woman honked and pointed menacingly at her. In the fall of 2008, Zandra was nominated for a Rhodes Scholarship and she asked me to write in support of that nomination, an honor I will always cherish. I'm still beaming. It's the wearing of the Super Bowl ring and the holding of an Academy Award Oscar all rolled into one.

Erika Geihe has not relented in her desire to do everything for everyone all the time. She didn't run XC her senior year at Harvard, compliments of a bulging disc that held up through her final season of track. Her mother had the same disc malfunction at the same age—and it still grabs. In Erika's junior year she was no longer doing long sprints and had been converted to a 1500 runner. She concluded her career on May 11, 2008 at Harvard by helping to win the 4x800 at the Heptagonal Championships and was named All-Ivy. After four years of work, Erika Geihe finally beat her high school PR. She'll be a hero some day, too. The last week of August, 2008, she and her mom drove across the country to Stanford where she'll take up residence for her grad work in Chemistry.

Julie Lynch is enrolled at Syracuse University but never ran for the 'cuse. Her experience at American had clawed its way far deeper into her psyche than anyone realized. Doubt defeated confidence.

Cadie Cargile of Bucknell taught kindergarten in Norway as she grew closer and closer to her boyfriend. Long nights during the winter were relieved by long hours at the bars and nightclubs in the Scandinavian country, but she grew to love the midnight sun that slays nightfall for a few months of the year. Still running for fun and health, she's returned after a year abroad to look for a job and enter grad school just north of New York City.

Brett Searing entered boot camp and was ranked third in his class. He, too, may one day be draped in medals and be called a hero by some oppressed people overseas. In late fall 2008, Brett shipped out to Afghanistan to fight the terrorists who bombed the World Trade Center.

Simone Bras of Williams College got married and was hit by several severe maladies that had her incapacitated for months. Her good friend and teammate, Merritt Haswell, dropped everything and left her vacation-life in Hawaii to take care of Simone for months. Simone improved enough for Merritt to return to Skaneateles and resume her life. Merritt's already a hero for selflessly turning her back on her own life to help a friend in desperate need. Simone's fight was valiantly won and maybe she can return one day to coaching cross country in her adopted state of Texas. Simone had surgery during her trials and suddenly her incessant headaches stopped and she was a few inches taller. The spinal problem was cured. Merritt left Skaneateles and headed to Drexel University in Philadelphia on September 13th 2008 to begin the rugged task of becoming a physical therapist.

Lia Cross finished her Colgate academic and athletic career and is living and working in Boston. The last time I saw her was in the spring of 2008. We met, hugged and chit-chatted on the shoulders of West Lake Road during April as we both ran out our frustrations. Her father, Don Cross, recently returned from Africa where he and a small group of Skaneateles residents spent months building a hospital on the outskirts of the savagery in Darfur, the genocidal catastrophe that the world has inconveniently ignored for far too long. The slaughter, at times, grew tensely close. Don and his cohorts, Ted Kinder and Mark Dewitt, are heroes. Inspired by John Dau, a major figure in the film, *God Grew Tired of Us*, and who was 'adopted' by the Skaneateles Presbyterian church, the Skaneateles men headed to a forlorn region just east of the

White Nile and got a clean, productive well dug while building the medical center.

Lopez Lemong became a citizen of the United States in a ceremony in Syracuse. USA Today had a huge feature on him and it was well-deserved for one of the Lost Boys of the Sudan. Fresh off his national NCAA championship in the 1500, he set his sights on becoming a member of the US Olympic team. He made it and became a media celebrity when he was chosen to carry the flag of the United States in the opening ceremony in Beijing. His Tully high school coach, Jim Paccia, is justifiably proud.

Olympian and National Champion Jonathon Riley from Skaneateles continues to be an impact player on the national running scene. His streak of three straight national championships in the indoor 3000 meter run has ended but in 2007 he still finished 2nd. He moved to Wisconsin from the Nike Farm Team training camp on the west coast to be closer to his wife's family. With two children, he's sticking to his game plan and trying to take the next step by working with a different coach. In the summer of 2008, he moved west again, this time to Beaverton, Oregon to continue training. He continues to make all of us proud in Skaneateles. His 13:19 5k in Belgium during late July 2006 thrust him into the picture for the 2007 Olympic Trials. Unfortunately, his wife divorced him and after watching Jonathon drop out of the Prefontaine 2-mile on TV, I knew he was in trouble. He ran a good race in the first round at the Olympic Trials but didn't have enough starch in the finals and stayed home with the rest of us. Taryn Phelps, a former teammate of Jon's in Skaneateles, is still trying to keep up with him and is advising him to enter the coaching field. Taylor Strodel is also trying to keep in touch with Jon during this awful time of loneliness. Taryn is doing some military consulting work and enjoying her two boys. Taylor is a special ed teacher in New York City. I never saw that coming.

Mary Crowley has moved farther into the clenches of crew at Fairfield. After being a part of a 'rebellion' to have a coach replaced, she and the team are now happy with the direction the program is taking. She continues to be a training dynamo who summers at Lourdes Camp on the southeast side of Skaneateles Lake while entering mini-triathlons.

We met at 8 AM again the summer of 2007 as the girls prepared to defend their incredible league victory skein that spanned 14 years, and their sectional title from 2006. Third at last year's state championship, I wondered how we'd do in the new year. The three seniors were gone, Hannah to Middlebury, Rachel to Bates and Sofie to Lynchburg. Our turnout was meager and disappointing after working to bolster the egos of so many members of the team all last year. Several who we were counting on just dropped from the scene in an inexplicable manner.

With Beatrice Walton coming off a real solid spring track season and apparently going through her final body growth change, she looked very promising. I doubted that the mental mayhem that sunk her boat in 2006 would get out of the harbor in 2007. She'd simply come too far I thought. But what I liked most in 2007 was her attitude. She'd become a leader who was spitting in the face of doubt. After a season that was up and down, she didn't run XC sectionals and we were seemingly back to square one. But the girl didn't quit and Bea just got better and better throughout indoor track and then outdoor track. She made it to the state championship in the spring of 2008 and started her senior XC season with a major breakthrough at the Central Square Invitational. The girl has more than game. She's a winner.

Alexis Mazzeo was a near clone of Bea in Cross Country but she, too, persevered and made it to the track state championship. Faithful and devoted and unwilling to disappoint me, she, too, had a good race in the 2008 XC season opener and she looks ready to break free from any remaining shackles.

Rachel Hosie continued to nibble on the lure and ran with it as a new competitive attitude took over in 2007. Having her way with everyone all season long, she met her Waterloo at XC sectionals and ended her junior year with disappointment. Running in the top 5, she suddenly puked twice and dropped back to 39th. Regaining her poise, she finished in 8th, one spot from moving on to the state meet. She again skipped indoor track but found her niche in the spring and it was called the 2000-meter steeplechase. She hit her stride with a convincing win at the State Qualifier in 7:13 but had the worst race of her season at the state meet and finished out of the money. She led for all but the final 800 meters in the opening race of her final XC season and clocked a 19:17 during a monsoon-like downpour at Central Square. Three days later she ran three threshold miles in 6:13, 6:11 and 6:11. She's ready. On October 11th, she won the East Syracuse-Minoa Invitational with a time of 18:37.8. She placed 6th at 'states in November '08 and was named to the all-state first team.

Kristin Roberts was suddenly different in XC practice during 2007. She, along with Hosie and Mazzeo, had begun taking iron and the transformation, especially in Roberts, was stark. On Wednesday, August 1st, Kristin came over a hill and floated to the track. "Where are the girls?" I asked. In time, they showed up after having been categorically dropped. Kristin had a look of wonder on her face. With a mixture of pride and surprise, she was obviously happy with herself. For the past two years I think she'd been running on empty as her oxygen-starved body was pushed to its physical limits. But that moment was the highlight of her senior season. She again had a great summer before heading to RIT.

The girls lost the league championship in 2007 as Westhill clobbered us 20-35. We'd been first since 1993 and the loss wasn't close. We laid an egg by starting too fast as emotion over-ruled logic and then we just ran in agony for the final 2.5 miles. It didn't get any better in the sectional championship as we failed to take any of the top spots as the Tully Black Knights took the sectional crown in both '07 and '08. We won the league title again in 2008.

Sam and Calvin Davis were the only boys showing up during the summer of 2007, though Luke Edson was out there every day on his own as he fit his runs into his busy schedule. Sam was the senior I was counting on. He'd understood that he was in far better shape than in his junior year, when he was felled by testicle surgery, and he was doing workouts in such a spectacular manner that I knew he was on the verge of qualifying for the state championships. You couldn't miss it when he came charging up a hill wearing the face of unconquerable confidence glaring straight ahead that dared the best to match his stride. Calvin was in Sam's shadow and would be hard-charging down the last half of the race as his 55-mile weeks soaked up the punishment and dissolved it. The rest of the boys? Only eight showed up to start the season, the consequence of three straight modified seasons with only one boy joining each year. The deep well had dried up. And when some seniors quit, it left a hole that couldn't be filled. I feared this would be the worst showing from Skaneateles in over 30 years but I expected some good times from the boys who had committed themselves to wearing the blue and gold. The season did, in fact, stink. We were 3-5 in league competition and were never really a factor in any big race.

As long-time supporter Mike Homeyer said to me, "I don't remember it being that difficult," referring to teammates getting together and doing the summer runs as they piled up base like Warren Buffet piles up the profits for Berkshire Hathaway. Mike was one of those 1960-era runners with heart and a granite-hard will. 1000 mile summers were more the norm than not. He had 'nads and was a scholarship runner when he was a kid four decades ago. His brother has run the Comrades Ultra Marathon in South Africa, both ways. He's hard as nails. Mike always like watching Amanda race. He liked her toughness. He liked that she didn't save anything in reserve. Amanda did save one thing; she saved her best race for last and placed 9th at the 2007 Sectional championship while missing out on a trip to the state championship by two places.

After building homes for the poor in the Philippines, Josh Youle returned 6 inches taller. With speed reps run faster than he'd ever run, and after motoring quickly on several long runs, I thought Josh was ready to make his presence known. He was already a presence in the Philippines where he was known as a hero. He graduated and moved to Colorado College where he's loving life.

Gary Martin, our faithful, energetic and knowledgeable driver, had once again decided to retire. Reversing himself quickly, he agreed to one more season of cross country but after that, he said he was done for sure. On September 6th, 2008, Gary pulled the bus into the driveway in front of the school Commons and we loaded everyone up at 8AM sharp. Perhaps we're either just too dumb or stubborn to call it quits.

Held hard in the clutches of this life-altering sport known as cross country, we move in unison together every autumn and then go our separate ways as life pulls us in different directions. We all hit the wall from time to time, get up, and move forward with a quiet resolve. It's just what we do and the fight never ends until it ends.

Acknowledging My Heroes

None of us has been raised in isolation. We're all truly the products of our communities, circle of friends and families. And we're the collective sum of our experiences. This book is the result of lots of pushing and pulling by many people, in particular my friend and editor Dave Sipley, an English teacher at J-E High. All the grammar mistakes in the text are his fault.

Brian Kinney, who now serves in the military defending our land and values, worked himself to the core to get the cover just right while a high school senior and before he shipped out.

My trip began on a 100 meter long Shaw Place in Chenango Bridge, NY where we spent summer evenings racing around the half-mile block for fun. It was shortly after World War II and the neighborhood was alive with the human by-products of many rekindled relationships as the war-weary but triumphant soldiers returned to their wives and propagated the species. In a steady progression that lasted for years, the Baby Boomers were brought onto this Earth and now they are ready to retire. You never wanted for something to do as a kid in the 50s and 60s. It was an amazing time to be alive.

I've been blessed with memorable teaching colleagues, co-coaches and opposing coaches who have inspired me, humored me and made me laugh at the silliness of everything we take so seriously. All of them have made me want to improve my 'game'. Competing with these great people has been an absolute blast to tell you the truth. And despite an enormous amount of reluctance on my part to learn the lessons taught so ably by so many teachers, especially junior high English teacher, Mr.

Keltos, I've continually made progress. Learning to learn is the greatest gift of all, and, as I matured, I learned to research effectively. Special recognition must go to Mr. Dixon, my energetic and highly intelligent high school history teacher and a strong supporter of cross country back at my alma mater, Chenango Valley, just north of Binghamton, NY. As I got older and became a teacher myself, I realized that the educators during my youth were just guys like me who enjoyed working with kids. I liked discovering that truism.

Any exactitude that I possess came from dear Mrs. Lawrence, my junior high social studies teacher who was a contemporary of my maternal grandmother, Ina Miller Kirkendall, a fellow social studies teacher by way of Johnson City who taught me all about having pride in your work.

A special thanks to my mother, Avis Arlene Kirkendall Reed, who begged me to hold my athletes to a lesser standard than I hold for myself; my expectations for my life having been a bit off the chart at times. I have to remember that the kids join my teams more for fun than for winning state championships. When I stopped to listen, I discovered mom really did know best.

My thanks to those who have always pushed me including legendary coach Bob McDaniel who drove so many teams to the promised-land from my high school. Those runs through the mountain meadows were majestic and boy did they hurt. Running up the middle of the Chenango River against the current and then up the embankment onto an uncompleted Interstate 81 was just plain tough. But we did it because we believed in him and were utterly afraid to disappoint him.

Dave Sweet, a senior XC rookie and close high school friend who somehow befriended Syracuse University hall-of-fame basketball coach Jim Boeheim while working in Myrtle Beach, got me on the roads all summer before our senior year. He taught me that late-comers to the great sport of cross country can turn into special senior-surprises—if they dare. When Jim Horsington showed up as a rookie senior in my second year of coaching at Marcellus, I had my first of several senior-surprises. When my oldest son, Kirk, was looking to enter the collegiate ranks as a sports information officer, Sweeter called his friend, Jim Boeheim, and within 30 minutes we received a call from a basketball coach in Texas who was willing to help.

We learn a lot from watching kids grow and mature while running six years for us. The transformation is nothing short of the rebuilding of West Berlin after the destruction of World War II. We coaches are blessed to bear witness to a child's growth. The Marshall Plan, by the way, may have been our greatest hour as a nation.

As a coach, you get to watch kids grow up in every imaginable way. Some of it is funny, some is painfully sad, and some is just plain ugly like a newborn horse trying to stand up and walk for the first time. Having the privilege of watching kids and teams rebound, regroup and move on, after failure has tried to bring them down, gives me the feeling that America will survive because there's a lot of great kids getting things done the right way, the old fashioned way; by working for it and working together.

As a coach you get to watch kids move around in their small homogenous social groups as everyone tries to fit in comfortably. Eventually you see them branching out, seeking the non-familiar, crossing some stark lines and hanging out with kids from other social, ethnic, economic and peer groups as they begin to show respect for hard work and achievement instead of inherited social ranking. And you know it's a good thing. Watching my sons Kirk and KC run for me was the most special gift that I could have received--except for watching my brave little wife of 34 years give birth to both hulks. I look at them with all their mass, muscle and cool-under-fire and wonder who the father really was. They're good men. Together, my wife and two boys-turned-men have taught me what life is all about. Even though running was the most important thing in my boys' lives while they were at practice or competing, I watched them maintain a healthy balance in their lives. My boys were two of the most devoted athletes who willingly sweat the small stuff in order to have a chance at grabbing the big prize. I was constantly amazed by how detailed and careful they were before a meet. They constantly reminded me, through their actions, that kids are trying to do the right things and they're complex and more than just a running machine serving at my behest. Rachel Hosie is the latest to remind me of that important life lesson and the important truism about balance that often gets lost in the heat of the chase for the championship. I learned to see and listen from my sons like I'd never done before in my life. They're my heroes who also fulfilled the

American dream by becoming better than their parents. I've told Kirk that he's the man I always wanted to be and I'm seeing the same good things from KC after a year living in Boston.

Watching KC run his last 100-meter stride in practice was rough because I knew I'd never again gaze down the track at my boys in that special, privileged way, the complicated relationship involving coach, athlete, dad and son. As KC's 4x800 teammates—all great kids who have added luster to the Skaneateles name—came down the track on a warm and sunny June afternoon, I only saw KC. I desperately tried to memorize each stride, his posture, the way his hands moved while helping to propel his body forward with sleek efficiency. I admired his stride, the feet stepping over the opposite knee in a bike-pedaling movement that was to be admired. I tried to appreciate everything he has meant to me. But the mind, as wondrous as it is, can't meet all the heart's demands or the pleadings of a soul that was growing increasingly somber at the thought of coaching without him by my side. The visions I tried to etch into my brain of KC's power and Kirk's smooth baton passes fade so damn fast but the love never diminishes.

Way before anyone wanted to be "Like Mike," (NBA great Michael Jordan) I wanted to be like a bunch of older guys who wore white shorts and a white jersey with a red slash. I wanted to be a state champ just like them. They were my heroes just as much as Mickey Mantle in Yankee pinstripes.

Those guys from Chenango Valley planted a seed in me. I wanted so desperately to be a state champ. I was never the runner they were, but the seed was planted and it did things beneath the surface that would surprise me decades later.

They gave me memories and goals. The bespectacled John Reid let me tag along on a run up River Road in Chenango Bridge. He was my hero. Somewhere near Wisconsin Drive, after thoughtfully shouting encouragement to me in 7th grade as his 6 foot 4 frame started to pull inexorably away, he dropped me like a bad habit. He was all alone doing his thing on roads that wouldn't see hordes of runners for another decade or two as the Arthur Lydiard and Bill Bowerman jogging craze hadn't yet developed northeastern roots. Once again, a seed was planted. I knew what 'good' felt like. I knew what 'good' was supposed to look and act like. Sure, John was a good guy with a state title and eventually a spot on the Chenango Valley Board of Education where he paid attention to the big picture unlike so many board members who get lost in their petty personal battles that subtract from real education. I enjoyed kidding him at a recent state championship testimonial about his basketball career at Colgate University and his record for leading the nation in fouls per game. He won't admit it but he was a long-armed hacker.

I remember Marv Berg and his New York Times Sunday newspaper route that weaved up and down the myriad of roads in Chenango Bridge just north of a mountain and across the river from our training trails. His younger brother, Doug, bequeathed the route to me upon his graduation from high school. I remember thinking, "If a state champ did this job, then so can I." Both Bergs were my heroes. They were just cool guys. Marv, a graduate of Swarthmore in Pennsylvania, has never said a word to any of his ex-teammates. He's as mysterious as he was back in high school when he got suspended before a big basketball game for refusing to salute the flag during the Vietnam War. Constitutionally he was right and society and the school administration were red-neck wrong. By the way, there is no credible evidence that anyone spit on those brave, honorable Vietnam soldiers upon their return to a nation that was terribly torn by our participation in that war. Some things just don't change.

Mike Satterthwaite was always trying to get out from his little sister's shadow. Patty was the world baton-twirling champion who often made television appearances on The Ted Mack Amateur Hour and the Ed Sullivan Show—the same show that debuted a British group calling themselves The Beatles who sported radical, non-conforming mop-tops. American teens couldn't get enough of them. And I was one who valued their trading cards, but never as much as I valued baseball cards.

I was with Patty on a date drinking wine on the night when my life almost ended as a duodenal ulcer broke through an artery just below my stomach. Thankfully my doctors, General Practitioner Alfred Edward Peterson—a World War II bomber pilot who shredded Germany with reluctance on his many night missions—and James McGuire—my up-to-date surgeon from across the street—saved my life with a new technique that left me with my stomach fully intact and my Vagus nerve cut. Mike Satterthwaite, post-high school, helped to keep our Chenango

Valley Invitational alive. Peterson, McGuire and Satterthwaite all remain my heroes. Doc MacGuire's first wife died a gruesome death. Doc Peterson was kicked out of intensive care at Wilson Hospital when his life-long companion, June Meadows, lay dying. "Can I stay if I put on the white coat," he pleaded; his once massive frame shriveled by age and personal grief. It was a hospital he was instrumental in founding. Medical care in this powerful and plentiful nation so often leaves trusting, desperate patients asking, "What the hell happened?" We can do better. And we must. I mourn Dr. Peterson's loss and the grief, helplessness and lack of humanity he suffered as his wife died. He fought the Germans but chose not to fight his medical colleagues because he trusted them. Never stop fighting and never stop speaking for those who you love. I failed my mother in that regard and I'll regret not standing up much more forcefully as she suffered that long excruciating, misery-filled last week of her proud life.

Dave Brinsko, a 9:17 two miler in the early 60s, was big-time. But what was bigger was riding with him while he shifted effortlessly through all four gears as we crossed the Chenango River in his blazingly cool convertible. He isn't my hero. He veered from the righteous path and got himself arrested for breaking and entering after a stellar career at Emporia State in Kansas. He even raced against Jim Ryun. His son ran well for Syracuse University and I almost went up to him at a meet. But I didn't. I regret that decision. I wonder what he's doing today?

Ray Smith was more than a hero; he was a God. He was a state champ like Brinsko. And I liked his little sister, Maureen, a lot. I mean, a lot. He ran the mile in 4:14 on cinders and he ran to school in the morning along the railroad tracks. But it was at a summer race at Union-Endicott's Ty Cobb Stadium when he taught me all I needed to know about college and running. While in Happy Valley (Penn State) on a full-ride, he said that the coach served up a beer after his races. It was carbo-loading he said. He was a thundering running stud who would have been a senior as the legendary coach Harry Groves began his 38 year career.

My friend and coaching mentor, Jack Daniels, once said that the difference between winners and all the rest is preparation and being ready to seize opportunity when it unexpectedly presents itself. I pass on that invaluable lesson to my students and teams as many times as my feeble mind can remind me. He's a wise, classy gentleman and hero to all distance runners and coaches worldwide. And even in the last stages of his life, he's as intrigued by research as ever. What a mind he must possess.

All these guys have sacrificed, worked hard, gone on to do great things in life like Chenango Valley runner Jim Brown who toiled and sweat with that state championship team back in 1963. Later, this champion took the reigns as mayor of Rome. He's dealt with the city losing its biggest partner, the United States Air Force, with dignity and hard work that has led to the rebuilding of that once great city. Jim was at my childhood home on one occasion when he 'helped' a girlfriend babysit me and my younger brothers, Hugh and Dave. Uh huh. We know what he was up to. He once promised me, as I lay in bed as a young punk, that he'd shoot hoops with me some day. I'm still waiting.

My dad, Bill Reed, is my hero for any number of reasons. He got the fire stoked when he began driving me the 50 miles on narrow, winding, two-lane back roads to Cornell's Barton Hall for the Ivy League's Heptagonal Championships. What a thrill to be sitting amongst those incredibly huge crowds—the men in tuxedos and suits while the woman wore dresses, splendid hats and sparkling jewelry—as those purest of athletes like Yale's 440-yard specialist Wendell Motley did their thing for the love of the sport and not for street credibility, money or lucrative shoe endorsements. My dad also gently woke me in the middle of the night to watch ABC's live broadcast of the Tokyo Olympics half a world away. NBC needs to study that concept.

During the fiercest, scariest moments of the Cold War we summered on the shores of DeRuyter Lake just south of Cazenovia in the middle of New York State. Somehow, amidst all the isolation at that little camp situated between some rugged hills, we got the black and white television tuned-in to the USA vs. USSR track dual meet as I sprawled across the porch bed on my stomach. Those races entranced me with the incredible level of competitiveness and amazing civility that surely defied the wishes of their political leaders.

Coaching produced many lonely weekend days and quiet weekday nights for my wife, Patty, the former Patricia Keefe from North Syracuse. Patty, was my girl and love at Oswego State College where we both trained to be teachers along the shoreline of Lake Ontario. I can still remember the deep feelings that overcame me on a spring break as a song by *Chicago* played on the car radio. Patty was up north with her family and I was standing in a Binghamton parking lot at McDonalds. Right then and there I knew my fate was sealed and I realized just who had my heart. I knew we'd be married, and we were, soon after she asked me.

I tried over 30 years ago to teach her to run according to the workouts developed by Dr. Kenneth Cooper—author of the 1968 best seller, *Aerobics*. It didn't take. Today, on her own, she runs twice as far as me and is as tempted by the stopwatch as anyone I've seen. She's tough. She's also my heroine.

I've coached a while now, seen some great runners pass my way and applauded some incredibly talented and successful teams here in Skaneateles where blue and gold rules the day. I've loved cheering frontrunners and some who wore a Skaneateles uniform who brought up the rear. I've always respected those who ignore their physical limitations and try hard to improve, happy with the noble effort and understanding of running's place in their life. We've won and earned ten state championships in cross country and track and helped produce one Olympian. But I will offer this layman's observation about my Chenango Valley predecessors, those guys who were Warriors before I became one and wore that distinctive satiny-red sweat suit. That team, those seniors and their coach, those Chenango Valley Warriors, would be just as successful today. Well done champs. I am what I am partly because of you.

Some childhood dreams, inspired by heroes, never die. And some even come true.

Printed in the United States
219807BV00002B/1/P